Early Modern Toleration

C000182513

This book examines the practice of toleration and the experience of religious diversity in the early modern world.

Recent scholarship has shown the myriad ways in which religious differences were accommodated in the early modern era (1500–1800). This book propels this revisionist wave further by linking the accommodation of religious diversity in early modern communities to the experience of this diversity by individuals. It does so by studying the forms and patterns of interaction between members of different religious groups, including Christian denominations, Muslims, and Jews, in territories ranging from Europe to the Americas and South-East Asia. The book is structured around five key concepts: the senses, identities, boundaries, interaction, and space. For each concept, the book provides chapters based on new, original research plus an introduction that situates the chapters in their historiographic context.

Early Modern Toleration: New Approaches is aimed primarily at undergraduate and postgraduate students, to whom it offers an accessible introduction to the study of religious toleration in the early modern era. Additionally, scholars will find cutting-edge contributions to the field in the book's chapters.

Benjamin J. Kaplan, Professor of Dutch History, University College London. He has published widely on the history of relations between religious groups in early modern Europe. Among his books is *Divided by Faith: Religious Conflict and the Practice of Toleration in Early Modern Europe* (2007).

Jaap Geraerts, Digital Humanities Lab, Leibniz Institute of European History, Mainz. His research interests comprise the Protestant and Catholic Reformations, religious toleration, and the digital humanities. Publications include *Patrons of the Old Faith: The Catholic Nobility in Utrecht and Guelders, c. 1580–1702* (2018).

Early Modern Themes

Books in the *Early Modern Themes* series are aimed at upper level under-graduate and postgraduate students who are looking more deeply at thematic topics in the early modern period. They combine chapters offering a synthesis of the topic as it stands, the key historiographical debates, and the cutting edge research which is driving the field forward.

Early Modern Emotions
An Introduction
Edited by Susan Broomhall

Early Modern Childhood
An Introduction
Edited by Anna French

Early Modern Things
Objects and Their Histories, 1500-1800, 2nd edition
Edited by Paula Findlen

Early Modern Court Culture
Edited by Erin Griffey

Early Modern Streets
A European Perspective
Edited by Danielle van den Heuvel

Early Modern Toleration
New Approaches
Edited by Benjamin J. Kaplan and Jaap Geraerts

For more information about this series, please visit: https://www.routledge.com/Early-Modern-Themes/book-series/EMT

Early Modern Toleration
New Approaches

Edited by Benjamin J. Kaplan
and Jaap Geraerts

Routledge
Taylor & Francis Group

LONDON AND NEW YORK

Designed cover image: The interior of St. Peter's Cathedral in Bautzen. Oil on copper, 58 × 51,5 cm. Museum Bautzen. Alamy image ID: MW9XJ3

First published 2024
by Routledge
4 Park Square, Milton Park, Abingdon, Oxon OX14 4RN

and by Routledge
605 Third Avenue, New York, NY 10158

Routledge is an imprint of the Taylor & Francis Group, an informa business

© 2024 selection and editorial matter, Benjamin J. Kaplan and Jaap Geraerts; individual chapters, the contributors

British Library Cataloguing-in-Publication Data
A catalogue record for this book is available from the British Library

ISBN: 978-0-367-46708-1 (hbk)
ISBN: 978-0-367-46707-4 (pbk)
ISBN: 978-1-003-03052-2 (ebk)

DOI: 10.4324/9781003030522

Typeset in Sabon
by KnowledgeWorks Global Ltd.

Contents

vi   *Contents*

List of Figures

List of Contributors

Allyson F. Creasman is an Associate Professor of History at Carnegie Mellon University, USA. Her publications include *Censorship and Civic Order in Reformation Germany, 1517-1648: "Printed Poison and Evil Talk"* (Ashgate, 2012).

Jaap Geraerts is a postdoctoral fellow at the Leibniz Institute of European History, Mainz (Germany), and a member of its Digital Humanities Lab. He has published on early modern Dutch Catholicism and interconfessional interaction in the Dutch Republic. His publications include *Patrons of the Old Faith: The Catholic Nobility in Utrecht and Guelders, c. 1580–1702* (2018).

Benjamin J. Kaplan holds the Chair in Dutch History at University College London, United Kingdom. He has published widely on the history of relations between religious groups in the Netherlands and Europe generally in the early modern era. Among his books are *Divided by Faith: Religious Conflict and the Practice of Toleration in Early Modern Europe* (2007) and *Cunegonde's Kidnapping: A Story of Religious Conflict in the Age of Enlightenment* (2014).

Susanne Lachenicht is a Professor of Early Modern History at Bayreuth University, Germany. She works on Europe and the Atlantic World with a special focus on diasporas, religious migrations, knowledge transfer and transformation, and temporalities in the early modern world.

Matthew Laube is an Assistant Professor of Music at Baylor University, USA. Prior to this, he held postdoctoral positions in history and music in London, Brussels, and Cambridge. Matthew's publications have appeared in *Past & Present* and *Early Music History*, and he is currently preparing a monograph on music in Reformation Heidelberg.

Carolina Lenarduzzi is a historian and lawyer. She earned her PhD in history from Leiden University with a thesis on the lived religion of the Catholic minority in the Dutch Republic. She is the author of the book *Katholiek in de Republiek* (2019) and of various articles on religious and cultural history in the early modern Netherlands. She is a Visiting Member of Staff at the Institute for History at Leiden University.

David van der Linden is an Assistant Professor in Early Modern History at the University of Groningen, the Netherlands. His research focuses on religious conflict, peacebuilding, and memory in the early modern world. His current project *Building Peace: Transitional Justice in Early Modern France* examines the strategies used by French authorities and citizens to restore peace after the French Wars of Religion.

David M. Luebke is a Professor of History at the University of Oregon (USA), and he writes about political and religious cultures in early modern Germany. His recent publications include *Hometown Religion: Regimes of Coexistence in Early Modern Westphalia* (2016) and an edited volume, *Archeologies of Confession: Writing the German Reformation, 1517-2017* (2017).

Natalia Muchnik is a Professor at the EHESS in Paris, France. She has written on religious minorities and diasporas in Early Modern Europe, including Sephardi Jews, Moriscos, Recusants, and French Huguenots. Her current research focuses on early modern prisons and confinement, especially in Spain, France, and England.

Hendrik E. Niemeijer is a senior researcher of Indonesian Religious History at the HDC Centre for Religious History, Vrije Universiteit Amsterdam, the Netherlands. He is a specialist in the archives of the Dutch United East India Company (VOC, 1605–1799) and Indonesian History. He currently works in Indonesia as a digital archive and heritage specialist.

Giada Pizzoni is a research associate at the University of Exeter (UK) working on European trade and religion. Between March 2019 and March 2020, as part of the AveTransRisk project, she investigated the British presence in nineteenth-century Malta. In September 2015, she obtained her Doctorate at the University of St. Andrews. Her PhD thesis entitled "Economic and Financial Strategies of the British Catholic Community in the Age of Mercantilism, 1672-1781" investigated the crucial role of Catholic merchants in the first British commercial expansion. After completing her PhD, she worked as a teaching fellow at the University of Warwick. Her first monograph *British Catholic Merchants in the Commercial Age, 1670–1714* was published in 2020.

Jesse Spohnholz is a Professor of History at Washington State University (USA) and the Director of the *History for the 21st Century* project. His research focuses on social practices of toleration and the experiences of religious refugees in Reformation-era Germany and the Netherlands.

Nicholas Terpstra is a Professor of History at the University of Toronto (Canada) exploring questions at the intersection of politics, religion, gender, and charity in early modern Europe, especially as these deal with marginalised individuals and groups. He has written on the experiences of religious refugees and the dynamics of Global Reformation.

Felicita Tramontana is an Associate Professor at the University Roma Tre (Italy) and Honorary Fellow at the Centre for the Study of the Renaissance of the University of Warwick (UK). She is the PI of the ERC-funded project "HOLYLAB. A Global Economic Organization in the Early Modern Period: The Custody of the Holy Land through its account books."

Anat Vaturi is a faculty member at the Department of Jewish History and Interdisciplinary Unit for Polish Studies at the University of Haifa and a teaching fellow at the Department of Jewish History at the Beit Berl Academic College (Israel). She specialises in early modern Polish-Jewish history. Her research interests include interreligious coexistence and the interplay of law, economics, and religion.

Introduction

Early Modern Toleration

Benjamin J. Kaplan and Jaap Geraerts

"Toleration" is the act of allowing or accepting things that one disapproves of or dislikes. Outside specialised realms such as medicine, the term is used mostly in relation to human behaviour: we tolerate certain ways that people think, act, or live their lives that differ from our own. Such toleration is generally regarded in today's world as a good thing; indeed, it enjoys the status of an ethical norm. If pressed, most people could probably articulate some principled grounds that justify, or even necessitate, our practising toleration. They may, for example, believe it would be unjust if some people could impose on others their own beliefs and practices, or that diversity is beneficial to society. Perhaps most commonly, people tend to think of toleration as the way to show respect for the freedoms we believe every individual has a right to enjoy. This sort of principled toleration, based on fundamental values, was originally conceived as the correct response to other religions. Over the past century or so, it has been extended to other forms of human variety, including culture, lifestyle, and sexuality. In it, political theorists recognise one of the fundamental principles underlying the modern liberal state.[1]

To look before the eighteenth century for this modern type of toleration, even in the restricted area of religion, is a problematic endeavour. Many a historian has attempted to find its antecedents and track its emergence over the long haul, but their efforts have usually produced histories distorted by anachronism and teleology. Whether it was, in the nineteenth and early twentieth century, Protestantism that historians chiefly credited for the "rise of toleration" or, later, the Enlightenment and secularisation, historians populated their writings with heroic champions of toleration who anticipated modern values and fanatical persecutors with primitive mindsets. In either case, the result was a master narrative of historical development in which, as toleration rose, civilisation itself advanced.[2] Today, most scholars reject this narrative. They recognise its mythical elements and its implicit function: to lend historical legitimacy to modern liberalism. So strong has the reaction been that some historians now eschew the very word "toleration" and its variant, "tolerance." Instead, to designate what they find in premodern eras, they have coined a variety of alternatives, such as "religious coexistence," "accommodating

DOI: 10.4324/9781003030522-1

religious difference," "living with religious diversity," "the ecumenicity of everyday life," "intercommunality," and "multiconfessionalism," as well as simpler terms such as "pluralism" and "diversity."[3] In all these cases, scholars are trying to find a more neutral designator, one divested of ideological commitments and unburdened by whiggish historiographic traditions.[4]

"Toleration" and "tolerance," though, and their equivalents in other languages were the terms used in the era with which this book is concerned, the early modern, which ran from roughly 1450 to 1750 CE. They were by no means the only terms, but by some point in the seventeenth century they emerged as the most important ones in Europe and its colonies, and so long as we understand them in their original, early modern sense, we can avoid idealisation and anachronism. "Toleration" in the early modern world meant, as contemporary dictionaries explained, a grudging sufferance of something one considered evil and wished did not exist. It was used chiefly (though not exclusively) with reference to religion, specifically to religions other than one's own – systems of belief and worship that one regarded as at best erroneous and at worst vehicles of satanic influence. In the Middle Ages, ecclesiastic authorities had applied this concept to non-Christians, especially Jews, whose continued presence in some parts of Europe was understood as part of a divine plan, to end only with the Last Days. The concept took on greater importance, though, the issue it addressed greater urgency, in the wake of the Protestant and Catholic Reformations, which split a formerly united western Christendom into rival denominations, also known as "confessions." This schism forced millions of Christians to confront for the first time differences of religious belief and practice within their own communities – differences made all the more bitter by the common Christian heritage of the confessions, each claiming their form of Christianity to be the only true one. At the same time, Europeans' expanding commercial enterprises and empire-building activities put them into contact with previously unknown religions such as those of native Americans, while dramatically intensifying their engagement with other religions around the globe, such as Islam, Hinduism, and Buddhism. How to think about religious differences and to handle them in practice was for Europeans arguably the most burning issue of the era.

Far from an ideal or norm, early modern toleration suffered from a basic illegitimacy. It was justified mostly commonly as a least-worst approach to regrettable circumstances, namely the failure so far of the "true" religion (however one construed it) to triumph over false ones. "Necessity" was said to require it – at least for now, in some places. Toleration was supposed to be a temporary expedient, although where religious divisions stubbornly persisted decade after decade, the notion that one day it would no longer be needed grew increasingly theoretical. Ruling elites pleaded sheer incapacity – that it was beyond their means to suppress "heresy" and "unbelief," and it is true that the administrative, pedagogic, and military tools available to early modern governments were lilliputian compared to those wielded by twenty-first century ones. Rulers and their apologists argued also that the alternatives to toleration, such as expelling religious dissenters from their lands, carried an unbearably heavy cost. To be sure, some advocates of toleration proposed more positive justifications as well, based on religious teaching and philosophical argument, and one state, the Dutch Republic, came to pride itself on its toleration, which became part of Dutch national identity. Until the eighteenth century, though, most advocates of toleration found themselves in the position of dissenters, opposing the teachings of the main Christian churches, the claims of rulers to authority in religious affairs, and the common sense of most people. The first construed toleration as tantamount to condoning heresy and idolatry, the second equated religious dissent with political subversion, while the third doubted that a community could remain united and harmonious if its members were fighting one another religiously. In the eighteenth century, toleration underwent a revaluation and, for those who participated in Enlightenment culture, took on the status of a cardinal virtue. But those participants formed a modest minority of the population. For most people, toleration remained what it had always been: an awkward concession of dubious propriety to the complexities of life in a religiously mixed society.

For this reason, and to distinguish early modern toleration from modern, some historians have taken to characterising the former as "pragmatic" or "practical."[5] These adjectives are useful in that they capture how the practice of toleration required compromise and entailed the transgression of norms and ideals to which the practitioners of toleration themselves subscribed. Early modern toleration seemed to contradict its practitioners' declarations of commitment to the religion they professed, their acceptance of its claims of unique validity, and their desire for its triumph over other faiths. Terms such as "pragmatic" and "practical" can be misleading, though, if they are taken to mean that early modern toleration was really incompatible with sincere piety or that it was motivated purely by economic or political self-interest. These accusations are no recent invention: they were voiced loudly in the sixteenth and seventeenth centuries, for example, when critics applied the pejorative label of "politique" to rulers who sought to avert civil war by accommodating religious diversity. When scholars echo the accusation, though, they fall into the error of reductionism. More than a few, for example, have suggested that the Dutch practised toleration simply because it was good for commerce and they profited by it. This is to conflate moral complexity with immorality and to ignore the wider sociocultural context. Toleration violated some early modern values but by no means all. On the contrary, values such as charity, Christian love, neighbourliness, and the "common humanity" of people of different faiths favoured toleration. So did other considerations, such as the duty of rulers to maintain peace and order, and of common folk to obey the law. According to all the Christian churches, such duties were divinely imposed, sacred obligations. The religious valence they carried, though, did not suffice to remove from toleration the stigma of impiety.

Early modern discourse did not distinguish between "toleration" and "tolerance," and indeed the distinction did not exist in some languages. It has become a common convention, though, for historians writing in English to use the former term to refer to actions and the latter to ideas and attitudes. This book looks at both: on the one hand, the ways in which people of different religions interacted and behaved towards one another; on the other, their sentiments and perceptions regarding religious difference. The latter has always been a subject of inquiry in the form of studies dissecting the ideas of influential authors who articulated arguments in favour of toleration. The former too has long been a subject of inquiry, but in an equally restricted sense, focusing on the laws and policies of rulers and governments. Common to both these approaches was an implicit elitism that pervaded the historical discipline generally. Intellectual historians presupposed that the ideas of philosophers, theologians, and other writers shaped the culture of their day through a process of diffusion in which ordinary people were passive recipients. Likewise, historians supposed that only princes and magistrates had it in their power to tolerate people of other religions. In this respect, they resembled their subjects, the writers and rulers of early modern Europe, who construed toleration as something bestowed (or not) from on high by those figures vested with the authority to regulate human affairs. Only in the past two or three decades have scholars rediscovered the agency of non-elites in these matters. Following (somewhat belatedly) a seismic shift in the discipline as a whole, a wave of revisionist historiography has recognised that everyone who lived in a religiously mixed community perforce interacted with people of other faiths and held attitudes regarding religious difference.[6] This book is part of that revisionist wave and aims to propel it further.

Not that one can ignore the vast differentials of power and influence that were inherent in the structures of early modern society. These profoundly shaped the sorts of agency that people of different ranks and roles could exercise in the negotiation of religious differences. It is, though, a signal advance that we now see toleration as an interactive process in which arrangements for accommodating religious differences were not simply imposed by ruling elites, who themselves were often divided in various ways, but negotiated between diverse parties, including the rank-and-file adherents of the different religions present in a community. Nor do we see these arrangements as fully established by one-off, time-delimited events such as the issuing of an edict or concluding of a treaty. Rather, toleration can best be considered an ongoing practice involving patterns of peaceful activity and interaction that persisted as long as they continued to be reaffirmed and re-enacted.

Those patterns, though, were subject at times to questioning, testing, challenge, and renegotiation by their participants. This helps explain why, in so many religiously mixed communities, we find an alternation between toleration in day-to-day life and occasional bouts of overt conflict that break out abruptly. For invariably, early modern toleration involved the managing and containing of religious tensions, not their resolution. "Stable, persisting, and often vitally important social relations" could be maintained for extended periods across the boundaries dividing groups, but differences of belief and practice created an ever-present subcurrent of strife. That was never more true than in the wake of the Reformations, when the rival Christian confessions defined themselves to an extraordinary degree in terms of their mutual oppositions and enmities.[7] If one defines toleration to denote behaviours that contributed to patterns of peaceful coexistence, then it was in no way incompatible with conflict that was confined to discursive or legal spheres. To the contrary, such conflict was the norm rather than the exception, and indeed some "regimes of toleration," such as that in the Holy Roman Empire after 1648, arguably encouraged legal wrangling as a safe alternative to extra-legal action. One of the most profound changes in our understanding of early modern toleration has been to see it no longer as the opposite of intolerance, in the sense of an incompatible alternative. The two terms can be simultaneously valid as descriptors of different aspects of relations between coexisting religious groups.[8]

Once we define early modern toleration as a practice rather than an ideal, and once we accept that it was anything but conflict-free, we find that it was far more common than scholars traditionally realised. Despite the continuing power of religious uniformity as a normative assumption, the Protestant and Catholic Reformations left thousands of communities, large and small, from the British Isles to the Commonwealth of Poland-Lithuania, religiously mixed. Subsequent migrations increased their number. In addition, wherever states with different official religions had a common border, there were communities whose inhabitants might be of one religion and yet have regular contact with people of another religion who lived just across that border in a neighbouring state. Such borders could be found in western Europe, separating, for example, the Dutch Republic from the Habsburg Netherlands, but were especially dense in the fragmented political landscape of central Europe, where some entities smaller than states – for example, parishes in the Swiss Grisons – also had the right to maintain different official religions. Empirical studies are still needed for a great number of places within Europe, never mind beyond it, where religious groups encountered and coexisted with one another.

These changes in how we think about and write the history of toleration have mostly been pioneered by historians of Europe. That is unsurprising given that the very notion of a "history of toleration" had its origins in the whiggish narratives described above, which credited the rise of toleration to developments in European culture and indeed located in Europe the cutting edge of all progressive historical change. As a subject of inquiry, the history of toleration was traditionally Eurocentric, and even today the majority of works treating the subject focus on Europe. Consequently, they focus also on relations between the religious groups found in Europe: the rival Christian confessions above all, plus Christian-Jewish relations. Happily, though, the past two decades have seen a growth of studies that look beyond those confines. The global, transnational, trans-imperial, and macro-historical approaches that have come to inform the historical discipline as a whole have begun to reshape the historiography of toleration.

The Mediterranean and Middle Eastern regions have been major beneficiaries of this shift in focus. Numerous studies now examine interactions between Christians, Jews, and Muslims in the vast zone that lay between and along the edges of the Christian and Muslim states lining the Mediterranean Sea. Samuel Huntington's claim that this zone was the site of a "clash of civilisations" inherently, perpetually opposed to one another, has given way to an appreciation for the amount of peaceful interaction and fruitful engagement that took place there between Christians and Muslims. Of course, the largest and most powerful Muslim state in those regions was the Ottoman Empire, whose subjects included from the beginning large numbers of Christians, mostly eastern Orthodox. Histories of the Empire have always given prominent consideration to the so-called "millets," Christian and Jewish minorities who enjoyed special protected status. The revisionist wave of historiography on toleration in Europe has strongly influenced how historians now write about religion in the Ottoman Empire. Ottomanists have moved away from regarding the Empire as a mosaic of self-governing, mutually isolated millets, towards conceiving it as a "plural society" characterised by extensive interreligious contacts. This has gone together with a focus on everyday life, documented using archival sources; on the practice of toleration rather than on ideas and laws; on the agency of religious minorities and their mutual interactions; and on topics that have commanded the attention of Europeanists in recent years, such as migration, conversion, and religious identity.

Some Ottomanists have also drawn comparisons between religious developments in the Empire and contemporaneous ones in Europe, applying to their own field the concept of "confessionalisation" first developed by German historians. This concept has several variants, but in its core meaning it denotes a process through which norms of religious belief and practice become more precise and rigid, boundaries between religious groups become sharper and less permeable, and people are subjected to a mix of pedagogic and disciplinary measures that leads them to internalise more fully the teachings of their religion. This "formation of confessions" is seen as occurring in most, if not all, the versions of Christianity that emerged from the Reformations. Despite, and indeed partly because of their bitter enmities, these religious rivals underwent similar, parallel developments. There is a further, "strong" version of the confessionalisation paradigm that sees this religious process occurring in tandem with political and social changes. Where this version prevails, three fundamental changes in early modern society – the formation of confessions; the rise of more powerful institutions of political rule; and the emergence of stricter, more inhibiting norms of behaviour – mutually reinforce each other. Ironically, even as it has come to be adopted by some Ottomanists, the confessionalisation paradigm has been subjected to much critique by European historians. Both its utility and limitations are highlighted in several contributions to this volume.

Historiography on the Mediterranean and Middle Eastern regions can be contrasted to historical writing on Southeast Asia and, to a lesser extent, the

Americas. The former continues to be dominated by a missionary perspective. In addition to the many studies on Catholic missions across this vast area, which continue to roll off the presses, Protestant missions increasingly receive scholarly attention as well, and comparative studies have shown the differences and similarities between the missions launched by various Christian confessions.[9] This missionary perspective has important ramifications for the ways in which relations between religious groups are examined: most attention goes to cross-cultural exchange and how missionaries adopted strategies that involved the accommodation of religious differences. This accommodation could be textual; hence, a number of studies focus on how religious, cultural, and linguistic differences were bridged in (translations of) catechisms and devotional texts.[10] It could also be liturgical and ritualistic; scholars have, therefore, paid attention to religious syncretism and hybridity.[11] As the Chinese and Malabar Rites controversies illustrate, topics such as these were already highly charged in the early modern period, generating conflicts that have yielded precious primary source material. In addition to using these sources to show intra-Catholic differences, disputes, and competition, historians have creatively employed them to unearth information about native religious beliefs and practices.[12]

Far less prominent in this historiography, however, is the kind of granular investigation of relations and everyday interactions between different religious communities that has become common in the European context.[13] Another difference is the very limited influence of the confessionalisation paradigm. To be sure, there still is some overlap between the two historiographies: phenomena such as religious syncretism, mobility, and conversion are studied by scholars working both on Southeast Asia and on Europe. Nevertheless, the historiographic differences are striking and noteworthy.

In comparison, although historiography on the Americas is partly characterised by a similar interest in religious missions, its concerns and methods overlap to a greater extent with those of its European counterpart. One reason for this is the realisation by historians that European states tended to export the ways of dealing with religious diversity they developed at home to the new territories that came under their control.[14] This pattern has been identified in Asia as well, for example in studies of the religious policies applied in Dutch overseas territories. Another reason for the closer relation between the historiographies on (North) America and Europe is the presence in many colonies of European settlers with different national, cultural, and religious backgrounds. As a result, scholars have focused more on the relationships between different Christian confessions and less on how indigenous beliefs and practices were accommodated within a Christian framework or how Christianity was translated and tailored to specific missionary contexts.

Because of this difference in historical contexts, studies on North America concern themselves more than do studies on Asia with the daily reality of religious diversity, governmental policies in relation to it, and interactions between different religious communities. These topics have customarily been studied within the context of a particular colony or locality, but more recently a comparative approach has become *en vogue*.[15] As in the European context, studies interested in the practice of religious toleration exist alongside intellectual histories of religious tolerance. Despite the points of contact and overlap between these historiographies, though, the confessionalisation paradigm has not been very influential in the American one. Arguably, this has resulted from the insistence of the "strong" version of this paradigm on close cooperation between church and state, institutions which needed to be established in colonial contexts and tended not to be as powerful as the ones at "home" (at least not immediately). Ultimately, the profoundly different contexts in which religious diversity and forms of toleration emerged have resulted in historiographies that sometimes partially overlap and interact, but at other times (sharply) diverge.

In spite of the differences between these historiographies outlined in the brief survey above, the field as a whole has been influenced by a number of overarching historiographic developments. The increased prominence of social history and "history from below" as well as changing views about the role of church and state – about which more below – have resulted in a major historiographic shift: a focus on the agency of religious groups and the individual members thereof, including those who were not part of secular or clerical elites. No longer seen as playthings in the hands of the ruling classes, religious minorities have been shown to have responded creatively to the measures taken by church and state, and also – crucially – to have influenced and shaped those measures. Examples abound, ranging from members of religious minorities who used their social and economic capital to mitigate the effects of hostile legislation to those who appealed to overseas co-religionists in foreign capitals to defend their interests and intercede with authorities on their behalf.[16] By employing strategies such as dissimulation and partial or occasional conformity, some minorities managed to exert political influence and maintain their religious identities as well as their religious practices and customs, ensuring their own survival even in adverse circumstances.[17] Moreover, there were many individuals who refused to be cowed by attempts at coercion, transgressing – sometimes flagrantly – the norms and rules formulated by church and state. This led to various kinds of interreligious interaction, ranging from illegal visits to Jewish ghettos to marrying a spouse of a different faith, or attending religious services in the church of a rival religion while travelling abroad.

Focus on the laity and their agency has changed scholars' perception of the policies of secular authorities regarding religious difference and diversity. Rather than simply being imposed from above, government policies were often the dynamic outcome of interactions between different interest groups, including government officials, church authorities, and religious minorities themselves. Moreover, early modern states were fragmented, highly complex entities that comprised various layers and institutions, which by no means acted consistently in unison. Different governmental institutions collided and competed over rights, privileges, and jurisdictions. Moreover, the religious sentiments of their officers varied, in part because the exclusion of members of religious minorities from political offices tended to be a gradual and drawn-out process. As a result, the genesis of the political and legal framework in which interreligious interaction took place in any particular state is invariably a complex, non-linear story. This fact emerges clearly from recent research on the religious peace treaties that were concluded in response to the fragmentation of western Christendom and the religious wars that erupted in its wake.[18] Historians of the Holy Roman Empire, for example, have devoted much attention to the Peace of Augsburg (1555) and Peace of Westphalia (1648).[19] In addition to scrutinising the text of such treaties, scholars have studied their subsequent interpretation and implementation at different levels of government. Regional and local studies have made clear how such laws and their varied interpretation influenced social and cultural relations between religious groups.[20] Similar research on the Edict of Nantes and its eventual revocation as well as on the measures taken against Moriscos in Spain, to mention just a couple of examples, has likewise yielded new insights into the complex interplay between different actors in relation to the treatment of religious minorities and their position in society.[21] Comparative studies, made possible by the existence of such a rich body of secondary literature, have started to trace the similarities and dissimilarities in the ways in which religious diversity was "managed" in different countries.[22]

The importance of the interplay between different actors and groups is also borne out when examining how relations between religious groups were temporally and spatially mediated. Expressions of religious belonging, in particular when they were highly visible and occurred in the public sphere, could be flashpoints for antagonism and violence between people of different religions. In some cases, both secular authorities and the dominant church joined forces in attempts to root out public manifestations of rival religions, but quite often the policies and the ways in which they were enforced in practice left much to be desired. Even when secular authorities adopted a policy of rigid spatial separation, the agency of religious minorities is apparent. The most prominent example is the Jewish ghettos that were established in some early modern European cities. Some Jews, medical doctors in particular, obtained permission to enter and exit the ghettos during times of day when this officially was prohibited. The expansion of the ghetto in Venice was prompted not only by the commercial and economic interests of the city government, but also by the complaints lodged by the Jewish community about the lack of space.[23] The ways in which interreligious interaction was temporally mediated were likewise products of dynamic engagement between groups. Relationships between different religious communities could be particularly fraught during certain times in the liturgical year, when interreligious interaction could turn violent.[24] The ensuing regulations, which might include stipulations about where and when members of a religious community could go to church or prohibitions to work on certain days, often were influenced by the demands of the clergy and requests made by religious minorities.[25]

In addition to the policies of the state, the ones advocated by ecclesiastical institutions and clergy continue to receive their due attention, and for good reason: they did exert influence, albeit in varying degrees, on the coexistence of, and actual interaction between, members of different religions.[26] In areas characterised by religious diversity, several churches and their clergy vied to influence both the policies of the state and the behaviour of the laity. In some cases, the leaders of rival churches were in agreement (as in the rejection of mixed marriage), but often their views clashed. Moreover, every church comprised different, often competing institutions, while its clergy was diverse in its training, institutional affiliation, theology, style of pastoral care, and other characteristics.[27] Nevertheless, clergy invariably subjected laity to norms and rules that prescribed what types of interreligious interaction were allowed. Almost every church erected some sort of bureaucratic apparatus to police the laity and punish wrongdoers. Still, because of the differences between and within churches, the influence exerted by "the" clergy on the particular forms of toleration that emerged was varied.

While church and state are still regarded as important factors in the forms of toleration that came into being, the assessment of their influence has become more nuanced as recent historiography has increasingly highlighted the roles played by non-elites. Moreover, scholars disagree about the exact roles played by church and state in the practice of religious toleration. This is partly a result of the mounting critique of the confessionalisation paradigm, in particular its "strong" version, which posited the close cooperation between church and state in the creation of pious, obedient citizens.[28] Historians have been keen to note the absence of such cooperation, even arguing that opposition between church and state created fertile ground for the existence of religious diversity.[29] Other scholars, though, point out that even in the absence of a strong, confessionalising state, confessional identities could emerge as people internalised the teachings of their respective churches.[30]

A number of other factors contributed to the different forms of toleration that emerged in the early modern world. The socio-economic profile of a religious group, although often partly affected by the policies of the state, was important, influencing their physical distribution in a locality and the kind of economic transactions and social interactions they engaged in.[31] Recent research has also emphasised the heterogeneity of religious groups. Their internal stratification meant that individuals who were part of the same group were engaged in different types of interreligious interaction, were impacted by legislation in different ways, and experienced religious diversity differently. High social status could mitigate the negative effects of belonging to a religious minority, while the fundamental inequality between religious majority and minorities could be "complicated by competing hierarchies of age, gender and occupation."[32] The attitudes, stances, and viewpoints of individuals were important, too: ultimately, the decision whether or not to interact with the religious other was in their hands. As a result, even within a particular form of toleration and specific religious group, the experience of religious diversity could be highly varied.

Taken as a whole, recent historiography has thus shown that toleration emerged in the context of dynamic processes of interaction and negotiation between a variety of actors, including government officials, clergymen and -women, and members of religious groups. Due to the complexity of this process, the precise genesis of particular forms of toleration can be hard to uncover; indeed, attempts to locate their origin sometimes produce distorting stories of linear development.[33] Irrespective of their genesis, the various forms of toleration practised in the early modern world influenced what interreligious interaction consisted of (its nature), and where and when it occurred (its context). In other words, the ways in which religious diversity was accommodated in early modern communities influenced how religious diversity was experienced by individuals in those communities.

Examining the various ways in which religious difference was accommodated, the experience of religious diversity, and the link between the two, this volume is structured on the basis of five key concepts: the senses, identity, boundaries, space, and interaction. These concepts underlay many of the key shifts and innovations in recent historiography. They help us understand the complex, multilayered phenomenon of interreligious interaction in a range of highly different circumstances and societies and enable us to tease out the ways in which such interaction was perceived and experienced. They can be applied to study relationships and interactions on the level of the group and on that of the individual. And as the paragraphs below show, they offer ways to connect forms of toleration with the experience of religious diversity.

The first concept is the *senses*, which played essential roles in expressing, encountering, and perceiving religious diversity. Religious difference could be expressed and perceived in many different ways, including through material culture and soundscapes. The sound of worship in particular had the ability to protrude into the public sphere, imposing on people there an experience of religious difference they did not always desire. Even more private spaces such as houses provided ample opportunities for encountering other religions through architectural features, artistic decor, and books, as well as through the presence of slaves, servants, or family members with different religious affiliations.[34] Because the experience of religious diversity was fundamentally shaped by the context as well as the content of interreligious interaction, the role of the senses is highly significant. Some occasions for noticing religious diversity could be regarded as more invasive than others. To be sure, the effects of perceiving and encountering religious diversity were not unidirectional: the spatial proximity of and regular points of contact between religious groups might set in motion trajectories of differentiation and rejection, but they also might spur processes of cross-fertilisation and exchange.

The concept of *identity* has been widely adopted by scholars because it has enabled them to study how perceptions of oneself and others influenced relationships with and behaviour towards other people. Scholars have studied identity from a variety of angles, but in general the earlier top-down perspectives that focused on the role of secular and religious elites in processes of identity-formation have given way to approaches more attuned to non-elite participation. Furthermore, by studying the multiplicity of identities people had and the ways in which different identities intersected, recent studies challenge the thesis that confessional identities invariably trumped other ones.[35] In this volume, the employment of the concept of identity serves two purposes. First, by examining the range of media and other forms of communication used by members of religious communities to express and assert their religious affiliations, we gain a greater understanding of how religious diversity was encountered and expressed. Second, by studying the content of religious identity – i.e. what it meant to be part of a religious group – we learn about its role in shaping human behaviour in the context of interreligious interaction.[36] Since identities had the power to connect and divide, their examination uncovers important aspects of how religious difference was articulated and experienced.

The solidification of group identities could lead to the emergence of *boundaries* between groups. The existence of various boundaries – not only legal and political ones but also social, cultural, and indeed religious ones – structured interreligious interaction.[37] While the formation of sharp boundaries often entailed a decreasing willingness to interact with members of other groups, even the clearest boundaries were sometimes crossed – both metaphorically and physically – through conversion, mixed marriage, or simply by everyday sociability. Whereas some boundaries were made explicit, for example through governmental legislation or rules of conduct prescribed by clergy, others were invisible and reflected the distinct behaviour of different religious groups. The cultural divides that resulted could have many dimensions, including name-giving practices and dress codes, to give but two examples. Often boundaries of different sorts coincided and were traversed simultaneously: recent studies of conversion, for example, have emphasised the frequency with which it was accompanied by physical migration and mobility.[38] While boundaries hampered certain interactions, their very existence highlighted societal differences. Thus, paradoxically, even when they were not transgressed, boundaries created occasions where religious differences were accentuated and experienced.

Interaction is the fourth concept around which the analyses offered in this volume revolve. Social historians have painted a detailed, albeit still incomplete, picture of the circumstances in which interaction between members of different religious groups took place. Their work has teased out some of the factors that shaped such interaction, which included the religious composition of local communities, demographic and economic trends, the presence of powerful institutions and rulers, the attitudes of secular and ecclesiastical elites, the brand of piety advocated by clergymen and -women, and the legal parameters established by peace treaties. Despite the great variety shown by these studies, which often have a local or regional focus, they have revealed distinct patterns of interaction between members of different religions that were widespread. Spurred by the insight that religious communities were heterogeneous and internally stratified, scholars have also examined particular subgroups within these communities, unearthing still other forms of interaction, some of which were specific to a group of people that shared a certain socio-economic profile or status.

The fifth and last concept, *space*, is predominantly used to examine the spatial contexts of interreligious interaction. Interactions that took place in sacred spaces, such as participation in the religious rites of another confession, tended to be viewed differently, by both lay participants and ecclesiastical authorities, than were forms of engagement that occurred in a more "neutral" context in the public sphere. Because different spaces were subject to different rules, scholars now conceive space as a cultural construct as much as a physical entity, something created through the attachment of meanings and patterning of behaviours. Some spaces, moreover, existed primarily in the imagination; devotional techniques such as mental prayer spring to mind. Still, religious communities operated within spatial and legal frameworks that established parameters regarding what they were allowed to do and where. To understand better the spatial contexts in which religious diversity was encountered and experienced, scholars have started to map the spatial distribution of religious communities (sometimes aided by digital technologies such as GIS) and study their spatial practices.[39] Where spaces were shared by different religious groups, their members intermingled, interacted, and sometimes collided. Interreligious interaction, then, was clearly mediated by space.

These five concepts make it possible to study interreligious interaction, the experience of religious diversity, and the relation between these two across space and time. We have therefore chosen to use these concepts to structure this volume. Each of the five sections, entitled "Sensing the Other," "Asserting Identities," "Crossing Boundaries," "Interacting and Engaging," and "Sharing Space," comprises two or three chapters. The use of gerunds in the sections' titles highlights the dynamic nature of the relationships between individuals and groups of different faiths, which were continually in a process of negotiation and renegotiation. In order to increase the volume's accessibility and utility for a wide audience, each of the sections is preceded by a concise historiographic introduction that explains the theme of its section, traces the historiographic developments relevant to it, and provides context for the chapters that follow. Each of the chapters then presents a detailed case study of the interaction between particular religious groups in a specific place and time. By covering different geographic regions and by studying the relationships between Christians, Jews, and Muslims as well as between different Christian denominations, the chapters encourage comparisons. Each of them is at the cutting edge of historiographic development regarding the practice of religious toleration in the early modern world. Drawing on new insights and knowledge generated by recent research, each chapter is an original contribution to the field, expanding the boundaries of our understanding.

Notes

1 The sort of modern, principled toleration we describe in this opening paragraph is a product principally of liberal political thought as developed from John Stuart Mill to John Rawls and beyond; in recent years, Rainer Forst has been perhaps its most distinguished advocate: Rainer Forst, *Toleration in Conflict: Past and Present*, trans. Ciaran Cronin (Cambridge: Cambridge University Press, 2013). It is, of course, not the only definition of toleration formulated in the modern era and has been critiqued extensively by theorists such as Williams, Nagel, Sandel, Kymlicka, and Heyd: see David Heyd, ed., *Toleration: An Elusive Virtue* (Princeton: Princeton University Press, 1996); see also Jeffrey R. Collins, "Redeeming the Enlightenment: New Histories of Religious Toleration," *Journal of Modern History* 81 (2009), 607–36. It remains, however, the dominant definition of toleration in western culture. For a philosophical introduction, see Catriona McKinnon, *Toleration: A Critical Introduction* (London: Routledge, 2006). A trenchant critique of the political functions served by the liberal concept is offered in Wendy Brown, *Regulating Aversion: Tolerance in the Age of Identity and Empire* (Princeton: Princeton University Press, 2006). Hayden distinguishes between "active" toleration, which fits our characterisation of modern toleration, and "passive" toleration, which conforms to what we will describe as the early modern concept; however, he sees the latter widely prevalent around the globe today: Robert M. Hayden et al., *Antagonistic Tolerance: Competitive Sharing of Religious Sites and Spaces* (London: Routledge, 2016).
2 Classic narratives crediting Protestantism include works by Thomas Macaulay, John Lothrop Motley, William Lecky, Wilbur Kitchener Jordan, and William Haller. The most forceful exponent today of a narrative crediting the Enlightenment and secularism is Jonathan Israel; see his monumental trilogy of books on the Enlightenment, beginning with Jonathan I. Israel, *Radical Enlightenment: Philosophy and the Making of Modernity 1650–1750* (Oxford: Clarendon Press, 2001).
3 See i.a. Keith P. Luria, *Sacred Boundaries: Religious Coexistence and Conflict in Early-Modern France* (Washington, D.C.: Catholic University of American Press, 2005); Wayne P. Te Brake, *Religious War and Religious Peace in Early Modern Europe* (Cambridge: Cambridge University Press, 2017); C. Scott Dixon, Dagmar Freist, and Mark Greengrass, eds., *Living with Religious Diversity in Early Modern Europe* (Farnham: Ashgate, 2009); Willem Frijhoff, *Embodied Belief: Ten Essays on Religious Culture in Dutch History* (Hilversum: Verloren, 2002); Nicholas Doumanis, *Before the Nation: Muslim-Christian Coexistence and Its Destruction in Late-Ottoman Anatolia* (Oxford: Oxford University Press, 2012); Thomas Max Safley, ed., *A Companion to Multiconfessionalism in the Early Modern World* (Leiden: Brill, 2011); Richard Bonney and D.J.B. Trim, eds., *Persecution and Pluralism: Calvinists and Religious Minorities in Early Modern Europe, 1550-1700* (Oxford-Bern: Peter Lang, 2006); Evan Haefeli, *Accidental Pluralism: America and the Religious Politics of English Expansion, 1497–1662* (Chicago: University of Chicago Press, 2021); Katsumi Fukasawa, Benjamin J. Kaplan, and Pierre-Yves Beaurepaire, eds., *Religious Interactions in Europe and the Mediterranean World: Coexistence and Dialogue from the Twelfth to the Twentieth Centuries* (Abingdon: Routledge, 2017). The varied terminology that has been applied to interreligious relations in the Ottoman Empire is surveyed in

Eleni Gara, "Conceptualizing Interreligious Relations in the Ottoman Empire: The Early Modern Centuries," *Acta Poloniae Historica* 116 (2017), 57–91.

4 A similar fate has befallen "convivencia," used to designate the harmonious relations between Christians, Jews, and Muslims said to exist in Spain before the late medieval period. In the minds of many historians, it has been discredited by its romanticisation and the Iberian nationalist myths with which it is associated. See Maya Soifer, "Beyond *convivencia*: Critical Reflections on the Historiography of Interfaith Relations in Christian Spain," *Journal of Medieval Iberian Studies 1*, no. 1 (2009), 19–35.

5 E.g. Isabel Karremann, Cornel Zwierlein, and Inga Mai Groote, eds., *Forgetting Faith? Negotiating Confessional Conflict in Early Modern Europe* (Berlin: De Gruyter, 2012); Victoria Christman, *Pragmatic Toleration: The Politics of Religious Heterodoxy in Early Reformation Antwerp, 1515–1555* (Rochester: University of Rochester Press, 2015); Victoria Christman and Marjorie Plummer, eds., *Topographies of Tolerance and Intolerance: Responses to Religious Pluralism in Reformation Europe* (Leiden: Brill, 2018); Ole Grell and Bob Scribner, eds., *Tolerance and Intolerance in the European Reformation* (Cambridge: Cambridge University Press, 1996), essay by Scribner; Charles J. Halperin, "The Ideology of Silence: Prejudice and Pragmatism on the Medieval Religious Frontier," *Comparative Studies in Society and History* (1984), 442–66; Ernst H. Kossmann, "Toleration and Tolerance in the Netherlands," *The Low Countries: Arts and Society in Flanders and The Netherlands, A Yearbook* (1997), 31–7; Charles P. Hanson, *Necessary Virtue: The Pragmatic Origins of Religious Liberty in New England* (Charlottesville, Va.: University Press of Virginia, 1998).

6 For a work of synthesis embodying this revisionism, see Benjamin J. Kaplan, *Divided by Faith: Religious Conflict and the Practice of Toleration in Early Modern Europe* (Cambridge, Mass.: Harvard University Press, 2007).

7 On the importance of looking at toleration over time and its alternation with bouts of violent conflict, see Hayden et al., *Antagonistic Tolerance*. On the concept of "negotiating religious differences," see François Guesnet, Lois Lee, and Cécile Laborde, eds., *Negotiating Religion: Cross-Disciplinary Perspectives* (Abingdon: Routledge, 2016). On relations across boundaries, see Fredrik Barth, *Ethnic Groups and Boundaries: The Social Organization of Culture Difference* (London: Allen & Unwin, 1969), quotation from p. 10; Patrick Geary, "Living with Conflicts in Stateless France: A Typology of Conflict Management Mechanisms, 1050–1200," in *Living with the Dead in the Middle Ages*, ed. Patrick Geary (Ithaca: Cornell University Press, 1994), 125–60.

8 A key work conceptually is David Nirenberg, *Communities of Violence: Persecution of Minorities in the Middle Ages* (Princeton: Princeton University Press, 1995); see also Alexandra Walsham, *Charitable Hatred: Tolerance and Intolerance in England, 1500–1700* (Manchester: Manchester University Press, 2006). The term "regimes of toleration" is from Michael Walzer, *On Toleration* (New Haven: Yale University Press, 1997).

9 For Catholic missions, see the references in footnote 10. For Protestant missions, see e.g. Charles H. Parker, *Global Calvinism: Conversion and Commerce in the Dutch Empire, 1600–1800* (New Haven-London, 2022). For Protestant missions in other parts of the world, see e.g. D.L. Noorlander, *Heaven's Wrath. The Protestant Reformation and the Dutch West India Company in the Atlantic World* (Ithaca: Cornell University Press, 2019); Simone Maghenzani and Stefano Villani, eds., *British Protestant Missions and the Conversion of Europe, 1600–1900* (Abingdon: Routledge, 2020); Alec Ryrie, "The Missionary Problem in Early Modern Protantism: British, Irish and Scandinavian Perspectives," in *Northern European Reformations: Transnational Perspectives*, ed. James E. Kelly, Henning Laugerud, and Salvador Ryan (London: Springer, 2020), 377–403. Comparative

studies include Charles H. Parker, "Converting Souls across Cultural Borders: Dutch Calvinism and Early Modern Missionary Enterprises," *Journal of Global History* 8, no. 1 (2013), 50–71; Catherine Bal);ériaux, "'Tis nothing but French Poison, all of it': Jesuit and Calvinist Missions on the New World Frontier," in *Encounters between Jesuits and Protestants in Asia and the Americas*, ed. Jorge Cañizares-Esguerra, Robert Aleksander Maryks, and R.P. Hsia (Boston-Leiden: Brill, 2018), 275–305.

10 Recent studies include: Anand Amaladass and Ines G. Županov, eds., *Intercultural Encounter and the Jesuit Mission* in *South Asia* (16th – 18th *Centuries*) (Bangalore: Asian Trading Corporation, 2014); Antje Flüchter and Rouven Wirbser, eds., *Translating Catechisms, Translating Cultures: The Expansion of Catholicism in the Early Modern World* (Leiden: Brill, 2017); R. Po-chia Hsia, ed., *A Companion to Early Modern Catholic Global Missions* (Leiden: Brill, 2018). More generally on missionaries and the practice of cultural translation: Joan Pau Rubiés, "Ethnography and Cultural Translation in the Early Modern Missions," *Studies in Church History* 53 (2017), 272–310.

11 E.g. Ines G. Županov and Pierre Antoine Fabre, eds., *The Rites Controversies in the Early Modern World* (Leiden: Brill, 2018).

12 E.g. Tara Alberts, *Conflict and Conversion: Catholicism in Southeast Asia, 1500–1700* (Oxford: Oxford University Press, 2013).

13 This might also have to do with a lack of written sources originating in other religious traditions. Luke Clossey, "Religious Expansion in Islam, Catholicism, and Buddhism," in *Global Reformations: Transforming Early Modern Religions, Societies, and Cultures*, ed. Nicholas Terpstra (London-New York: Routledge, 2019), 16.

14 For a recent study that emphasises the European dimension of developments in North America, see Haefeli, *Accidental Pluralism*; "A European turn in early American History? A Discussion of Evan Haefeli's *Accidental Pluralism: America and the Religious Politics of English Expansion, 1497–1662*," *Journal of Early American History* 12, no. 1 (2021), 1–43. Earlier studies already remarked on the importance of taking this European dimension into account. E.g. George L. Procter-Smith, *Religion and Trade in New Netherland: Dutch Origins and American Development* (Ithaca: Cornell University Press, 1973), 237.

15 Procter-Smith, *Religion and Trade in New Netherland*; Joyce D. Goodfriend, "Practicing Toleration in Dutch New Netherland," in *The First Prejudice: Religious Tolerance and Intolerance in Early America*, ed. Chris Beneke and Christopher S. Grenda (Philadelphia: University of Pennsylvania Press, 2011), 98–122; Evan Haefeli, *New Netherland and the Dutch Origins of American Religious Liberty* (Philadelphia: University of Pennsylvania Press, 2016); Mark Häberlein, *The Practice of Pluralism. Congregational Life and Religious Diversity in Lancaster, Pennsylvania, 1730–1820* (University Park: Pennsylvania State University Press, 2009). For a comparative study, see Haefeli, *Accidental Pluralism*.

16 Raymond A. Mentzer, *Blood & Belief: Family Survival and Confessional Identity among the Provincial Huguenot Nobility* (West Lafayette, Purdue University Press, 1994); Bastian Gillner, *Freie Herren – Freie Religion: der Adel des Oberstifts Münster zwischen konfessionellem Konflikt und staatlicher Verdichtung, 1500 bis 1700* (Münster: Aschendorff, 2011); Jaap Geraerts, *Patrons of the Old Faith: The Catholic Nobility in Utrecht and Guelders, c. 1580–1702* (Leiden: Brill, 2018); Goodfriend, "Practicing Toleration in Dutch New Netherland."

17 E.g. Alexandra Walsham, *Church Papists: Catholicism, Conformity and Confessional Polemic in Early Modern England* (Woodbridge: Boydell Press, 1993); Enrique Soria Mesa, *Los últimos moriscos: pervivencias de la población de origen islámico en el Reino de Granada (siglos XVII-XVIII)* (Valencia: Publicacions de la Universitat de València, 2014). Natalia Muchnik, "Conversos versus Recusants:

Shaping the Markers of Difference (1570–1680)," *in Religious Changes and Cultural Transformations in the Early Modern Western Sephardic Communities*, ed. Yosef Kaplan (Leiden: Brill, 2019), 43–70.

18 For recent studies of religious peace treaties, see e.g. Te Brake, *Religious War and Religious Peace*, and the multi-year project "Europaische Religionsfrieden Digital" (https://eured.de/en/startseite-english/, last accessed November 14, 2022).

19 R.G. Asch, "Religious Toleration, the Peace of Westphalia and the German Territorial Estates," *Parliaments, estates & representation / Parlements, états & représentation* 20, no. 1 (2000), 75–90; Whaley, "A Tolerant Society? Religious Toleration in the Holy Roman Empire, 1648–1806," in *Toleration in Enlightenment Europe*, ed. Ole Peter Grell and Roy Porter (Cambridge: Cambridge University Press, 2000), 175–95.

20 Paul Warmbrunn, *Zwei Konfessionen in einer Stadt. Das Zusammenleben von Katholiken und Protestanten in den paritätischen Reichsstädten Augsburg, Biberach, Ravensburg und Dinkelsbühl von 1548 bis 1648* (Wiesbaden: F. Steiner, 1983); Peter Zschunke, *Konfession und Alltag in Oppenheim: Beiträge zur Geschichte von Bevölkerung und Gesellschaft einer gemischtkonfessionellen Kleinstadt in der frühen Neuzeit* (Wiesbaden: F. Steiner, 1984); C. Scott Dixon, "Urban Order and Religious Coexistence in the German Imperial City: Augsburg and Donauwörth, 1548-1608," *Central European History* 40, no. 1 (2007), 1–33; David Mayes, "Divided by Toleration: Paradoxical Effects of the 1648 Peace of Westphalia and Multiconfessionalism," *Archiv für Reformationsgeschichte* 106, no. 1 (2015), 290–313; and the chapters by Alyson Creasman and Jesse Spohnholz in this volume.

21 Keith P. Luria, "France: An Overview," in *A Companion to Multiconfessionalism*, 207–38, and the literature cited there; see also the chapter by David van der Linden in this volume. For Moriscos in Spain, see e.g. Mercedes García-Arenal and Gerard Wiegers, eds., *The Expulsion of the Moriscos from Spain: A Mediterranean Diaspora* (Leiden: Brill, 2014); Már Jónsson, "The Expulsion of the Moriscos from Spain in 1609–1614: The Destruction of an Islamic Periphery," *Journal of Global History* 2, no. 2 (2007), 195–212.

22 E.g. Charles H. Parker, "Paying for the Privilege: The Management of Public Order and Religious Pluralism in Two Early Modern Societies," *Journal of World History* 17, no. 3 (2006), 267–96.

23 Benjamin Ravid, "The Religious, Economic and Social Background and Context of the Establishment of the Ghetti of Venice," in *Gli Ebrei e Venezia*, ed. Gaetano Cozzi (Milan: Edizioni Comunita, 1987), 222–3.

24 Nirenberg, *Communities of Violence*; Id., "Violencia, memoria y convivencia: los judíos en el medioevo ibérico," *Memoria y civilización* 2 (1999), 31–53; Daniel Jütte, "'They Shall Not Keep Their Doors or Windows Open': Urban Space and the Dynamics of Conflict and Contact in Premodern Jewish–Christian Relations," *European History Quarterly* 46, no. 2 (2016), 209–37.

25 For examples of such regulations, see Benjamin J. Kaplan, "Fictions of Privacy: House Chapels and the Spatial Accommodation of Religious Dissent in Early Modern Europe," *The American Historical Review* 107, no. 4 (2002), 1047. Benjamin Ravid, "Cum Nimis Absurdum and the Ancona Auto-da-Fé Revisited: Their Impact on Venice and Some Wider Reflections," *Jewish History* 26, no. 1–2 (2012), 90. For an example of the agency of religious minorities, see e.g. Nirenberg, "Violencia, memoria y convivencia," 46.

26 See e.g. Johann Gamberoni, *Der Verkehr der Katholiken mit den Häretikern. Grundsätzliches nach den Moralisten von der Mitte des 16. bis zur Mitte des 17. Jahrhunderts* (Brixen: A. Weger, 1950); Thomas Kaufmann, "Religious, Confessional and Cultural Conflicts among Neighbors: Observations on the Sixteenth and Seventeenth Centuries," in *Orthodoxies and Heterodoxies in Early Modern*

German Culture, ed. Randolph C. Head and Daniel Christensen (Leiden: Brill, 2007), 91–115; Charles H. Parker and Starr-LeBeau, eds., *Judging Faith, Punishing Sin: Inquisitions and Consistories in the Early Modern World* (Cambridge: Cambridge University Press, 2017).

27 For the (institutional) conflicts within the early modern Catholic Church, see e.g. Craig Harline and Eddy Put, *A Bishop's Tale: Mathias Hovius among His Flock in Seventeenth-Century Flanders* (New Haven: Yale University Press, 2000).

28 For the distinction between a "strong" and "weak theory of confessionalisation," see e.g. Philip Benedict, "Confessionalization in France? Critical Reflections and New Evidence," in *Society and Culture in the Huguenot World, 1559–1685*, ed. Raymond Mentzer and Andrew Spicer (Cambridge: Cambridge University Press, 2002), 44–61.

29 In particular in the historiography on the Dutch Republic, this opposition has been emphasised. E.g. Christine Kooi, *Liberty and Religion: Church and State in Leiden's Reformation, 1572–1620* (Leiden: Brill, 2000).

30 Randolph C. Head, "Catholics and Protestants in Graubünden: Confessional Discipline and Confessional Identities without an Early Modern State?," *German History* 17, no. 3 (1999), 321–45.

31 For example, many Muslims who arrived in Sevilla in the years 1569–70 ended up on the outskirts of this city. The small number of them who lived in the centre often were slaves or servants in well-to-do Catholic families. Manual F. Fernández Chaves and Rafael M. Pérez Garcia, *En los márgenes de la ciudad de Dios. Moriscos en Sevilla* (Valencia: Publicacions de la Universitat de València, 2009), 222.

32 Alexandra Walsham, "Cultures of Coexistence in Early Modern England: History, Literature and Religious Toleration," *The Seventeenth Century* 28, no. 2 (2013), 123.

33 A point convincingly made by David Luebke in his contribution to this volume.

34 Tara Hamling, *Decorating the "Godly" Household: Religious Art in Post-Reformation Britain* (New Haven: Yale University Press, 2011); Richard L. Williams, "Cultures of Dissent: English Catholics and the Visual Arts," in *Catholic Communities in Protestant States: Britain and the Netherlands c. 1570–1720*, ed. Benjamin J. Kaplan et al. (Manchester: Manchester University Press, 2009), 230–48; P.J.A.N. Rietbergen, "The Library of a Dutch Country Squire, Thomas Walraven van Arkel (1615–1694). A Contribution to the Study of Dutch Aristocratic Culture in the 17th Century," *Lias* 9 (1982), 271–84. For Jewish homes in Venice as sites of multireligious encounter, see Francesca Francesconi, "The Venetian Jewish Household as a Multireligious Community in Early Modern Italy," in *Global Reformations: Transforming Early Modern Religions, Societies, and Cultures*, ed. Nicholas Terpstra (London-New York: Routledge, 2019), 231–48.

35 Mentzer, *Blood & Belief*; Craig Harline, *Conversions: Two Family Stories from the Reformation and Modern America* (New Haven: Yale University Press, 2011); David M. Luebke, *Hometown Religion: Regimes of Coexistence in Early Modern Westphalia* (Charlottesville: University of Virginia Press, 2016); Geraerts, *Patrons of the Old Faith*.

36 For studies that examine what it actually meant for people to be part of a religious community, see e.g. Judith Pollmann, "Being a Catholic in Early Modern Europe," in *The Ashgate Research Companion to the Counter-Reformation*, ed. Alexandra Bamji, Geert H. Janssen, and Mary Laven (Farham: Ashgate, 2013), 165–82; Alec Ryrie, *Being Protestant in Reformation Britain* (Oxford: Oxford University Press, 2013); Bernard Vincent, "Ser morisco en España en el siglo XVI," in *El río morisco*, ed. Bernard Vincent (Valencia: Publicacions de la Universitat de València, 2015), 155–62.

37 Luria, *Sacred* boundaries; Etienne François, *Die unsichtbare Grenze: Protestanten und Katholiken in Augsburg 1648–1806* (Sigmaringen: Thorbecke, 1991). According to Christine Kooi, the crystallisation of clear boundaries between religious groups contributed to their peaceful coexistence. Christine Kooi, *Calvinists and Catholics during Holland's Golden Age: Heretics and Idolaters* (Cambridge: Cambridge University Press, 2012), 220.

38 Duane Corpis, *Crossing the Boundaries of Belief: Geographies of Religious Conversion in Southern Germany, 1648–1800* (Charlottesville, Va.: University of Virginia Press, 2014). Kim Siebenhüner, "Conversion, Mobility and the Roman Inquisition in Italy Around 1600," *Past & Present* 200, no. 1 (2008), 5–35. Alberts, *Conflict and Conversion*, 155. The study of mobility in the context of Reformation and post-Reformation culture is burgeoning. See e.g. Geert H. Janssen, *The Dutch Revolt and Catholic Exile in Reformation Europe* (Oxford: Oxford University Press, 2014). Liesbeth Corens, *Confessional Mobility and English Catholics in Counter-Reformation Europe* (Oxford: Oxford University Press, 2019).

39 Nicholas Terpstra and Colin Rose, eds., *Mapping Space, Sense, and Movement in Florence: Historical GIS and the Early Modern City (London: Routledge, 2016)*; David Frick, *Kith, Kin, and Neighbors: Communities & Confessions in Seventeenth-Century Wilno* (Ithaca-London: Cornell University Press, 2013); Justine Walden, "Before the Ghetto: Spatial Logistics, Ritual Humiliation, and Jewish-Christian Relations in Early Modern Florence," in *Global Reformations: Transforming Early Modern Religions, Societies, and Cultures*, ed. Nicholas Terpstra (London-New York: Routledge, 2019), 97–115; Timothy Fehler, "Coexistence and Confessionalization. Emden's Topography of Religious Pluralism," in *Topographies of Tolerance and Intolerance. Responses to Religious Pluralism in Reformation Europe*, ed. Marjorie Elizabeth Plummer and Victoria Christmann (Leiden: Brill, 2018), 78–105.

Part I

Sensing the Other

Historiographic Introduction

Developing a new and exciting field of research, scholars have begun in recent years to examine ideas about the senses and the role of the senses over the course of human history. Known as the "history of the senses" or "sensory history," the field is predicated on the idea that, to echo Mark M. Smith, the senses "are not universal but, rather, a product of place and, especially, time, so that how people perceived and understood smell, sound, touch, taste and sight changed historically."[1] In other words, the senses should not be understood in a transhistorical fashion, but rather be conceived of as products of specific cultures. Hence many scholars speak of "sensory cultures" or their equivalent for one of the senses, e.g. "sonic cultures."[2]

The studies produced in this field are characterised by differences in approach, scope, and topic. Some take either a particular sense or all the senses as their starting point. In tracing how the senses were understood across cultures and historical periods, many of these studies engage with the so-called great divide theory. Proposed by Marshall McLuhan and Walter Ong, among other scholars, this theory holds that, due to factors such as the invention of the printing press and the changes wrought by the religious reformations of the sixteenth century, sight became the predominantly important sense in western cultures, creating a divide with non-western cultures where this supposedly did not happen.[3] Historical change has, therefore, often been understood as a mutation in the hierarchy of the senses, the order of which changed in accordance with shifting ideas about and attitudes towards individual senses.

More closely related to the themes of this volume are the publications that investigate the ways in which attitudes about the senses changed as a result of the Protestant and Catholic Reformations.[4] Due to sharply diverging theologies and ritual practices, the role of the senses differed among the Christian confessions that emerged in the early modern world, not to mention the different values attributed to the senses in other, non-Christian religious traditions.[5] Other studies adopt a sensory perspective in order to enhance our understanding of religious worship, showing that the practice and experience of religion were multi-sensory affairs.[6] Departing from the older focus on the hierarchy of senses, these studies show that the different

DOI: 10.4324/9781003030522-2

senses often worked in tandem and should be understood and examined in relation to each other.[7]

This scholarship is based to a considerable extent on books authored by intellectuals and treatises written by reformers of various stripes, as well as on normative and prescriptive sources such as the decrees of ecclesiastical and governmental institutions. To be sure, these sources can to some extent be read against the grain in order to discern existing practices that were thought to be commendable or contemptible (often the latter). A widely held notion that the senses are not innate but need to be trained spurred the output of texts that aimed to do exactly that.[8]

More recently, scholars have been keen to move beyond the normative framework created by reformers, taking religious difference and diversity as the starting point of their analysis. As part of the growing scholarship on confessional coexistence in the early modern world, they have started to pay more attention to the sensory dimensions of religious diversity, i.e. the various ways in which religious differences were enacted and perceived sensorily. In what ways, for example, did people give sensory expression to their religious affiliation, and how and in which context was their affiliation perceived by others? A good example of research of this kind is the work done on processions, which, as sensory and public events with clear visual and auditory markers, were hard not to notice. The study of processions informs us about the constitutive elements of religious identities and how these were asserted as well as about reactions from the other side of the confessional divide.[9] In addition to studies that focus on religiously mixed regions, other publications focus on the sensory practices of religious exiles and refugees, thus showing the "national" traits of religious identities and practices.[10]

Still other research aims to complement earlier studies on programmes of sensory reform by examining how people reacted to the changing sensory cultures fashioned by the Protestant and Catholic Reformations.[11] This change in perspective and focus has been accompanied by the inclusion of other, more personal sources such as chronicles and diaries, which help one to include the experiences of people who were subjected to the sensory expressions associated with religions different from their own. In combination, then, with a comparative perspective, the history of the senses helps to uncover important dimensions of confessional coexistence in the early modern world.

The three chapters in this section mainly focus on one of the senses, namely hearing, but do so from different perspectives. In her contribution, Allyson Creasman studies religious invective in Augsburg, one of the multi-confessional imperial cities in the Holy Roman Empire. Augsburg's secular authorities adopted various strategies in order to maintain civic peace, such as the enforcement of the Peace of Augsburg (1555), which included, like many other religious peace treaties, a clause which prohibited the use of insulting and disparaging language about members of other confessions. Other strategies included resorting to existing laws of defamation, the invocation of notions of civic honour, and a formal reconciliation procedure for those who had transgressed the rules. The many court cases that ensued are indicative of the fact that religious insult was difficult to root out in Augsburg and that people felt wronged by verbal abuse based on their religious affiliation. Religious invective was one of the ways – and a problematic one in the eyes of local authorities – in which religious difference was experienced on a daily basis by early modern Augsburgers.

Whereas Creasman examines the spoken – and, one imagines, sometimes shouted – word, the contributions by Matthew Laube and Carolina Lenarduzzi analyse the sung word in the Southern Netherlands and the Dutch Republic, respectively. Whereas the latter country is known for its religious diversity, the former is not, yet throughout most of its history pockets of people belonging to religious minorities continued to exist.[12] As a result, in both countries, Catholic singing developed partly in response to the "acoustic presence," to borrow Laube's phrase, of other confessions. When discussing the sonic profile of Catholicism in the two countries, Laube and Lenarduzzi use the term "soundscape," a term that permeates studies on Reformation and post-Reformation "sonic cultures." Often departing from the more prescriptive meaning and use of this term by R. Murray Schafer, the scholar who coined it, this concept is now customarily taken to denote the sounds relevant in a given context and/or for a particular group of people.[13] Hence scholars speak about the soundscape of early modern Catholicism, the soundscapes of early modern cities and towns, and so forth.[14]

Often the term soundscape is connected to the notion of space, based on the idea that space influenced which sounds were heard, by whom, and how.[15] The dimension of space – a concept to which a separate section in this volume is dedicated – features in the contributions by Laube and Lenarduzzi as well. Catholic music was performed in different spatial contexts and served various ends. Songs were used not only for internal purposes, such as to inculcate a greater understanding of religious doctrine, but for external ones as well, including the conversion of non-Catholics. Songs thus constituted another means by which people were exposed to religious differences, in particular because the ability of sound to protrude into the public sphere was eagerly taken advantage of.

In different ways, the three authors incorporate and further develop the insights offered by recent work on religious diversity and coexistence in the early modern world. Creasman examines the concrete policies put in place by local authorities to govern speech, a topic that has been analysed largely from the perspective of intellectual history.[16] By analysing the spatial contexts in which Catholic songs were performed, Laube and Lenarduzzi address an important theme that frequently appears in the relevant scholarship, namely the distinction between public and private spheres.[17] Moreover, they show the prominence of certain trans-confessional strategies, such as the use of *contrafacta* (substituting a new text for a song's original one while leaving its music unchanged). Lastly, each of the contributions in its own way emphasises the role and agency of the laity in interreligious relationships, partly through the inclusion of sources that are individual rather than institutional or normative in nature.

Taken together, the three chapters thus weave together and fruitfully combine several recent trends in diverse academic fields, including the history of the senses and the history of confessional coexistence. In doing so, they make clear how the experience of religious difference was mediated through the senses and how everyone involved, ranging from secular authorities to laypeople, was aware of and actively tried to shape the sensory dimensions of religious diversity.

Notes

1 Mark M. Smith, *Sensing the Past: Seeing, Hearing, Smelling, Tasting, and Touching in History* (Berkely: University of California Press, 2007), 3. For the subtle differences between the "history of the senses" and "sensory history," see Ibid., 4.

2 Wietse de Boer, "The Counter-Reformation of the Senses," in *The Ashgate Research Companion to the Counter-Reformation*, ed. Alexandra Bamji, Geert H. Janssen, and Mary Laven (Farham: Ashgate, 2013), 258. Daniele V. Filippi and Michael J. Noone, "Introduction," in *Listening to Early Modern Catholicism: Perspectives from Musicology*, ed. Daniele V. Filippi and Michael J. Noone (Leiden: Brill, 2017), 1–17.

3 Smith, *Sensing the Past*, 8–10; Mark M. Smith, *A Sensory History Manifesto* (University Park: Pennsylvania State University Press, 2021), 68; Andrew Kettler, *The Smell of Slavery. Olfactory Racism and the Atlantic World* (Cambridge: Cambridge University Press, 2020), 8–12. Frequently studies also situate themselves in relation to Norbert Elias' idea of the civilising process. E.g. Robert Muchembled, *Smells: A Cultural History of Odours in Early Modern Times*, trans. Susan Pickford (Cambridge: Polity Press, 2020), 1–4.

4 Jacob M. Baum, *Reformation of the Senses: The Paradox of Religious Belief and Practice in Germany* (Urbana: University of Illinois Press, 2018); Philip Hahn, "Sensing Sacred Space: Ulm Minster, the Reformation, and Parishioners' Sensory Perception, c. 1470 to 1640," *Archiv für Reformationsgeschichte* 105, no. 1 (2014), 55–91.

5 Hence, the great efforts to which Catholic missionaries in South-East Asia went in order to determine which (aspects of) native religious customs were and were not superstitious. E.g. Tara Alberts, "Missions in Vietnam," in *A Companion to Early Modern Catholic Global Missions*, ed. R. Po-chia Hsia (Leiden: Brill, 2018), 292–301.

6 Wietse de Boer and Christine Göttler, eds., *Religion and the Senses in Early Modern Europe* (Leiden: Brill, 2013); Robin Macdonald, Emilie K.M. Murphy, and Elizabeth L. Swann, eds., *Sensing the Sacred in Medieval and Early Modern Culture* (Abingdon: Routledge, 2018); Marcia B. Hall and Tracy Elizabeth Cooper, eds., *The Sensuous in the Counter-Reformation Church* (Cambridge: Cambridge University Press, 2013).

7 Robin Macdonald, Emilie K.M. Murphy, and Elizabeth L. Swann, "Introduction," in *Sensing the Sacred*, 4. For a couple of interesting examples of the interaction between senses pertaining to the use of rosaries, see Rachel King, "'The Beads with Which We Pray Are Made from It': Devotional Ambers in Early Modern Italy," in *Religion and the Senses in Early Modern Europe*, ed. Wietse de Boer and Christine Göttler (Leiden: Brill, 2013), 168–70.

8 For the idea that the senses need to be trained and thus are products shaped by particular ideas and considerations which varied over time and among cultures, see Muchembled, *Smells*.

9 The work of Alexander J. Fisher is particularly relevant. See Alexander J. Fisher, *Music and Religious Identity in Counter-Reformation Augsburg, 1580–1630* (Aldershot: Ashgate, 2004); Alexander J. Fisher, "Reworking the Confessional Soundscape in the German Counter-Reformation," *Basler Jahrbuch für historische Musikpraxis* 38 (2014), 105–16; Alexander J. Fisher, *Music, Piety, and Propaganda: The Soundscapes of Counter-Reformation Bavaria* (Oxford: Oxford University Press, 2014); Alexander J. Fisher, "'Mit singen und klingen': Urban Processional Culture and the Soundscapes of Post-Reformation Germany," in *Listening to Early Modern Catholicism*, 187–203.

10 Emilie K.M. Murphy, "A Sense of Place: Hearing English Catholicism in the Spanish Habsburg Territories, 1568–1659," in *Sensing the Sacred*, ed. Robin Macdonald, Emilie K.M. Murphy, and Elizabeth L. Swann (Abingdon: Routledge, 2018), 136–57.

11 A good example is Hahn, "Sensing Sacred Space."

12 Roman Roobroeck, "Confessional Coexistence in the Habsburg Netherlands. The Case of the Geuzenhoek (1680–1730)," *BMGN – Low Countries Historical Review* 136, no. 4 (2021), 3–26.

13 Ary I. Kelman, "Rethinking the Soundscape. A Critical Genealogy of a Key Term in Sound Studies," *The Senses and Society* 5, no. 2 (2010), 212–34. In order to apply this term to all the senses, Wietse de Boer coined the term "sense-scapes." De Boer, "The Counter-Reformation of the Senses," 252.

14 David Garrioch, "Sounds of the City: The Soundscape of Early Modern European Towns," *Urban History* 30 (2003), 5–25. For recent work on early modern religious soundscapes, see the literature cited in this historiographical introduction.

15 See, e.g. the definition of soundscape provided by Fisher, "Reworking the Confessional Soundscape," 105. For the link between architecture and "sensory environments," see, e.g. Pamela Graves, "Sensing and Believing: Exploring Worlds of Difference in Pre-Modern England: A Contribution to the Debate Opened by Kate Giles," *World Archaeology* 39, no. 4 (2007), 515–31.

16 Teresa M. Bejan, *Mere Civility: Disagreement and the Limits of Toleration* (Cambridge, MA: Harvard University Press, 2017).

17 Benjamin J. Kaplan, "Fictions of Privacy: House Chapels and the Spatial Accommodation of Religious Dissent in Early Modern Europe," *The American Historical Review* 107, no. 4 (2002), 1031–64; Genji Yasuhira, "Transforming the Urban Space: Catholic Survival Through Spatial Practices in Post-Reformation Utrecht," *Past & Present* 255, no. 1 (2021), 39–86.

1 "To Preserve and Instill the Beloved Peace"

Religious Invective and Confessional Coexistence under the Peace of Augsburg

Allyson F. Creasman

As the 200th anniversary of the Religious Peace of Augsburg approached in 1755, the Lutheran clergy in Brandenburg-Ansbach prepared a catechism instructing parishioners on the history and significance of the Religious Peace. We must thank God for the Peace of Augsburg, the faithful were told, because "this precious Peace is an unshakable pillar not only of our religious freedom, but also the welfare of the entire Holy Roman Empire; after the intolerable perils [of religious war], it established peace and trust between the estates and protected the entire German Nation from further destruction and ruin."[1]

Religious freedom, peace, and trust between the confessions: such was the perception of the Peace of Augsburg in the middle of the eighteenth century, when the so-called "Age of Religious Wars" was but a distant memory and the Age of Enlightenment seemed to beckon. In the ensuing years, this understanding of the treaty's significance featured prominently in standard narratives of the rise of religious tolerance. This historiography charted a story of progress that privileged intellectual history and legislative settlements and culminated in the Enlightenment embrace of liberty of conscience.[2] More recent historians have challenged this paradigm, seeing toleration as a contested and contingent social practice balancing the countervailing impulses unleashed by the Reformation.[3] While the Reformation ushered in religious pluralism, it also reinforced the long-standing conviction that civil and moral order demanded uniformity in religious belief and practice. Indeed, the Reformation intensified the impulse to stamp out religious dissent.[4] To the extent that early modern communities accommodated religious diversity, they did so grudgingly and on tentative, pragmatic grounds. As historians such as Alexandra Walsham have shown, ordinary people could both cling to their confessional hostilities and contain conflict, as circumstances required. This "tolerance of practical rationality," as Robert Scribner put it, emphasised putting differences aside in the interest of the common good, but in no sense entailed acceptance of religious difference.[5] Keeping the peace was thus a fraught process, involving constant negotiation between these competing impulses. What emerged was not an ideological commitment to religious freedom, but a reluctant recognition of the practical need for coexistence.

DOI: 10.4324/9781003030522-3

Seen in this light, the Peace of Augsburg and the other religious settlements that emerged in this period were not legislative milestones in the progress of religious tolerance, but fragile compromises that generated near-constant controversy and required careful negotiation to maintain. Indeed, far from guaranteeing religious freedom, the Peace of Augsburg recognised only two lawful confessions in the Empire. And rather than establishing peace and trust between those confessions, the treaty sparked divisive sparring between the very parties it was supposed to pacify. To help defuse these conflicts, authorities at both imperial and local levels used the Peace of Augsburg to regulate confessional invective. Although efforts to encourage civil discourse have received some attention from scholars of early modern tolerance,[6] the practical enforcement of such measures has received comparatively little analysis. This chapter examines the regulation of religious insult in the bi-confessional city of Augsburg as a means of negotiating religious coexistence. Invoking the Peace of Augsburg and the civic rhetoric of honour, Augsburg magistrates tried to keep the peace by prosecuting religiously motivated insults between members of the city's two protected faiths. What emerged in this community was a fitful, pragmatic settlement that imperfectly negotiated the line between tolerance and intolerance.

"Brotherly love and Christian peace" – the Peace of Augsburg

Formally adopted on September 25, 1555, the Religious Peace of Augsburg extended legal recognition within the Empire to the "old Catholic faith" and the "faith of the Augsburg Confession." In a principle jurists later summed up as *cuius regio, eius religio* – "whose realm, his religion" – the treaty authorised the princes of the Empire to determine which of the two recognised faiths would be practised within their territories. To secure the peace between the Empire's Catholic and Lutheran powers, each was to let the other "enjoy their religious beliefs, liturgy, and ceremonies as well as their estates and other rights and privileges in peace; [for] a unanimous Christian understanding and agreement shall be obtained only by Christian, friendly, peaceful means..."[7]

The Peace of Augsburg was intended as a temporary compromise until religious unity could be restored or a more lasting solution to the Empire's religious divisions was negotiated. But the treaty raised almost as many questions as it settled. In the quest to find agreement, the negotiators had left a number of important issues either unaddressed or deliberately vague; in the ensuing decades, competing interpretations of the document engendered almost unceasing litigation between Catholics and Protestants in the imperial courts.[8] The treaty's ambiguities thus stoked divisions between the very parties it was intended to pacify, and to some degree institutionalised religious conflict within the Empire's judicial system.

The basic structure of the Religious Peace also ensured that the focus would remain squarely on confessional differences, rather than points of agreement. The Peace of Augsburg accorded legal rights and protections to members of the "old Catholic faith" and adherents of "the faith of the Augsburg Confession" – and to no one else. Claiming the treaty's protections therefore necessarily entailed an inquiry into how far the claimants conformed to one of these permitted theological categories. As a result, the Peace "favored a culture of painstaking observation of both one's own religion and the other" that highlighted the points of division between them.[9]

The Religious Peace also struck a political bargain that neither protected party could justify in religious terms: two confessions legally recognised in one Empire. In an age that saw religious uniformity as basic to the social and spiritual good of the community, the Peace was anomalous. Ideally, all members of society were to be integrated into a sacral community, a *corpus Christianum* united in Christian faith for the common good.[10] In this moral vision, the tolerance of false belief could call down divine wrath on the entire community. As the spiritual and moral integrity of the community was the foundation upon which all civic order rested, the public good demanded that the magistracy protect society from the potentially disruptive influence of unorthodox belief. While the religious conflicts of the Reformation era would generate significant debate as to the limits of the magistrate's power to compel private conscience, a broad consensus among both Catholics and Protestants held that Christian authorities had not only the right, but also the duty to police opinion and belief for the public good.[11]

So the Religious Peace was religiously problematic from the start. But the imperative to crush unbelief was tempered by the equally important Christian obligation to show charity and forbearance, even towards one's enemies.[12] These were Christian ideals presumably cherished across the confessional divide, and it was in these concepts of peace, brotherhood, and Christian love that the Peace of Augsburg found its moral force. In calling on both sides to show each other "Christian love and true friendship,"[13] the treaty sought to incorporate the protected confessions into a single legal community, mutually bound to honour each other's rights as fellow Christians, citizens, and neighbours. The Peace of Augsburg was not unique in this. From the Bohemian Wars to the Edict of Nantes, similar language was to be found in the many treaties, pacification edicts, and "friendship pacts" that sought to quiet the religious conflicts raging across Europe.[14] To promote Christian concord, these treaties prohibited religious insults and invective between the protected confessions. Such provisions drew on long-standing legal precedents outlawing defamatory words or writings, as these were deemed potentially disruptive of the public peace.[15] The law of defamation provided a useful foundation for these peacekeeping efforts, as such laws were understood to define and enforce the obligations of respect and civility owed to each member of the community.[16]

In the Holy Roman Empire, officials at both imperial and local levels interpreted the Peace of Augsburg's mandate that Catholics and Lutherans leave each other in peace as a general prohibition of religious invective by either side. Jurists and magistrates extended the long-standing prohibition of

Schmähschriften (scandalous or libellous texts) to include religious polemic deemed contrary to the spirit of the Peace of Augsburg.[17] The 1570 Diet of Speyer, accordingly, banned partisan polemical texts.[18] Further, legislation adopted at the Frankfurt Diet of 1577 prohibited writings that violated doctrines common to both the Catholic faith and the Augsburg Confession, the "spirit" of the Peace of Augsburg, or that otherwise promoted unrest and breaches of the peace.[19]

"To preserve and instill the beloved peace" – honour and civic order

The Peace of Augsburg legitimised itself with an appeal to Christian values of charity and goodwill that were common to both protected confessions. But, as noted above, both the treaty's design and operation tended to underscore points of division, rather than consensus. If there was to be peace between the confessions, the Religious Peace alone would not suffice to secure it. What was needed was a framework within which these conflicts could be aired and, if not fully resolved, then at least contained. At the imperial level, conflicts between the Catholic and Lutheran estates played out in the courts, especially in the Imperial Cameral Court (*Reichskammergericht*).[20] But the most direct challenge to implementing the Peace came at the local level, particularly in those cities with religiously-mixed populations. According to the treaty's so-called "City Article," in those imperial cities where Lutheranism and Catholicism were both practised,

> the same should henceforth remain so observed in such cities, and the citizens [...] should live peacefully and quietly with each other, and neither side shall attempt to abolish the other's religion, church practices, or ceremonies, or attempt to force them from them; rather, each side shall allow the other, according to this Peace, to remain quietly and peacefully in its religion, faith, church practices, ordinances, and ceremonies, as have been decreed and granted herein to both religions by the Imperial Estates.[21]

In effect, the Peace of Augsburg called on these religiously-mixed communities to maintain the confessional status quo but was vague on precisely how they were to achieve that. No guidance was provided, for example, on the relative political and legal rights of the two faith communities. Were they to share power or have proportional representation in civic governance? How much independence would each church have to decide its own affairs? And what protections would safeguard the rights of the minority faith? The absence of these guarantees bred significant confusion and insecurity about how such bi-confessional settlements could be maintained.[22]

The challenge facing these imperial cities in keeping the peace is perhaps best illustrated in the city that gave the Peace of Augsburg its name.[23] With a population of nearly 40,000 in the mid-sixteenth century, Augsburg was among the Empire's largest and most prosperous cities. Augsburg had officially adopted evangelical reform in 1537, but its defeat in the Schmalkaldic War and the subsequent imposition of the 1548 Interim reopened the city to Catholicism. Also in that year, Emperor Charles V established a new civic constitution ensuring a Catholic majority in the Augsburg city council, although Catholics then comprised less than 10% of the city's population.

The Religious Peace of 1555 required Augsburg to redirect its religious policies from enforcing Lutheran orthodoxy towards fostering community between the two protected confessions.[24] But in an era that valued religious unanimity, the maintenance of two confessions in one city undermined commonly held expectations of civic order. And as the Peace itself provided little practical guidance on how it was to be implemented, Augsburgers had to develop their own strategies for keeping the peace. What emerged in Augsburg was an ad hoc, pragmatic settlement developed through negotiation, accommodation, and resistance between the confessions and between the citizenry and civic government. The daily interactions between Catholics and Lutherans in the Augsburg streets reveal a form of practical coexistence, shaped less by an ideological commitment to religious tolerance but as a pragmatic necessity for keeping the peace. In this framework, Augsburgers of both confessions – Catholic and Protestant – could temporarily put aside their differences as social circumstances required, without at the same time abandoning the very real religious commitments that divided them. Willem Frijhoff has described this adaptability as the "ecumenicity of everyday life," that is, an ability to coexist with people of different religious backgrounds as a normal part of daily life and temporarily "put brackets around" confessional differences "in the interests of civil order and the welfare of the local community."[25] But this toleration was temporary and situational – in different settings and circumstances, that forbearance could be withdrawn, and confessional tensions flared. Judith Pollmann has noted that it was thus entirely possible for individuals to be simultaneously both tolerant and intolerant – depending on the settings and social roles in which they found themselves, Catholics and Protestants could interact with members of the other faith in ways that either smoothed over their religious differences or brought them to the fore.[26]

Thus, in confessionally mixed communities like Augsburg, neither religious conflict nor coexistence could be assumed as the normal state of affairs. Both were among the possible modes of interaction in everyday life, and individuals were in every case presented with a choice that involved a calculation of costs and benefits "in which the destructive potential of conflict over religion was deemed to outweigh the advantages."[27]

To encourage Augsburgers to choose peace, the city council emphasised the call to concord and Christian love that was basic to the Religious Peace. Within days of the treaty's announcement, Augsburg's city council summoned the city's clergy before it and laid down the law that was to govern confessional relations under the new regime. It decreed that, henceforth, both the adherents of the Catholic faith and the Augsburg Confession were to live together in peace and were in no way to hinder each other in the exercise of their faiths. Lutheran and Catholic clergy were to refrain from any insulting or incendiary preaching against each other, as such talk might tend to stir up confessional hatred. Instead, the council instructed that they should, at all times, exhort their congregations to brotherly love and Christian peace. It decreed that:

> [The clergy of both faiths shall exhort] the common citizenry [...] in dutiful obedience, to [that] Christian patience and humility, and also brotherly love, which Christ so often and earnestly commanded, and which we are obligated, for the sake of our soul's salvation, to show to one another [...][28]

The Augsburg city council legitimised its bi-confessional policies by invoking the Peace of Augsburg's call to Christian charity, affirming publicly that the obligations of civility and respect bridged the confessional divide. They found an especially useful framework for enforcement in the civic code of honour, which had long had the force of law. Just as the law of defamation provided a means of framing these accords at the national level, honour set forth the obligations of civility and respect that burghers were expected to show to each other, and it did so in theologically neutral terms. Although not incompatible with Christian values, the code of honour made few theological demands on believers' consciences – both Catholics and Lutherans could recognise their neighbour's honour without having to approve their religious choices. And when conflicts did arise, the rhetoric of honour furnished a means to de-escalate and defuse them, facilitating reconciliation and restoration of the status quo. Thus, honour could sometimes be won by making peace, ignoring an affront, or by forgiving an offender.[29] Honour was, therefore, a pliable concept – a "rhetoric" – that individuals selectively invoked to escalate or defuse a conflict.[30] And as the Peace of Augsburg itself provided little guidance on how these communities were to keep the peace, the civic code of honour offered one pragmatic support.

In Germany, as elsewhere in early modern Europe, honour was basic to urban sociability, as public reputation defined who was entitled to acceptance in their community, the full rights of citizenship, and the respect of their peers.[31] In this context, an assault on a person's honour was both a sin and a crime, as it violated the Christian and civic obligations that neighbours owed to one another. Augsburg's 1537 Discipline Ordinance reflected this moral understanding of the offence, holding that insults were "unchristian and unjust." As a result of this evil, "good policy, peace, and brotherly love are destroyed and torn asunder, and also countless other nuisances and mischiefs arise to overwhelm all authority and public morals."[32]

To facilitate peacemaking, honour offences could be settled with a formal retraction and apology sworn before the magistrates. These remedies drew heavily on the theological understandings of the sacrament of reconciliation and were intended to reconcile the parties, restore lost honour, and reintegrate them within the civil community.[33] In Augsburg, the defendant was required to offer his or her hand to the victim and swear:

> In that I disgraced and humiliated you, and thereby improperly attacked and injured your honour, I confess my wrong. I am sorry, and I ask you to forgive me. It will never happen again, and you should suffer no disadvantage from this, for I know you to be nothing other than an honourable, upright citizen.[34]

But honourable status also turned on one's reputation for piety, and religious leaders – both Catholic and Protestant – encouraged the faithful to call out false belief. The pamphlet wars of the Reformation and the increasingly strident confessional debates that followed flooded the literary marketplace with polemical religious tracts, often written in highly personal and insulting terms. Religious invective permeated the theological discourse of the age and encouraged the laity to speak in kind.[35]

In confessionally mixed communities such as Augsburg, such religious insults were seen as particularly destructive of "good policy, peace, and brotherly love."[36] These types of insults singled out the victim's religion as the most salient and objectionable thing about them, suggesting that their beliefs were somehow deviant and disreputable. Most commonly, religious insults framed the victim as un-Christian and thus not entitled to the same respect and fellowship accorded to other believers.[37] Calling someone a "heretic" (*Ketzer*) – a common term of abuse in these years – obviously functioned in this way. Likewise, labelling a convert a "fallen Christian," an "apostate," or a "Mameluke"[38] suggested that they now stood outside the true, Christian faith. But even the denominational labels commonly accepted today had pejorative meanings in the confessional era.[39] Calling someone a "Lutheran" (or sometimes, a "Martinist") or a "Calvinist" implied that they were a follower of Martin Luther or John Calvin, and not Jesus Christ. The Protestant usage of the term "Papist" instead of "Catholic" carried exactly the same meaning.[40] And for the same reasons, German Protestant polemicists often rendered *Jesuiter*, the German word for "Jesuit," as *Jesuwider*, meaning literally "against Jesus."[41]

By placing individuals outside the Christian fold, these types of insults repudiated the duties of Christian charity and civility on which the public order was thought to rest. As such, religious insults were considered particularly troublesome forms of abuse in confessionally mixed communities, where keeping order depended on the mutual recognition of such obligations. And in an era when beliefs were so hotly contested, magistrates assumed that abusive language could easily lead to physical violence or even riots. In a

large, religiously-mixed community such as Augsburg, where opportunities
for friction abounded, officials policed religious insults carefully. Such talk
was no minor matter, the Augsburg magistrates asserted, "but an act of high
malice and disorder, which is in no way to be tolerated in an imperial city,
lest all forms of disorder and evil may arise."[42]

To combat this problem, the city council prosecuted religious invective
as a violation of the Peace of Augsburg. In dozens of cases from the 1560s
through the 1640s, the council's deputies arrested individuals dealing in
anti-Catholic or anti-Lutheran polemical writings or overheard making re-
ligiously-motivated insults or threats against members of the other confession. All such cases were referred to the city council for adjudication, as the
expression of such views was considered likely to disrupt the fragile peace
between the confessions and erupt into violence.[43]

In these cases, Augsburg's magistrates used the Religious Peace as a tool
of indoctrination to educate the populace in an ethic of communal harmony
and mutual respect, whereby Catholics and Lutherans at all levels of society
acknowledged a duty to one another to coexist peacefully and maintain the
civic order. Using pre-written questions, officials followed a standard formula
of interrogation, leading defendants through a kind of civic catechism explaining their duties under the Religious Peace. These questions stressed commonly
shared values of Christian charity and underscored each citizen's obligation
to treat their neighbours with honour, regardless of their religion. Defendants were reminded that the Religious Peace protected Catholic and Lutheran
citizens equally and that both confessions shared the same duty to respect the
laws. The magistrates' questions typically rehearsed the following points:

- Did the defendant not know "both religions are practiced here and that
  each resident was responsible to leave each other in peace and respect each
  other's rights?"
- Why, then, had he "tried to injure his neighbour's honour?"
- What dishonourable things did he know about this person that would
  justify this behaviour, and how can he prove it?
- Does he think that he, as a citizen here, should be allowed to treat another
  citizen in this way? And how does he expect to answer for this before the
  authorities?
- Is he willing to retract what he said?[44]

Almost invariably, the accused admitted that they knew that the Peace
of Augsburg protected both confessions in Augsburg. Very few Augsburgers
claimed to be unaware that religious insults were banned under the Religious Peace. Even fewer defended their comments; most tried to excuse their
behaviour, often claiming that they were angry or drunk and hadn't really
meant what they said. Sixt Hernberger's 1601 prosecution was typical. Hernberger, a woodcutter, had been overheard in a beer hall complaining that
"Satan has led the Jesuits, the monks, and the other rogues into the city!"

Hernberger went on to say that the Capuchins were "especially great rogues" and that there would be no good in the city until Satan led them all away again.[45] Hernberger allegedly repeated more of the same "evil speech" in a neighbour's house. The man was so affronted by Hernberger's comments that he drew his weapon and warned him "if you were in any other place, someone would stick a knife in you and let you bleed!"[46]

The magistrates asked Hernberger whether he knew that "one is obligated here to extend the same protections to both religions?"[47] He knew this, he said, and had therefore behaved with all propriety "all the days of his life." He was so drunk on the night in question, however, that he could remember nothing of what he was supposed to have said. He was truly sorry, he stated, and affirmed that he had no quarrel with the Catholic clergy. He only had good experiences with them almost daily, in fact.[48] Hernberger begged for mercy, stating that he was a "broken man" and did not know how he would carry on his trade.

Of course, Hernberger had every incentive to tell the magistrates what they wanted to hear – and these expressions of contrition were, indeed, what the authorities wanted. With his confession, Hernberger accepted his fault and reaffirmed his obligations to his Catholic neighbours; the council released him with a warning, "this time."[49] This was the magistrates' preferred result, for by giving the defendant the opportunity to apologise and make amends, the council could reconcile the parties and restore their injured honour. And couching the offence as a violation of the mutually recognised obligations of fellowship and honour, the council could sidestep the fraught questions that divided the confessions. The rhetoric of honour emphasised the points of agreement between these confessions, rather than their differences.

Although Hernberger gave the magistrates the response they wanted, he wasn't necessarily insincere. He stressed that, most of the time, he got along perfectly well with his Catholic neighbours. Like many Augsburgers, he was able to put aside his own religious opinions to deal peacefully and productively with members of the other faith. But when drink had loosened his tongue, out came his religious prejudices. Hernberger, like so many others in this period, was simultaneously both religiously tolerant and intolerant. When sober, he was able to choose between these two modes of interaction as circumstances required.

For the Augsburg magistrates, one of the advantages of handling these cases as honour offences was that the laws against insults provided a means to de-escalate and resolve these conflicts. The Augsburg ordinance expressly recognised drunkenness or anger as mitigating factors, suggesting that defendants could not fully control themselves in such a state and, thus, were not really responsible for their hurtful words.[50] This formulation provided an opportunity for the offender to disavow the full import of what they said and establish a basis for reconciliation. And as the formula of reconciliation in the Augsburg statute spoke only in terms of reaffirming the victim's honour, it elided the religious differences between the parties.

Although these prosecutions presented the Peace of Augsburg as a religiously neutral basis for confessional relations, the realities of sharing this city severely tested this incorporative ideal. A review of the criminal prosecutions in Augsburg reveals an upturn in prosecutions under the Peace of Augsburg of anti-Catholic speech and polemical writings coinciding with the increasingly public profile of Catholic religious orders in the city. The first of these prosecutions stemmed from the 1560s, following closely upon the arrival of the Jesuits in Augsburg in 1559.[51] A similar upturn in prosecutions of anti-Catholic polemic may be noted around 1600, coinciding with the beginnings of a Capuchin mission in Augsburg.

Although there is little evidence that the activities of these religious orders were deliberately provocative, Augsburg's Protestant community seems to have seen their arrival as an attempt to undermine the Religious Peace of Augsburg. Indeed, however much he sought to disavow his comments, Sixt Hernberger's complaint about the influx of "Jesuits and monks" into Augsburg alluded to this very issue. Although Lutherans made up more than 80% of Augsburg's population at mid-century, Catholics controlled the city's government for most of this period and many of the city's wealthiest and most powerful families also adhered to the "old faith."[52] The fact that many of these families were also public supporters of the Jesuit mission in Augsburg fuelled Protestant concerns that the city council was giving the Jesuits free rein to tilt the confessional balance in the city back to the Catholic church.[53]

As a mostly Catholic institution governing a mostly Lutheran city, the Augsburg city council was sensitive to charges of religious favouritism. Despite its efforts to be even-handed, rumours circulated in some quarters that Catholic officials were conniving with the Jesuits in a secret plan to expel the Lutheran clergy and force the city's return to Catholicism.[54] To assert its legitimacy and ensure support across the religious spectrum, the Augsburg city council was ever careful to remind its citizens that it acted impartially under an imperial mandate to enforce the Religious Peace. For the council, the treaty functioned as a religiously neutral source of authority in an environment where the very perception of religious partisanship was politically explosive.

The 1569 prosecution of George Taschner is a case in point. A member of the city watch, Taschner was arrested for telling other members of the guard that the city council kept a watch in the city solely to protect the Catholic clergy. The only solution was to replace the council, he said, and he allegedly let loose a string of vulgar insults against the Mass, priests, and Catholics in general.[55] In interrogating Taschner, the magistrates stressed that the council was merely carrying out the imperial will, citing the Peace of Augsburg as proof of its neutrality. They reminded him that "the Imperial Majesty, the Electors, the princes, and the estates of the Empire have ensured that the old religion and the Augsburg Confession are to be tolerated equally and that no one should attack the other."[56] He admitted that he knew this well. How, then, did he expect to avoid punishment for "saying such dishonourable things and telling good, honourable people" to go to the Devil?[57]

Perhaps unwittingly, the council's reliance on imperial authority implicitly recognised the limits of its authority and the uncertain appeal of its call to confessional coexistence. With the council's very legitimacy under question in some quarters, it could not assume that all citizens would respect its authority. Nor could the council assume that appealing to civic virtues of Christian fellowship, neighbourliness, and honour would suffice to keep the peace. In such a context, the weight of imperial authority was a necessary support.

Given the anxieties over the city's religious identity, conversion was an especially fraught subject in Augsburg, and the city council enlisted the Peace of Augsburg to police the issue. In 1580, for example, Hieronymus Österreicher was arrested for publicly insulting David Abele, a convert to Catholicism, as a "fallen Mameluke." Österreicher's interrogators asked him whether he understood the terms of the Peace of Augsburg and emphasised that the law carried the weight of imperial authority. Did he not know, they asked, that both the Catholic religion and the Augsburg Confession were permitted in the Empire and that the Imperial Recesses expressly provided that members of each confession were to allow the members of the other faith to "hold fast to their religion without injury or offense?"[58] Österreicher admitted that he knew this very well, although he didn't know exactly what the Imperial Recesses said about it. Was it not also true, they asked, that "both religions have existed in this very city for many years, and that the Imperial Recesses require that each citizen let the others practice their own religion without being attacked for it?"[59]

The interrogators stressed Österreicher's neighbourly duty to show goodwill. In attacking Österreicher's assertion that converts to Catholicism were "fallen Mamelukes," they challenged his suggestion that Catholics were not Christians, and presumably, outside the bonds of Christian fellowship. Although Österreicher admitted that both religions had been practised side by side in Augsburg for many years, he added that, in his experience, "each side had attacked the other on account of religion."[60] The interrogators also stressed Österreicher's duties as a citizen, asking whether he understood that it was the command of the City council, his lawful ruling authority, that the Peace of Augsburg be obeyed within the city. Österreicher admitted that he knew this, too, but noted that, in his opinion, the council's will had been ignored all too often over the years.[61]

Österreicher's comments highlighted both the anxieties over conversion that were latent in this community and the challenges the authorities faced in policing these conflicts. He said he had worried as soon as he had insulted Abele that he would be punished for it. But he not only said it anyway, he told the magistrates that lots of other people used such insults, too. Fear of the law was evidently not enough to silence Österreicher or, it seems, many others. Still, he claimed he had not meant to hurt anyone, and he was released after making a sworn apology to Abele.[62]

This case must be understood in the context of wider concerns about the religious demographics in Augsburg. By the 1580s, Augsburg's Lutheran community still held a strong majority in the city, but it had seen its numbers steadily whittled away by immigration from the Catholic countryside and high-profile conversions.⁶³ By codifying the religious divide in the city, the Peace of Augsburg had, ironically, helped to harden the boundaries separating the two faiths, and any encroachment by one faith into the preserve of the other was seen as a violation of its rights under the Religious Peace. The city council was sensitive to these concerns and invoked the Peace of Augsburg to regulate the clergy's missionising among adherents of other faiths. It interpreted the Peace of Augsburg's prohibitions against interference in the religious practices of another officially-sanctioned confession to include efforts to dissuade another from his own faith. Thus, the council discouraged religious disputations as an attempt to interfere with or hinder another person in the practice of a protected religion. In particular, authorities feared that religious debates among the laity devolved all too often into name-calling. Thus, the council prosecuted Michael Benedict under the Peace of Augsburg in 1603 for debating Conrad Ess about religion in a public street. Benedict, a Catholic servant, asked Ess, a Lutheran shoemaker, which faith was better. When Ess, predictably, chose his own, Benedict replied that "God must be a Lutheran fool, then, if that faith is sent from God!"⁶⁴ Benedict then declared that Lutherans "belonged to the Devil" and that he could prove "with heaven and earth and the four elements" that the Catholic religion was the true faith. Benedict's interrogators demanded to know "why was it necessary for him to insult all these people and debate about religion? Why can't he hold to his own religion and let others remain undisturbed in their own faith?"⁶⁵

To the Augsburg authorities, religious disputation required scrutiny not simply because it infringed on the Religious Peace but because it raised the potential for violence and unrest. By publicly calling the truth of a protected faith into question and challenging the credibility of its clergy, religious debate aroused indignation on both sides and created the risk that outraged bystanders would come to the defence of their faith not with arguments but with violence. Augsburg's magistrates informed the city council that violence between Catholic and Protestant citizens was an increasingly common problem. Reporting on a May 1603 street fight between a Catholic and a Protestant over the Catholic's anti-Lutheran remarks, the magistrates opined that the case was an especially bad one, as it involved people "molesting and irritating" each other over religion. This problem, they noted, "had now unfortunately become very common and was completely out of control in almost all the inns and beer halls." Nothing good could come of it, they concluded, if this "evil" were tolerated or allowed to worsen over time.⁶⁶

The limits of peace

The magistrates' report indicates that officials saw religious conflict as an endemic problem in Augsburg. Indeed, in these years, religious contest seemed to gain ever greater prominence as a means of affirming confessional identity. Both Catholics and Lutherans sought to lay claim to the city's public spaces to assert the primacy of their own beliefs in the city's spiritual and public life. Through public rituals, symbols, placards, and songs, Catholics and Protestants in Augsburg each appropriated the city's streets and forums to claim moral – if not legal – hegemony over the city and its institutions.

This development was by no means confined to Augsburg, as a hardening of confessional divisions is discernible across much of Europe in the late sixteenth and early seventeenth centuries.[67] But in Augsburg, where neither confession clearly dominated, the bi-confessional settlement opened up a space to compete for the city's religious identity. The Peace of Augsburg had premised political rights on confessional affiliation, but didn't fully spell out what rights each protected confession would enjoy in Augsburg.[68] This reality highlighted religion as the fundamental component of individual and communal identity, helping to crystallise the religious divide in the city. The ensuing tensions severely tested the incorporative ideal underlying the city council's political and social agenda through the end of the Thirty Years' War.

These tensions came to a head in the 1580s and 1590s, when Augsburg was rocked by a series of protests that demonstrated how earnestly Augsburgers had adopted the ideology of the Religious Peace, but how differently they had come to interpret it. In 1582, Pope Gregory XIII sponsored a reform of the Julian calendar, and Augsburg's city council adopted the new "Gregorian" calendar early the next year. Although the council cited practical economic reasons for its decision, the adoption of the reformed calendar unleashed a storm of protest among the city's Lutherans. Leaders of the Lutheran community argued that accepting the new calendar required them to accept the Pope's authority to define the liturgical year within the Lutheran churches. This, they argued, violated the Peace of Augsburg, which they interpreted as granting the Lutheran churches exclusive authority to define their own rituals and practices without interference or hindrance from the Catholic Church.[69]

For those Protestants who resented the political hegemony of Catholics in the city council, the "Calendar Conflict" (*Kalenderstreit*) reinforced their doubts about the council's even-handedness between the confessions. To silence the dissent, the city council tried in April 1584 to expel its most vocal critic, the Lutheran pastor Georg Müller, triggering a major riot.[70] Further conflict arose between the council and the Lutheran community over the council's assertion of its right to appoint and remove the Protestant clergy. At stake in this so-called "Vocation Conflict" (*Vokationstreit*) were the same issues looming in the Calendar Conflict: the independence of the Lutheran churches from the interference of a supposedly Catholic-leaning council.[71]

In part, the conflict arose from the very policies the council had tried to advance since 1555. In stressing the mutual rights and obligations of Catholics and Lutherans under the Peace of Augsburg, the council had sought to promote a spirit of accommodation between the confessions, in which respect for the Religious Peace was a duty shared by every citizen. But an imperial commission investigating the 1584 riot discovered that many Lutherans also believed that, under the Peace of Augsburg, both confessions were supposed to share political power as well. They argued that the treaty had envisioned that power would be shared between Catholics and Lutherans "half and half," but that the Catholics had manipulated council elections to ensure their control of the government.[72] The disconnect between the reality of civic governance and the rhetoric of civic cooperation bred resentment, widening the divisions between the confessions.[73]

Augsburg's bi-confessional settlement collapsed almost completely over the course of the Thirty Years' War, as political power shifted between Catholic and Lutheran regimes. In August 1629, following a series of imperial victories, Emperor Ferdinand II ordered a sweeping policy of re-Catholicisation in Augsburg. Over the objection of the city council, the emperor issued a "special command" that all "un-Catholic" teaching be suppressed in Augsburg. The Lutheran churches were closed and their clergy dismissed; Lutheran officials were removed from civic offices and all exercise of the Lutheran faith was banned.[74]

With the Religious Peace now suspended in Augsburg, the city's magistrates nonetheless continued to invoke its authority. Less than a month after the announcement of the emperor's edict, Augsburg magistrates prosecuted Georg Neumair for insulting a visiting Jesuit. They reminded him that the law prohibited anyone from attacking "another, regardless of their religion … with sharp, dishonouring, and threatening words."[75] In his defence, Neumair noted that the Peace itself had been effectively set aside, as only one religion was now protected. He admitted he insulted the Jesuit "partly" because he was drunk, but "partly" out of "the general dislike of the Jesuits that is present in this world, since they are said to be the primary agents of the current religious prohibition" of Lutheranism in Augsburg.[76] The council concluded that Neumair's comments could have "caused a great disorder and dangerous riot," and it expelled him from the city for three months.[77]

Augsburg magistrates also drew on the Religious Peace in prosecuting Martin Haller for insulting a Catholic priest. With "un-Catholic" services now banned in Augsburg, Lutheran parents had little choice but to baptise their children in Catholic churches. Although a staunch Lutheran, Haller agreed to serve as godfather for his landlord's children "out of Christian duty."[78] But during the ceremony, he heatedly berated the priest for using chrism and holy water without, in his view, scriptural warrant. He was also found in possession of several illegal anti-Catholic pamphlets and songs. Under arrest, Haller was reminded by the magistrates that under the Peace of Augsburg "for years now, it's been forbidden to hinder the Catholics in their worship, ceremonies, and churches."[79] Haller insisted that he had never meant to hinder the Catholics in their worship – if only they had accorded Lutherans the same respect. He spoke only out of "proper zeal for Christ's word," he said, to defend the truth and to maintain "the innocent little child" in the faith.[80]

With Augsburg's capitulation to the Swedish army in April 1632, the emperor's edict against "un-Catholic" teaching was set aside and the all-Catholic city council was replaced with a new, all-Lutheran regime. The Lutheran ascendancy was short-lived, however. Catholic armies retook the city in 1635, and an all-Catholic city council governed until the end of the war. Although Augsburg's churches returned to Catholic control, Lutherans were permitted to worship publicly. The new council set aside the re-Catholicising agenda of 1629–32, focusing less on maintaining an officially-sanctioned orthodoxy than on maintaining internal security and social order.[81]

By the end of the Thirty Years' War, it had become clear that, whether they liked it or not, both Catholics and Lutherans in Augsburg had come to accept the bi-confessional settlement of the Religious Peace. Catholics and Lutherans may not have genuinely embraced the truths of each other's faiths, but both groups had come to understand the practical necessity of accommodating both confessions in the city. Both groups expected that their rights to live and worship in Augsburg would be legally recognised and that their neighbours would be bound to accommodate them. Neither side was prepared thereafter to accept the legitimacy of either group's exclusive rule. Both Catholic and Lutheran regimes thus had to allow for diversity of belief and expression, at least within the narrow limits of the Peace of Augsburg.

In 1648, the treaties of Osnabrück and Münster, known collectively as the Peace of Westphalia, brought the Thirty Years' War to an end. After decades of fighting, the Empire finally had peace, and in Augsburg, Catholics and Lutherans had the legal parity over which they had so long contended.[82] The Peace of Westphalia ratified the Religious Peace of Augsburg, recognising it as "valid, and to be held sacred and inviolate," and extended its protections to Reformed Christians.[83] In Augsburg, most city offices were to be staffed equally by Lutherans and Catholics, and each confession was to have exclusive authority over their respective schools and churches.[84] Both sides were forbidden to use civic authority to oppress members of the other confession.[85]

The Augsburg city council followed the treaty with a new decree governing religious invective. As it had done before under the Peace of Augsburg, the council sought to enforce its decrees under the Peace of Westphalia by appealing to the citizenry's duty to preserve communal harmony and concord. But the council's May 20, 1649 decree made clear that the arrival of confessional parity had not brought peace between the confessions. Indeed, the council complained that, despite multiple prohibitions of religious insults, the problem had only become worse since the new Peace. The council reiterated that religious insults "serve only to create mistrust, embitterment ... [and] destroy the peaceful life of the citizenry." It warned that "not only are neighbours and fellow citizens sorely injured by this, but [...] [s]uch [conduct] is deeply contrary to good policy, the welfare of the citizenry, and communal harmony." Once again, the council commanded that Catholics and Lutherans were to "refrain from all defamations and insults [...] and shall instead show to everyone all appropriate decorum, peaceful and neighbourly trust."[86]

Once again, the council's warnings went unheeded. In August 1649, Augsburg officials arrested Hans Zeberle for insulting two Lutheran clergymen and denouncing the Peace of Westphalia. Zeberle was a day labourer who had been arrested twice before in neighbouring villages for "telling the truth about the authorities," as he put it.[87] According to Leonhart Fußnegger, the pastor of the Lutheran church of St. Jacob, Zeberle had come to his home in late July asking to learn about the Augsburg Confession, suggesting he meant to convert. But Zeberle soon began to rant about the Peace of Westphalia. He wished to punish all those who upheld the "damned, godless Peace," he said, for it "offended God, trampled the Queen of Heaven underfoot, held the saints up to contempt, and also overthrew His Holiness the Pope."[88]

One week later, Zeberle visited the home of Lutheran pastor Johann Mair. Again, he asked the pastor to explain the true religion to him. Before the pastor could fully answer, Zeberle interjected that the Peace of Westphalia was damned, for "nothing of the Mother of God stands therein," and shouted that the Lutheran preachers were "heretics, soul-killers, and thieves and preach a devilish, damned doctrine!"[89]

Before the magistrates, Zeberle admitted everything. They demanded to know who had instructed Zeberle to bait the pastors, but he swore he had simply drawn these ideas out of various sermons he heard. Such talk was everywhere, he said: "talk like this comes not only from the pulpit, but on the public streets from the common people and even in the workplace, and [I can't help but] listen to it."[90] The magistrates reminded him that the council's May 20 decree threatened serious punishment for making insults or threats against members of either religion. Zeberle retorted that he "marvels that they prohibit much, but punish little – to tell the truth, [this kind of talk] should have cost him his life ten times over already!"[91] At least according to Zeberle, however much the council tried to legislate against religious invective, such talk was "everywhere" – in the churches, the streets, and the workplaces. And the council's many decrees were toothless – they "prohibit much, but punish little." To the magistrates, Zeberle's reckless and unrepentant speech cast some doubt on his sanity. The council concluded that Zeberle "was not always in his right mind" but nonetheless expelled him.[92]

Meanwhile, the news of Zeberle's confrontation with the pastors had created a small uproar within the Lutheran community. Soon a Lutheran, Colman Stritzel, was under arrest for making threats against the Catholics. Stritzel's neighbours informed authorities that he was going about after the Zeberle incident saying that "it would be no wonder if someone stuck a knife in a Papist, because they're all thieves."[93]

The council prosecuted Stritzel's comments against "the Papists" as a violation of its May decree prohibiting religious invective. Stritzel admitted that he knew about the decree; he could not read it, but he had heard of its contents. "Even if there had been no decree," they asked, "would he not be obligated as a citizen to leave others in peace?"[94] The council pressed home the communal responsibilities fundamental to the preservation of the Peace: "does he think that, with behaviour like this, he can properly be called a decent, peaceful citizen? [...] Does he think it is permissible to insult and dishonour members of the

Catholic faith, thereby violating the laws providing for peace and unity among the citizenry?"[95] Stritzel affirmed that he always sought to resolve all differences with his neighbours, both Catholic and Protestant, in a peaceful way. He assured the council he was a good citizen, trying always to refrain from all "un-peaceful" behaviour. With that, they released him with a warning.[96]

The arrests of Stritzel and Zeberle demonstrated that, although the war was over, the confessional tensions that had divided Augsburgers for decades were not soon forgotten. As it had before the war, the new government sought to use its regulatory powers to promote acceptance of the new political and religious order, looking this time to the Peace of Westphalia to instruct Augsburgers in their mutual rights and obligations to keep the peace. Although this regulatory strategy had a long history in the city, events in Augsburg since the Calendar Conflict had crystallised confessional identities and deepened the rifts within the community. The confirmation of legal parity between the confessions was expected to provide Augsburg's authorities with a more effective means of policing and negotiating these conflicts by more clearly delineating each protected group's rights.[97] This helped eliminate some of the main triggers of conflict, such as political representation in civic offices, use of churches, and oversight of clergy and church administration. But to the extent that parity defined each group's political rights in confessional terms, it served also to reinforce religious division within the community. The new, post-war order in Augsburg fostered the organisation of communal life around exclusive, confessional identifications, leading to sharply delineated Catholic and Lutheran subcultures in Augsburg. This created, in Étienne François's words, an "invisible boundary" in Augsburg, as Catholics and Lutherans differentiated themselves not only in their religious choices, but also in their occupations, dress, and naming practices.[98]

Conclusions

As ratified in the Peace of Westphalia, the Peace of Augsburg remained a foundation of imperial law until the dissolution of the Empire in 1806. But far from the "unshakable pillar of religious freedom" that it seemed in the eighteenth century, the protections of the Peace of Augsburg were deeply contested in Germany's "long Reformation." While modern historians have sometimes hailed the Peace as a milestone in the history of religious tolerance, early modern Germans understood it to be a narrowly crafted and fragile compromise. It endorsed neither liberty of conscience nor the equal dignity of all faiths. Nor was the Peace of Augsburg particularly innovative. In many ways, the Religious Peace looked backwards, recalling age-old values of Christian charity and civic order, and it found its legal force in long-held understandings of the law of honour and defamation.

But by joining the ideal of Christian amity with the legal proscription of defamation, the Peace of Augsburg emerged as an important tool in pacifying the confessional battles of the early modern age. In Augsburg, the city council's efforts to suppress division and promote consensus under the Religious Peace of Augsburg were both an expression of the long-held public ideal of civic harmony and an effort to create and promote new concepts of community. The city had accommodated religious difference to the extent it could be incorporated within certain commonly-held notions of honour, Christian concord, and civic cooperation. Toleration of religious pluralism, however, was grounded essentially on pragmatic considerations; legal or moral recognition of individual rights in matters of belief was still ill-defined.

Although the Peace of Augsburg could not completely pacify the religious conflicts in the city, it put the treaty's call to religious accommodation at the very centre of debate. These cases prosecuting religious invective in Augsburg suggest that, to some degree, Augsburgers internalised the values of the Religious Peace. Despite the tensions over the city's religious identity and the allocation of political power between the confessions, the Peace of Augsburg remained the touchstone of political legitimacy in that city. Even in spearheading protests against the city council over the introduction of Gregorian calendar reform in the 1580s, for example, Lutheran civic leaders sought to justify their defiance in terms of the Peace of Augsburg's guarantees of religious self-determination. Although the disputes over the meaning of the Peace of Augsburg could themselves serve confessional interests, the Peace of Augsburg's fundamental principle – that Catholics and Lutherans should each be allowed the peaceful practice of their faiths without interference or intimidation – validated the ideal of communal harmony as the primary civic goal.

Notes

1 Landeskirchliche Archiv der Evangelisch-Lutherischen Kirche in Bayern (LAELKB), Markgräfliches Dekanat Leutershausen, Nr. 36, Rep. Nr. 16, ff. 3ᵛ-4ʳ.
2 See, for example, W. K. Jordan, *The Development of Toleration in England, 1640–1660* (Cambridge, MA: Harvard University Press, 1932–40); Perez Zagorin, *How the Idea of Religious Toleration Came to the West* (Princeton: Princeton University Press, 2003). For a historiographical overview, see Benjamin J. Kaplan, *Divided by Faith: Religious Conflict and the Practice of Toleration in Early Modern Europe* (Cambridge, MA: Harvard University Press, 2007), 1–12; Alexandra Walsham, *Charitable Hatred: Tolerance and Intolerance in England, 1500–1700* (Manchester: Manchester University Press, 2006), 6–13.
3 See, for example, Kaplan, *Divided by Faith*; Walsham, *Charitable Hatred*; Stuart Schwartz, *All Can Be Saved: Religious Tolerance and Salvation in the Iberian Atlantic World* (New Haven, CT: Yale University Press, 2008); Jesse Spohnholz, *The Tactics of Toleration: A Refugee Community in the Age of the Religious Wars* (Newark: University of Delaware Press, 2011).
4 Walsham, *Charitable Hatred*, 1–5, 40–9.
5 Robert W. Scribner, "Preconditions of Tolerance and Intolerance in Early Modern Germany," in *Tolerance and Intolerance in the European Reformation*, ed. Ole Peter Grell and Robert W. Scribner (Cambridge: Cambridge University Press, 1996), 38; Judith Pollmann, "The Bond of Christian Piety: The Individual Practice of Tolerance and Intolerance in the Dutch Republic," in *Calvinism and Religious Toleration in the Dutch Golden Age*, ed. R. Po-Chia Hsia and H.F.K. Van Nierop (Cambridge: Cambridge University Press, 2002), 58, 70–1.

6 See, for example, Teresa M. Bejan, *Mere Civility: Disagreement and the Limits of Toleration* (Cambridge, MA: Harvard University Press, 2017).

7 Karl Brandi, ed., *Der Augsburger Religionsfriede vom 25. September, 1555. Kritische Ausgabe des Textes mit den Entwürfen und der königlichen Deklaration* (Göttingen: Vandenhoeck & Ruprecht, 1927), 36–8. For analyses of the treaty's historical and contemporary significance, see Axel Gotthard, *Der Augsburger Religionsfrieden* (Münster: Aschendorff Verlag, 2004); Wolfgang Wüst, Georg Kreuzer, and Nicola Shümann, eds., *Der Augsburger Religionsfriede 1555. Ein Epochenerignis und seine regionale Verankerung* (Augsburg: Wißner, 2005); Heinz Schilling and Herbert Smolinsky, *Der Augsburger Religionsfrieden 1555* (Münster: Aschendorff, 2007).

8 Gotthard, *Augsburger Religionsfrieden*, 240–80. On the litigation of disputes over the Peace of Augsburg in the imperial courts, see Bernhard Ruthmann, *Die Religionsprozesse am Reichskammergericht (1555–1648)* (Köln: Böhlau Verlag, 1996); Stefan Ehrenpreis, *Kaiserliche Gerichtsbarkeit und Konfessions Konflikt: Der Reichshofrat unter Rudolf II (1576–1612)* (Göttingen: Vandenhoeck & Ruprecht, 2006).

9 Thomas Kaufmann, "Religious, Confessional and Cultural Conflicts among Neighbors: Observations on the Sixteenth and Seventeenth Centuries," in *Orthodoxies and Heterodoxies in Early Modern German Culture: Order and Creativity 1550–1750*, ed. Randolph C. Head and Daniel Christensen (Leiden: Brill, 2007), 104.

10 Bernd Moeller, "Imperial Cities and the Reformation," in *Imperial Cities and the Reformation: Three Essays*, trans. H.C. Erik Midelfort and Mark U. Edwards (Durham, N.C.: Labyrinth Press, 1982), 46; Kaplan, *Divided by Faith*, 60–72.

11 Walsham, *Charitable Hatred*, 1–5, 40–9.

12 Ibid., 228–99.

13 Brandi, *Der Augsburger Religionsfreiden*, 8.

14 Ernst Walder, ed., *Religionsvergleiche des 16. Jahrhunderts*, I, Quellen zur Neueren Geschichte, Hft. 7 (Bern: Verlag Herbert Lang & CIE, 1960), 5–13. On "friendship pacts" in the French Wars of Religion, see Olivier Christin, *La paix de religion: L'autonomisation de la raison politique au XVIe siècle* (Paris: Seuil, 1997). For a comparative analysis of these treaties and accords, see Wayne P. Te Brake, *Religious War and Religious Peace in Early Modern Europe* (Cambridge: Cambridge University Press, 2017).

15 Günther Schmidt, *Libelli Famosi. Zur Bedeutung der Schmähschriften, Scheltbriefe, Schandgemälde und Pasquille in der deutschen Rechtsgeschichte* (Diss., Universität Köln, 1985), 131–41, 253–4.

16 Debora Shugar, *Censorship and Cultural Civility: The Regulation of Language in Tudor-Stuart England* (Philadelphia: The University of Pennsylvania Press, 2006), 140.

17 Allyson F. Creasman, *Censorship and Civic Order in Reformation Germany, 1517–1648: "Printed Poison and Evil Talk"* (Farnham: Ashgate, 2012), 109–19; Ulrich Eisenhardt, *Die kaiserliche Aufsicht über Buchdruck, Buchhandel und Presse in Heiligen Römischen Reich Deutscher Nation (1496–1806)* (Karlsruhe: Verlag C.F. Müller, 1970), 55–6.

18 Reichsabschied Speyer 1570, § 154, in *Neue vollständige Sammlung der Reichs-Abschiede, welche von den Zeiten Kayser Conrads des II. bis jetzo auf den Teutschen Reichs-Tagen abgefasset worden*, Bd. 3 (1747) (Osnabrück: Otto Zeller, 1967), 308.

19 Reichspolizeiordung 1577, XXXV, § 3, in ibid., 396.

20 See Ruthmann, *Die Religionsprozesse am Reichskammergericht*.

21 Brandi, ed., *Der Augsburger Religionsfriede*, 49–50.

22 C. Scott Dixon, "Urban Order and Religious Coexistence in the German Imperial City: Augsburg and Donauwörth, 1548–1608," *Central European History* 40, no. 1 (2007), 8–11.

23 Of the imperial cities subject to the "City Article" of the Religious Peace, Paul Warm-brunn identifies only eight cities that can be properly considered "parity cities" in the sense that they protected the religious practices of both faiths, granted full civil rights to members of the minority faith, and allowed members of both faiths at least some participation in civic governance. These included: Ulm, Donauwörth, Kauf-beuren, Leutkirch, Augsburg, Biberach, Ravensburg, and Dinklesbühl. Paul Warm-brunn, *Zwei Konfessionen in einer Stadt: das Zusammenleben von Katholiken und Protestanten in den paritätischen Reichsstädten Augsburg, Biberach, Ravensburg und Dinklesbühl von 1548 bis 1648* (Weisbaden: F. Steiner, 1983), 11–5.

24 Ibid., 108–13; Bernd Roeck, *Eine Stadt in Kreig und Frieden. Studien zur Ge-schichte der Reichsstadt Augsburg zwischen Kalenderstreit und Partität* (Göttin-gen: Vandenhoeck & Ruprecht, 1989),1: 239–62.

25 Willem Frijhoff, "How Plural Were the Religious Worlds in Early Modern Europe? Critical Reflections from the Netherlandic Experience," in *Living with Religious Diversity in Early-Modern Europe*, ed. Dagmar Freist and C. Scott Dixon (Alder-shot: Ashgate, 2009), 33–4.

26 Pollmann, "The Bond of Christian Piety," 58, 70–1.

27 David M. Luebke, *Hometown Religion: Regimes of Coexistence in Early Modern Westphalia* (Charlottesville: University of Virginia Press, 2016), 6.

28 Stadtarchiv Augsburg (StAA), Literalien, "Schwenkfeldiana & Reformations-acten," Oct. 4, 1555.

29 Robert B. Shoemaker, "Reforming Male Manners: Public Insult and the Decline of Violence in London, 1660–1740," and Elizabeth Foyster, "Boys Will Be Boys? Manhood and Aggression, 1660–1800," in *English Masculinities 1660–1800*, ed. Tim Hitchcock and Michele Cohen (London: Longman, 1999), 147–50, 157–9, 162–3; Julie Hardwick, "Early Modern Perspectives on the Long History of Domestic Violence: The Case of Seventeenth-Century France," *The Journal of Modern History* 78, no. 1 (2006), 15.

30 Scott Taylor, *Honor and Violence in Golden Age Spain* (New Haven, CT: Yale University Press, 2008), 9.

31 James R. Farr, "Honor, Law, and Custom in Renaissance Europe," in *A Com-panion to the Worlds of the Renaissance*, ed. Guido Ruggiero (Oxford: Oxford University Press, 2006), 127.

32 StAA, Evangelisches Wesensarchiv Augsburg, Akten Nr. 147, Nr. 2, f. Aiii^v.

33 Mario Müller, *Verletzende Worte. Beleidigung und Verleumdung in Rechtstexten aus dem Mittelalter und dem 16. Jahrhundert* (Hildesheim: Georg Olms Verlag, 2017), 238.

34 StAA, Schätze, Nr. ad 36/3, f. 5^v.

35 Bejan, *Mere Civility*, 23–6.

36 StAA, Evangelisches Wesensarchiv Augsburg, Akten Nr. 147, Nr. 2, f. Aiii^v.

37 Kaplan, *Divided by Faith*, 34–7.

38 "Mameluke" refers to enslaved warriors recruited from non-Muslim families and converted to Islam to serve in the armies of medieval Egyptian caliphs. It was an insult commonly directed against converts in early modern Germany.

39 Bejan, *Mere Civility*, 5.

40 Amy Nelson Burnett, "Picards, Karlstadians, and Oecolampadians: (Re-)Naming the Early Eucharistic Controversy," and David Mayes, "Triplets: The Holy Roman Empire's Birthing of Catholics, Lutherans, and Reformed in 1648," in *Names and Naming in Early Modern Germany*, ed. Joel F. Harrington and Marjorie Elizabeth Plummer (Oxford: Berghan, 2019).

41 See, for example, BayHStA, General Register, Fasc. 787, Nr. 7/1, ff. 18^r-20^r. On anti-Jesuit propaganda in the era, see Eric Nelson, "The Jesuit Legend: Superstition and Myth-Making," in *Religion and Superstition in Reformation Europe*, ed. Helen Parish and William G. Naphy (Manchester: Manchester University Press, 2002), 94–111.

42 StAA, Strafamt, Urgichten (Urg.), Caspar Thoman, Jan. 13, 1581, "Bericht der verordenyen an die Zucht unnd Straffordnung," Jan. 10, 1581.
43 StAA, Schätze Nr. ad 36/9, "Zucht und Policey Ordnung," f. 33ᵛ.
44 StAA, Strafamt, Urg. Caspar Thoman, Jan. 13, 1581; Urg. Jacob Erhard, Feb. 3, 1612; Urg. Casper Weickmann, July 20–7, 1615.
45 StAA, Strafamt, Urg. Sixt Hernberger, July 23, 1601.
46 Undated, unsigned note filed in ibid.
47 Urg. Sixt Hernberger, July 23, 1601, Question Nr. 6.
48 Ibid., Answer Nr. 10.
49 StAA, Strafbuch Nr. 103, 1596-1605, f. 146ᵛ.
50 StAA, Schätze, Nr. ad 36/3, f. 48ʳ; Allyson F. Creasman, "Fighting Words: Anger, Insult, and 'Self-Help' in Early Modern German Law," *Journal of Social History* 51, no. 2 (2017), 277–8.
51 Placidus Braun, *Geschichte des Kollegiums der Jesuiten in Augsburg* (Munich: Jakob Giel, 1822), 3–11.
52 Although Protestants gained a slight majority in the Privy Council in the early 1570s, thereafter the balance shifted decidedly towards the Catholics. Warmbrunn, *Zwei Konfessionen*, 132–7; Katarina Sieh-Burens, *Oligarche, Konfession und Politik im 16. Jahrhundert: zur sozialen Verflechtung der Augsburger Bürgermeister und Stadtpfleger 1518–1618* (Munich: Verlag Ernst Vögel, 1986), 183–5.
53 Warmbrunn, *Zwei Konfessionen*, 248–9; Sieh-Burens, *Oligarche*, 195, 200–3; Carl A. Hoffmann, "Konfessionell motivierte und gewandelte Konflikte in der zweiten Hälfte des 16. Jahrhunderts – Versuch eines mentalitätsgeschichtlichen Ansatzes am Beispiel der bikonfessionellen Reichsstadt Augsburg," in *Konfessionalisierung und Region*, ed. Peer Frieß and Rolf Kießling (Konstanz: Universitätsverlag Konstanz GmbH, 1999), 99–100.
54 See, for example, StAA, Strafamt, Urg. Veit Goppoldt, April 12, 1564; Urg. Magdalena Geslerin, April 17, 1564; Urg. Gedeon Mair, Nov. 7, 1583; Urg. Christof Widenman, Nov. 10, 1583; Urg. Christof Wörter, Aug. 22, 1584.
55 Report of Witnesses dated Aug. 19, 1569, filed in StAA, Strafamt, Urg. Georg Taschner, Aug. 19–27, 1569.
56 Urg. Georg Taschner, Aug. 19, 1569.
57 Ibid.
58 StAA, Strafamt, Urg. Hieronymus Österreicher, March 2, 1580.
59 Ibid.
60 Ibid.
61 Ibid.
62 StAA, Strafbuch Nr. 100, 1571-1580, f. 76ᵛ.
63 Warmbrunn, *Zwei Konfessionen*, pp. 135–6. On conversion in Augsburg post-1648, see Duane J. Corpis, *Crossing the Boundaries of Belief: Geographies of Religious Conversion in Southern Germany, 1648–1800* (Charlottesville: University of Virginia Press, 2014).
64 StAA, Strafamt, Urg. Michael Benedict, April 13, 1603.
65 Ibid. Claiming that he was drunk and didn't know what he was saying, Benedict received only a short imprisonment. StAA, Strafbuch Nr. 103, 1596-1605, f. 214ᵛ.
66 Report of *Strafherren*, filed in StAA, Strafamt, Urg. Hans Scheurer, May 5, 1603.
67 Kaplan, *Divided by Faith*, 28–47.
68 Dixon, "Urban Order," 8–11.
69 Ibid., 11–2.
70 Creasman, *Censorship and Civic Order*, 147–84; Ferdinand Kaltenbrunner, "Der Augsburger Kalenderstreit," *Mittheilungen des Instituts für österreichische Geschichtsforschung* 1 (1880), 497–540.
71 Warmbrunn, *Zwei Konfessionen*, 360–75; Roeck, *Eine Stadt in Krieg und Frieden*, 1: 125–33.

72 StAA, Kalenderstreitacten Nr. 28, "Relatio. Der Ro: Kay: Mt: verordneter Comissarien der alhie anno 1584 nach dem auflauf verrichter Inquisition und Commission," ff. 138^v, 142^v. By the 1580s, Lutheran jurists throughout the Empire were increasingly arguing that the Peace of Augsburg had envisioned just such a power-sharing arrangement, but this argument anticipated by several decades the system of strict confessional parity that would ultimately be codified in the Peace of Westphalia at the conclusion of the Thirty Years' War. M. Frisch, "Zur Rechtsnatur des Augsburger Religionsfriedens," *Zeitschrift der Savigny-Stiftung für Rechtsgeschichte*, Kanonistische Abteilung, 79 (1993), 448–58.

73 Roeck, *Eine Stadt in Krieg und Frieden*, 1: 169–88.

74 Ibid., 2: 615–30.

75 StAA, Strafamt, Urg. Georg Neumair Sept. 6, 1629.

76 Ibid., Urg. Georg Neumair, Sept. 12, 1629.

77 Ibid.; StAA, Strafbuch 1615-1632, f. 663.

78 StAA, Strafamt, Urg. Martin Haller, Oct. 21, 1630.

79 Ibid., Question 6.

80 Ibid., Answer 6.

81 Roeck, *Eine Stadt in Krieg und Frieden*, 2: 771–5, 869–80.

82 On commemorations of the Peace of Westphalia in Augsburg, see Emily Fisher Gray, "Celebrating Peace in Biconfessional Augsburg: Lutheran Churches and Remembrance Culture," in *Topographies of Tolerance and Intolerance: Responses to Religious Pluralism in Reformation Europe*, ed. Marjorie Elizabeth Plummer and Victoria Christman (Leiden: Brill, 2018), 176–200.

83 Instrumentum Pacis Osnabrugense (IPO), Art. V, § 1, in *Kaiser und Reich: Verfassungsgeschichte des Heiligen Römischen Reiches Deutscher Nation vom Beginn des 12. Jahrhunderts bis zum Jahre 1806 in Dokumenten*, Teil II, ed. Arno Buschmann, 2nd ed. (Baden-Baden: Nomos Verlagsgesellschaft, 1994), 34.

84 Warmbrunn, *Zwei Konfessionen*, 173–4; Roeck, *Eine Stadt in Krieg und Frieden*, 2: 949–74.

85 IPO, Art. V, §§ 4; 6-9.

86 SStBA, 2°Aug. 324, Bd. 4, "Statutes," Nr. 21.

87 StAA, Strafamt, Urg. Hans Zeberle, Aug. 5, 1649.

88 Ibid.

89 Ibid.

90 Ibid.

91 Ibid.

92 StAA, Strafbuch, 1633-1653, ff. 332-333.

93 StAA, Strafamt, Urg. Colman Stritzel, Aug. 5, 1649, Report of Witnesses, Dated Aug. 13, 1649.

94 Urg. Colman Stritzel, Aug. 5, 1649, Question 7.

95 Ibid., Questions 17 and 19.

96 Ibid., Answer 17; StAA, Ratsbücher, Nr. 71, 1648–1650, Aug. 12, 1649, f. 262.

97 On legal parity as an important condition for confessional coexistence, see Kaplan, *Divided by Faith*, 217–34.

98 Etienne François, *Die unsichtbare Grenze: Protestanten und Katholiken in Augsburg 1648–1806* (Sigmaringen: Jan Thorbecke Verlag, 1991).

2 The Acoustics of Peace
Singing and Religious Coexistence in Seventeenth-Century Mechelen*

Matthew Laube

In 1622, Benedict van Haeften, provost of the Benedictine abbey in Affligem, was alarmed by the sounds he had been hearing in Mechelen, a city some 30 km distant from his abbey in the Southern Netherlands. In the preface to *Den Lusthof der Christelycke Leeringhe (The Pleasure Garden of Christian Doctrine)*, a musical setting of the Jesuit Mechelen catechism (1610), Van Haeften lamented that, in the years surrounding the Twelve Years' Truce (1609–21), Mechelen had been resonating not with the recognizable sounds of Catholicism but with "*amoureuse*, worldly and heretical songs" which "seduced" the laity away from Catholicism.[1] According to Van Haeften, heretics since antiquity had used song to entice lay believers away from Catholic orthodoxy. With the Truce, however, the movement of people and goods from the Protestant Northern Netherlands into the Catholic southern provinces had increased, and with it the sounds of heresy. Van Haeften blamed Mechelen's mixed soundscape on those who, like heretics "in previous ages, have sought to spread their false doctrine through songs" that contained ideas contrary to Catholicism and disturbed the hearts and minds of lay Catholics through inordinate sensuality.[2]

At first blush, Van Haeften's depiction of Catholic Mechelen as a religiously diverse environment sits uneasily with scholarship that has emphasised the conservatism of Mechelen, a city which served as the territorial centre of both judicial and ecclesiastical powers, and its strong loyalty to royal authority compared to other cities in Flanders and Brabant.[3] Yet, although religious toleration in the Southern Netherlands has attracted far less scholarly attention than in cities of the Calvinist north, confessional coexistence in Mechelen and across the south should not be surprising. Catholic writers in Tournai lamented the continued presence of Protestants into the first half of the seventeenth century.[4] Protestants lived and worshiped in Antwerp in the decades after the final official abolition of Protestantism in 1589. With the arrival of the Truce in 1609, several hundred local Protestants made themselves more visible, travelling by boat from Antwerp to Lillo in the north for weekly services, baptism, weddings, and communion.[5] On the southern borderlands of the Low Countries, Lille's community of Protestants in 1612 numbered roughly 50 people who met in eight houses across the city.[6] In the university

DOI: 10.4324/9781003030522-4

town of Douai, a local community of Protestants whom authorities claimed had arrived from "infected lands under the shadow of commerce" became more vocal during the opening years of the peace between 1609 and 1614.[7]

Singing, moreover, was far from a secondary concern in minority contexts in Mechelen and elsewhere. Despite possible dangers, Protestants across the Catholic Southern Netherlands maintained an acoustic presence before and during the Truce. As Protestants from Antwerp sailed to Lillo, they sang psalms to make their presence known as a demonstration of defiance and solidarity while passing Catholic soldiers on the embankments.[8] In addition to meeting regularly with one another, Calvinists in Douai used psalm singing to catechise their children at home. They owned books containing anti-Catholic songs against the Pope, the Eucharist, and the saints, which they distributed to others.[9]

Scholars now accept that not all Protestants went into exile after the restoration of Catholicism in the Southern Netherlands in 1585 under Alessandro Farnese. Nor did Catholic authorities systematically check whether everyone in the south was reconciled.[10] Although uncertainty may have remained regarding who was reconciled with Catholicism and who was not, far less ambiguity existed about the aims of the Catholic restoration and the plurality of media and mechanisms – beyond the persecution of dissidents – by which clergy and laity sought to implant Catholic doctrine and culture. According to Judith Pollmann, after 1585 the clergy for the first time gave lay believers an active role in fighting heresy in the south.[11] Members of Jesuit sodalities learned in earnest how to recognise heretics and counter Protestant arguments, and Catholic organisations asserted control by appropriating formerly Protestant spaces.[12] Catechism teaching formed a major component of lay education, not just for elite men who were viewed as particularly susceptible to Protestantism, but also for the "simple people" who, according to Catholic leaders, had been the target of Protestant efforts.[13] Catholic reforms became more pressing during the Twelve Years' Truce as goods and people flowed more freely across the border, which brought religious "others" closer and turned the experience of religious diversity into a daily reality.

In this environment, singing formed an essential part of engaging laymen and -women and mobilising them during the Catholic restoration in the south. This included the singing of plainchant with Latin texts, sung both in liturgical contexts and outdoors in processions and on pilgrimage.[14] In addition, Catholic songs in Dutch marked the passage of the liturgical year and enabled lay believers to catechise themselves about theological matters of individual import, such as the four last things.[15] Singing also helped lay Catholics to engage in confessional polemic, which permeated devotional singing even in religious houses. To take a slightly late example, when in 1663 a beguine known only as J.G. composed a devotional song for use within the walls of her beguinage in Brussels, she selected the melody entitled "Calvinist Vespers," a well-known anti-Calvinist song which had circulated in the Southern Netherlands since at least 1545.[16] Catholic songwriters even attempted to alter collective memory and Catholicise sounds previously associated with Protestantism. Nearly half of the melodies used by the Leiden priest Rumoldus Batavus in his *New Songbook Containing Diverse Songs*, a Catholic devotional songbook targeted at "simple Dutch people," are also found in the *Souterliedekens*.[17] First published in 1540, the *Souterliedekens* was the first full psalter in Dutch and was popular among Protestants and Catholics alike in both north and south, and, like Batavus's later songbook, it was also aimed at "all Christian people," including the "uneducated."[18]

Despite the ubiquity of Catholic singing following the restoration after 1585, lay Catholic singing still attracts only scant attention in scholarship of Catholic reform, religious toleration, or music history in the Southern and Northern Netherlands.[19] This chapter will explore what religious diversity in Mechelen sounded like in the years surrounding the Twelve Years' Truce. Instead of concentrating primarily on Mechelen's community of Protestants, this chapter will investigate Catholic responses to the physical and acoustic presence of religious "others," arguing that local religious diversity stimulated Catholic musical creativity and generated new modes of Catholic singing which, in addition to demarcating religious lines with greater clarity, prepared laymen and -women for everyday encounters with Protestants living in their midst. This chapter takes as its premise that lay believers played an active role in developing, implementing, and challenging local strategies for toleration and that tolerance and intolerance, like peace and conflict, were not diametrically opposed phenomena but were themselves coexisting and interlinked. Examining rubrics of sound can help shed fresh light on local definitions of toleration, especially in mundane situations of urban life, and enrich existing interpretations of religious diversity in Mechelen, put forth by Craig Harline and Eddy Put, among others, who emphasise that Catholic authorities relied heavily on secular powers to regulate and counteract diversity during the Twelve Years' Truce.[20] A critical examination of *Den Lusthof der Christelycke Leeringhe* (Antwerp, 1622), Van Haeften's musical setting of the Mechelen catechism, will illuminate how Catholic leaders also turned directly to members of the laity, and to the medium of song, as a means of managing conflict, catechising local residents, and instructing lay Catholics in how they should engage directly with "others" through the sensory media of singing and sound.

Dissident singing in Mechelen

The historiography of music in sixteenth- and seventeenth-century Mechelen has painted a picture not of a vibrant lay faith or religious coexistence, but of Catholic triumph through elite and professional musical activity, which swelled following the arrival of Protestantism and the city's designation as the seat of the archbishopric. Within five years of the Iconoclastic Fury in 1566, authorities had expanded the cathedral's musical forces. In 1571, the number of permanent singers rose from nine to twelve, while from 1570 the number of choirboys increased from six to ten. Organs were constructed or restored in 1565, 1586, 1588, and again in 1612, while notable choirmasters such as George de La Hèle, Jan van Turnhout, and Nicolas Rogier joined the cathedral between 1572 and 1585.[21] However, other documentation reveals that Mechelen was a strikingly pluriconfessional environment where Protestant belief and resistance – not just orthodox devotion – strongly conditioned local Catholic activity and innovation. Protestants silenced and removed bells that marked Catholic rhythms of the city. During the English Fury in 1580, Protestant soldiers removed the bells of the Abbey of Roozendaal, which were sold to St Peter's church in the small fishing village of Arnemuiden in Zeeland.[22] Indeed, Protestant singing had formed part of Mechelen's acoustic environment since the 1520s when Mechelen "still glittered" with the sights and sounds of late medieval Catholicism.[23] In 1529, the Lutheran Willem van Zwolle penned before his execution a Protestant martyr-song which was quickly reproduced in Luther's Wittenberg in 1530.[24] Not only does Willem's song apear to be the first known example of a Lutheran songwriter directly referencing Luther's hymn "A Mighty Fortress" ("Ein feste Burg"), which Luther also composed *c.*1529. It also called on Netherlandish Protestants to engage in a lifelong, Word-based acoustic campaign and labour to ensure that "God's word might be heard everywhere."[25]

By the 1560s, local residents interacted with – and heard – Protestants with regularity in both extraordinary and mundane circumstances. Sometimes local Catholics confronted Protestants during heated moments of confessional tensions, as when an angry sculptor, according to Marcus van Vaernewijck's recounting, confronted an image breaker in Mechelen in 1566.[26] Other times, cross-confessional encounters occurred as part of daily life in streets, taverns, and workshops, or as part of neighbourhood and friendship networks. In the late 1550s, a Protestant carpenter named Jan Boots regularly mixed with fellow carpenters and neighbours in Adegemstraat and is known to have spoken with friends about religious matters and openly taunted beguines on city streets.[27] His taunting of Beguines likely included singing anti-Catholic songs. When Boots was apprehended and his home searched in 1560, he was found in possession of a Dutch Bible, letters exchanged with his Lutheran brother in Lübeck, and six songs condemning the Virgin, the Pope, and "false prophets," which Boots confessed to having composed himself and kept hidden at home in a cupboard.[28]

After 1585, a plurality of religious "others" lived in and passed through Mechelen, even as the Catholic town council and clerical authorities began to implement Tridentine reforms across the city and archbishopric. As Craig Harline and Eddy Put have observed, disturbances during the Truce frequently came from Calvinist visitors to the city. In 1610, sailors from the north mixed with local residents in city streets and openly mocked the Eucharist during a public procession, an act which resulted in only two days of jail time and in being read the terms of the Truce, before the sailors were released.[29] One year later, a statue of the Virgin was smashed outside St Rombout.[30] Disturbances came not only from male visitors to the city; during the Truce, a woman from Brussels openly argued with Archbishop Mathias Hovius about whether Christ was actually present in the Eucharist.[31] It is worth speculating that such protests, as sensory events, may have included – or been incited by – any number of pre-existing or newly composed songs criticising the Pope, the Virgin, and the Eucharist, or later by anti-Catholic songs celebrating the Reformation centenary in 1617, which fell in the middle of the Truce.[32]

In addition to visitors, Mechelen was also home to local residents who not only held Protestant views but also sought out Protestant and Orangist political songs. When Benedict van Haeften lamented the mixed confessional soundscape of Mechelen in 1622, he may have known about the manuscript songbook of Willem De Gortter (1585–after 1637), a Calvinist merchant, native of Mechelen, and member of *De Peony*, a local chamber of rhetoric which championed the prolongation of the Twelve Years' Truce.[33] In 1620 *De Peony* organised a cross-confessional, inter-city poetry competition that brought together chambers from the north and south and facilitated the regular cross-confessional mixing of De Gortter and others with both Protestants and Catholics who shared a desire for peace.[34] Although his songbook is best known for containing the first manuscript appearance of the Dutch anthem, *Wilhelmus*, De Gortter also recorded songs written by other rhetoricians, especially the Antwerp Lutheran Willem van Haecht (*c*.1530–after 1585), which carefully interlaced the language of religious peace with undercurrents of anti-Catholicism and veiled references to religious violence.[35] For instance, De Gortter copied down Van Haecht's "Listen, You Heathen Nation," a Protestant *Geuzenlied* which championed the Protestant ideals of the Word and salvation by grace, but did so without reference to the Pope, Virgin, saintly intercession, or other topics that Catholic audiences might find scandalous.[36] However, even as Van Haecht eschewed overtly anti-Catholic language in order to manage conflict or avoid censors, De Gortter and others likely did not miss that Van Haecht's chosen melody for "Listen, You Heathen Nation" – the melody which set Van Haecht's own setting of Psalm 11 – itself encoded messages of intolerance and anti-Catholic violence through its association with Psalm 11.[37] Here King David writes that the Lord "tests the righteous" but "hates […] the wicked and also all their servants." "The wicked," whom Van Haecht defined as Catholic "enemies of the church," "shall cry as God rains down lightening and sulphur with a loud clamour; a storm will be their lot."[38] In 1622, therefore, what may have concerned Benedict van Haeften about Mechelen's soundscape was not simply that some local residents like De Gortter held Protestant views or that they mixed with Catholic residents, but that these Protestants appeared to be advancing two different causes simultaneously: openly working for a cessation of religious violence and a prolongation of peace through their public activities as rhetoricians, while privately copying Protestant songs that contained only thinly veiled references to religious violence and divine judgement.

Intolerance and coexistence in Mechelen

By the beginning of the Twelve Years' Truce, Mechelen had long possessed a reputation as a city hostile to religious nonconformity of any kind. In part, this reputation was a Protestant construction, generated in response to the numerous executions of Lutherans, Reformed Protestants, and Anabaptists that occurred between 1520 and 1580 and fuelled by Protestant depictions of Spanish violence in 1572.[39] However, as Bram Caers and others have emphasised, Mechelen's conservative religious and social outlook also corresponded to its symbolic function as the seat of central religious and judicial authorities.[40] In 1559, Mechelen became the seat of an archbishopric, with the church of St Rombout elevated to cathedral status, while the *Grote Raad* was located in Mechelen from the late fifteenth century to the French Revolution.[41] Mechelen's intolerance and conservativism continued between 1578 and 1585 and took new forms before and during the Truce.[42] Local policies after 1600 reflected the position of the Archdukes, who in 1607 reaffirmed their commitment to cleanse the south of heretics and, in 1610, famously declared a desire to have no subjects at all, rather than permitting Protestants.[43] As Harline and Put have written, Archbishop Hovius supported the production of polemical pamphlets against Calvinism and actively enforced the terms of the Truce and attempted to punish those who caused public scandal through mockery and protest.[44] Some magistrates stood firmly against the Twelve Years' Truce, and it was to these "dear fathers and guardians of the collective prosperity" that members of *De Peony* directed their efforts to prolong the Truce and create "lasting peace" beyond 1621.[45]

Policies governing the production of sound, evidenced in church reform and in municipal and diocesan regulations, further reveal an attitude of intolerance. At St Rombout, it was when Catholic authorities felt under greatest threat that organs were installed or refurbished – in 1565, 1586, and 1612 – in order to reinforce and widen the confessional divide with Protestants. In 1607, the synod of Mechelen restricted the melodies played from local carillons only to Catholic hymns, reissuing an ordinance from 1570 by which the synod forbade "licentious, military or tasteless music from the carillon."[46] In 1608, the synod reissued a placard from 1601 which gave authorities the power to screen all songs being printed, stipulating that "No chamber plays, comedies or other recreational plays, dances, or songs should be printed or represented" without proper "visitation and preceding consent."[47] Although not stated explicitly, the synod of Mechelen most likely had in mind to restrict songs with religiously heterodox words and associations. In 1597, similar ordinances were issued in Flanders forbidding all "chamber plays, songs, comedies, sonnets, ballads, morality plays and the like" that contained "things offensive directly or indirectly to the Catholic

religion or religious people" and that were produced by "the evil and repro-
bate sects [that] increasingly come up and multiply on a daily basis."[48]

Beneath this veneer, however, Mechelen's conservatism was neither fixed
nor widely accepted among the local Catholic laity. Indeed, song served to
bolster flagging adherence to central authority at critical moments of confessional conflict. In 1567, in the wake of the Iconoclastic Fury, an anonymous
pro-Catholic pamphleteer created *Advertissement ende loffelycke verman-
inghe*, which used poetic verse to delineate confessional communities by
denouncing Protestant heretics, praising locals for confronting image break-
ers, and calling Catholic Mechelaars to arms to fight against the Reformed
church.[49] However, it has gone unnoticed that the poetic verse – whose opening lines begin "Doemen schreef vyfthien hondert zeffentzestich Jaer" – may
have been inspired by the similarly titled "Doemen schreef M.V. hondert
ende eenen veertich Iaer," a popular song from the 1540s which sought to en-
gender feelings of political mistrust of anyone who allied themselves against
central authorities. Using a similar (though not identical) rhyme scheme as
the later 1567 verse, "Doemen schreef M.V. hondert ende eenen veertich
Iaer" first circulated in the Antwerp Songbook of 1544 and was written following the alliance of the French king and Duke of Jülich in 1541, which
excluded Charles V.[50] Although it is unclear whether the 1567 verse from
Mechelen was ever meant to be sung, it is likely that its opening words –
nearly identical to the 1544 song – tapped into popular knowledge in order
to elicit feelings of mistrust of anyone, especially Protestants after 1566, who
positioned themselves against central authorities of church and state.

As early as the 1560s, secular and church authorities also initiated forms of
toleration which have thus far gone unnoticed. Indeed, although local authorities sought to rid the city of Protestantism, it would be wrong to conclude
that Catholic leaders disapproved of every element of local Protestant culture
or that they always painted Protestants with the same broad brush. Despite
the close association of vernacular psalms with Protestantism, Mechelen's
Catholics were given their own approved book of versified Dutch psalms and
Catholic hymns in 1566, "for the profit of all people in Mechelen," not just
Protestants.[51] Six years earlier, when the sheriff and church courts examined
the six songs written by Jan Boots, only five of the six were declared criminal.[52] Authorities did not condemn Boots's sixth song, "How Wondrous Are
the Works of God," which, in contrast to the other five songs, contained no
reference to the Pope or "false prophets" who "appear like sheep."[53] Instead,
"How Wondrous Are the Works of God" praises the generous nature of God
the Father – as opposed to Christ – in phrasing reminiscent of Old Testament
wisdom literature which Catholic authorities appear not to have found objectionable.[54] Nevertheless, through using the broad language of scripture, the
Lutheran Boots also encoded messages into "How Wondrous Are the Works
of God" about the hardships and mortal risks of religious dissent, reminding
singers and hearers to "call to the Lord in your trouble," because "in him you
will retreat; he alone is the one who kills and brings again to life," not any

earthly authority.[55] Therefore, Boots's song not only reveals that Mechelen's authorities did not condemn every creative output of Protestants, even songs written by individuals who confessed to writing sharp anti-Papal propaganda. It also suggests that, had Boots been anticipating execution upon being arrested and tried in Mechelen courts for his Protestant beliefs, his fears proved to be unfounded. Following his trial in 1561, Boots was not executed but was punished in ways designed to draw him back to Catholicism and enable him to continue to work and provide for his family.[56]

Accommodation of religious diversity also continued after 1600. Hovius grounded his own local toleration of Protestants in the fear that Catholics in the north would be treated poorly. "I do not think that heretics must be banned to the last person; this would disturb the peace too greatly and cause retaliation against our co-religionists in the north."[57] Throughout the Truce, clergy came into direct contact with Protestants and, to some degree, tolerated Protestants in the hope it would advance the Catholic cause on the level of individual conversions. While visiting his Catholic grandparents in Mechelen, the Amsterdam Protestant Frans Boels embraced Catholicism while lodging with Jean de Froidmont, a canon from Mechelen cathedral, despite repeated threats from his Protestant mother of being cut off both financially and personally.[58] Cross-confessional contact was not limited to the clergy. Catholic residents encountered religious "others" in urban spaces as part of everyday life: on the streets, as well as in hotels, taverns, and other places that provided basic subsistence for Protestant visitors when staying in Mechelen. When Maria Boels travelled from Amsterdam to win her son back to Protestantism, she likely encountered not just diocesan officials but also innkeepers and fellow lodgers and diners at The Little Windmill where she and her friend, a "robust Dutch woman," were staying.[59]

Religious officials were aware of the regular exposure of local residents to Protestants and heterodox ideas. One tool designed to help Mechelaars navigate life with religious integrity was the Mechelen catechism, *Den Schat der Christelicker Leeringhe* (*The Treasure of Christian Doctrine*).[60] Created by the Jesuit Lodewijk Makeblijde (1565–1630), *Den Schat* was commissioned in 1607 by the synod of Mechelen to make doctrinal instruction more uniform and deepen the faith of lay Catholics in Mechelen and across the archbishopric. Aimed primarily at the young, the catechism was envisioned for use by teachers and priests in schools and churches that organised catechism lessons for parishioners. It was also to be used by Mechelaars of all ages in lay homes across the social spectrum. In a lengthy preface addressed to house fathers (*Huysvaders*), Makeblijde enjoined them to read the catechism to family members and other household residents as part of communal life at the domestic table throughout the year, on "every holy day in the evenings, before or after the meal" in order to bring forth "beautiful fruit of lasting devotion."[61]

The Mechelen catechism had a sharply polemical tone. It conditioned Mechelaars to expect all Protestants to be "quarrelsome," characterising them uniformly as "those who cause division among you," drawing on the words of the Apostle Paul in Romans and 2 Timothy.[62] Makeblijde's catechism was designed, therefore, to present the "uniform perfection of [the] upright doctrine of Christ, in which [we] should hold fast, under all stormy attacks of heretical errors."[63] While adherents to Protestantism were labelled as universally quarrelsome, Catholics were granted considerable latitude to decide for themselves when and how best to interact with "heretics you might find in your midst."[64] In general, disputing with heretics should be left to "teachers of the holy church." However, lay believers may debate with Protestants if it "happens to the honour of God, and the blessedness of souls."[65] Makeblijde subdivided lay Catholics into two groups and created differentiated instruction for how each was to interact with Protestants. On the one hand were lay Catholics who eagerly sought out debates with Protestants. For them, Makeblijde advised that disputes with Protestants should not "happen at every occasion, with everyone," but that when a confrontation did take place, lay Catholics were to use "this treasure very gently, with humility and thankfulness from your heart to God."[66] On the other hand, Makeblijde recognised that some lay Catholics could not avoid rubbing shoulders with Protestants in daily life. Their regular domestic devotion should be strongly orientated towards preparing them and safeguarding them against heresy. These men and women should "daily ask God for his grace and protection, with all humility, in the morning, at Holy Mass, and in the evening."[67] They were to cling to the ingrained routines and customs of Catholicism, "Never [letting] go of your Christian habits; nor [doing] anything that goes against God's honour or obedience to the Holy Church."[68] Lay Catholics should avoid being indebted to Protestants and were encouraged to confessionalise everyday material objects, "never [taking] anything from heretics, in order that you don't sell your freedom, and lose your soul."[69]

Singing the Mechelen catechism

First published in abridged form in 1609, the Mechelen catechism appeared in expanded form in 18 editions between 1610 and 1716.[70] It found use locally in the city and archbishopric of Mechelen, as well as Catholic communities further north, including Makeblijde's own Jesuit mission in Delft. Extending the reach of the catechism into the Francophone south was a dual Dutch-French edition published in Antwerp in 1644.[71] In 1622, Benedict van Haeften published his musical setting of Makeblijde's catechism in *Den Lusthof der Christelycke Leeringhe*, moved by a deep concern for "worldly and heretical" songs in Mechelen as well as the ignorance of the children of the city and archbishopric, whom Van Haeften described as "blunt in understanding and short of memory."[72] Published in Antwerp in 1622 by Hieronymus Verdussen, a prolific printer of Catholic devotional works, *Den Lusthof* contained 112 songs in five main sections and formed the backbone of Benedict van Haeften's efforts in 1622 to "implant" Catholic doctrine in the hearts of lay believers and Catholicise Mechelen's soundscape.

Through *Den Lusthof*, Van Haeften sought to widen the audience and appeal of the Mechelen catechism by combining Makeblijde's doctrinal content with entertaining and "sweet sounding" songs that were designed for use in schools, churches, and lay homes across social categories. For nearly every song text, readers were able to choose which melody to use. They could choose either a two-voice polyphonic setting with musical notation or one or more suggested popular tunes printed without musical notation. For all song texts, Van Haeften indicated at least one popular tune, but for some texts five or more possible melodies were given.[73] Through providing multiple modes of musical engagement, Van Haeften enabled individual households to self-differentiate and sing in a way that best suited the social and cultural make-up of the home. The two-voiced polyphonic compositions, so-called *Bicinia*, indicate that Van Haeften likely intended *Den Lusthof* to support curricular programmes in Mechelen's schools in order to facilitate the learning not just of Catholic doctrine, but also of basic musical skills such as singing, reading musical notation, and understanding basic compositional techniques such as counterpoint.[74]

Regardless of which musical setting was chosen, these songs were designed to help establish devout domestic routines that allowed for the daily articulation of collective faith. They also helped to restrain excessive sensuality at mealtimes. According to Van Haeften, immoderation brought on attacks of the devil, which might make a person susceptible to heresy.[75] Van Haeften, therefore, advised house fathers to "teach your children and wife to sing such songs [of praise to God], not only when they are afraid or are doing some other work, but above all at the table," where "the devil spies and induces his cunning lies at meal times" through "drunkenness, overeating, immoderate laughing, and worldliness of the heart." In order to fend off the devil, "one must, most of all, arm oneself with psalms, before eating when at the table. And with wife and children rising from the table" to finish eating, "sing sacred songs of praise to God."[76] Because warding off inordinate sensuality through singing psalms carried strong resonances with Calvinist and Lutheran practices, Van Haeften differentiated Catholic table singing by localising it, connecting Catholic table song with local cultures of devotion. In his "Song After the Meal," Van Haeften instructed readers to use the melody to "Dulce sacrato mea lingua pange," a well-known musical setting used for an ode of praise to St Rombout, the patron saint of Mechelen. Van Haeften also incorporated specifically Catholic references to the worship of saints into the song text and interrupted verses five and six with the instruction that singers recite the *Pater Noster* together.[77]

Beyond the home, *Den Lusthof* also equipped Mechelaars to engage with Protestants living amongst them, providing lay Catholics with material to counter Protestant attacks against two aspects of Catholic theology: the honouring of relics and the theology of images. The text of the song "Of Relics, or the Bones of Saints" begins by addressing Protestants directly, asking "Heretics evil and weak from Satan, without reason, what do you think happens at shrines?"[78] Giving lay Catholics the ability to counter Protestant claims that bones are inanimate matter unworthy of veneration, Van Haeften clarified that Catholics do not honour bones *per se*, but instead "the body that here has fought, and much pain has suffered" for God and his church.[79] And in order to rebut the view that relics were a Catholic invention, Van Haeften cited the Biblical example of King Josiah who, when he toppled Israel's altars to other gods, "held onto the bones of the prophets, and let all the others burn, when he destroyed all the idols in his lands."[80] Similarly, Moses "with honour transported the body of Joseph in a wagon [...] may we not then confer on the deceased a single honour?"[81] Relics were, finally, powerful intercessory weapons which gave courage to fight heresy and secured one's eternal blessedness. The final verse admonished singers "to pray to God with humility through them who still fight with us, That He let us enjoy the pleasures of heaven forevermore."[82]

Similarly, the song "Of the Honour of Images" enabled lay Catholics to refute Protestant arguments against the veneration of images. Van Haeften encouraged Catholic believers not to self-fashion their own faith as Protestants did, but to view the lives of past Catholics as a kind of living image and reflect on "how God's friends, going before us" serve as a "powerful mirror."[83] Countering the Protestant emphasis on the Word, the song taught that an image is "often better than the word" for "bring[ing] forth its fruits" and "awaken[ing] our hearts to God."[84] According to Van Haeften, to deny the Catholic theology of images would also be to deny that God had woven images into the very nature of humankind as a reflection of himself. In asking "A human, is that not God's image?," referencing the creation account in Genesis 1:27, the song sought to turn Protestants' rootedness in the Word back against them, using Old Testament scripture itself to challenge Protestants, who frequently grounded their condemnation of images solely in the Decalogue while neglecting the subject of images found in other parts of scripture.[85]

Despite the Mechelen catechism's admonition that lay debates with Protestants should be rare and characterised by humility, Van Haeften penned one polemical song intended to be sung directly to Protestant hearers. Using pronouns such as "Your" and "You," the "Song Against the So-Called Reformed Church" openly heckles Protestants, accusing that "Your doctrine is not as pure, false heretic, as you declare [...] Each now sees before their eyes, you are not in God's church."[86] Emphasising the ancient origins of Catholicism, the song criticises Protestants for the "freshly baked goods that one sells in your churches" to "curious people." Catholics, by contrast, could claim that "The ancient origins serve me," while Protestants "go and search for a new song."[87] The concluding verse of the song implored Protestants to "leave the liar's nest: Follow God's church, it is best for you [...] Do not sway like a reed, Because God's church is not anywhere else."[88] Clearly distinguishing Catholicism from Protestantism were the two refrains of the text: "You are not in God's church" (vv. 1–3) and "God's church is not there [with the Reformed]" (vv. 4–6). Further deepening a sense that Protestants were wayward and untrustworthy was the melody itself. Van Haeften chose the melody of the popular song "Your Love is Not as Pure" (*Uwe liefd' is niet so puere*) as both his popular tune option and the basis of his polyphonic setting for two voices. This melody is almost certainly from a Flemish song based on "Si c'est pour mon pucelage," a widely known song about a young girl who sees through the "beautiful promises" (*belles promesses*) and "disappointing speeches" (*discours decevans*) of an untrustworthy suitor from the city and instead promises her love to a boy from the village.[89] Here Van Haeften invites audiences familiar with the original message of the song, Protestant and Catholic alike, to equate the "beautiful promises" of Protestants with those of a deceptive man who sought to force himself on others.

In *Den Lusthof*, Van Haeften differentiated Catholicism from Protestantism not only through his use of recognizably Catholic ideas and musical material, such as the melody he chose for Catholic table singing, but also by Catholicising beliefs and melodies that were shared with Protestants locally and further afield. In his preface, Van Haeften echoed Luther and later Protestant writers when he praised the universality of music to all humankind, writing that "we have by nature an inborn appetite and affection towards song; as St Chrysostom declared, are not the young suckling children crying in the cradle or in the arms of their nursemaids relieved through song?"[90] Nearly a century earlier, Luther had argued that music was "impressed on or created with every single creature, one and all."[91] Likewise, the "inborn appetite" of which Van Haeften wrote mirrored comments by his contemporary, the Moravian Amos Comenius, who wrote that "music is the most natural thing. For as soon as we are born into the world, we begin to sing the Paradise song. Crying is our first music."[92] Yet, looking beyond surface resemblances, Van Haeften was seeking to confessionalise ideas shared across confessional lines and redeploy them for his own, Catholic purposes. Rather than song being a vehicle for communicating the Word and worshiping God, as Luther and others had claimed, Van Haeften praised the universality of song, in part to argue that corporate singing and learning doctrine through song were not Protestant inventions, but were rooted in the ancient practices of the Catholic past. Van Haeften cited the example of Athanasius who had set "the articles of faith psalm-wise in song." Similarly, St Ambrose had written that "there is nothing more powerful than such *lof-sanghen* in which the confession of the holy trinity daily is sung through the mouth of all the people." Citing a more recent example, Van Haeften praised Wilhelmus Lindanus, the first Bishop of Roermond, who in 1587 "set the catechism in Dutch rhyme for the youth of these Netherlands" so that they "should sing the catechism in schools, churches and after catechism lessons."[93] Framing corporate singing as a historical Catholic practice, rather than a Protestant invention, not only countered Protestant claims and justified Van Haeften's efforts, but also emboldened lay singers who may have believed older Catholic messages that lay singing was itself a marker of Protestantism.[94]

In addition to adopting ideas shared across confessional lines, Van Haeften integrated popular melodies known and used by local Protestants. *Den Lusthof* even included some melodies composed by Protestants. Van Haeften used the melody to "Hoe zalig zijn de landen," a *Geuzenlied* by Willem van Haecht, for two of his Catholic catechism songs: one teaching on the Catholic Eucharist and the other about the church being the bride of Christ.[95] He also included several melodies found in the *Souterliedekens*. The tune "Christe est die et lux" – which set the *Te Deum* in the *Souterliedekens* – set Van Haeften's Dutch setting of the Compline hymn, "Wy roepen tot u's avonds laet" (*Te lucis ante terminum*). Similarly, Van Haeften used the melody of Psalm 150 in the *Souterliedekens* – "Die bruyt en wou niet te bedde" – to set an eschatological song about the joyful entry of a soul into Heaven.[96] Even after 1600, melodies and texts from the *Souterliedekens* continued to circulate among local Protestants in Mechelen, who incorporated the *Souterliedekens* into their musical activities and confessional identity. In 1560, Jan Boots drew the melodies for all six of the songs from the *Souterliedekens*. Willem van Haecht, whose songs were known and copied by Willem De Gortter *c*.1600, used the melody "Christe est die et lux" as a musical setting in his own Dutch psalter.[97]

The fact that Van Haeften used melodies known to local Protestants should not be interpreted as a personal expression of tolerating Protestant communities and culture. Instead, Van Haeften may, in part, have been tapping into popular repertoires of local knowledge as a means of enticing Protestants and easing the reception of Catholic ideas. Through borrowing melodies known by Protestants and Catholics alike, Van Haeften may also have been seeking to Catholicise the soundscape of Mechelen by altering and de-Protestantising collective memory through fitting these songs with new Catholic words and "forgetting" their previous religious associations. Van Haeften was far from alone in doing this. In fact, Van Haeften likely did not assemble the repertoire of popular tunes in *Den Lusthof* himself. Van Haeften instead created the bank of popular melodies in *Den Lusthof* most likely by consulting and imitating Jesuit songbooks produced earlier in the Truce, such as *Het Prieel*, published first in Bruges in 1609 and then Antwerp in 1614 and 1617 by Verdussen.[98] The anonymous compiler of *Het Prieel* specifically selected tunes known to Protestants because "the old tunes" were widely known across the population and "are sometimes very pleasant and lovely."[99] Desiring to use the best of the old tunes, the creators of *Het Prieel* – and Benedict van Haeften – hoped to alter collective memory through "alienating" (*vervreemden*) and erasing memories of the original texts that appealed across confessional lines.[100] According to the compiler of *Het Prieel*, "very many songs we have left with the old tunes, so that [...] the old frivolous song [texts] are gladly left behind and more easily forgotten, since one can sing other sacred songs to the same lovely tune."[101] While change was not instantaneous, it should be permanent, as "the people should gradually let go of these dishonourable words which should be eternally forgotten."[102]

Conclusions

The foregoing discussion has highlighted that the experience of early modern religious diversity had important sensory dimensions. The composite sound of singing, including the text of a song and its melody, demarcated local religious groups from one another, even as individual elements were frequently shared across confessional lines. This chapter has contributed new material to the growing scholarly literature on religious diversity in the Catholic Southern Netherlands in the seventeenth century. It has also outlined some ways in which minority religion itself exerted considerable influence over Catholic cultures after 1585. The adoption by Catholic writers of ideas and musical material used by Protestants, even in their efforts to erase the past meanings of songs from public memory, illustrates that Catholic cultures of song were formed in relation to Protestantism, not just according to the Council of Trent or local cultures of devotion. Protestants in Mechelen sang, but so did lay Catholics. They sang songs that deepened their Catholic faith, and likely even sang directly to religious "others" who lived in or visited the city. Unlike the polemical songs composed by the Lutheran Jan Boots, the anti-Protestant song "Of the So-called Reformed Church" in *Den Lusthof* was not written by a lay person but by a leading Catholic cleric who composed the song for lay Catholics. It is true that, during the Twelve Years' Truce, Catholic authorities in the South sought to limit lay action to a narrow field of acceptable activities, for example, limiting the reading of the Bible only to those given permission to do so.[103] At the same time, it would be wrong to conclude that Catholic authorities intended to curtail lay agency and choice entirely. One notable feature of *Den Lusthof* is that it presented lay believers with a range of choices for how to engage with the musical text in a way most suitable to them, through their ability to choose musical settings they would use. Within the pluriconfessional environment of Mechelen, *Den Lusthof* illustrates that the sphere of music was one area where lay Catholics enjoyed a relatively wide (though not limitless) space for individuality and lay decision-making, which individualised the experience of Catholic singing while also forging a city-wide religious community.

Notes

*   I would like to thank Marianne C.E. Gillion for commenting on a draft of this chapter. This research was funded by The Leverhulme Trust (ECF-2018-237) and their support is gratefully acknowledged.
1   Preface of Benedict van Haeften, *Den Lusthof der Christelycke Leeringhen* (Antwerp: Hieronymus Verdussen, 1622), **3ʳ. Lodewijk Makeblijde, *Den schat der christelicker leeringhe tot verklaringhe van den catechismus* (Antwerp: Joachim Trognesius, 1610).
2   Ibid.
3   Bram Caers, "Three 'Forgotten' Cityscapes of Mechelen in the Late Sixteenth Century: The Spanish and English Furies in Mechelen (1572, 1580) through the Eyes of Contemporaries," *Monte Artium: Journal of the Royal Library of Belgium* 10 (2017), esp. 66–7; Guido Marnef, *Het calvinistisch bewind te Mechelen* (Kortrijk-Heule: UGA, 1987).

4 Erika Kuijpers, "Between Storytelling and Patriotic Scripture. The Memory Brokers of the Dutch Revolt," in *Memory Before Modernity: Practices of Memory in Early Modern Europe*, ed. Erika Kuijpers et al. (Leiden: Brill, 2013), 196.

5 Marie-Juliette Marinus, "Het verdwijnen van het protestantisme in de Zuidelijke Nederlanden," *De Zeventiende Eeuw* 13, no. 1 (1997), 264–5.

6 Werner Thomas, "The Treaty of London, the Twelve Years Truce and Religious Toleration in Spain and the Netherlands (1598–1621)," in *The Twelve Years Truce (1609): Peace, Truce, War, and Law in the Low Countries at the Turn of the 17th Century*, ed. Randall Lesaffer (Leiden: Brill, 2014), 293.

7 Matthew Laube, "The Musical Cultures of Dissent and Anti-Catholicism in Counter-Reformation Douai," in *Theatres of Belief: Music and Conversion in the Early Modern City*, ed. Iain Fenlon, Marie-Alexis Colin, and Matthew Laube (Turnhout: Brepols, 2021), 193–215.

8 Marinus, "Het verdwijnen van het protestantisme," 265.

9 Laube, "Musical Cultures of Dissent," 193–215.

10 Judith Pollmann, *Catholic Identity and the Revolt of the Netherlands, 1520–1635* (Oxford: Oxford University Press, 2011), 129.

11 Ibid., Chapters 5 and 6.

12 Ibid., 140, 146–9.

13 Ibid., 143, 147.

14 Marianne C.E. Gillion, "Protests, Processionals, and Plainchant: Reconciling the Counter Reformation in Early Modern Antwerp" (in preparation). I am grateful to Dr Gillion for sharing this paper with me.

15 Rumoldus Batavus, *Nieu Liedt-Boecxken/Inhoudende verscheyden Liedekens op de principaelste Feest-daghen ende ander Heylighe daghen van den Jaere [...]* (Antwerp: Gheleyn Janssens, 1617), 162–76.

16 *Het Lieffelyck Orgel-Pypken, Spelende alder-hande schooner Gheestelijcke Liedekens [...]* (Brussels: Philip Vleugaert, 1664), 90–9. A translation and discussion is found in *Women's Writing in the Low Countries, 1200–1875: A Bilingual Anthology*, ed. Lia van Gemert et al. (Amsterdam: Amsterdam University Press, 2010), 267–75.

17 *Souter Liedekens Ghemaect ter eeren Gods, op alle die Psalmen van David: tot stichtinghe, ende een gheestelijcke vermakinghe van allen Christen mensch* (Antwerp: Symon Cock, 1540), 27 of the 56 melodies chosen by Batavus have concordances with the *Souterliedekens*. For the concordances, see the entry for *Nieu liedt-boecxken* in the Dutch Song Database (http://www.liederenbank.nl).

18 Batavus, *Nieu liedt-boecxken*, 3.

19 One recent study is Carolina Lenarduzzi, *Katholiek in de Republiek: De belevingswereld van een religieuze minderheid, 1570–1750* (Nijmegen: Vantilt, 2019), 211–44; see also Karel Porteman and Gilbert Huybens, "Het Zuidnederlands geestelijk lied in de 17e eeuw. Een vergeten bladzijde uit de Nederlandse literatuur- en muziekgeschiedenis," *Revue Belge de Musicologie/Belgisch Tijdschrift voor Muziekwetenschap*, 32/33 (1978), 121–42; Gilbert Huybens, "'Spieghel der ghenade Gods': Psalmzang en psalmbeleving in Vlaanderen in de zestiende en zeventiende eeuw," in *Psalmzingen in de Nederlanden van de zestiende eeuw tot heden*, ed. J. de Bruijn and W. Heuting (Kampen: Kok, 1991); Judith Pollmann, "Hey Ho, Let the Cup Go Round: Singing for Reformation in the Sixteenth Century," in *Religion and Cultural Exchange in Europe, 1400–1700*, ed. Heinz Schilling and István György Tóth (Cambridge: Cambridge University Press, 2006), 294–316; and Charles Parker, *Faith on the Margins: Catholics and Catholicism in the Dutch Golden Age* (Cambridge, MA: Harvard University Press, 2008), 145.

20 Craig Harline and Eddy Put, *A Bishop's Tale: Mathias Hovius Among His Flock in Seventeenth-Century Flanders* (New Haven, CT: Yale University Press, 2000), 167.

21 G. van Doorslaer, "Historische aantekeningen betreffende de orgels in de St. Romboutskerk te Mechelen," *Mechlinia*, 3 (1926), 38–123; Eugeen Schreurs, "Mechelen," *Grove Music Online* (2001), accessed June 2, 2023. https://www.oxfordmusiconline.com/grovemusic/view/10.1093/gmo/9781561592630.001.0001/omo-9781561592630-e-0000042619.

22 Luc Rombouts, *Singing Bronze: A History of Carillon Music* (Louvain: Lipsius Leuven, 2014), 79.

23 Harline and Put, *A Bishop's Tale*, 9.

24 *Artickel der Doctorn von Louen/zu welchen/Wilhelm von Zwollen/Konigs Christiernen Forirer/Christlich hat geantwort [...]* (Wittenberg: Joseph Klug, 1530).

25 Ibid., E^r–Eii^r. Like the final verse of "Ein feste Burg," Willem's song speaks of "letting go" (*lass fahren*) of "goods and honour" (*gut und ehr*) and finding refuge in God's Word.

26 Cited in Geert Janssen, *The Dutch Revolt and Catholic Exile in Reformation Europe* (Cambridge: Cambridge University Press, 2014), 27.

27 E. van Autenboer, *Een Ketterproces te Mechelen: Jan Boots alias Lepelaar* (Mechelen: N.V. Mech. Drukkerijen, 1943), 15.

28 Ibid., 8, 21–4.

29 Harline and Put, *A Bishop's Tale*, 163–9.

30 Ibid., 166.

31 Ibid.

32 See, for instance: "Waeckt op ghy banghe, Nederlanden blint," in *Toetsteen: Waeraen men waerlick beproeven mach* (s.l.: 1603); or "Pater grijp toch een moed," in *Beelzebubs Testament, Het welcke hy Antechrist synen Sone nae ghelaten heeft* (Haarlem: Pieter Arentsz., 1612). For the Reformation centenary, see the six songs in *Reynier Telles Vrede-Zangh Ofte Jaer-Liedt* (Amsterdam: Porcevant Morgan, 1617).

33 Caers, "Three 'Forgotten' Cityscapes," 68–9.

34 Marc Van Vaeck, "*De Schadt-Kiste Der Philosophen Ende Poeten* (Mechelen 1621): een blazoenfeest aan de vooravond van het einde van het Bestand," *De Zeventiende Eeuw* 8, no. 1 (1992), 75–80. The entries were reproduced in *De Schadt-kiste der philosophen ende poeten waer innetevindensynveelschoone leerlycke Blasoenen, Refereynenende Liedekens [...]* (Mechelen: Henry Jaye, 1621).

35 Brussels, KBR Ms. 15662. *Wilhelmus en de anderen: Nederlandse liedjes 1500–1700*, ed. Marijke Barend-van Haeften et al. (Amsterdam: Amsterdam University Press, 2000), 23.

36 Brussels, KBR Ms. 15662, f. 112^v.

37 Willem van Haecht, *De CL. Psalmen Dauids, in dichte ghestelt Door Willem van Haecht* (Antwerp: Aernout s' Conincx, 1579), 27.

38 Ibid., 29.

39 Engravings of the Spanish fury of 1572, many of which were produced in the north, proliferated during the Truce. See, for example, *Mecchelen wert geplondert* (Rijksmuseum RP-P-OB-78.991), which was created near the end of the Truce, *c.*1618–1624.

40 Caers, "Three 'Forgotten' Cityscapes," 66–7.

41 Ibid., 66.

42 On the conservatism of Mechelen between 1578 and 1585, see Marnef, *Het calvinistisch bewind*, esp. 115 and 141–6; Caers, "Three 'Forgotten' Cityscapes," 66–8; and Harline and Put, *A Bishop's Tale*, 16; Paul Rosenfeld, "Review of Guido Marnef, *Het Calvinistisch bewind te Mechelen 1580–1585*," *Revue belge de philologie et d'histoire* 68, no. 4 (1990), 1006–7.

43 Thomas, "Treaty of London," 286.

44 Harline and Put, *A Bishop's Tale*, 167.

45 Van Vaeck, "*De Schadt-Kiste Der Philosophen Ende Poeten* (Mechelen 1621)," 80.
46 Rombouts, *Singing Bronze*, 77, 80.
47 *Placcaet ende Ordinancie vande Eertzhertoghen [...]* (Rutgeert Velpius: Brussels, 1608), Aiii.
48 *Placcaet Sconijncx ons gheduchts Heeren [...]* (Ghent: Jan vanden Steene).
49 British Library Ms. Add. 18.291. Pollmann, *Catholic Identity*, 83; Jan Bloemendal and Arjan van Dixhoorn, "Literary Cultures and Public Opinion in the Early Modern Low Countries," in *Literary Cultures and Public Opinion in the Low Countries, 1450–1650*, ed. Jan Bloemendal, Arjan van Dixhoorn, and Elsa Strietman (Leiden: Brill, 2011), 31–3.
50 *Een schoon liedekens. Boeck inden welcken ghy in vinden sult. Veelderhande liedekens* (Antwerp: Jan Roulans, 1544), Qi^v.
51 *Den psalter Davids na dalder correcxte copie overghesedt [...]* (Antwerp: Jan van Waesberghe, 1566).
52 Autenboer, *Een Ketterproces*, 21–6.
53 Ibid., 23–4.
54 Ibid., 23.
55 Ibid., 24.
56 Boots was later executed in 1568 following his involvement in Mechelen's Iconoclastic Fury. Ibid., 19.
57 Quoted in Harline and Put, *A Bishop's Tale*, 168.
58 Ibid., 169–73.
59 Ibid., 172.
60 Makeblijde, *Den Schat der Christelicker Leeringhe.*
61 Ibid., **2^r.
62 Ibid., 24.
63 Ibid., *7^v.
64 Ibid.
65 Ibid., 23–4.
66 Ibid., **1^r.
67 Ibid., 27.
68 Ibid.
69 Ibid.
70 L. Loosen, *Lodewijk Makeblijde, 1565–1630: Hymnen en Gezangen* (Zwolle: W.E.J. Tjeenk Willink, 1964), 285–7.
71 Lodewijk Makeblijde, *Catechismvs oft christliicke leeringhe [...] catechisme ov doctrine chrestienne [...] pour la jeunesse [...] de Malines* (Antwerp: Widow of Joannes Cnobbaert, 1644).
72 Van Haeften, *Den Lusthof*, unpaginated preface.
73 For example, the song "The First Song about Belief and the Holy Sacraments" could be sung to six different tunes, in addition to a two-voice polyphonic setting. Van Haeften, *Den Lusthof*, 13.
74 On *Bicinia*, see Bruce Bellingham, "The Bicinium in the Lutheran Latin Schools During the Reformation Period" (PhD diss., University of Toronto, 1972).
75 In his emphasis on unrestrained sensuality rather than the Galenic humours, Van Haeften adopts language similar to some writers – including Reformed writers – who saw the 'idolatrous body as the locus of inordinate sensuality'. See Charles Parker, "Diseased Bodies, Defiled Souls: Corporality and Religious Difference in the Reformation," *Renaissance Quarterly* 67, no. 4 (2014), 1265–97.
76 Van Haeften, *Den Lusthof*, **2^v.
77 Ibid., 154–5.
78 Ibid., 186.
79 Ibid.
80 Ibid.

81 Ibid., 187.
82 Ibid.
83 Ibid., 189.
84 Ibid.
85 Ibid., 190.
86 Ibid., 81.
87 Ibid.
88 Ibid.
89 The Dutch text to "Uwe liefd' is niet so puere" does not survive but resembles the later religious song "Waer uwe liefd also puure" found in *Het Prieel*, which may also have been based on "Uwe liefd' is niet so puere." *Het Prieel der gheestelicker melodiie; Inhoudende veel schoone Leysenen, ende Gheestelijcke Liedekens [...]* (Antwerp: Hieronymus Verdussen, 1614), 177.
90 Van Haeften, *Den Lusthof*, 1**^{v}.
91 J. Andreas Loewe, "*Musica Est Optimum*: Martin Luther's Theory of Music," *Music and Letters* 94 (2013), 598.
92 Cited in Linda Maria Koldau, *Frauen-Musik-Kultur: ein Handbuch zum deutschen Sprachgebiet der Frühen Neuzeit* (Cologne: Böhlau Verlag, 2005), 350.
93 Van Haeften, *Den Lusthof*, 1**^{r}.
94 Pollmann, *Catholic Identity*, 27. In some cities, authorities silenced all Catholic singing as a means of suppressing heresy. See Gérard Moreau, ed., *Le Journal d'un bourgeois de Tournai: Le second livre des chroniques de Pasquier de la Barre (1500–1565)* (Brussels: Palais des académies, 1975), 431.
95 Van Haeften, *Den Lusthof*, 228, 306. Van Haecht's song first appeared in a 1564 collection of his plays and was included in numerous Beggars' songbooks beginning with *Een nieu Geusen Lieden Boecxken* (s.l.: s.p., 1581).
96 Van Haeften, *Den Lusthof*, 170, 355.
97 Van Haecht, *Psalmen Dauids*, 131.
98 There are significant concordances between melodies used in *Den Lusthof* (1622) and *Het Prieel de[r] Gheestelijcke Melodie* (Bruges: Pieter Soetaert, 1609) and its later editions.
99 *Het Prieel der Gheestelicker Melodiie* (Antwerp: Hieronymus Verdussen, 1617), 2^v.
100 Van Haeften, *Den Lusthof*, **3^r.
101 *Het Prieel*, 5^r.
102 Ibid., 3^r. "Dishonourable words" also included bawdy lyrics, not just Protestant songs. Yet for Van Haeften, "worldly and heretical" songs were grouped together as a common concern.
103 Pollmann, *Catholic Identity*, 191.

3 Tuning Catholicism in the Dutch Republic

Catholic Soundscapes in a Calvinist Society, c. 1600–1750

Carolina Lenarduzzi

In "De Patria" (c. 1624), a long poem in Latin about pre-Reformation Amsterdam, the Catholic lawyer, poet, and amateur-musician Cornelis Plemp (1574–1638) lamented that his faith was no longer audible in the city. The church bells that used to "celebrate eternity" were now mostly silent. The organ in Amsterdam's Old Church that his beloved teacher, the musician and composer Jan Pietersz Sweelinck (1562–1621), used to play so beautifully did not enchant his ears anymore with Catholic tunes. And perhaps most of all, he mourned the loss of the precious hymns that were performed during Holy Mass.[1] In his poem, Plemp invoked feelings of nostalgia for a time when Catholic soundscapes were omnipresent, not only in the churches, but also on the streets where religious chant accompanied the numerous urban processions, where litanies were sung by pilgrims on their way to holy shrines and where chimes and church bells were continuously ringing.

This sonic landscape changed dramatically in the last quarter of the sixteenth century when the Northern Netherlands became a Calvinist state. The rebellion against their sovereign Philip II of Spain – the Dutch Revolt – resulted in the creation of the Dutch Republic and the ascendancy of the Reformed Church as the privileged, public church. By the early 1580s, all forms of Catholic worship and all activities associated with Catholicism were banned from the public arena, including the Catholic soundscapes that Plemp referred to in "De Patria." Catholic gatherings were prohibited and priests were no longer allowed to say Mass or administer the sacraments. Catholics lost their church buildings and convents to the new church or the secular authorities and had to worship in secret in private houses. Yet, unlike their fellow believers in Britain, Dutch Catholics were granted freedom of conscience and were never required to become members of the official Reformed Church. So, in theory, they could practise their faith with impunity as long as they confined their religious allegiance to the private sphere. In practice, however, they were quite creative in developing multiple strategies to manifest themselves as Catholics in the public arena as well.

Nevertheless, living in a Reformed environment and having transformed almost overnight from the dominant culture in society into a marginal subculture, Catholics were forced to reflect on what they regarded as

DOI: 10.4324/9781003030522-5

fundamental to their identity, and how they could express this in daily life. They had to reconsider their centuries-old, self-evident habitus – the internalised set of cultural and social dispositions and values that governed how Catholics behaved in the world and how they viewed society.[2] Which practices and rituals were still meaningful to them? Did this habitual repertoire acquire new functions after the Reformation? In short, Catholics had to reinvent themselves, both vis-à-vis their co-religionists and the outside world. One way to explore what it meant to be a Catholic in the Dutch Republic is through soundscapes, by which I mean (potentially) significant sounds that shape religious identity and sacred space.[3]

   The last few decades have witnessed a surge of historical interest in Dutch minority Catholicism, to use a term coined by Christine Kooi.[4] Initially, historians and literary scholars focused mainly on Catholics' interactions with Protestants and the practice of religious coexistence.[5] Recent historiography has shifted its attention to the dynamics within the Catholic community itself, covering such diverse subjects as the relation between clergy and laity, the agency of religious and semi-religious women, and Catholicism in specific regions (Utrecht, Guelders) and within specific groups, such as nobles and migrants.[6] New concepts and methodologies such as material culture, memory, and identity have been introduced, expanding the study of early modern Catholicism into stimulating new arenas of academic enquiry.[7]

   As a window to explore the Catholic experience in the Calvinist Dutch Republic, Catholic music has not yet been the subject of much historical research, unlike Protestant music and psalm singing.[8] Opening up this area of research will enrich our understanding of the Dutch Catholic experience. Recent scholarship has demonstrated that post-Reformation devotional music contributed greatly to the formation of confessional identities.[9] This chapter, therefore, analyses how Dutch Catholics employed sacred music in everyday life to articulate and solidify their identity in a hostile environment. But in the multi-confessional Dutch Republic, sacred soundscapes had a divisive quality too.[10] Since the acoustic horizon extended beyond the visible, Catholic soundscapes had the potential to affect the outside world as well. The second part of this contribution argues that the strong Calvinist aversion to Catholic musical culture turned the latter into an excellent instrument to provoke Protestant ears, enabling Catholics to assert the continuity and vitality of their community in the urban domain. At the same time, the society-wide sensitivity to spiritual music meant that the latter could not only be exploited as a polemical weapon in the confessional conflicts, but also utilised as a tool for reconciliation and even conversion.

   Of all the arts it is probably music that speaks most directly to the human soul. Because of its associations with the divine, early modern sacred music generated even deeper feelings. According to prevailing concepts of the so-called Harmony of the Spheres, based on neo-Platonic ideas that music reflected the divine ordering of the universe and all things in it, sacred music was regarded as the resonance of the heavenly choirs on earth.[11] But it is the singing voice in particular that has always been a medium to express and invoke devout emotions. The combination of sacred music and lyrics greatly enlarged the emotional impact of sound.[12] As Augustine wrote in his *Confessions*: "I realize that when they are sung these sacred words stir my mind to greater religious fervour and kindle in me a more ardent form of piety than they would if they were not sung [...]."[13] In what follows, therefore, I will focus on sacred songs. As Chiara Bertoglio has rightfully pointed out, sacred song culture in the early modern period was not a stable category: was it limited to songs performed in church, or did it include songs for processions and private devotion, or even polemical songs against competing confessions? For the purpose of this chapter, I will adopt her broad definition of sacred song as including all songs based on religious texts.[14] Within this definition, I will distinguish between the age-old liturgical songs in Latin, exclusively performed during worship, and contemporary non-liturgical Catholic songs in the vernacular.[15]

As to sources, it is my aim to capture the individual Catholic experience. Therefore, I have not organised this contribution around (secular or religious) institutional archives. Instead, I have called upon the voices of individual Catholics as they speak to us from personal documents such as chronicles, diaries, letters, and autobiographical poetry. Although early modern Dutch personal texts are in general not very introspective, these sources do show us how Dutch Catholics engaged with their spiritual song culture to cope with the trauma of the Dutch Revolt, to reshape their religious identity, and to respond to Reformed challenges.

Sensing each other: sacred songs within the Catholic community

Liturgical songs in Latin

Gregorian chant and polyphonic motets were integral to the Catholic liturgy. With the ban on Catholicism, however, these liturgical songs had lost their traditional setting: churches and convents had either been demolished or requisitioned and, especially in the first decades after the Reformation, the clergy was decimated. Many priests had fled the Dutch Republic or converted to the new church. Traditional music colleges and choirs had been dissolved. Liturgical songbooks were sparse, being either destroyed or hidden in private homes, and until the 1680s no new songbooks were printed.[16] Yet Catholic clergy and laity alike considered the songs of the Mass an indispensable ingredient of the Catholic habitus. Not only did the post-Tridentine church emphasise eucharistic culture and music in order to distinguish Catholic from Protestant eucharistic theology, but Dutch Catholics also realised that through religious music they could buttress their fragile community.[17] The musical culture of the Catholic liturgy helped define their identity, but its universal character also created a spiritual bond with Catholics in other countries.[18] Listening to the familiar Latin lyrics bridged geographical distances and created a community with fellow believers beyond the Republic's borders. The knowledge that they were linked to an international network of co-religionists who shared the same past and rituals provided Dutch Catholics with comfort.[19] In this respect, it is meaningful that Catholic memoirs repeatedly stress the efforts made to save the musical rites of the liturgy.

Key to the survival of the traditions of Catholic liturgical music were the semi-religious women known as spiritual virgins ("kloppen" or "klopjes" in Dutch). These spiritual virgins were unmarried women who took no vows but lived together in communal households as if in a religious order, thus occupying a place "in the middle" between nuns and lay women. It is widely acknowledged that these women were immensely important to the survival of Dutch Catholicism.[20] Historical research has focused mostly on their role behind the scenes as teachers of Catholic doctrine to children and as patrons and protectors of the priests of the so-called Holland Mission (the clandestine Catholic Church in the Dutch Republic). Much less attention has been paid to the prominent role these women played in preserving the Catholic musical heritage for future generations.

The decisive role they attributed to music in rebuilding the Catholic community is highlighted in a large collection of biographies of *kloppen* in Haarlem, a city in Holland with an exceptionally large community of spiritual virgins. Their life stories were written in the second quarter of the seventeenth century by Tryn Oly (1585–1651), a member and spiritual mother of this community.[21] Oly's biographies stress how the emotional impact of religious songs stimulated devotion and (re)kindled Catholic beliefs:

> Who is able to count how many fruits [religious songs] have borne [...] how many hearts sacred music has pulled away from worldly idleness, and guided to spiritual purity; how many people it has led from sin to virtue; how many lukewarm Catholics it has ignited with the love of God; how many fallen hearts it has picked up and reunited with God [...].[22]

For these reasons, their confessors considered it vital that talented virgins learnt to read musical notation, to play the organ and violin, and to sing the liturgy and the *Officium Divinum* (the official set of prayers marking the hours of the day). For that purpose, the virgins also studied Latin. The Council of Trent had decreed that Latin was to remain the exclusive language of the liturgy, and the Holland Mission strictly supervised the implementation of this decree.[23] Officially, singing the liturgy was the exclusive domain of the celebrant and a choir consisting of ordained male singers, usually lower clergy.[24] From Oly's biographies, however, we learn that in Haarlem the liturgical songs were actually performed by the *kloppen*, who occupied also in a literal sense the priest's place near the altar.[25] The shortage of priests in the early stages of the Dutch Reformation apparently allowed the *kloppen* to fill the resulting musical vacuum in the liturgical rites.

Oly explicitly states that the Haarlem virgins were instrumental in the revival of liturgical music and its dissemination to other cities. Whether this is local chauvinism or not, personal chronicles confirm that throughout

Figure 3.1 Joannes Stalpaert van der Wiele, *Gulde-jaers feest-daghen of den schat der geestelycke lof-sanghen [...]* (Antwerp, 1635).

Courtesy of Digitale Bibliotheek voor de Nederlandse Letteren.

the Northern Netherlands *kloppen* assumed a leading role in preserving and performing liturgical chants. The spiritual virgin Wilhelmina Reeck, for example, informs us that Delft priest Joannes Stalpaert van der Wiele (1579–1630) supervised a choir of 20 spiritual virgins, who regularly accompanied Mass in house churches with Gregorian chants and other liturgical songs (Figure 3.1).[26] In Gouda, home town to a large community of *kloppen*, the latter also took the musical initiative, leading in 1643 and 1645 to Reformed complaints about the singing of Catholic hymns during Mass by the spiritual virgins.[27]

But the role these semi-religious women claimed for themselves was not unproblematic within the Catholic community either. In his personal chronicle, Catholic hardliner Franciscus Dusseldorpius (1567–1630) recounts that some priests had filed complaints with the papal nuncio in Brussels regarding the liturgical role of the virgins. The nuncio demanded an explanation from the embarrassed apostolic vicar (the head of the Holland Mission), who had to admit that in the Calvinist context of the Dutch Republic, such liberties were unavoidable.[28] It may well be that the confessors of the Haarlem virgins

Figure 3.2 Hendrick van Vliet, *Group portrait of Michiel van der Dussen, Willemina van Setten and their five children*, 1640.

Courtesy of Museum Prinsenhof Delft.

were not always pleased either. This would explain why Oly recorded that they occasionally required sopranos to sing the alto voice, and vice versa, and why they replaced talented singers with virgins who had no musical gifts at all. As these decisions detracted from the emotional appeal of sacred songs, which was highly valued by the priests, I think it likely that these were in fact disciplinary measures. Through such "exercises in humility," the women were forced back into their traditional role of serving the clergy.

A portrait of the wealthy Catholic Van der Dussen family from Delft, painted in 1640 by Hendrick Cornelisz van Vliet, demonstrates that lay people too contributed to keeping the liturgical soundscapes alive (Figure 3.2). The painting is resonant with Catholic symbolism. The two older daughters, for instance, wear a chain with a small crucifix, a visible demonstration of their faith. But the most prominent Catholic marker is the song to which father Michiel van der Dussen points his finger and which he and his sons are about to perform. It is called "In festo S. Michaelis," a Gregorian antiphon in honour of the feast day of S. Michael, after whom Michiel is named. As the Calvinist authorities made it impossible to perform this liturgical piece in church, the appropriate setting, the painting functioned as a substitute, transforming, as it were, the domestic sphere into a sacred space.[29] Just as Cornelis Plemp re-appropriated the Catholic soundscape of pre-Reformation Amsterdam through his poetry, Van der Dussen claimed through this portrait

the musical heritage of his church. The fact that father and sons were portrayed as playing traditional church music symbolised the continuity and
viability of Catholicism.

Sacred songs in the vernacular

Singing was also something Catholics could actively *do*. In a groundbreaking
essay, emotion scholar Monique Scheer has convincingly argued that emotions are not so much expressed as shaped in bodily practices.[30] To relate her
point to the subject of this chapter, one could say that the embodied practice
of singing sacred songs mobilised feelings of devotion. Dutch Catholics realised that the physical experience of singing songs triggered feelings of devotion and shared identity.[31] The *collective* nature of the experience of singing a
shared repertoire added to this mechanism.[32] Consequently, vernacular song
culture metamorphosed into an important tool to mobilise Catholics and nurture Catholicism. Poetically gifted priests composed new lyrics to well-known
pre-existing tunes (so-called *contrafacta*). The above-mentioned Stalpaert van
der Wiele, author of three voluminous religious songbooks, explicitly referred
to the power of vernacular songs to stir people's feelings.[33] Even more than
worldly tunes, he wrote, songs in praise of God had the capacity "to spark and
ignite human hearts." He therefore encouraged his readers to sing his songs
in order to experience "a special love for God [...] and also His saints," dem-
onstrating that in his view the practice of singing intensified the devotional
emotions his lyrics evoked.[34] Precisely because of this effect, he considered
sacred song in the vernacular an excellent instrument to catechise and instruct
his fellow believers.[35] And, indeed, Stalpaert's songs guided Catholics through
the ins and outs of their religion, ranging from very basic instructions on how
to make the sign of the cross to complex doctrines on transubstantiation and
free will. The saints were portrayed as exemplary Catholics whose suffering
for their faith merited imitation by ordinary believers. Catholics were thus
urged to steadfastly practice their faith despite their difficult circumstances.
Stalpaert's more polemical songs provided Catholics with ammunition against
Protestant attacks on Roman doctrine and rituals.[36]

Other priests, too, recognised that in mission territory like the Northern
Netherlands, with few priests available, devotional songs in the vernacular
were an invaluable medium to teach doctrine, to anchor the Catholic past in
people's memories, and to counter Protestant arguments. In his *Nieu Liedt-
Boecxken* [New Song-Book] (1614), the Leiden priest and songwriter Rumoldus van Medenblick (?–1640/42) – writing under the pseudonym Rumoldus
Batavus – states that his tunes were meant to be sung during Catholic gatherings when a priest was not available.[37] Songs could then serve as a substitute for sermons. Furthermore, songs were an ideal vehicle to reach out to
children and ordinary people. Gouda priest Willem de Swaen (c. 1610–1674)
authored a collection of songs dedicated to the saints, titled *Den Singende
Swaen* [The Singing Swan] (1655). In his foreword he explicitly acknowledges

the attraction of singing and songs to young people. Song's capacity to touch their soul, he explains, turned it into an excellent tool to stimulate their faith.[38] Rumoldus van Medemblick composed his songs especially for lay Catholics who were unable to understand Latin.[39] In his collection of devotional songs *De Nederlandtsche Weergalm* [The Dutch Echo] (1664), the Jesuit Franciscus Mijleman (1610–1667), who worked for 30 years as a missionary in the north of the Dutch Republic, used simple lyrics that were easy to memorise in order to reach uneducated and illiterate believers.[40] The use of existing popular tunes further facilitated this memorisation process. It also heightened devotional feelings. Stalpaert set his lyrics to the "sweetest and most popular melodies" so that his songs would fall on even more fertile ground.[41] Such melodies would intensify the emotional potency of singing, confirming that the bodily performance of singing was a necessary ingredient of his musical repertoire.[42]

Finally, these priests recognised another important asset of religious songs: they could be performed anywhere and under all sorts of conditions without leaving any trace. Catholics could thus practice their faith without attracting the attention of the authorities. Saints and relics could no longer be worshipped openly, but their glory could be praised in songs. In the same way, songs enabled Catholics to perform an inner pilgrimage to their former holy places.

Composing sacred songs in the vernacular as a vehicle for religious experience was not the exclusive domain of priests: lay Catholics contributed to this genre as well. Netherlandish society knew a long tradition of amateur music-making and poetry-writing, both before and after the Reformation, and amongst believers of all denominations.[43] Standing in this long tradition was the Amsterdam Catholic Herman Verbeecq (1621–1681). His oeuvre consisted of a long autobiographical poem, several plays, and poems for social occasions. In addition, Verbeecq wrote a collection of religious songs, mostly *contrafacta*, which he titled *Sang Godin* [Song Goddess] (1662). Just like the songs by his clerical fellow-composers, Verbeecq's work focused on specifically Catholic subjects like the Eucharist and the saints. But he also highlighted the Catholic past of the Republic and vehemently attacked Calvinist "heretics" and their offences against the Holy Mother Church.[44] We do not know if Verbeecq's handwritten songs reached an audience. Most likely, his (and other) manuscript songbooks were not as widely disseminated as the priests' printed (and often reprinted) editions, if at all. Still, through his songs Verbeecq could channel his personal religious emotions, finding an alternative route to practice his faith.

Sensing the other: transgression of confessional boundaries

Singing provocation

We can conclude from the previous section that the reception, circulation, and performance of sacred music consolidated the identity and culture of the Northern-Netherlandish Catholic community. Music not only exemplified shared devotional ideals, but it was also an excellent medium to transcend confessional boundaries and appropriate public space. Soundscapes did not stop at the threshold of private houses or hidden churches, but drifted through walls and doors into the outside world, challenging Protestant ears. In Tryn Oly's biographies, we read that the *kloppen* often played the organ until deep into the night. Anna Sicxtus, in whose living quarters the organ was housed, complained about the "noise" she had to endure during the many hours of practice.[45] Since the virgins lived right in the centre of Haarlem, it is safe to assume that their Protestant neighbours had to endure (or enjoy) the same organ practice as well. Catholic diarist Jan de Boer (1694–1764) recorded more than once his vocal and instrumental contributions to the clandestine Masses in Amsterdam's hidden churches, sometimes accompanied by a full orchestra with strings, winds, and percussion. Undoubtedly, this abundant music-making did not escape passers-by.[46]

The Haarlem virgins and Jan de Boer, who emerges from his diary as both a passionate Catholic *and* a loyal citizen of the Republic, probably did not mean for their music to invade the public domain.[47] To activist Catholics, however, music was an excellent instrument to make Catholic beliefs reach Calvinist ears and thus prove that the Holy Mother Church had definitely survived the Reformation, despite all efforts to the contrary. In his memoirs, the Jesuit Willebrord van der Heijden (1595–1638), who worked as a missionary in Friesland from 1627 to 1638, recorded that in 1614 devotional singing during an illegal Catholic conventicle had drawn the attention of the Calvinist authorities. But when the bailiff and his men angrily entered the premises, the congregation kept on singing, openly provoking the Calvinist authorities with their religious convictions – and in the process enabling the priest to escape.[48] The experience of singing the religious hymns together will have emboldened them. A similar incident happened in 1628.[49]

The effectiveness of music as a polemical strategy is highlighted by the many consistorial complaints to city magistracies about loud Catholic music-making.[50] From both Catholic memoirs and legal documents, it appears that ordinary citizens were less troubled by Catholic soundscapes than authorities were. Oly, for example, recorded that the organ in Anna Sicxtus' house was tuned by a "heretic" with whom she was on a friendly footing.[51] Of course, this Protestant organ tuner had business interests at heart, but not once in her biographies does Oly mention that the frequent Masses with vocal and instrumental music caused any friction with the virgins' neighbours or other fellow citizens; neither does Dusseldorpius or any other diarist.

Not surprisingly, Calvinist preachers were especially angered by musical accompaniment of illegal Masses.[52] Having banned the use of church organs in religious worship, condemning them as a typically Catholic instrument, organ music, in particular, was offensive to their ears. Their wrath intensified if the organs were played by *kloppen* since the Reformed ministers (rightly) considered these semi-religious women instrumental to the survival of Catholicism in the Dutch Republic. More than once city organists as well were caught accompanying "popish ditties and idolatrous hymns." They were told in no uncertain terms to refrain from such actions.[53] Incidents such as these confirm that music provided Catholics with a very effective strategy to stay behind the walls of their houses or hidden churches, but at the same time openly propagate the Catholic cause: invisible to the outside world, but audible in the public arena.

Singing conversion

Because religious music was so emotionally charged, Catholics exploited song as a tool of conversion as well. The Jesuit Willebrord van der Heijden understood well the potential of song to proselytise Protestant listeners. In his memoirs, he described the public exorcism in 1634 of a Mennonite girl named Anna van Ezumazijl, whose body had been possessed for many years by no less than eight devils. Only after her conversion to the Church of Rome did a priest succeed in driving the evil spirits away. Under the watchful eye of both Catholic and Protestant bystanders, the devils left Anna's body and, very surprisingly, started to sing songs. One devil, in particular, sang about the girl's conversion and the Catholic faith – which he called "the only true faith" – in such a moving way that, according to Van der Heijden, even the "heretics" started to cry. The emotional impact was such that some Protestants decided there and then to convert to Catholicism. The religious feelings expressed by the singing devil affected, as it were, his listeners as well and evoked in them similar emotions.[54] Moreover, the emotional quality of song gave extra force to the Catholic monopoly on exorcism, an instrument Calvinists had also banned from their repertoire, but to which ordinary people were still very receptive.[55]

Interestingly, not all Catholics were happy with the musical games some of their fellow believers played with the outside world. In 1613 the civil authorities of Utrecht heavily fined some female religious for, amongst other things, singing evening vespers at illegal conventicles. Franciscus Dusseldorpius feared all Utrecht Catholics would have to pay for such irresponsible behaviour: financially, because the women had insufficient funds to pay the fine themselves; in terms of religious freedom, because the provocation would incite the authorities to enforce the anti-Catholic placards more strictly than before. The militant Dusseldorpius was usually not one to compromise with the Reformed "enemy," but in this case he believed the "nuns" should be excommunicated for their irresponsible behaviour.[56] Some 50 years later, the archpriest Arnold Waeijer (1606–1692) from Zwolle, in the east of the Republic, attacked a Jesuit colleague for encouraging his parishioners to sing devotional songs that were audible in the streets. Waeijer, too, worried about the repercussions for Zwolle's Catholic community.[57] In the mid-eighteenth century, the more adaptive Jan de Boer complained in his diary about fellow believers who openly sang the *Te Deum laudamus* and other Catholic hymns whilst on a pilgrimage to a demolished chapel in a nearby village. De Boer labelled his singing co-religionists "fake-Catholics," whose blatant devotional display would reduce what little freedom the Catholic community enjoyed.

These cases show that Catholics across the spectrum, from militant to accommodating, criticised loud music-making.

In addition, these cases illustrate change over time. Despite his harsh criticism of the singing pilgrims, De Boer was not at all troubled by his own musical contributions to illegal Catholic conventicles. Nowhere in his diary did he problematise these church performances. Apparently, he did not consider such vocal transgression of the line between private and public devotion offensive. In his eyes, the setting in which sacred music was performed made a fundamental difference. This had everything to do with the relative freedom the Catholic Church enjoyed since the beginning of the eighteenth century. Around 1700, the intra-Catholic controversy between the (mainly regular) Roman Catholic and the (mainly secular) Jansenist clergy intensified, culminating in 1723 in a formal schism. In the disputes leading up to this schism, Dutch secular authorities supported the predominantly Dutch-born Jansenists who favoured a "Batavian" over a Roman church. Sensing an opportunity to eliminate the presence in the Republic of the foreign-based religious orders, the States of Holland issued two edicts in which they *de facto* legalised the apostolic vicar of the Holland Mission as well as the secular priests, on condition that they were born in the Dutch Republic and were "admitted" by the secular authorities.[58] Tolerant Amsterdam, however, admitted regular priests as well and even allowed them to be assisted by foreign priests from their order. Unhindered by the authorities, they continued celebrating Mass, for example, in the hidden church "De Papegaai" that was frequented by ardent Roman Catholic De Boer.[59] Against this backdrop, De Boer must have felt justified not only in attending Mass, but in accompanying the liturgy with abundant music as well. In this respect, the Catholic experience of living in a hostile society had significantly changed by 1750 compared to the previous century, when Dusseldorpius and Waeijer feared the authorities' wrath over music-making in hidden churches.

Singing bridges

Jan de Boer shows us that music embodied not only devotion and resistance, but peaceful engagement with non-Catholics as well. Obviously, Catholic song culture, with its devotional-polemical lyrics, could not function as a medium to bridge the confessional divide. Yet, despite its Catholic associations for zealous seventeenth-century Calvinists, the church organ could. De Boer moved to Amsterdam in 1738 but was born and raised in Haarlem. In his autobiographical poems – just like Herman Verbeecq, De Boer devoted his spare time to poetry as well as music – his lively participation in Haarlem's musical culture figures prominently. Particularly his exuberant poem in honour of the new Müller organ in the city's formerly Catholic St. Bavo Church reflects De Boer's feeling that music could bring together people of all denominations. This poem, entitled "On the glorious new organ" ["Op het overheerlijk nieuw orgel"] (1738), does not show any of the anti-Calvinist resentments

that resonate in other works by his hand.⁶⁰ There is no trace of bitterness at
the sequestration of the former Catholic church or the second-class position
of the city's Catholic community. Instead, De Boer praises the magistrates for
the exceptional instrument they commissioned for the St. Bavo Church, which
put Haarlem ahead of other cities in the competition for the most prestigious
organ. To him, the church organ, the former focal point of the forbidden Catholic liturgy, embodied Christian unity and urban patriotism instead of confessional strife. In other words, his loyalty to the Church of Rome, so often at
the forefront of his poetry and diary, was not incompatible with loyalty to his
home town. On other occasions too, he employed music to show his solidarity
with his fatherland, for example in 1747 when in the wake of the War of the
Austrian Succession (1740–1748), the country faced an invasion by French
armies, a threat that revived painful memories of the Disaster Year 1672. To
demonstrate his feelings for his fatherland, De Boer took his violoncello outside and in front of his house played "Wilhelmus van Nassouwen," a polemical song from the late sixteenth century directed against the King of Spain and
the Catholic Church. "Nothing surpasses the Wilhelmus," De Boer stated, not
hindered by its anti-Catholic origins.⁶¹ In 1749, the Peace of Aachen, which
had ended the war the year before, was celebrated in all Dutch churches. In the
Catholic church of the French Carmelites, De Boer participated in a *Te Deum*
that moved all churchgoers to tears of joy for the long-wished peace.⁶² These
records show that Jan de Boer had more than one identity: he nourished both
subcultural *and* mainstream loyalties. Recent historical research confirms that
Catholic identity in general was a multilayered affair.⁶³

Conclusions

Because of its potential to stir emotion, in combination with its performative
qualities, sacred soundscapes were a particularly powerful tool to rebuild the
Catholic community in the Dutch Republic. On a personal level, sacred hymns
intensified feelings of devotion. Within the Catholic community as a whole,
they served as identity marker, mnemonic aid, and didactic tool for children
and illiterate or simple people. Liturgical chant in particular fostered a sense of
belonging to a wider Catholic world. Hearing the music of the liturgy bound
Catholics not only to co-religionists that were physically present, but also to
Catholics beyond the Republic's borders. Furthermore, the age-old tradition
of Gregorian chant underlined the continuity of the Old Church. It confirmed
that in the struggle for "seniority," the Catholic Church had the upper hand.

But in post-Reformation Dutch society, music could also function as a medium to transport Catholic beliefs from the domestic sphere into the public
domain. Turning the straitjacket the Dutch Reformed authorities had forced
upon them into an opportunity, religious, semi-religious, and lay Catholics
creatively and actively exploited music to transgress the line between private
and public space, and to plead their case in the public arena. These "cross
border" claims show that their musical culture enabled Catholics to reinvent

themselves in a Protestant context and reclaim their position in society. Sacred music, in other words, demonstrates that Catholics were not passive victims of marginalisation, but active agents of their own lives.

At the same time, religious soundscapes reveal the dynamics and heterogeneity of the Catholic subculture. Although all Catholics considered sacred music to be an integral part of their devotional repertoire, its performance was a bone of contention. This chapter has shown that not all believers appreciated music as a weapon against Protestant domination, sometimes to the point that they no longer recognised each other as fellow Catholics. Furthermore, this heterogeneity was a complex affair: militant and accommodating Catholics alike spurned musical challenges. Franciscus Dusseldorpius, who wholeheartedly rejected the Dutch Republic, and Jan de Boer, who embodied both Catholic and Dutch loyalties, shared the same position, though De Boer's eighteenth-century self-confident views on music in hidden churches differed greatly from Dusseldorpius' fear of discovery of such transgressions 150 years earlier.

Conflicting interpretations of what it meant to be a Catholic and how this should be expressed in a hostile environment were not limited to soundscapes. We see similar developments with regard to the cult of relics. Whereas Catholics across the spectrum recognised the veneration of relics as an important aspect of their habitus, they disagreed about what this meant in the context of the Dutch Republic. Some believers felt that these sacred remains of saints and martyrs should be transported to Catholic safe havens abroad, where they could be openly worshipped. Others were convinced that they should stay "at home" where they had been revered for centuries, even if that meant that these holy objects had to be hidden in attics or under floors to protect them from Protestant destruction.[64]

Finally, this chapter has demonstrated that Catholicism was – and is – a multisensory experience: smelling incense, looking at visual representations of suffering saints and crying martyrs, touching rosaries, sprinkling holy water, and hearing sacred songs. In Protestant territories such as the Dutch Republic, these sensory aspects of the Catholic habitus became contested and had to be reconsidered by adherents of the Catholic Church. The promising results from exploring Catholic experience in the early modern Northern Netherlands through sacred soundscapes should serve as a stimulus to investigate other sensory experiences as well, such as taste, smell, and touch, and the emotions they evoked.

Notes

1 Cornelis Gisbertus Plemp, *C.G. Plempii Poemata Deuter authographa*, 2 vols. (Special Collections University of Amsterdam, inventory number ms II A 51 (1638) and 52 (1624–1628)), vol. II A 52, f. 328.
2 The concept of habitus was introduced by French sociologist Pierre Bourdieu in 1971 and has since become an influential theoretical tool across the academic spectrum. Bourdieu has further expounded his habitus theory in *La distinction. Critique sociale du jugement* (Parijs: Les Editions de Minuit, 1979).

3 The term "soundscape" is coined by the Canadian composer R. Murray
   Schafer, *The Tuning of the World* (Toronto: McClelland & Stewart Limited,
   1977); republished in 1994 as *The Soundscape. Our Sonic Environment and
   the Tuning of the World*. Although the concept has been used in a number of
   ways, this chapter builds on Alexander Fisher's interpretation; Alexander Fisher,
   "Reworking the Confessional Soundscape in the German Counter-Reformation,"
   Basler Jahrbuch für historische Musikpraxis 38 (2014), 103. For a survey of the
   different approaches to the notion soundscapes, see Ari Kelman, "Rethinking the
   Soundscape. A Critical Genealogy of a Key Term in Sound Studies," *Senses &
   Society* 5, no. 2 (2010), 212–24.
4 Christine Kooi, "Sub jugo haereticorum: Minority Catholicism in Early Modern
   Europe," in *Early Modern Catholicism. Essays in Honour of John W. O'Malley,
   S.J.*, ed. Kathleen M. Comerford and Hilmar M. Pabel (Toronto: University of
   Toronto Press, 2001), 147–62. The term refers to the type of Catholicism that
   emerged after the Reformation in non-Catholic countries such as the Dutch
   Republic.
5 For example, Willem Frijhoff, "The Treshold of Toleration. Interconfessional
   Conviviality in Holland during the Early Modern Period," in *Embodied belief*,
   ed. Willem Frijhoff (Hilversum: Verloren, 2002), 39–65; R. Po-Chia Hsia and
   H.F.K. van Nierop, eds., *Calvinism and Religious Toleration in the Dutch Golden
   Age* (Cambridge: Cambridge University Press, 2002).
6 For example, Charles Parker, *Faith on the Margins: Catholics and Catholicism in
   the Dutch Golden Age* (Cambridge, MA: Harvard University Press, 2008); Geert
   Janssen, *The Dutch Revolt and Catholic Exile in Reformation Europe* (Cambridge: Cambridge University Press, 2014); Jaap Geraerts, *Patrons of the Old
   Faith: The Catholic Nobility in Utrecht and Guelders, c. 1580–1702* (Leiden:
   Brill, 2019); Genji Yasuhira, "Catholics' Survival Techniques in Utrecht, 1620s–
   1670s" (PhD diss., Tilburg University, 2019).
7 For a historiographic analysis, see Carolina Lenarduzzi, "Katholiek in de Republiek. Subcultuur en tegencultuur in Nederland, 1570–1750" (PhD diss., Leiden
   University, 2018), 12–28. For a discussion of the new methodological and con-
   ceptual tools, see Jaap Geraerts, "Early Modern Catholicism and Its Historiogra-
   phy. Innovation, Revitalization, and Innovation," *Church History and Religious
   Culture* 97 (2017), 381–92.
8 For example, Andrew Pettegree, *Reformation and the Culture of Persuasion*
   (Cambridge: Cambridge University Press, 2005); Judith Pollmann, "'Hey Ho,
   Let the Cup go Round!' Singing for Reformation in the Sixteenth Century," in
   Religion and Cultural Exchange in Europe, 1400–1700, ed. Heinz Schilling and
   István György Tóth (Cambridge paperback, 2012), 294–316; Alexander Fisher,
   Music, Piety and Propaganda in Bavaria (Oxford: Oxford University Press,
   2014). For music as a window on Dutch Catholicism, see Lenarduzzi, "Katholiek
   in de Republiek," 249–86.
9 Anna Kvicalova, *Listening and Knowledge in Reformation Europe* (London: Pal-
   grave Macmillan, 2019); Chiara Bertoglio, *Reforming Music* (Berlin/Boston: De
   Gruyter, 2018), 519–64; D. van der Poel, L.P. Grijp, and Wim van Anrooij, eds.,
   Identity, Intertextuality, and Performance in Early Modern Song Culture (Leiden/
   Boston: Brill, 2016).
10 Alexander Fisher, "Mit singen und klingen; Urban Processional Culture and
   the Soundscapes of Post-Reformation Germany," in *Listening to Early Modern
   Catholicism*, ed. Daniele Filippi and Michael Noone (Leiden/Boston: Brill, 2017),
   187–201; David van der Linden, "The Sound of Memory: Acoustic Conflict and
   the Legacy of the French Wars of Religion in Seventeenth-Century Montpellier,"
   Early Modern French Studies 41, no. 1 (2019), 7–20.

11 Jacomien Prins and Mariken Teeuwen, eds., *Harmonisch labyrinth. De muziek van de kosmos in de Westerse wereld* (Hilversum: Verloren, 2007), 33–46.

12 James Caccamo, "The Responsorial Self: Christian Ethics and Ritual Songs" (PhD diss., Loyola University Chicago, 2004), 10.

13 Augustinus, *Confessiones*, Book 10, Chapter 33.

14 Bertoglio, *Reforming Music*, 103–5.

15 Ibid., 104–5, for debates on the meaning of the concept of liturgical music.

16 This posed serious problems as both Gregorian chant and the polyphonic motets were too complex to learn by heart. R. Rasch, Geschiedenis van de muziek in de Republiek der Verenigde Nederlanden, Chapter 9, 2–3, http://www.hum.uu.nl/medewerkers/r.a.rasch/My-Work-on-the-Internet.htm.

17 Alexander Fisher, "The Sounds of Eucharistic Culture," in *A Companion to the Eucharist in the Reformation*, ed. Lee Palmer Wandel (Leiden/Boston: Brill, 2016), 443.

18 For this mechanism, see Liesbeth Corens, "Saints Beyond Borders: Relics and the Expatriate English Catholic Community," in *Exile and the Formation of Religious Identities in the Early Modern World*, ed. Jesse Spohnholz and Gary Waite (London: Pickering & Chatto, 2014), 25–38; Lenarduzzi, "Katholiek in de Republiek," 126; Renée Vulto, "Waer vriendenmin gaet, hand aen hand, met liefde voor het Vaderland," *Tijdschrift voor Geschiedenis* 133, no. 4 (2020), 631.

19 For the role of music in creating communities beyond geographical borders, see S. Whitely, A. Bennett, and S. Hawkins, eds., *Music, Space and Place. Popular Music and Cultural Identity* (Aldershot: Ashgate, 2004), 4.

20 Parker, *Faith on the Margins*, passim; Joke Spaans, *De Levens der Maechden. Het verhaal van een religieuze vrouwengemeenschap in de eerste helft van de zeventiende eeuw* (Hilversum: Verloren, 2012); Lenarduzzi, "Katholiek in de Republiek," passim.

21 Tryn Jans Oly, *Levens der Maechden*, 3 vols. (Library Museum Catharijneconvent Utrecht, Collectie Preciosa Warmond, inventory numbers 92B13-14, 92C10).

22 Oly, *Levens der Maechden*, vol. 2, f. 59ʳ, "Leven van Josina Willems."

23 Council of Trent, Session XXII, chapter VIII. For the Dutch implementation of this decree, see L.P.M. Loosen, *Lodewijk Makeblijde (1565–1630). Hymnen en gezangen* (Zwolle: Tjeenk Willink, 1964), 93.

24 Boys that were part of the choir were ordained as well. In Catholic territories, nuns who had taken solemn vows were allowed to sing the Hours of the Day, preferably in accordance with the strict enclosure stimulated by the church authorities; Kimberlyn Montford, "'Holy Restraint'. Religious Reform and Nun's Music in Early Modern Rome," *The Sixteenth Century Journal* 37, no. 4 (2006), 1007–26.

25 Oly, *Levens der Maechden*, vol. 3, f. 122ᵛ, "Leven van Cornelisgen Alberts dochter."

26 A. Hensen, ed., "Levensverhaal van J.B. Stalpaert v.d. Wielen, op verzoek van pastoor Rumold van Medenblick door het Delftsche klopje W.D. Reeck, in 1630–1632 geschreven," *Bijdragen Geschiedenis van het Bisdom Haarlem* [hereafter *BGBH*] 46 (1929), 321–49.

27 A. van Lommel, "Bouwstoffen voor de kerkelijke geschiedenis van verschillende Parochiën thans behoorende tot het bisdom van Haarlem," *BGBH* 7 (1879), 350.

28 *Annales sive historiae de tumultibus Belgicis annis 1566-1615 Francisci Dusseldorpii*, 2 vols. (Keulen 1615–1616, University Library Utrecht, inventory number coll. hss. 775), vol. 2, f. 315.

29 This interpretation builds upon Emily Murphy's argument that through the physical performance of spiritual music in a household, the domestic space became sacred; Emily Murphy, "Music and post-Reformation English Catholics. Place,

Sociability, and Space, 1570–1640" (PhD diss., York University, 2014), 277. We do not know whether Van der Dussen family actually performed the antiphon, but ultimately the painted performance functioned in the same way.

30 Monique Scheer, "Are Emotions a Kind of Practice (and Is That What Makes Them Have a History)? A Bourdieuian Approach to Understanding Emotion," *History and Theory* 51 (2012), 193–220.

31 L.P. Grijp and D. van der Poel, "Introduction in *Identity, Intertextuality, and Performance in Early Modern Song Culture*, ed. Van der Poel, Grijp, and Van Anrooij, 4–17.

32 Grijp and Van der Poel, "Introduction," 26; Vulto, "Waer vriendenmin gaet," 626.

33 Jan Baptist Stalpaert van der Wiele, *Gulde-jaer ons Heeren Jesu Christi op alle de Zonnen-dagen des jaers* (Den Bosch, 1628); Id., *Extractum katholicum, tegen alle Gebreken van Verwarde Harsenen* (Leuven, 1631); Idem, *Gulde-jaers feest-daghen, of Den Schat der Geestlycke Lof-sangen, Gemaeckt op Elcken Feestdagh van 'tgeheele Jaer* (Antwerpen, 1635).

34 Stalpaert, *Gulde-iaers feestdagen*, "voorrede" (preface), ff. iij^v and iv^r.

35 Ibid., ff. iij^v and iij^r.

36 Especially in *Extractum katholicum*.

37 Rumoldus Batavus [Rumoldus van Medenblick], *Nieu Liedt-Boecxken, inhoudende verscheyden liedekens op de principaelste feest-daghen ende andere heylighe daghen van den iaere [...]* (Antwerpen, 1614), 138.

38 Willem de Swaen, *Den singende Swaen, dat is Den lof-sangh der heyligen, die als singende swaenen de doodt blygeestigh hebben ontfangen / Gemaeckt door G.D.S.* (Antwerpen, 1664), "Approbatie," *3^r–*4^r.

39 Batavus [Van Medenblick], *Nieu Liedt-Boecxken*, 138.

40 Victor à Campis [Franciscus Mijleman], *De Nederlandtsche Weergalm, Toegesongen ende opgedragen met de Engelsche choorzangers, aen de H. Altijt gepresen Moeder Godts-Maeghd Maria, omhelsende in 't Hemels Hof haere beminde Soon, Vleesch en Bloet Jesus Christus* (Antwerpen [Amsterdam], 1664), 4.

41 Stalpaert, *Extractum katholicum*, x.

42 Ibid., x–xi. See also Una McIlvenna, "The Power of Music. The Significance of Contrafactum in Execution Ballads"; Katie Barclay, "Performance and Performativity," in *Early Modern Emotions. An Introduction*, ed. Susan Broomhall (London: Routledge, 2016), 14–7.

43 Grijp and Van der Poel, "Introduction," 3. See also Eddy de Jongh, *Muziek aan de muur. Muzikale voorstellingen in de Nederlanden 1500–1700* (Zwolle: Waanders, 2008), 27–8.

44 Herman Verbeecq, *Sang Godin, bestaande in verscheijde liedekens zo geestelijk, als werelsz.* (Amsterdam, 1662, Stadsbibliotheek Haarlem, inventory number Hs. 187 A4).

45 Oly, *Levens der Maechden*, vol. 2, f. 87^r, "Leven van Annetge Sicxtus."

46 Jan de Boer, *Chronologische historie van alle hetgeene is voorgevallen bij de komste van Willem Karel Hendrik Friso, prince van Oranje etc [...]* (Amsterdam, 1747–1748, Royal Library, The Hague, inventory number Hss. 71).

47 On many occasions, De Boer described himself in his diary as a "loyal citizen" (see paragraph "Singing bridges" below).

48 H. Amersfoordt and U.A. Evertsz, eds., *Verhaal van de verrigtingen der jezuïeten in Friesland door pater Willebrordus van der Heijden, lid van de orde der jezuïeten* (Leeuwarden: J.W. Brouwer, 1842), 39. The original manuscript has been lost.

49 Ibid., 73.

50 In 1656, for example, the Reformed Church of Amsterdam complained how in many house churches Catholics sang liturgical songs and played organs, violins, and other instruments in such a loud way that they could be heard not only in the adjoining houses but also in the street; I.H. van Eeghen, "De eigendom van de katholieke kerken in Amsterdam ten tijde van de Republiek," *BGBH* 64 (1957), 268–9. See for more examples, A. van Lommel, "Bouwstoffen voor de kerkelijke geschiedenis van verschillende Parochiën thans behoorende tot het bisdom van Haarlem," *BGBH* 7 (1879), 54–99, 340–90 and *BGBH* 9 (1881), 322.

51 Oly, *Levens der Maechden*, vol. 2, ff. 84^{r-v}, "Leven van Annetge Sicxtus." The hidden churches in Gouda also employed the city organist to tune their instruments; Lommel, "Bouwstoffen," 350.

52 See Lommel, "Bouwstoffen," passim.

53 Christine Kooi, *Calvinists and Catholics during Holland's Golden Age* (Cambridge: Cambridge University Press, 2012), 166–7.

54 This mechanism is related to the emotional contagion theory; see, for example, Patrick Hunter and Glenn Schellenberg, "Music and Emotion," in *Music Perception. Springer Handbook of Auditory Research 36*, ed. M.R. Jones et al. (New York: Springer, 2010), 129–64.

55 Lenarduzzi, "Katholiek in de Republiek," 271–2.

56 Dusseldorpius, *Annales*, vol. 2, f. 415-6.

57 Arnold Waeijer, "Nopende het Aerts-priesterschap van Swolle naer de Beroerten deser Nederlanden mitsgaders van eenige gedenckweerdige voorvallen", ed. G.A. Meijer, *Archief voor de Geschiedenis van het Aartsbisdom Utrecht* [hereafter *AAU*] 46 (1921), 271.

58 Wiltens, *Kerkelyk Plakaat-boek*, vol. 1, 641; Cornelis Cau, *Groot Placaetboeck [...]*, vol. 6 (The Hague, 1746), 367. In 1737, another step towards formal recognition was taken when the Catholic Church became a tax subject and was thus acknowledged as a legal entity.

59 B.H. Klönne, "De toelating der Roomsche priesters in Amsterdam tusschen 1730 en 1794," *BGBH* 15 (1888), 21–7.

60 Jan de Boer, "Op het overheerlijk nieuw orgel," in *Alle de Gedigten. Liederen. Invallende Gedagten. en Poëzij van Jan de Boer* (Haarlem 1736, 1745, Library Archive Noord-Holland, inventory number 60041), ff. 184-6.

61 De Boer, *Chronologische historie*, f. 7.

62 W.P.C. Knuttel, "Uit het verleden der Amsterdamsche katholieken," *BGBH* 26 (1901), 276–7.

63 Lenarduzzi, "Katholiek in de Republiek," 418–22.

64 Lenarduzzi, "Katholiek in de Republiek," 223–45, 248.

Part II

Asserting Identities

Historiographic Introduction

In recent decades, the term "identity" has become ubiquitous both within and outside academia. Its proliferation, however, is anything but a sign of its uncritical adoption. The author of a recent introduction to "identity" speaks of an "obsession with identity," reflecting the doubts that exist about both the utility of this concept and the nonchalance with which it often is invoked.[1] Due to the different ways in which a range of academic disciplines, including anthropology, history, political science, psychology, and sociology, conceive of and use this concept, its meaning runs the risk of becoming ambiguous and obscure. As a result, some scholars simply refrain from providing a definition whereas others intervene with the explicit aim of restoring a degree of conceptual clarity.[2]

Nowadays scholars are accustomed to distinguishing between a range of different identities, including gender, racial, and social ones. Particularly relevant for this volume is the notion of religious identity, according to which people saw themselves and were seen through the prism of religion. In line with recent theories of identity, according to which identities are historically contingent social constructs,[3] historians have emphasised the changing nature of religious identities: politico-religious circumstances and other variables affected what religious affiliation meant and how it was expressed. Religious identities were complex, layered, and had multiple roots. Membership of a particular church, participation in public or clandestine religious rituals, refusal to act in certain capacities (e.g., the refusal of most Mennonites to hold political office or serve in militias), clothing styles, name-giving practices, and many other things could become markers of religious identity.

To complicate matters further, individuals' religious identities are influenced by their gender, socio-economic status, nationality, and other attributes. Even though religious identities were often shared among a group of people, they did not necessarily carry the same meaning, substance, or relevance for every individual group member. Religious identities did not exist in isolation, but rather formed part of a constellation of identities people had. Recent research has therefore aimed to enhance our understanding of the interplay between a person's religious and other identities and how this

DOI: 10.4324/9781003030522-6

interplay influenced their behaviour and relationships with other people.[4] It has been shown, for example, that the confessional identities formed among European Christians in the wake of the Reformations by no means always negated or overrode civic, familial, and other identities.

The ways in which the concept of religious identity has informed scholarship in the field of (Post-)Reformation studies reflect broader historiographic developments over the last half a century or so. Traditional church historians tended to focus on the theological building blocks of religious identities. Applying the methodologies of their sub-discipline, their research was largely guided by and based on the authoritative and often normative documents and decrees issued by the various Christian churches, such as confessions of faith, papal bulls, and catechisms.[5] As the field of church history evolved into that of religious history,[6] the earlier top-down framework gave way to attempts to understand the emergence of religious identities from below by looking at the contributions made by "ordinary" people to (nascent) religious identities. Not only did people creatively appropriate, modify, and internalise the teachings of their church, but they also actively shaped elements of religious identities, for example, by expressing their preferences for certain acts of piety or styles of pastoral care and by criticising theological innovations.[7] The religious identities that emerged should be seen at least partially as the outcome of a dynamic process of exchange between clergy and laity.[8] Due to the greater focus on the laity and other historiographic shifts, such as the increased interest in material culture, historians have gradually widened the range of their source materials, which now comprise material objects and images as well as texts, through which religious identities are studied.[9]

Religious diversity forms the background in many of these studies against which the development of religious identities in the early modern era is understood. This is because the substance of these identities was almost invariably influenced by the existence of rival religions. Even without the physical presence of people adhering to different faiths, religious identities were often defined in relation and, indeed, opposition to other religions.[10] In fact, though, an increasing number of societies across the world were characterised by varying degrees and forms of religious diversity, and studies that concern themselves with religious coexistence and the practice of toleration are keen to situate and study religious identities in the context of the relationships between members of different religious communities.[11] Religious identities influenced the attitudes and behaviour of people towards those of other faiths and in turn could be significantly influenced by the relationships people had with religious "others."

In her chapter, Natalia Muchnik studies the process of identity formation and the role in it of contextual factors, such as repression and persecution. She does so by focusing on the religious identities of crypto-Jews and crypto-Muslims (often called "Moriscos") in early modern Spain. These two communities were commonly grouped together under the label "New Christians" in order to distinguish them from the people who claimed to have no Jewish or Muslim ancestors, known as "Old Christians." This distinction reflected the attempts of Iberian society to come to terms with the destabilisation of religious identities and boundaries caused by episodes of mass, often forced conversions, which rendered it more difficult to identify the "religious other." Combined with a general distrust in the sincerity of many of these conversions, this difficulty resulted in a preoccupation with lineage and a "genealogical mentality."[12] It also led to the emergence of certain mechanisms, such as the "purity of blood" (*limpieza de sangre*) statutes, to determine to which group a person belonged (e.g., whether their blood was "tainted" by having Jewish or Muslim ancestors) and thus to counteract this "crisis of classification and identification."[13]

In this context, Muchnik emphasises the "ethnic dimension" of religious identity, studying how the stigmatisation of lineage and blood fostered the particular self-understandings and senses of belonging characteristic of crypto-Jews and -Muslims. On the one hand, New Christians, crypto-Jews in particular, started to regard their blood as a container and transmitter of positive values and virtues and began to conceive of their lineage as superior to other ones.[14] The focus on lineage and genealogy, and the idea that religion was biologically codified in one's physical body, as it were, enabled the adoption of religious ideas and practices that were formally at odds, or at least in tension, with Jewish and Islamic orthodoxy and orthopraxy. On the other hand, attempts by the Inquisition to sniff out New Christians who were secretly practising Judaism or Islam encouraged clandestinity and dissimulation. These practices contributed to processes of identity formation and to group cohesion. Pressure from the Inquisition resulted also in what Muchnik aptly calls the "ritualisation of everyday life," as certain religious practices, in particular those that could be performed within the relatively safe confines of the domestic sphere, gained in significance. In spite of the substantial differences within and between the two communities, crypto-Jews and crypto-Muslims, one finds that in terms of socio-economic status, access to (normative) religious texts, and other variables, the group and individual identities of both crypto-Jews and crypto-Muslims emerged in relation to and constant interaction with the wider society they were part of.

Whereas Muchnik situates the formation of religious identities against the backdrop of persecution and repression, David van der Linden examines the formative role played by memory. While some of the most important students of memory, including Maurice Halbwachs and Frederick Bartlett, wrote their canonical texts as long as a century ago, it was in the last two decades of the twentieth century that cultural memory studies emerged as a scholarly sub-discipline.[15] It has been gaining in popularity ever since. Interdisciplinary in nature, this sub-discipline concerns itself with numerous aspects of memory, ranging from its biological and psychological dimensions to sociocultural processes of remembering. Many studies originating in this field have examined the nexus between memory and identity, which is unsurprising given the importance of memory for the self-understanding of individuals and human collectives.[16] Annual remembrances of martyrs, memories of persecution, and the cults of founders of religious movements are all examples of the ways in which memory practices buttress and shape religious identities.

By shaping identities and the remembrance of past events, memories influence relationships between individuals and between groups of people. For this reason, Van der Linden argues, the concept of memory can enhance our understanding of the practice of religious toleration. His chapter focuses on the competing "memory cultures" in the French city of La Rochelle, a Huguenot (Calvinist) stronghold that was conquered by Catholic forces in 1628. The Catholic and Protestant identities that emerged in La Rochelle were underpinned by different and often conflicting memories of the sixteenth-century French Wars of Religion. It mattered not only *what* but also *how* something was remembered.[17] Certain acts of remembering soured relationships between Catholics and Protestants, in particular those acts that were public in nature and that therefore expressed a competing memory culture in a decidedly visible way. An example is the different "material vectors," including paintings and plates, through which Catholics in La Rochelle remembered past victories over their confessional rivals. The annual procession that celebrated the 1628 conquest of the city was an act of remembrance that particularly aroused the ire of Protestants. The existence of competing memory cultures thus threatened the fragile coexistence of the two religious communities in this city.

The two chapters in this section, then, exemplify some of the ways in which religious fragmentation and diversity influenced both the content of religious identities and the ways in which those identities were asserted and expressed. In the case of New Christians in Spain, the expression of religious identity was largely restricted to the private sphere, thus fuelling suspicions among Old Christians about the New Christians' religious and political loyalties. By contrast, in France the principal source of friction and conflict was the public assertion of religious identity. Both chapters thus reveal the importance of the circumstances in which religious identities were shaped, asserted, and experienced.

Notes

1 Florian Coulmas, *Identity: A Very Short Introduction* (Oxford: Oxford University Press, 2019), 1, 27. Rogers Brubaker and Frederick Cooper, "Beyond 'Identity'," *Theory and Society* 29 (2000), 1–47.
2 For an example of the former, see Coulmans, *Identity*; for the latter, see Nathalie Heinich, *Wat onze identiteit niet is* (Amsterdam: Prometheus, 2020), the Dutch translation of *Ce que n'est pas l'identité* (Paris: Gallimard, 2018). See also Peter J. Burke and Jan E. Stets, *Identity Theory* (Oxford: Oxford University Press, 2009).
3 Coulmans, *Identity*, Ch. 3.

4 E.g. David M. Luebke, *Hometown Religion: Regimes of Coexistence in Early Modern Westphalia* (Charlottesville, VA: University of Virginia Press, 2016), esp. 18. Jaap Geraerts, *Patrons of the Old Faith: The Catholic Nobility in Utrecht and Guelders, c. 1580–1702* (Leiden: Brill, 2018), 16–9. Craig Harline, *Conversions: Two Family Stories from the Reformation and Modern America* (New Haven: Yale University Press, 2011), 246–51.

5 The confessionalisation paradigm was also characterised by a top-down, statist perspective. See, e.g. Wolfgang Reinhard, "Pressures towards Confessionalization? Prolegomena to a Theory of the Confessional Age," in *The German Reformation: The Essential Readings*, ed. Scott Dixon (Oxford: Blackwell, 1999), 169–92. For a succinct summary of this paradigm and some of the critique it received, see Ute Lotz-Heumann, "The Concept of 'Confessionalization': A Historiographical Paradigm in Dispute," *Memoria y Civilización* 4 (2001), 93–114.

6 For this development, see, e.g. Willem Frijhoff, "Van Histoire de l'Eglise naar Histoire Religieuse: De invloed van de Annales-groep op de kerkgeschiedenis in Frankrijk en de perspectieven daarvan voor Nederland," *Nederlands Archief voor Kerkgeschiedenis* 61 (1981), 113–53.

7 For an example of the latter, see B. Nischan, "The Exorcism Controversy and Baptism in the Late Reformation," *Sixteenth Century Journal* 18, no. 1 (1987), 31–52.

8 A number of historians have emphasised the cooperation between clergy and laity. E.g. Marc R. Forster, *The Counter-Reformation in the Villages: Religion and Reform in the Bishopric of Speyer, 1560–1720* (Ithaca: Cornell University Press, 1992); Marc R. Forster, *Catholic Revival in the Age of the Baroque: Religious Identity in Southwest Germany, 1550–1750* (Cambridge: Cambridge University Press, 2001); Charles H. Parker, *Faith on the Margins: Catholics and Catholicism in the Dutch Golden Age* (Cambridge, MA: Harvard University Press, 2008); Judith Pollmann, *Catholic Identity and the Revolt of the Netherlands, 1520–1635* (Oxford: Oxford University Press, 2011).

9 E.g. Bridget Heal, *A Magnificent Faith: Art and Identity in Lutheran Germany* (Oxford: Oxford University Press, 2017).

10 David Nirenberg, *Anti-Judaism: The History of a Way of Thinking* (London: Head of Zeus Ltd, 2018).

11 The number of publications that could be cited here is vast. For a good indication, see the chapters by Bertrand Forclaz and Dagmar Freist in C. Scott Dixon, Dagmar Freist, and Mark Greengrass, eds., *Living with Religious Diversity in Early Modern Europe* (Farnham: Ashgate, 2009).

12 David Nirenberg, "Mass Conversion and Genealogical Mentalities: Jews and Christians in Fifteenth-Century Spain," *Past & Present* 174, no. 1 (2002), 3–41.

13 Nirenberg, "Mass Conversion," 16. See also Stuart B. Schwartz, *Blood and Boundaries: The Limits of Religious and Racial Exclusion in Early Modern Latin America* (Waltham: Brandeis University Press, 2020), 61–2. The existence of mixed marriages contributed to the emergence of complex identities and further eroded the distinction between Old and New Christians. Luis F. Bernabé-Pons, "Identity, Mixed Unions and Endogamy of the Moriscos: The Assimilation of the New Converts Revisited," *Mediterranean Historical Review* 35, no. 1 (2020), 79–99; Max Deardorff, "The Ties That Bind: Intermarriage between Moriscos and Old Christians in Early Modern Spain, 1526–1614," *Journal of Family History* 42, no. 3 (2017), 250–70.

14 This was also expressed by members of Jewish diaspora in other states. E.g. Miriam Bodian, *Hebrews of the Portuguese Nation: Conversos and Community in Early Modern Amsterdam* (Bloomington: Indiana University Press, 1999).

15 Astrid Erll, "Cultural Memory Studies: An Introduction," in *Media and Cultural Memory. An International and Interdisciplinary Handbook*, ed. Astrid Erll and

Ansgar Nünning (Berlin-New York: De Gruyter, 2008), 9–10; Judith Pollmann, *Memory in Early Modern Europe, 1500–1800* (Oxford: Oxford University Press, 2017), 3–4.

16 Erll, "Cultural Memory Studies," 2, 6. For case studies on the relation between memory and civic identity after episodes of religious strife and upheaval, see David de Boer, "Between Remembrance and Oblivion: Negotiating Civic Identity after the Sacks of Mechelen (1572, 1580)," *Sixteenth Century Journal* 51, no. 4 (2020), 963–81; Erika Kuijpers and Judith Pollman, "Why Remember Terror? Memories of Violence in the Dutch Revolt," in *Ireland: 1641: Contexts and Reactions*, ed. Micheál Ó Siochrú and Jane Ohlmeyer (Manchester: Manchester University Press, 2013), 176–96.

17 Erll, "Cultural Memory Studies," 7.

4   At the Crossroads of Identity

Conversos and Moriscos in Inquisitorial Spain (Sixteenth and Seventeenth Centuries)*

Natalia Muchnik

During the auto-da-fé staged on October 18, 1570 in Logroño, Galicia, it was learned that Gracia de Gabiria, a resident of La Guardia, of the "generation of Jews" and daughter of a man condemned "for Judaism," had "publicly boasted of being of the Jewish caste" and of having praised "the Jews and their Law," saying that "Jewish meant righteous, and that the Jews were better than Christians [...] and that the greatest honour that could be paid to her and her children, was to call them Jews."[1] Three years later, this time in Baza, Andalusia, a Morisco slave from Rincon (Malaga) reportedly declared: "Every night my master mistreats me and canes me to teach me the [Catholic] doctrine and thinks he must make me a Christian," but "I am a Moor and daughter of a Moor [...] and a Moor I will die."[2] These two testimonies (though they must be interpreted with caution given the conditions under which they were expressed – recourse to torture, the structuring of the Inquisitors' questionnaires, distortions introduced by scribes)[3] are nonetheless significant. Indeed, they shed light on the very foundations of the identity-construction of crypto-Jews and crypto-Muslims – usually called Moriscos – New Christians[4] whom the Inquisition accused of secretly practicing Judaism or Islam.[5] In the case of both Gracia and the Morisco slave, what emerges is the importance attached to family and origin, the ethnic dimension of identity, the affirmation of self in the face of oppression, and a valuing of difference. Crypto-Jews and Moriscos shared a quasi-ethnic conception of religion and group membership that stressed memory and collective identity. Here, belonging is as much social as strictly religious. Thus, rather than examining the syncretism that has already been the subject of numerous studies, the focus in this chapter is on the performative dimension of identity-construction and the ways in which groups establish properties recognised as their own, as explicated by Fredrik Barth.[6] As debates among historians testify, though, it remains difficult to measure degrees of assimilation, assess the reality of clandestine religious practices, or establish the degree of distortion in sources.[7]

Certainly, like the ritual practices of the Moriscos and, even more so, those of the crypto-Jews, the sense of belonging to these groups was labile, varying according to context and moment or, more prosaically, relative to

DOI: 10.4324/9781003030522-7

their socio-economic position, interlocutors, and the forms of repression to which they were subjected. The repression was the result of the Inquisition, instituted in 1478 in Spain, and the Purity of Blood statutes that, beginning in the mid-fifteenth century but even more so from the mid-sixteenth century, divided Hispanic society into Old and New Christians, who have been stigmatised ever since.[8] That said, there were notable differences between conversos and Moriscos, particularly their distinct sociological characteristics. While conversos were mainly artisans or merchants and mostly lived in cities, Moriscos were primarily farmers and craftsmen, residing in the countryside or in small towns where they were, if not the majority, large in number. Before their expulsion from Spain in 1609–1614, Moriscos could also be found in cities in Morisco-majority regions, such as the *albaicin* quarter of Pastrana, in the region of Guadalajara.[9] This neighbourhood was created at the time of the deportation of the Granada Moriscos following the Second War of the Alpujarras (1568–1571) to accommodate around 200 families. A dozen of them, among the richest and most integrated, managed to stay in the city in 1614, seemingly living in harmony with the conversos (including crypto-Jews) who occupied the quarter at that time.[10]

This chapter argues for viewing this identity-mosaic as a construct in perpetual renewal, as diverse as there were individuals, and not as a specific social position or product. First examined in its collective dimension, through belonging to stigmatised groups and being thereby singled out in Spanish society, identity-construction is then assessed through the lens of origin. For, if genealogy and blood are what stigmatise Moriscos and conversos, they are also what bind them together and define them in their eyes. Likewise, the inquisitorial repression and clandestinity in which some of them lived had a certain cohesive effect. Finally, the role of religion should not be underestimated, even if it was transformed by secrecy and relative distance from normative sources, a situation that manifested itself in a ritual complexification of everyday life.

Reversing the stigma

Perception of self is not, as we know, enough to define ourselves. It is necessarily accompanied by a consideration of others, the mirror of difference, and by reputation, known to be important in early modern societies, whether stigmatising or inclusive. Identity is, above all, a relationship with a plural Other. Without reducing the identities of crypto-Jews and Moriscos to mere reactions to the stigma perpetuated by the Purity of Blood statutes or to products of inquisitorial action, as argued by certain historians,[11] the burden of repression remains undeniable in explaining the groups' cohesion. It is also possible that the Holy Office actually perpetuated certain clandestine religious practices, notably through the Edicts of Faith. Posted or read, these texts issued by the Holy Office listed clues to identify supposed heretics. As their content (the rites listed) remained mostly unchanged from the sixteenth to the eighteenth century, they may have been a source of inspiration for Moriscos and crypto-Jews.[12] It is also worth noting that the forms of religion practised by these same populations differed where there was less repression, for example, among the crypto-Jewish communities of France or in the Southern Netherlands in the sixteenth and seventeenth centuries.[13] Whatever their actual religious practices and despite their manoeuvres to assimilate via marriages to Old Christians, falsification of genealogies, changes of surnames,[14] et cetera, conversos and Moriscos remained marked by the stain of their origins. Though indubitably, in certain periods and at least until the 1570s, Moriscos were more visible than conversos in certain respects, especially in appearance and clothing.

Conversos and Moriscos were, nonetheless, reminded of their origins whenever they wanted to accede to certain positions, such as that of "familiar" of the Holy Office or municipal *regidor* (alderman), or to enter certain institutions such as religious orders, university residential colleges, military orders, or various brotherhoods. Furthermore, due apparently to the devaluation of *hidalguía* (nobility) by the integration of newcomers, often of converso origin, and the impoverishment of some of its members, the importance of *limpieza* (purity) increased significantly in the sixteenth century. This manifested itself particularly in the multiplication of *linajudos* (experts in genealogies) and genealogical compilations such as the green books (*libros verdes*). Both tracked down and compiled "dishonourable" genealogies, especially those with New Christian elements.[15] This stigmatisation, which produced a form of naturalisation of traits, occurred daily and was reflected in one's reputation in the eyes of neighbours, especially in villages. Such distinction was probably particularly evident in the small towns where Moriscos often lived, mostly found in the kingdoms of Valencia and Murcia and, after the Second War of the Alpujarras and the subsequent deportation of the Granada Moriscos, in western Andalusia, Extremadura, and Castilla-la-Mancha. The continuation of their distinctive cultural and religious features was, in fact, one of the justifications given for the expulsion of 1609–1614,[16] although this difference cannot be generalised systematically.[17]

Though not every New Christian was necessarily a crypto-Jew or crypto-Muslim in the making – far from it – the authorities and population tended to equate origin/ethnicity with religious affiliation. In reaction, stigmatisation produced in some New Christians a process of inversion. Resistance involved the affirmation of identity and a dialectical relationship with the stigmatising other: a posing of oppositions. In inquisitorial documentation we, thus, find numerous affirmations of pride that go beyond the usual framework of expectations held by the court, resembling the "reversal of stigma" analysed by Georg Simmel.[18] "Pride of origin" is reinforced by the opposition that, in the account of the Morisco slave presented in the introduction, is embodied in the master and his caning his slave to inculcate Christian dogma. Religious belonging, therefore, takes on an ethnic dimension, already present in the Purity of Blood statutes. This in part explains

why fervent Moriscos and crypto-Jews were able to defend spiritual or dogmatic postulates that, if not "heterodox," at least ran contrary to Islam or
Judaism.[19] The blood of the New Christian, usually depreciated and rejected
by Spanish society, is on the contrary valued in the extreme, especially
among the crypto-Jews. Indeed, the New Christian is the bearer of a "quality," a virtue, a righteousness in the case of Gracia de Gabiria, who claims
to be of the "Jewish caste," the caste here being the lineage, the ancestry,
the tribe. The infamy of "impure" blood (*manchado*) in Spanish society
becomes synonymous with honour and noble origins. This was often linked
to the revindication of a form of anchoring, of autochthony, as found, for
example, in the *plomos* of Sacromonte, lead tablets engraved with mysteri-
ous designs and Arabic and Latin characters, discovered on the Sacromonte
hill in Granada between 1595 and 1599. They were commonly associated
with the relics, consisting of a parchment with an image of the Virgin Mary
dressed as a Morisco, discovered in 1588 during the demolition of the Torre
Turpiana, the remains of the city's old mosque.[20] Yet, the *plomos* were in
fact forgeries created by Moriscos to prove the presence of Arabs at the
time of the Apostles and their conversion by Saint James: the books supposedly contained a fifth gospel, that of Barnabas, with the relics being
those of the disciples of Saint James. These claims of being older Christians
and more long-standing natives than the Spanish Old Christians themselves
were made in the hope of avoiding imminent expulsion.

This autochthony and reversal can also be found among the crypto-Jews,
somewhat paradoxically since many of them who lived in sixteenth- and
seventeenth-century Spain actually came from Portugal during the Iberian
Union (1580–1640). They created extraordinary genealogies that made
them out to be descendants of biblical figures, David in particular. Like the
Jews of medieval Spain, they claimed to originate from the tribes of Judah
and of Benjamin, the Levites or the ten lost tribes, combining desire for im-
mortality, antiquity, and messianic destiny. This ancestral nobility, or "aristocracy of anteriority," was added to the affirmation of a specifically Jewish
purity of blood. It explains why the crypto-Jews gave themselves the code
name of Basques, a symbol of antiquity. Indeed, the Basques were considered to be Old Christians *par excellence*, whose blood was said to be pure
of any mixing and to whom collective (universal) nobility was attributed,
by virtue of the alleged arrival in their land of the biblical patriarch Tubal,
grandson of Noah, who was said to have begun the populating of Spain.[21]
This valorisation of blood was also reflected in matrimonial alliances, which
privileged (though not exclusively) endogamy in both populations.[22] Among
the *chuetas*, crypto-Jews of Mallorca, those who entered into mixed marriages (with Old Christians), were described as "badly mixed" (*malmes-
clats*); their children were called "apple-peaches" and often had to marry
amongst themselves.[23]

Just as they celebrated the antiquity of their origins by creating their
own myths, Moriscos and crypto-Jews developed eschatological narratives

announcing their deliverance. The quest for individual salvation was also a quest for the salvation of an entire people. As with other European populations, where *translatio electionis* (the transfer of chosenness) often appears at moments of crisis, linked with eschatological expectations, the crypto-Jews likened themselves to the oppressed Hebrews of Egypt awaiting their liberation by a providential figure. Overwhelmed by suffering – beginning with the expulsions of the fifteenth century – the crypto-Jews established themselves as martyrs *par excellence*, an image reflected in the Judeo-Iberian diaspora, which was permeated by a culture of martyrdom. As for the Moriscos, their misfortunes were to end with the arrival of the *mahdi* (or *Al-Fatimi*), the "Divinely Guided One," sometimes confused with the Ottomans. He was to reconquer Spain, defeat the Christians, and restore the purity of original Islam. These beliefs were expressed particularly in *jofores*, prophecies announcing the universal victory of Islam, numerous during the War of the Alpujarras.[24]

Stigmatisation and inquisitorial repression reinforced cohesion and a feeling of belonging among those who, more or less, clandestinely followed the faith and rites of their ancestors. For the Moriscos and crypto-Jews were not just groups of individuals who shared a conviction that their salvation lay in their Law; they formed imagined communities who gave themselves a common history and their own social fabric, one marked by secrecy.

Clandestinity and community cohesion

Forced into clandestinity, although, one imagines, to a lesser extent in the case of Moriscos, who more often lived "amongst themselves," crypto-Jews and crypto-Muslims constituted groups that, in many respects, resemble the secret societies analysed by Georg Simmel.[25] Welded together by secrecy, the group puts up a united front at different scales (local, regional, diasporic). The cohesive effect of clandestinity was all the stronger in that there was no internal partitioning, since reputation and mutual recognition were key principles, especially among the crypto-Jews. This helps to explain – independently perhaps of the reality of religious practices – the large number of arrests by the Inquisition. Indeed, the arrest of a single individual who testified even vaguely to what he had seen or heard could result in the arrest of all the others. This collective dimension of identity is akin to a form of co-substance where, according to Simmel, "the necessity of depending upon tradition from person to person, and the fact that the spring of knowledge flowed only from within the society not from an objective piece of literature – this attached the individual member with unique intimacy to the community. It gave him the feeling that if he were detached from this substance, he would lose his own, and would never recover it elsewhere."[26]

Certainly, as we shall see, the absence of traditional references to faith and ritual must be relativised among the Moriscos, in particular before the Expulsion. The metaphor of the body and a sense of quasi-mystical unity, seemingly stronger for the crypto-Jews, are found, for example, in the phrases "All are one" and "All make but one," recurrent in the inquisitorial trials when those giving testimonies sought to describe the interdependence of the crypto-Jews – unless this was an addition by the scribe of the Holy Office.[27] This notion similarly appears in texts written against both Moriscos and conversos. For instance, in 1674, Francisco de Torrejoncillo dedicated the eighth chapter of his *Centinela contra Judíos* to the Jews who "wherever they may be, stick together and form a mystical body." This notion is also used against the Moriscos, especially in relation to the Expulsion, where the Morisco stereotype is reified so as to facilitate their "elimination" from the body social.[28] Thus, for Pedro Aznar Cardona, in his *Expulsión justificada de los Moriscos españoles [...]* (Huesca, 1612), "the great and the small, all were one in error and apostasy."[29]

The sense of unity and the importance of collective identity were reinforced by the practices surrounding secrecy, including initiation rites, codes of recognition, and, for some Moriscos, the use of Arabic, which distinguished the insider from the outsider. In public places in Seville, for example, groups of Moriscos in 1580 reportedly spoke *algarabía*, an Arabic dialect progressively mixed with Spanish, so as not to be understood by the rest of the population.[30] This also explains the formula "to declare oneself as observant of the Law of Moses," which allowed the crypto-Jews to recognise one another as Judaizers and members of the group. In 1653 Lucrecia Nuñez, from Lamego, Portugal, confessed to having fasted in Madrid for the three days of Queen Esther (Purim) with the crypto-Jews who lived in the same house as her: "all of them revealed [*dieron quenta*] and told each other and each separately that they were fasting during those days out of observance and respect for the said law [...] and after this episode all of them were declared and known [*declarados y conocidos*] as observers and believers in the law of Moses and as such frequented and discussed with one another without any distrust."[31] This mutual recognition – with strong performative value since it "makes" the Judaizer, both in his or her own eyes and those of others – is simultaneously a profession of faith and a rallying symbol for the secret society formed by the community. It, moreover, enables, in a context of clandestinity, members of the group to satisfy their need to display their belonging.

When subjected to repression and the suspicious gaze of neighbours, the home becomes the place of self-revelation and clandestine practices, whereas the public space is one of simulation and dissimulation. Though usually involving only the immediate family, this domestic religiosity could also bring together members of the same network, creating what inquisitors called a "complicity" (*complicidad*). For instance, at the turn of the sixteenth and seventeenth centuries, the rich Morisco widow Maria Xaramfa hosted Friday night meetings in a large room of her house in the suburb of Segorbe, north of Valencia, an area with a strong Morisco presence. The town's Morisco community seemingly gave her 30 ducats to use her house as a "mosque" and paid "three poor women to wash and clean it for the four celebrations of the year." Black and white carpets with the hand of Fatima (*khamsa*) could also be found there, the hand being a symbol often found among the Moriscos, for whom the five fingers represented the five pillars of Islam.[32] The aforementioned meetings were led by Miguel Gavany (or Gavari), an *alfaquí* (doctor of Islamic law) who read the Koran and taught the "Mahoma ceremonies." Other Moriscos, including Geronimo Lupe *alias* Payo and Pedro Rasin *alias* Claves, were trained there to become *alfaquíes*.[33] The presence and knowledge of these *alfaquíes* – numerous in regions such as Valencia[34] – in ritual and dogmatic matters was one of the major differences between Moriscos and crypto-Jews.

An emphasis on the home and the rituals connected to it brought to the fore the role of women.[35] This was especially true for crypto-Jewish women, who took on important socio-religious functions, especially given the centrality of the purificatory rites they performed (feeding, body care, preparation of objects) and their transmission of the faith to children. Some women even became domestic preachers, as did Angela, a 70-year-old Morisco woman from Cordoba who was sentenced to burn at the stake during the auto-da-fé staged in Cordoba on January 21, 1590. A dozen of her supposed co-religionists are said to have described her as "teacher and dogmatist [*dogmatizadora*] of the sect of Mohammed and [to have said that] her house [served] as a mosque and [that] she alerted the others as to when the fast of Ramadan and the religious festivals of the Moors [*moros*] fell."[36] That said, this female ritual visibility seems to have been more predominant among the crypto-Jews, as it was closely tied to the professional mobility of husbands who were often merchants. In contrast, Moriscos were commonly craftsmen or farmers and generally more sedentary. It appears that Morisco women attracted less attention from the Holy Office than did converso women, with the exception of those designated as *dogmatizadoras* or *alfaquinas*.[37]

The quintessence of the crypto-Jewish woman was embodied by the figure of Queen Esther, the symbol and emblem of the crypto-Jewish soul and destiny. The wife of the Persian king Ahasuerus, whose name refers to the secret (*seter*), had concealed her Jewishness, but upon learning that the Jews in the Empire were threatened, she interceded on their behalf. This probably explains why the three days ritually dedicated to her dominate the crypto-Judaic calendar and why her fasting takes precedence over all other feasts. This importance of women in crypto-Judaism also manifested itself in the emergence of a new function, that of the professional faster. These were often poor, elderly, and widowed women who were paid to abstain from food in the name and place of a co-religionist, i.e. to perform the fundamental rite of crypto-Judaism. The fasts asked of them were paid for according to an established price scale. The fasting woman could also be hired to assist the dying, as did Ana Maria of Andujar, in Andalusia, who in July 1649 accompanied the wife of Pedro Marcos de Espinosa in her final moments, and for whom she fasted for eight days. Pedro then gave her some clothes, including a waistcoat and petticoats "left behind by the deceased."[38]

The impact of repression and clandestinity in terms of cohesion and affirmation of difference is certainly not specific to the Spanish case. It was also apparent during the same period among English Catholics, repressed since the Reformation of the mid-sixteenth century, and, in some respects, among the French crypto-Protestants after the revocation of the Edict of Nantes in 1685. As in the case of Moriscos and crypto-Jews, the place to practice a forbidden religion was often for these groups the home. An example is the residence of the Vaux, Catholics living in Harrowden, north of London, dedicated to the Virgin of Loreto in the 1590s. Baroness Vaux set up secret rooms for visiting priests, including her confessor, the Jesuit John Gerard.[39] Meanwhile, French (crypto-) Protestants used coded language to communicate, among other things, the date, place, and time of clandestine synods. In the 1730s and 1740s, they referred to such synods as the "general fair," the "sacred college," or the "class" while to refer to a gathering for worship ("assemblée," often in a clearing or in the forest), they spoke of "marriage."[40]

If religious clandestinity and inquisitorial repression were undeniable constraints for Moriscos and crypto-Jews, they were nonetheless fundamental. They structured forms of sociability and communal space and bound together the group and individuals. Clandestinity and repression also explain certain forms of solidarity and even occasional collaboration between Moriscos and crypto-Jews.[41] Through linguistic codes, initiation rites, and their own unique myths, they paradoxically constituted instruments of identity-construction. Nevertheless, the importance of ritual practices, both individual and collective, should not be underestimated. Belonging to the group was achieved through the intention of the gesture, tirelessly repeated and reinvented, each reiteration potentially leading to a change in details.

Ritualising everyday life

As a general rule, because they were obliged to simulate and dissimulate, crypto-Jews and Moriscos tended to resort to discreet religious practices confined to the home. Prayer and food – the preparation of dishes and meals, or their absence, fasting – were prioritised. Likewise, because they were often far from the normative sources of Judaism and Islam – at least after the Expulsion in the case of the Moriscos – they seemed to have focused on ritual at the expense of dogma. That said, the latter, centring on anxiety over salvation, was important too. This led to a certain complexification, in the sense of an increased ritualisation of daily practices, and even resulted in a degree of invention in each community, family, or individual. Particular objects, sacred or profane, thus saw their ritual significance increase as they became more clandestine, spurring the development of a new gestural corpus. This phenomenon similarly occurred among other clandestine religious minorities, such as the English Catholics with the rosary.[42] These recompositions and the instability of the ritual corpus were legitimised, in the eyes of the actors themselves, by the danger posed by the Inquisitorial threat and the suspicious gaze of the neighbourhood. The ritual modifications also explain the critiques conversos and Moriscos were subjected to outside of Spain. Thus, among the Iberian Jews, certain *responsa* indicate that rabbis considered the conversos as *meshumadim* (apostates), voluntary converts who, because they continued living in idolatry in Spain, had lost their status as *anusim* (forced converts).[43] Yet many among the Judeo-Iberian diaspora insisted instead on the sacrifice they had made in the name of the faith. For the Moriscos, two principles, *taqiyya*, which authorised dissimulation and the departure from Muslim precepts in situations of danger, and *niyya*, which prioritised internal intention over external practice, were legitimised by certain normative Muslim texts, including the *fatwa* addressed to the Moriscos of Granada by the Mufti of Oran in 1504. That said, the extent of the diffusion and use of these principles remains a point of debate among historians.[44]

A distinction should also be made between crypto-Jews and Moriscos in that the latter maintained a much more pronounced corpus of Islamic cultural and religious traditions, at least until the Expulsion, although this varied greatly from region to region.[45] For example, Arabic was still spoken in areas such as Granada and Valencia, as well as written in the form of *Aljamía* (or *Aljamiado*), Spanish in Arabic characters. Its use would have spread with the deportation of Moriscos from Granada to places where it was less common.[46] Moreover, the Moriscos had easier access to normative religious sources, chiefly because of the above-mentioned *alfaquíes*; the same was true of traditional texts. Thus, many of those accused by the inquisitorial court of Valencia in the years 1580–1600 had a Koran, which was sometimes found during their arrest. In the region of Zaragoza, until the Expulsion, scribes produced copies of the Koran and even translated them into Spanish in order to sell them to Moriscos in the area.[47] This was perhaps also the case for the Granadino Juan Valenciano who, in the early seventeenth century, had a shop in Seville and was accused of leading Muslim prayers in his home at night. While reading from the Koran, he would explain how to pray or perform Ramadan. According to one witness, they prayed together three times a day after their ablutions, heads bowed, punctuating their orisons with "God is great" in Arabic.[48] In addition to prayers and ablutions, it seems that it was food practices (especially the preparation of meat) and fasts[49] (particularly Ramadan) that most persisted – at least according to the inquisitorial trials. Finally, the customary use of "Moorish" names, which doubled Christian names for many Moriscos, helped create a specific communal space.[50]

Among crypto-Jews, food and its exclusion, the fast, seem to have had a much more central function in the calendar of worship than they did for Jews elsewhere who were not subject to repression. Even if crypto-Jews did not know or observe all the Judaic dietary prescriptions, they kept track of them, notably the prohibition of pork, as did Moriscos. Complexification of the ways in which meals were prepared contributed to the sacralisation of daily life and formed the bedrock of crypto-Judaism.[51] Thus, unable to perform the ritual slaughter, crypto-Jews nevertheless tried to slit the animals' throats with a perfectly sharp knife. The day before consumption, they would remove the blood, fat, and sciatic nerve from the meat and wash it thoroughly. This preparation brought some sixteenth-century crypto-Jews closer to the Moriscos. Indeed, some ate the animals that the Moriscos had slaughtered and prepared, claiming that their methods satisfied Mosaic custom. These ritual and sometimes spiritual similarities between the two groups appear on various occasions starting in the sixteenth century.[52] The making of unleavened bread (*cenceño*) was also of considerable importance, as was its placement on the table during the meal. The separation of the first portion of dough, thrown into the fire, in memory of the sacrifice in the Temple, seems to have been intermittently practised until the end of the sixteenth century. Yet, beyond these traces of Judaic ritual, certain innovations were strictly crypto-Judaic. For example, in Coria (del Rio), in the region of Seville, while kneading bread Manuel Ribero and his relatives (accused by the Holy Office in 1620)

> made little balls of dough and threw them into the embers and if they jumped from the fire, they took them out, and ground them and from their powder, [with] rosemary and cotton, made amulets in little bags and wore them hanging on their bodies, on their coats and belts, and the aforesaid Manuel Ribero wore it around his neck and another little ball wrapped in a paper on his belt.[53]

Besides amulets, which were common among the crypto-Jews, everything was, for them, potentially a "source of religious energy," and the making of even the smallest object of worship required a slew of operations.[54] The meticulousness of the gestures and scrupulous respect for their sequence gave the objects their sacredness. This is exemplified in the candles to which the crypto-Jews of Andujar, in 1649, added new wicks each Friday night: "especially one, which they put in a candleholder and placed in the room where they slept, [and that] burned all night without anyone touching it, as doing so was said to be a sin under the Law of Moses."[55] The same sacralisation surrounded the objects – as well as individuals – that came from the diaspora.

The religiosity of the crypto-Jews and Moriscos benefitted, in fact, from the inputs of their respective diasporas, through the circulation of objects and individuals. It is known that travel back and forth between, on the one hand, Muslim lands and Judeo-Iberian communities and, on the other, the Iberian Peninsula was not uncommon. For the crypto-Jews, it included both former conversos and Jews born and raised in Judaism.[56] The habitual nature of these trips is illustrated by the 1662 testimony of Francisco Roldan, who was born in Portugal and lived in the Judeo-Iberian community in Hamburg for about ten years before moving to Andalusia. When the inquisitorial court asked him which people in the Jewish congregations "where he had been, who were baptised and came from those kingdoms [Spain and Portugal], habitually came to trade there," Roldan replied that Antonio Lopez Gomez, a Lisbon native who had become a Jew in Amsterdam, often went to Murcia to buy silk, frequently with Isaac Castiel, a Jew born in Amsterdam.[57]

Although this circulation was less marked among the Moriscos, it nevertheless existed, as attested by the number of Moriscos from the Maghreb indicted for Muslim practices by the Holy Office.[58] Like Maghrebi Jews, such as the members of the Zaportas and Cansino families who served as mediators between Morocco and Spain until their expulsion from Oran in 1669[59] and travelled around Spain with a licence, official Muslims were also present in Spain. These were diplomats or, of course, the many slaves who had come from a Muslim country through the slave trade or war.[60] For instance, the Morisco Juan Valenciano, who we saw acting as an *alfaquí* in Seville, declared that he had been converted and instructed in Islam at the turn of the seventeenth century by a *"moro de galera* [galley]."[61] It is known, moreover, that from 1733 onwards a house used as a hospital and mosque existed in Cartagena for free Muslims. It was destroyed in 1770 at the request of the Inquisition when orders were given to expel the Moors from Muslim countries, though the protests of the Dey of Algiers led to its reconstruction in 1774.[62] In addition, the renegades who had resided in the Ottoman Empire and who lived in captivity until their redemption and return to Spain exerted ritual and spiritual influence. In short, though the status of these Muslims is often difficult to determine, their presence in the Peninsula seems nonetheless confirmed by different types of sources. Thus, in 1629, in Moron de la Frontera, Andalusia, there were those who complained that the Moors "live publicly under their Law, celebrate their marriages as if they were in Barbary, and encourage each other not to become Christians." In Cadiz, the local authorities counted 3000 Muslims and called for the number of slaves to be reduced to one per owner.[63]

Certainly, the religious input of these visitors and "foreigners" depended on their ritual knowledge, time spent in an official Jewish or Muslim community, and the length of their stay in Spain. They could actively transmit snippets of the normative religions or pass them on in a more diffuse way, through conversations or in a moment of their own religious life. Often, when they were aware of the necessity of clandestinity, they adapted their discourse and description of religious practices to their audience and their living conditions. These elements were then shared and altered along sociability networks. If it had less of an overall impact than, for example, the contribution of Catholic missionaries in the British Isles, the effect of these visitors was still far from negligible, as the Inquisition was well aware. This was all the more apparent in that these individuals sometimes carried ritual instruments or, more frequently, texts in the form of books or simple leaflets. In the 1630s and 1640s, for example, Jacob Cansino of Oran, interpreter for the King of Spain, and thus holding a license, gathered around him in Madrid a small circle of Maghrebi Jews. Using several ritual books in Hebrew, he instructed the crypto-Jews of the capital.[64] These texts were also sent clandestinely by relatives in the diaspora and then passed on from person to person or were recopied in Spain. This was what happened with a leaflet giving the equivalences between the Christian and Mosaic calendars that was published in Amsterdam in 1638 by Juda Machabeu under the title *Calendario de las fiestas que celebran los Hebreos*, as an appendix to his ritual book, and which was found in Malaga the following year.[65]

Conclusions

In the face of repression and stigmatisation, many conversos and Moriscos – though not all, far from it – resisted through their social and religious practices. The tightening of the community, accentuated by clandestinity, cannot, in fact, be read solely through the prism of religion. Certainly, spirituality and ritual had places in their own right, beyond the forms of syncretism that have often attracted the attention of historians. For their spiritual and ritual corpus must be considered as original constructions having established referents independent of their respective sources, Christianity, Judaism, and Islam. What is more, it is arguably the act and the belief that, above all, matter, as much as (or more than?) their normative content. The group, which cannot be considered an a priori and homogeneous given, only forms a "community of believers" insofar as the religious dimension is central to it. Yet, ultimately, belonging to the group seems more important than the truth on which it is based.[66] These practices and beliefs were, moreover, intertwined with a multiplicity of factors variably articulated in individuals' lives and according to context. In this regard, the socio-economic differences between these two populations should be underlined: the relative mobility, dispersion, and invisibility of the crypto-Jews, often in urban areas, versus the comparatively sedentary lifestyle, concentration, and visibility of the Moriscos, more commonly in the countryside. The strong internal heterogeneity of both of these groups, as much social as religious, must also be emphasised. Among them, there was the "main core," highly endogamous and deeply marked by religion and the defence of their clandestine identity, but there were also those at the margins, tied less strongly to the core group, where unions with Old Christians were not rare. As is often the case, here the construction of identity has a cumulative and unstable character that should neither be oversimplified nor reified. It was not binary. It took shape through constant interactions with multiple and shifting alterities: between crypto-Jews and Moriscos and their co-religionists outside Spain, but also between these clandestine communities and Hispanic Catholic society. That said, both groups did adopt certain traits specific to early modern Iberian societies, including the emphasis placed on origin and blood, shaped in this context by the effects of repression and clandestinity. Belonging is both given and constructed, individual and collective. The group becomes a mystical body whose survival is each and every member's responsibility.

Notes

* This research has been supported by the project *Ser Diáspora. Dispersión, Conexión e Integración de algunas minorías en los espacios euromediterráneos (ss. XVI-XVII)* [GV/2020/078].

1 Madrid, Archivo Histórico Nacional [hereafter AHN], Inquisition [hereafter INQ], Book 787, ff. 57–63, quoted in José Simón Díaz, "La Inquisición de Logroño (1570–1580)," *Berceo. Boletín del Instituto de estudios riojanos* I (1946), 98.

2 AHN INQ, Legajo 1953 (74), ed. José María García Fuentes, *Visitas de la Inquisición al Reino de Granada* (Granada: Universidad de Granada, 2006), 139–40.

3 The validity of inquisitorial trials as sources of information on the religious and social practices of the accused has been the subject of much discussion among historians, particularly with regard to crypto-Judaism. A more "traditional" line of research, led by Ytzak Baer, Haim Beinart, and Cecil Roth, supports the existence of crypto-Judaism, contrasts with the work of Antonio J. Saraiva and Benzion Netanyahu, among others, which contests its magnitude.

4 Note the difference between New Christians, conversos or Moriscos, descendants of converted Jews or Moors without religious connotation, and those accused of secretly practising the religion of their ancestors: crypto-Jews – in English and Spanish also called conversos – and crypto-Muslims similarly designated as Moriscos.

5 The bibliography on Moriscos and crypto-Jews is extensive. On Moriscos, see, e.g. Mercedes García-Arenal, *Inquisición y Moriscos: Los procesos del Tribunal de Cuenca* (Madrid: Siglo XXI, 1978); Miguel de Epalza, *Los Moriscos antes y después de la expulsión* (Madrid: MAPFRE, 1992); Bernard Vincent, *El río Morisco* (Valencia: Universitat de València, 2006); Isabelle Poutrin, *Convertir les musulmans. Espagne, 1491–1609* (Paris: Puf, 2012). About conversos, see notably David M. Gitlitz, *Secrecy and Deceit: The Religion of the Crypto-Jews* (Philadelphia: The Jewish Publication Society, 1996); Pilar Huerga Criado, *En la raya de Portugal. Solidaridad y tensiones en la comunidad judeoconversa* (Salamanca: Universidad de Salamanca, 1993); Renée Levine Melammed, *A Question of Identity. Iberian Conversos in Historical Perspective* (Oxford: Oxford University Press, 2004); Natalia Muchnik, *De paroles et de gestes. Constructions marranes en terre d'Inquisition* (Paris: EHESS, 2014).

6 Fredrik Barth, *Process and Form in Social Life* (London: Routledge & Kegan Paul, 1981), 79–81.

7 See footnote 3.

8 The first Purity of Blood statute was instituted in 1449 and banned New Christians from holding various offices in the jurisdiction of Toledo and then served as a model for the statutes of Toledo's Cathedral Chapter in 1547. These were then gradually adopted by most institutions. See, *inter alia*, Juan Hernández Franco, *Cultura y limpieza de sangre en la España moderna. Puritas Sanguinis* (Murcia: Universidad de Murcia, 1996) and *Sangre limpia, sangre española. El debate de los estatutos de limpieza (siglos XV-XVIII)* (Madrid: Cátedra, 2011); Albert Sicroff, *Les controverses des statuts de pureté de sang en Espagne, du XVe au XVIIe siècle* (Paris: Didier, 1960).

9 Bernard Vincent estimates that 30–40,000 Moriscos may have remained after the Expulsion, a number to which must be added those who returned. Bernard Vincent, "Les musulmans dans l'Espagne moderne," in *Les musulmans dans l'histoire de l'Europe, I. Une intégration invisible*, ed. Jocelyne Dakhlia and Bernard Vincent (Paris: Albin Michel, 2011), 615. See, among others, Trevor J. Dadson, *Los Moriscos de Villarrubia de los Ojos (siglos XV-XVIII). Historia de una minoría asimilada, expulsada y reintegrada* (Madrid-Frankfurt: Iberoamericana-Vervuert, 2007); James B. Tueller, "The Moriscos Who Stayed Behind or Returned. Post-1609," in *The Expulsion of the Moriscos from Spain. A Mediterranean Diaspora,*

ed. Mercedes García-Arenal and Gerard Wiegers (Leiden: Brill, 2014), 197–216; Esteban Mira Caballos, "Unos se quedaron y otros volvieron. Moriscos en la Extremadura del siglo XVII," *XXXIX Coloquios Históricos de Extremadura. Trujillo del 20 al 26 de septiembre de 2010* (Trujillo: Ayuntamiento de Trujillo, 2011), 459–88.

10 Esther Alegre Carvajal, *La villa ducal de Pastrana* (Guadalajara: Aache, 2003).

11 Some, like Antonio J. Saraiva (*The Marrano Factory. The Portuguese Inquisition and Its New Christians, 1536–1765*, Leiden: Brill, 2001) and Benzion Netanyahu (*The Origins of the Inquisition in Fifteenth Century Spain*, New York: Random House, 1995), focus on the political and economic factors of inquisitorial activity, reducing the reality of prosecuted faith crimes. Others stress the social or even "ethnic" bias of the charges, since it is often the inquisitorial gaze that classifies heresies according to the origin of individuals. The same elements are qualified as crypto-Judaism or crypto-Islam depending on the origin of the individuals – a process which could refute the reality of the crimes.

12 Charles Amiel, "Crypto-judaïsme et Inquisition. La matière juive dans les édits de la foi des Inquisitions ibériques," *Revue de l'Histoire des Religions* 210 (1993), 145–68.

13 Natalia Muchnik, "La conversion en héritage. Crypto-judaïsants dans l'Europe des XVIe et XVIIe siècles (Espagne, France, Angleterre)," *Histoire, économie & société* 4 (2014), 10–24.

14 See particularly the work of Enrique Soria, including "Falsificadores, usurpadores y herejes. La familia Baños de Granada, de Moriscos islamizantes a marqueses," *eHumanista* 40 (2018), 296–315.

15 Ruth Pike, *Linajudos and Conversos in Seville: Greed and Prejudice in Sixteenth- and Seventeenth-Century Spain* (New York: Peter Lang, 2000); Monique Combescure Thiry and Miguel Angel Motis Dolader, eds., *El libro verde de Aragón* (Zaragoza: Certeza, 2003).

16 The literature on the Expulsion is extensive. See, e.g. Luis Bernabé Pons, *Los Moriscos. Conflicto, expulsión y diaspora* (Madrid: Catarata, 2009); M. García-Arenal and G. Wiegers, eds., *The Expulsion*; Bernard Vincent, ed, *Comprender la expulsión de los Moriscos de España (1609–1614)* (Oviedo: Universidad de Oviedo, 2020).

17 Contrary to the image that is sometimes presented, Morisco difference cannot be caricatured. See, e.g. Israel Lasmarías Ponz, "Vestir al Morisco, vestir a la morisca. El traje de los Moriscos en Aragón en la Edad Moderna," *30 años de mudejarismo. Memoria y futuro (1975–2005), Actas del X Simposio Internacional de Mudejarismo. Teruel, 14–16 septiembre 2005* (Teruel: Instituto de Estudios Turolenses, 2007), 629–42; more broadly, Dadson, *Los Moriscos*.

18 Georg Simmel, *Stigma: Notes on the Management of Spoiled Identity* (Englewood Cliffs: Prentice Hall, 1963).

19 See, e.g. Natalia Muchnik, *Une vie marrane. Les pérégrinations de Juan de Prado dans l'Europe du XVIIe siècle* (Paris: Honoré Champion, 2005), 341–89; Stuart B. Schwartz, *All Can Be Saved: Religious Tolerance and Salvation in the Iberian Atlantic World* (New Haven, CT: Yale University Press, 2008).

20 Manuel Barrios Aguilera and Mercedes García-Arenal, eds., *Los Plomos del Sacromonte. Invención y tesoro* (Valencia: Universitat de València, 2006).

21 Muchnik, *De paroles*, 39–41.

22 Luis Bernabé Pons, "Identity, Mixed Unions and Endogamy of the Moriscos: The Assimilation of the New Converts Revisited," *Mediterranean Historical Review* 35 (2020), 79–99.

23 Enric Porqueres i Gené, *Lourde alliance. Mariage et identité chez les descendants de juifs convertis à Majorque (1435–1750)* (Paris: Kimé, 1995), 227–30.

24 Mercedes García-Arenal, *Messianism and Puritanical Reform: Mahdîs of the Muslim West* (Leiden: Brill, 2006), 315–24 and "Un réconfort pour ceux qui sont dans l'attente. Prophétie et millénarisme dans la péninsule Ibérique et au Maghreb (XVIᵉ-XVIIᵉ siècles)," *Revue de l'histoire des religions* 220 (2003), 445–86. Also, see Mayte Green-Mercado, *Visions of Deliverance: Moriscos and the Politics of Prophecy in the Early Modern Mediterranean* (Ithaca-London: Cornell University Press, 2019).

25 Georg Simmel, "The Sociology of Secrecy and of Secret Societies," *American Journal of Sociology* 11 (1906), 441–98.

26 Simmel, "The Sociology," 475.

27 Muchnik, *De paroles*, 57–60.

28 José María Perceval, *Todos son uno. Arquetipos, xenofobia y racismo. La imagen del Morisco en la Monarquía Española durante los siglos XVI y XVII* (Almeria: Instituto de Estudios Almerienses, 1997), 185; François Martinez, *La permanence morisque en Espagne après 1609* (Villeneuve d'Ascq: Presses Universitaires du Septentrion, 2002).

29 Biblioteca Nacional de España, R-2856, f. 112ʳ, quoted in Julio Caro Baroja, *Razas, pueblos y linajes* (Madrid: Revista de Occidente, 1957), 94.

30 Michel Boeglin, *Entre la Cruz y el Corán. Los Moriscos en Sevilla (1570–1613)* (Seville: Ayuntamiento de Sevilla-ICAS, 2010), 73.

31 AHN INQ, Book 1117, f. 13ʳ (Maria Lorenzo's Trial).

32 AHN INQ, Book 938, f. 416ᵛ, quoted in Raphaël Carrasco, *La monarchie catholique et les Morisques (1520–1620). Études franco-espagnoles* (Montpellier: ETILAL-Université Paul Valéry, 2005), 48–9; Ana Labarta, "La cultura de los Moriscos valencianos," *Sharq al-Andalus* 20 (2011–2013), 233–4.

33 AHN INQ, Legajos 548 (6) and 553 (16), quoted in Louis Cardaillac, *Morisques et chrétiens: un affrontement polémique (1492–1640)* (Paris: Klincksieck, 1977), 66; Rafael Benítez Sánchez-Blanco, "La fabulosa conjura morisca del Jueves Santo de 1605," in *Pasados y presente. Estudios para el profesor Ricardo García Cárcel*, ed. Rosa Maria Alabrús et al. (Barcelona: Universitat Autònoma de Barcelona, 2020), 255.

34 Around ten or so of these *alfaquíes* (or at least those designated as such) were condemned at the auto-da-fé of 1574, in AHN INQ, Book 936, ff. 111ʳ-113ʳ, quoted in Rafael Carrasco, "Historia de una represión. Los Moriscos y la Inquisición en Valencia, 1566–1620," *Areas. Revista internacional de ciencias sociales* 9 (1988), 40.

35 See Bernard Vincent, "Las mujeres moriscas," in *Historia de las mujeres en Occidente*, ed. Georges Duby and Michelle Perrot (Madrid: Taurus, 1991–1993), III: 585–95; Mary Elizabeth Perry, "Behind the Veil: Moriscas and the Politics of Resistance and Survival," in *Spanish Women in the Golden Age: Image and Realities*, ed. Magdalena S. Sánchez and Alain Saint-Saëns (Wesport: Grennwood Press, 1996), 37–53; Renee Levine Melammed, *Heretics or Daughters of Israel? The Crypto-Jewish Women of Castile* (New York: Oxford University Press, 1999).

36 AHN INQ, Legajo 1856 (33), ff. 18ᵛ-19ʳ, ed. Rafael Gracia Boix, *Autos de fe y causas de la Inquisición de Córdoba* (Cordoba: Diputación Provincial de Córdoba, 1983), 246–7.

37 Carrasco, "Historia de una represión," 32.

38 AHN INQ, Livre 1116, ff. 24ʳ⁻ᵛ.

39 John Gerard, *The Autobiography of an Elizabethan*, ed. Philip Caraman (London: Longmans, Green & Co, 1951), 163; Godfrey Anstruther, *Vaux of Harrowden: A Recusant Family* (Newport: Monmouthshire, 1953).

40 Edmond Hugues, *Les synodes du Désert* (Paris: Fischbacher, 1885), vols. LV and LVII.

41 Claude B. Stuczynski, "Two Minorities Facing the Iberian Inquisition: The 'Marranos' and the 'Moriscos'," *Hispania Judaica* 3 (2000), 134–5; Natalia Muchnik, "Judeoconversos and Moriscos in the Diaspora," in *The Expulsion*, ed. M. García-Arenal and G. Wiegers, 434–6.

42 See, e.g. Alexandra Walsham, "Beads, Books and Bare Ruined Choirs: Transmutations of Catholic Ritual Life in Protestant England," in *Catholic Communities in Protestant States. Britain and the Netherlands, c. 1570–1720*, ed. Benjamin Kaplan et al. (Manchester: Manchester University Press, 2009), 103–22; Natalia Muchnik, "*Conversos* vs. Recusants: Shaping the Markers of Difference (1570–1680). A comparison," in *Religious Changes and Cultural Transformations in the Early Modern Western Sephardi Communities*, ed. Yosef Kaplan (Leiden: Brill, 2019), 50–6.

43 Analysis of the *responsa* was been widely debated. See Benzion Netanyahu, *The 'marranos' of Spain from the Late XIVth to Early XVIth Century* (New York: American Academy for Jewish Research, 1966); Moisés Orfalí, *Los conversos españoles en la literature rabínica: problemas jurídicos y opiniones legales durante los siglos XII–XVIII* (Salamanca: Universidad Pontificia, 1982).

44 Youssef El Alaoui, "¿De Christo con el alma mora, o de Mahoma con el bautismo de Christo? Morisques et dissimulation: entre taquiyya et niyya," *Les cahiers du Framespa* 34 (2020) and "Taqiyya: Disimulo legal," *Al-Qantara* 34 (2013), 345–55.

45 Vincent, *El río*, 156–7.

46 Bernard Vincent, *L'Islam d'Espagne au XVIe siècle. Résistances identitaires des morisques* (Saint-Denis: Bouchène, 2017), 105–7.

47 Ronald E. Surtz, "Morisco Women, Written Texts, and the Valencia Inquisition," *The Sixteenth Century Journal* XXXII (2001), 421–33.

48 AHN INQ, Legajo 2075 (19) and (20), quoted in Mary Elizabeth Perry, *The Handless Maiden. Moriscos and the Politics of Religion in Early Modern Spain* (Princeton, NJ: Princeton University Press, 2005), 79; Boeglin, *Entre la Cruz*, 98–9.

49 Santiago La Parra López, "Las comidas y los ayunos de los Moriscos. Datos para una convivencia en el ducado de Gandía," *Mélanges de la Casa de Velázquez* 47 (2017), 233–53.

50 Bernard Vincent, "Les morisques et les prénoms chrétiens," in *Les morisques et leur temps*, ed. Louis Cardaillac (Paris: CNRS, 1983), 59–69.

51 See David M. Gitlitz and Linda Kay Davidson, *A Drizzle of Honey. The Lives and Recipes of Spain's Secret Jews* (New York: St. Martin's Press, 1999).

52 Stuczynski, "Two Minorities," 136–7.

53 AHN INQ, Legajo 2075 (25).

54 Emile Durkheim, *Les Formes élémentaires de la vie religieuse. Le système totémique en Australie* (Paris: Puf, 1968), 599, 698.

55 AHN INQ, Book 1112, f. 26ʳ.

56 See, e.g. Yosef Kaplan, "The Travels of Portuguese Jews from Amsterdam to the 'Lands of Idolatry' (1644-1724)," in *Jews and Conversos: Studies in Society and the Inquisition*, ed. Y. Kaplan (Jerusalem: The Magnes Press, 1985), 197–224; Natalia Muchnik, "Des intrus en pays d'Inquisition: présence et activités des juifs dans l'Espagne du XVIIe siècle," *Revue des Études Juives* 164 (2005), 119–56.

57 AHN INQ, Book 1131, ff. 198ʳ⁻ᵛ.

58 Bernard Vincent, "Musulmans et conversion en Espagne au XVIe siècle," in *Conversions islamiques. Identités religieuses en Islam méditerranéen*, ed. Mercedes García-Arenal (Paris: Maisonneuve et Larose-ESF, 2001), 193–205.

59 Jean-Frédéric Schaub, *Les juifs du roi d'Espagne. Oran 1509–1669* (Paris: Hachette, 1999); Mercedes García-Arenal, ed., *Entre el Islam y Occidente. Los judíos maghrebíes en la Edad Moderna* (Madrid: Casa de Velázquez, 2003).

60 The bibliography on slavery in Spain and renegades is extensive. See, e.g. Aurelia Martín Casares and Margarita García Barranco, eds., *La esclavitud negroafricana en la historia de España. Siglos XVI y XVII* (Granada: Comares, 2010); Alessandro Stella, *Histoire d'esclaves dans la péninsule Ibérique* (Paris: EHESS, 2000); Bartolomé Bennassar and Lucile Bennassar, *Les Chrétiens d'Allah. L'histoire extraordinaire des renégats, XVIᵉ et XVIIᵉ siècles* (Paris: Perrin, 1989).
61 Boeglin, *Entre la Cruz*, 99.
62 Maximiliano Barrio Gozalo, *Esclavos y cautivos. Un conflicto entre la cristiandad y el islam en el siglo XVIII* (Valladolid: Junta de Castilla y León, 2004), 154–8.
63 AHN, Consejos, Legajo 43775 and Archivo General de Simancas, Guerra Antigua, Legajo 1876, quoted in B. Vincent, "Les musulmans," 628.
64 N. Muchnik, "Des intrus," and AHN INQ, Books 1108 and 1135, ff. 177ʳ–179ʳ.
65 AHN INQ, Legajo 163 (14).
66 Muchnik, *De paroles*, 12.

5   Memory, Toleration, and Conflict after the French Wars of Religion

David van der Linden

In 1598 King Henry IV issued the Edict of Nantes, which famously ended the French Wars of Religion (1562–1598) by installing a regime of religious toleration. The edict allowed French Calvinists – also known as Huguenots – to publicly worship alongside the Catholic majority and granted them a range of civic rights, including access to the courts, public office, schools, and hospitals. Yet the king was well aware that if this state-sanctioned experiment in toleration was to succeed, both confessions had to refrain from seeking retribution for the massacres, forced displacements, and looting of property that had punctuated the wars. The first article of the Edict of Nantes thus ordered French men and women to forget the troubles, decreeing that "the memory of all things that have happened on either side shall remain extinguished and suppressed, as if they had never taken place."[1]

The aim of this chapter is to examine the relationship between toleration and memory in the aftermath of the French religious wars. Historians have often argued that the Edict of Nantes ushered in a period of coexistence, as they have found evidence in communities across France that toleration before the law translated into cross-confessional interactions. For example, Catholics and Protestants were able to regulate their religious differences through pragmatic arrangements, including parity in law courts and government, the sharing of cemeteries, and the construction of Protestant churches outside Catholic towns. In many cities, they also did business together and intermarried.[2] Yet the past was never entirely forgotten. As this chapter will argue, Catholics and Protestants continued to revisit the wars throughout the seventeenth century, in particular the violence and material losses they had suffered at the hands of the other. Tales of cold-blooded murder and iconoclastic fury allowed them to solidify a group identity based on victimhood, but they also fuelled religious hatred and undermined coexistence. These memories, moreover, were passed down to future generations who had not lived through the wars, thus perpetuating religious tensions for decades. As such, memories of civil war formed a major obstacle to toleration and had the potential to undo the fragile bonds between the two confessions.

To understand the relationship between memory and toleration, this chapter adopts a local approach. Given that both the remembering of past events and

DOI: 10.4324/9781003030522-8

the getting along with members of another faith are social practices above all – in other words, they are things that people *do* – we can only study these phenomena on the ground. My focus will be on the post-war memory cultures of La Rochelle, a port city on the Atlantic coast that initially refused to be drawn into the religious wars, until in 1568 the Huguenots seized control of urban government and banned Catholic worship. La Rochelle would remain a bastion of the Reformed movement for three decades, until the Edict of Nantes forced the Protestants to allow the reintroduction of Catholicism. Comparing the memory practices of Catholics and Huguenots in this bi-confessional city after 1598 reveals the extent to which the troublesome past could exert a powerful, even destructive influence on future generations.

Memory and toleration

Before exploring these local tensions, it is important to stress that the concept of "memory" has spawned a wide range of definitions and approaches, in large part because it has attracted scholarly attention from such diverse fields as psychology, sociology, philosophy, literary studies, and history. Strictly speaking, memory is individual and inaccessible to the historian: what people think or remember remains private, unless they choose to share their thoughts with others. Crucial to the study of memory, then, are the ways in which people communicate their memories, either in written form – such as chronicles, diaries, petitions, and court testimonies – or as a material vector, including devotional objects, paintings, and monuments. These "acts of remembering" offer a valuable, if imperfect, testimony of what individuals and communities deem important to remember and transmit to future generations. As Judith Pollmann has argued, memory can be defined as "a form of individual or collective engagement with the past that meaningfully connects the past to the present."[3]

Memory studies have indeed become a flourishing field of historical inquiry, as historians explore the ways in which communities throughout time have remembered their past. Much of this scholarship has focused on the emergence and evolution of a so-called "collective memory": a corpus of memories that is shared by a group of people to such an extent that it comes to define their communal identity and self-understanding. The term was first coined by the French sociologist Maurice Halbwachs. In his book *Les cadres sociaux de la mémoire* (1925), and again in his posthumous *La mémoire collective* (1950), Halbwachs argued that individual memories are dependent on what he called a "social framework": the people, beliefs, and culture to which we belong function as a blueprint that determines how we remember and transmit the past. Ultimately, Halbwachs suggested, our memories are social constructs, more like variations on a common theme than truly unique expressions of our lived past.[4]

Halbwachs' ideas have had a major impact on the field of memory studies as it has developed since the 1990s, especially through the work of the German historians Jan and Aleida Assmann. They have emphasised that remembering also requires forgetting: whenever people enshrine the past, they will select only the most memorable stories for safekeeping and discard those deemed unfit for remembrance. Jan Assmann has noted that historical events initially produce a wealth of personal testimonies that together constitute a "communicative memory"; some people will undoubtedly know more than others, but there are no obvious experts. Over the course of one or more generations, however, memory brokers will select the most relevant memories and weave them into a larger, canonical narrative, which Assmann has labelled "cultural memory." Aleida Assmann has likewise observed that although people have access to a vast reservoir of stories about the past – what she calls a "stored memory"– they will select just a few of these stories to create a "functional memory" and forget about the others.[5]

This creation of cultural and functional memories offers a fruitful avenue for studying the history of early modern toleration. By examining how Catholics and Protestants chose to remember the Wars of Religion, we can get a better sense of how both confessions asserted their religious identity and negotiated their relationship with others – what it meant to be a Catholic or Protestant in a multi-confessional society. Indeed, the link between memory and identity is crucial to understanding practices of toleration: we need memories to know who we are and where we belong, but memories can also set us apart from others and fuel conflict. Historians of the Reformation have called the process of carving out religious identities at the expense of other denominations "confessionalisation," as Catholics and Protestants increasingly stressed the doctrinal and ritual differences that separated them.[6] This chapter will suggest, however, that memories of suffering and past injustice also contributed to the erection of barriers between Protestants and Catholics. In the case of post-war France, two questions will guide this exploration. First, what choices did Huguenots and Catholics make when they remembered the past? And second, what impact did these memories have on religious coexistence between the two groups after 1598? As we shall see, post-war France was a nation divided by memory: although the Edict of Nantes had ostensibly pacified the kingdom, Catholics and Protestants developed antagonistic memories that stressed victimhood and called for retribution, which ultimately undermined the policy of religious toleration.

Remembering and forgetting the Wars of Religion

Although men and women in early modern France were unfamiliar with our modern concepts of collective and cultural memory, they were acutely aware that some form of memory management was required to avoid future conflict. King Henry IV in particular realised that publicly remembering the war's massacres, sieges, and profanation of sacred property would only perpetuate animosity between Catholics and Protestants, which explains why in the Edict of Nantes he ordered his subjects to leave the past behind. The king also prohibited Frenchmen from seeking redress in court and instructed public prosecutors not to investigate crimes committed during the troubles.[7] Henry's decision to bury the memory of the religious wars was hardly novel, as early modern rulers believed almost universally that the forgetting of wartime offences was the best way forward to secure peace and reconciliation. These so-called oblivion clauses were a key element of pacification treaties across Europe, including the Pacification of Ghent (1576) in the Low Countries, the Act of Oblivion (1660) after the English civil war, and the Westphalian Treaty of 1648.[8] The Edict of Nantes likewise drew on previous oblivion clauses, which had been included in each of the pacification edicts issued by the monarchy during the Wars of Religion. The 1563 Edict of Amboise that had ended the first religious war, for example, stipulated that "all insults and offenses, which the inequity of time and the occasions that have arisen as a result may have caused between our subjects, as well as all other things that have occurred or were caused by the present turmoil, shall remain extinguished, as if they are dead, buried, and never took place."[9] Subsequent peace edicts would repeat this clause, until it was integrated into the Edict of Nantes.

The most pressing reason for the monarchy to issue such oblivion clauses was to wipe the slate clean, ensuring that old hatreds would not destroy a hard-won peace. French legal scholars of the time amply theorised the necessity of forgetting the past, in order to transition France from civil war to durable peace and concord. Foremost among them was Antoine Loisel, a lawyer in the Parlement de Paris (the most important court of appeal in France), who, quoting the ancient orator Titus Labienus, argued that *optima belli civilis defensio oblivio est* ("the best defence against civil war is oblivion").[10] Because remembering past injustices only helped to "embitter and renew old wounds," Loisel argued that the best remedy was "to efface everything as quickly as possible, to ensure that nothing remains in the minds of the people on either side, and to never speak or think of it again."[11]

Yet Loisel's passionate defence of expunging the past does not explain how Henry IV expected people to forget about the religious troubles. After all, the monarchy could not police the minds of those who had experienced the wars. Scholars have argued, however, that the aim of these oblivion clauses was not necessarily to impose forgetfulness, but to control public discourse about the past. Both the Edict of Nantes and the preceding edicts of pacification issued a moratorium on evoking or investigating the troubles, which was not quite the same as ordering complete forgetfulness. Injustices committed during the wars were never formally pardoned; rather, by pretending they had never occurred, the monarchy prevented people from acting upon their knowledge of the past, in particular in courts of law. In essence, oblivion was a form of legal amnesia to prevent future conflict.[12] The monarchy essentially hoped that as long as Frenchmen conformed to the public fiction that the religious conflict had never existed, it was possible that its private memory would slowly fade away, too.

Yet despite attempts to police evocations of the past and promote religious coexistence, the wars were not easily forgotten. Recent scholarship has demonstrated that men and women in cities throughout France in fact continued to remember the wars and passed down memories of wartime injustices to future generations.[13] The remainder of this chapter will analyse how in one such locality – the city of La Rochelle – Catholics and Protestants evoked the troubles, and what impact these memories had on practices of toleration. To do so, I will draw on a wide range of memory vectors, including chronicles and petitions as well as material remains, processions, and paintings – at a time when the majority of the urban population was illiterate, material memories were crucial in transmitting stories about the troublesome past.

Chronicling massacre

An obvious way to understand how people remembered the religious wars is to examine the individual testimonies they left behind. Many French citizens composed chronicles to keep a chronological record of events in their city, which could take the form of diaries, retrospective memoirs, or full-fledged histories based on extensive archival research. These chronicles were seldom composed as introspective autobiographies that allowed the author to explore their emotional response to the violence; rather, they recorded their experiences as exemplary tales for future generations, confident in the belief that the past offered useful lessons.[14] Memories of religious violence figured prominently in these chronicles, in particular the many massacres that had occurred throughout the wars, as Catholics and Protestants attempted to purge the urban community of heresy – what, today, we would call ethnic cleansing. Chronicles that discussed these killings are highly indicative of local confessional tensions, since authors typically assigned blame for the violence and wrestled with the question whether or not they should exculpate their own community.

Most scholarship has focused on Protestant accounts of victimhood, in particular regarding the 1572 St Bartholomew's Day Massacre, when Catholics killed an estimated 10,000 Huguenots in Paris and other provincial cities. Yet historians have shown that Protestants also massacred Catholic clergy and citizens in many of the towns they seized by stealth, in particular during the second religious war of 1567–68.[15] Among the key cities affected by this wave of violence was La Rochelle, which was seized by the Huguenots in February 1568. The city's Reformed church had attracted a large number of followers since its official foundation in 1558, including the royal governor Guy Chabot de Jarnac, the city mayor Jean Pineau, and 60 of the 100 *pairs et échevins* (city councillors). Yet the outbreak of civil war in 1562 deeply divided the Huguenot party. A faction of radicals tried to seize control of the city and join the Protestant war effort, but they were thwarted by Jarnac and moderate Protestants on the city council, who successfully defended the city's neutrality and maintained an uneasy religious coexistence with La Rochelle's Catholic population. All of this changed during the second religious war, when the new Protestant mayor François Pontard orchestrated a coup to seize La Rochelle for the Huguenot commander-in-chief, the Prince of Condé. On the morning of January 9, 1568, Pontard led his supporters through the streets, calling the Huguenots to arms and spreading a rumour that the Catholics were plotting to massacre them. After Pontard had wrested control of the city, he invited the sieur Jean de Sainte-Hermine, a lieutenant of Condé, to rule La Rochelle as military governor. Pontard also arrested and imprisoned some 100 inhabitants, including prominent Catholics, all remaining priests and friars, and moderate Protestants who had opposed his coup. The massacre occurred towards the end of February (none of the sources report a precise date), when 27 clergymen held at the medieval Tour du Garrot – also known as the Tour de la Lanterne – were stabbed to death by Huguenot soldiers, who threw their mutilated bodies into the sea below. The men also killed the Protestant prisoner Jacques de la Roue, a *huissier* (usher) in the *présidial* court of La Rochelle and one of Pontard's most vocal critics.[16]

Perhaps not surprisingly, Protestants largely kept silent about the massacre. The city council's official apology for joining forces with Condé, written by the Huguenot *avocat* Jean de La Haize, made no mention of the violence but argued that the takeover of La Rochelle had been necessary to protect the freedom of conscience and defend the interests of the entire French nation.[17] The only contemporary mention of the massacre by a Protestant author occurs in an anonymous chronicle, known as the Baudoin manuscript (so named after its most likely owner), which covers the city's history from medieval times until 1589. The author tried to minimise Protestant culpability, arguing that the capture of La Rochelle had happened peacefully and blaming the massacre on the new governor Sainte-Hermine, who as an outsider had quickly antagonised the Rochelais by imposing heavy taxes and forcing them to construct new fortifications. The chronicler went on to claim that it was the governor who had ordered the priests to jump to their deaths from the Tour du Garrot, thus further absolving the city's Protestants from any wrongdoing.[18]

As perpetrators, the Protestants had every reason to forget the violence or deflect accusations of rebellion, but more surprising is that Catholics hardly spoke about their suffering either. One of the few Catholic sources to mention the massacre is a chronicle kept by the notary Antoine Bernard, who lived 200 km away in the town of Langon, southeast of Bordeaux. News of the killings was reported to him by an eyewitness, François Miglet, who told that the Huguenots had arrested 13 clergymen, "whom they led to the Tour du Garrot, and bound their hands behind their back, and, at the hands of the executioner, threw them down into the sea."[19] The main reason for the lack of Catholic memories in La Rochelle was the Huguenot coup of 1568, which had profoundly altered the confessional balance of power and put limits on what could be remembered. The new city council led by Pontard immediately banned Catholic worship and confiscated the property of those who had fled the city. Successive edicts of pacification only restored Catholicism temporarily, which meant its members struggled to survive in an otherwise Protestant city.[20] The Huguenot domination of La Rochelle also made it possible to impose a partisan memory of the wars and silence counter-narratives. The local Protestant consistory did not hesitate to censure histories that portrayed the wars too even-handedly or that cast doubt on the Huguenot cause. In 1581, for example, the city's leading minister Odet de Nort persuaded the national synod meeting in La Rochelle to censure and subsequently redact the *Histoire de France* by the local historian Lancelot Voisin de La Popelinière, who had suggested the Reformation was the result of popular rebellion and "opinionated" men.[21]

Although the 1598 Edict of Nantes permitted the re-establishment of Catholic worship in La Rochelle, thus making possible the potential recovery of memories about the 1568 massacre, it was not until after the royal siege of 1628 that most exiled Catholics returned to the city. By this time, however, 60 years had passed since the massacre occurred, which explains why it had almost disappeared from urban consciousness. It was precisely to rescue the massacre victims from oblivion that the Augustinian friar Simplicien Saint-Martin included a lengthy overview of friars martyred during the wars in his *Histoire de la vie du glorieux père St Augustin* (1641). Although Saint-Martin served as a professor of theology at the University of Toulouse, rather than in one of La Rochelle's monasteries, he regretted the lack of local chronicles that documented the massacre victims and chastised previous generations for not telling their story. It was crucial "to collect these precious fragments," he wrote, "lest in time their memory should be lost."[22] He began his martyrology with the massacre at La Rochelle, offering details not included in Protestant chronicles: Saint-Martin claimed that governor Sainte-Hermine had arrested no fewer than 77 members of the clergy and commanded them to abjure their faith. When they refused to recant, the Huguenots dragged them to the Tour du Garrot, where they were chained in pairs and thrown down into the sea. Based on documents Saint-Martin had consulted (but did not cite), he believed that as many as 20 Augustinian friars had perished in the massacre.[23] All in all, memories of the 1568 massacre followed a predictable confessional path: Catholics gradually came to identify as victims, while the Huguenots tried to avoid being portrayed as rebels who had resorted to violence.

The memory of iconoclasm

Whereas the 1568 massacre was nearly lost in the fog of time, memories of the material losses suffered by La Rochelle's Catholics persisted throughout the seventeenth century, fuelling tensions between the two faiths. The Protestant iconoclasm that had virtually obliterated the sacred landscape had left deep scars among Catholics, both physical and spiritual. Prior to the Reformation, La Rochelle comprised five parish churches and eight monasteries, all of which had been founded in medieval times; the nearest cathedral was located in Saintes, some 70 km to the southeast.[24] The first iconoclasm occurred in the spring of 1562, just after the outbreak of the civil war. La Rochelle's clandestine Reformed community still worshiped in private, but on 31 May the Huguenot ministers Pierre Richer and Ambroise Faget organised a public celebration of the Lord's Supper on the Place de la Bourserie, an event attended by several thousand Protestants and governor Jarnac. In their sermon, the ministers denounced the recent massacre of Huguenot worshippers at Vassy and the lacklustre efforts of the monarchy to prosecute the perpetrators. The sermon prompted a crowd of between 200 and 300 Protestants to sack all Catholic churches in town, pulling down statues and destroying altars.[25] A second round of destruction took place after the Huguenot coup of 1568. Under the leadership of mayor Pontard and governor Sainte-Hermine, Catholic worship was proscribed and virtually all the churches and monasteries were razed to the ground, their ecclesiastical goods appropriated, and their stones repurposed for the construction of military fortifications. Only the belltowers of St Sauveur and St Barthélémy were left standing, to serve as watchtowers and platforms to attack Catholic assailants with canon fire.[26]

Protestant chroniclers agreed that the less said about the iconoclasm, the better. Although Calvin had argued that worshipping images was idolatrous, he had also condemned acts of vandalism against Catholic churches. Theodore Beza, Calvin's successor in Geneva, likewise insisted that only public authorities were entitled to remove images, not individual worshipers in a frenzy of violence. In his *Histoire écclesiastique des églises réformées au royaume de France* (1580), Beza thus attributed most of the iconoclastic incidents to a few madmen, arguing that Protestant consistories had never condoned the violence.[27] Although he failed to mention the destructions in La Rochelle, local authors adopted his line of defence. The Protestant author of the Baudoin chronicle, for example, mentioned the destructions of 1568 only in passing, while he portrayed the 1562 iconoclasm as an orderly event, noting that "all the idols were torn down and the greater part of the altars destroyed in the churches of La Rochelle, without any tumult or death of any papist or anyone else."[28]

Following the re-establishment of Catholic worship in 1598, Huguenot authors who had not witnessed the events nonetheless felt compelled to defend the iconoclasm of the previous generation. The Huguenot magistrate Amos Barbot, who composed a chronicle of La Rochelle's history in the 1610s, unequivocally blamed the destructions on the *menu peuple* ("the common people") and argued that the Protestant leadership – although they agreed with the removal of images – had not participated in the iconoclasm for fear of being prosecuted. According to Barbot, governor Jarnac had publicly protested his innocence and promised to arrest the perpetrators, although in the end just two men were apprehended.[29] The Huguenot minister Philippe Vincent made a similar distinction in his local history of the Reformed church, written around 1650 (it was only published in 1693). He strongly condemned the iconoclasm as "a sickness that was almost universal," but at the same time he pointed his finger at a select group of image-breakers who had taken matters into their own hands, writing that "for private individuals to undertake this of their own accord, with violence and turmoil, is absolutely seditious and an attack on the authority of the magistrate." Having consulted the consistory acts of the Reformed church, moreover, he assured his readers that the Huguenot ministers had firmly denounced the iconoclasm.[30] This crucial distinction between seditious plundering and state-ordered iconoclasm explains why Vincent did not denounce the stripping of the altars in 1568, which had been sanctioned by the authorities: he noted matter-of-factly that on 9 January, mayor Pontard "issued an order to the inhabitants to enter the churches and break and destroy all the images."[31]

Whereas La Rochelle's Protestants tried to deflect accusations of guilt, Catholics never forgot the destructions. Because the Edict of Nantes granted them the right to worship in La Rochelle, their chief aim was to restore the sacred landscape and seek compensation for the destructions committed by the Huguenots. This campaign required the systematic recollection of past losses, which inevitably brought them into conflict with the city's Protestants. The immediate context for remembering the troubles was the arrival in the summer of 1599 of two royal commissioners, appointed by Henry IV to ensure that the terms of the edict – including the restoration of Catholic worship – were applied throughout France. Composed of one Catholic and one Protestant, these bipartisan commissions were also authorised to receive petitions and issue religious settlements. The commissioners sent to the Poitou and Aunis regions, the Catholic *maître de requêtes* Martin Langlois and the Protestant lieutenant-general Jean de la Parabère, arrived in La Rochelle on 25 July.[32] They were taken on a tour of the city by two Catholic delegates that lasted several days, during which they were shown the churches, convents, and cemeteries that were now either occupied by Protestants or laid to waste during the wars (Figure 5.1). The commissioners' report meticulously charted the Catholic losses: the parish church of St Nicolas, for example, was found "to be entirely ruined, without the foundations being visible, and the larger part of this church as well as the cemetery enclosed in the fortifications." Little more remained of the church of St Jean du Perrot, except "part of the belltower to about the second floor, which is all bricked up and currently serves as a gunpowder depot."[33]

After further consultations with both parties, Langlois and Parabère issued what they believed to be an even-handed settlement. Whereas the churches of Notre Dame de Cougnes and St Nicolas were considered lost, given that the Protestants had incorporated them into the urban fortifications, they allowed Catholics to rebuild the ruined churches of St Sauveur, St Jean du Perrot, and St Barthélémy. They would have to fund the reconstruction out of their own pocket, however, because no financial reparations were awarded – article 76 of the Edict of Nantes explicitly stipulated that the Huguenots could not be prosecuted for the "burning and destruction of churches." In the end, the commissioners only returned the surviving church of Ste Marguerite, which the Protestants had used for their own services.[34] The Protestant town council grudgingly accepted these conditions, but did not interfere when on August 4, a crowd of women, children, and artisans broke into Ste Marguerite to smash the windows, pulpit, and floorboards. The Catholics subsequently took

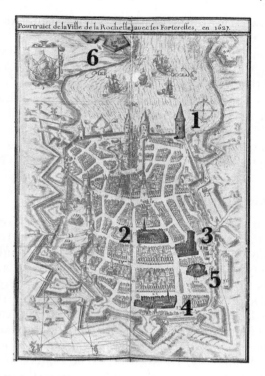

Figure 5.1 Map of La Rochelle in 1627. Médiathèque Michel Crépeau, La Rochelle, 3PL988-10. Design: Ruben Verwaal. Key sites: 1. Tour du Garrot; 2. Town hall; 3. Belltower of St Barthélémy; 4. Church of Ste Marguerite; 5. Huguenot Grand Temple; 6. Military camp of Coreille, site of the Minim monastery.

possession of their damaged building during a solemn Mass led by the bishop of Saintes, who also consecrated the ruins of St Barthélémy and organised a procession between the two recovered churches – a visual reminder that the Catholics were reclaiming their position in La Rochelle.[35]

The departure of Langlois and Parabère on August 9, revealed just how fragile religious coexistence was, as the Catholics remained a small minority in a city dominated by Protestant authorities reluctant to implement the edict. The ruined church of St Barthélémy became the focal point of the conflict over sacred space: while Catholics undertook the arduous task of rebuilding their church, Protestants tried to prevent its reconstruction. Matters came to a head in November 1603, when mayor Louis Berne entered the construction site accompanied by a group of archers, ordering the workmen to halt their work and imprisoning one of them without a warrant. When two of the workmen returned on Monday, they were beaten with clubs and chased out of the city. Meanwhile, a crowd of Protestants destroyed the newly carved saints' statues that had been placed inside the partially restored church.[36] In response, the

Catholic churchwardens began legal proceedings against the mayor in the local *présidial* court, demanding that the peace commissioners' settlement be respected and the ongoing reconstruction of St Barthélémy not be hindered.[37] Yet the cards were firmly stacked against them: in a petition to Henry IV, the Catholics noted that the presiding judge Jehan Pascault was a committed Huguenot, while his Catholic counterpart Jehan Cambin had recently converted to Calvinism. When royal commissioners visited La Rochelle again in 1617, the Catholics still complained that their church was "useless" because of ongoing Protestant opposition.[38] Memories of material loss thus fuelled religious conflict between the two confessions long after the wars had officially ended.

Material memories, old and new

The memory wars between La Rochelle's Catholics and Protestants entered a new round in the aftermath of the last war of religion. In 1620, King Louis XIII led his army across southern France to occupy the independent Protestant principality of Béarn, where he forcibly restored Catholic worship. Alarmed by this royal show of force, in December 1620 Protestant leaders headed by the Duke of Rohan met in La Rochelle, where they resolved to take up arms to defend the Reformed cause. Their uprising ended in spectacular defeat: between 1621 and 1629, royal armies besieged and occupied the rebellious Huguenot cities in southern France, including Montauban, Montpellier, and, most famously, La Rochelle.[39] The capture of La Rochelle in October 1628 did little to resolve the conflict between the two communities. As exiled Catholic citizens and clergy returned to rebuild their churches and monasteries, they developed a defiant memory culture that recalled both the losses they had suffered and their ultimate triumph over heresy. Given that Catholic identity, in contrast to Protestant self-understanding, was rooted more in the material – in particular, the maintenance of centuries-old ritual practices and the cherishing of objects – it is not surprising that Catholic memory was conveyed primarily through material vectors such as church buildings, inscriptions, and processions. Even under normal circumstances, processions and sacred space could spark conflict between the confessions, but they gained in commemorative significance in the aftermath of the wars, when Catholics also came to understand them as references to their recent suffering. Precisely because they used the public sphere to remember the wars, the simmering conflict with the city's Protestants was further escalated.

The importance La Rochelle's Catholics attached to remembering the wars is evident from the capitulation treaty that Louis XIII issued in November 1628. The king not only re-established Catholic worship in La Rochelle and banned the settlement of Protestant immigrants, but also decreed a series of measures aimed at restoring the sacred landscape and remembering the troubles through visual and material markers. First, he ordered the rebuilding of all ruined churches and monasteries and the restitution of confiscated Catholic property to their rightful owners. Furthermore, the Protestant church built on the Place du Château (known as the Grand Temple) was handed over to the Catholics, to be turned into a cathedral with a resident bishop, and a cross planted on the square bearing an inscription that commemorated the royal victory. In the decades following the siege, La Rochelle became a massive construction site, as Catholics rebuilt no less than three parish churches and nine monasteries.[40] The restoration of the sacred landscape was both an act of remembering and forgetting: on the one hand, it visually marked the triumph of Catholicism, but, on the other, it sought to efface the period of Huguenot rule and the destructions it had entailed.

The most poignant of these building projects was the establishment of a new monastery at the former military encampment south of the city, next to the graveyard of fallen Catholic soldiers. The monastery was headed by the Minim friars of Touraine, who had served Louis' army as chaplains during the siege. The king decreed that at the entrance to the future church of the Minims' monastery – aptly named Notre Dame des Victoires – two plates should be affixed to commemorate his victory and the soldiers who had fallen in battle.[41] By the early eighteenth century, the monastery had fallen into disrepair and was demolished, but when the royal engineer Claude Masse visited the site in 1711, the cemetery still remained, as did the inscription. Below the arms of Louis XIII, two tablets recalled the Catholic triumph of 1628: "Halt, Christians, and admire this trophy of piety and glory, whose worthy author is Louis XIII, who has subjected the rebellious, insolent, and heretical La Rochelle to the law of God and of his Church, as well as to that of his sceptre." The inscription went on to declare that "in order that the memory of such an august victory might be remembered for centuries to come, his majesty had this church and convent built, [...] wishing that the place which had been the scene of his battles should be an eternal mark of his piety."[42] The inscription thus drove home the message that the Minim monastery served as a monument marking the downfall of La Rochelle's Protestants.

Another key material memory appeared in the church of Ste Marguerite, the only one of the medieval parish churches to have survived the Wars of Religion. Although it had been returned to the Catholics in 1599, when war broke out in 1621, the Protestant city council again confiscated the building and voted to banish the Oratorian priests who served it. By the priests' own account, a Protestant crowd had threatened to massacre them, as they wrote that the monastery was "besieged by an infinite number of people who wanted that they be thrown over the walls, each of them shouting at the top of their voices that they would not allow them to leave their city alive."[43] The reconsecration of Ste Marguerite on All Saints' Day 1628 by Henri d'Escoubleau de Sourdis, the bishop of Maillezais and future archbishop of Bordeaux, thus held special significance for La Rochelle's Catholics, whose other places of worship still lay in ruins. Due to a lack of funds, it would take until mid-century before the churchwardens could afford to properly renovate the church interior. In 1665 they commissioned an altarpiece of their patron saint from the local artist Pierre Courtilleau, who delivered his work

Figure 5.2 Pierre Courtilleau, *Entry of Louis XIII in La Rochelle on November 1, 1628*, oil on panel, 185 × 143 cm.

Courtesy of Musée des Beaux-Arts, La Rochelle (MAH.1952.13.1).

in 1668 (Figure 5.2).[44] The painting depicts the key players in the Catholic reconquest of La Rochelle, framed against the cityscape in the background, including the belltowers of St Sauveur and St Barthélémy. In the foreground, Louis XIII is flanked by Cardinal Richelieu, while on the right the bishop of Maillezais is accompanied by father Jousseaume, the superior of the Oratorian priests. Towering in the sky is Saint Margaret the Virgin, martyred in AD 304 for refusing to renounce her Christian faith, as she straddles the dragon sent by Satan to devour her. The painting thus symbolically commemorated the wartime suffering of La Rochelle's Catholics, who despite Huguenot persecution had persevered in their faith as had Saint Margaret, until they triumphed over the monster of heresy.

While it is difficult to know how Protestants responded to these material memories, Catholic efforts to reclaim the public sphere by means of processions sparked immediate conflict. The first Catholic procession took place on November 1, 1628, the day Louis XIII entered his reconquered city: after Cardinal Richelieu had celebrated Mass at the reconsecrated church of Ste Marguerite, the king participated in a general procession led by Capuchin and Recollect friars carrying crosses and relics, while they sang the celebratory hymn *Te Deum laudamus*.[45] The king also decreed that henceforth, a commemorative annual procession was to be held on this date to celebrate the capture of La Rochelle.[46] Processions to commemorate the Wars of Religion – in particular foiled Huguenot sieges or deliverance from Protestant rule – were a common feature of post-war France. Catholics in Poitiers, for example, marched around the city walls on September 7, to commemorate that in the summer of 1569 the city had resisted a Protestant siege, while on October 20, Montpellier's Catholics organised an annual procession to celebrate the 1622 capture of their city by Louis XIII.[47]

More important, however, was the resumption of processions that marked the liturgical calendar. Although these processions were primarily linked to religious feast days, they were also part of a campaign to re-sacralise urban space and expunge the period of Protestant domination, when processions had been prohibited. Nor had La Rochelle's Catholics forgotten that despite the restoration of Catholic worship in 1599, the Protestant town council had frustrated their attempts to reintroduce processions. When in March 1600 the priests of Ste Marguerite petitioned to march through La Rochelle on Palm Sunday, the council refused their demand and posted soldiers outside the church to prevent the procession.[48] The Catholics protested this obstruction with the king, who duly ordered the city council to allow processions between Ste Marguerite and St Barthélémy, but to little effect: in 1617 they complained that the councillors were still dragging their heels in implementing the king's wishes.[49]

The 1628 capture of La Rochelle turned the tables on the Protestants, however, who were also forced to decorate their homes on religious holidays, when Catholics marched through their streets carrying the Holy Sacrament. An official city ordinance, first issued in June 1631, stipulated that all citizens along the processional route had to clean their street and "hang tapestries, white cloths, and other honourable things in front of their houses," or pay a hefty fine of 500 *livres*.[50] La Rochelle's Protestants had little choice but to acquiesce, which earned them a stern rebuke from the Huguenot national synod. By December 1637, therefore, the consistory resolved to send its minister Philippe Vincent to Paris to petition the king. Vincent pointed out that by virtue of secret article 3 of the Edict of Nantes, Protestants could not be forced to decorate their homes, nor could they be charged for decorations put up by municipal authorities. His mission was only partially successful: although Louis XIII conceded that La Rochelle's Huguenots did not have to deck their houses, he ordered them to pay for the decorations put up by Catholic officials instead.[51] Once Louis XIV had ascended to the throne, however, Vincent shrewdly managed to get this decision reversed, obtaining a royal letter in 1645 that suspended Protestant taxation and ordered the city council to use the proceeds of the municipal meat tax to subsidise the decorations. After protests from the Catholics, the king eventually fixed the Protestant contribution at 100 *livres* per annum.[52] These ongoing conflicts about processions reveal the extent to which deep-seated tensions inherited from the religious wars continued to divide Catholics and Protestants.

Conclusions

This chapter has sought to demonstrate that memories of religious conflict cast a long shadow over post-war France, undermining the policy of coexistence mandated by the Edict of Nantes. Although the monarchy nominally prohibited French citizens from remembering the troubles, thus hoping to promote peace and reconciliation, in practice Catholics and Protestants found it difficult to forget the violence they had witnessed. An exploration of these "acts of remembering" in the city of La Rochelle shows that both sides developed deeply partisan memories of the wars. Some of the most memorable events only helped to divide them along confessional lines, including the massacre of clergy, the Protestant destruction of the sacred landscape, and the prohibition of Catholic worship. Whereas Protestants sought to downplay their involvement in these events and avoid the stigma of rebels who had resorted to violence, Catholics purposefully memorialised their suffering through a range of memory vectors, such as the rebuilding of churches and monasteries, the placement of new commemorative monuments, inscriptions, and altarpieces, as well as the reintroduction of processions that had been outlawed by the Huguenots. These memories in turn fuelled disagreements long after the wars had ended: by mid-century, Catholics and Protestants were still locked in bitter conflict over the reconstruction of churches that had been destroyed a century before, the massacres committed during the wars, and the organising of processions that had been banned for decades. The Catholic reconquest of La Rochelle, and that of many other cities in post-war France, was thus fuelled in large part by the assertion of contested memories of the troubles – memories that slowly but surely eroded the monarchy's premise that Catholics and Protestants could live together in peace.

Notes

1 Edict of Nantes, article 1, in "L'édit de Nantes et ses antécédents," ed. Bernard Barbiche, École nationale des chartes, accessed July 7, 2021, http://elec.enc. sorbonne.fr/editsdepacification/edit_12. On the religious wars and the Edict of Nantes, see Mack P. Holt, *The French Wars of Religion, 1562–1629* (Cambridge: Cambridge University Press, 2005), esp. 166–71.
2 Gregory Hanlon, *Confession and Community in Seventeenth-Century France: Catholic and Protestant Coexistence in Aquitaine* (Philadelphia: University of Pennsylvania Press, 1993); Keith P. Luria, *Sacred Boundaries: Religious Coexistence and Conflict in Early Modern France* (Washington, D.C.: Catholic University of America Press, 2005); Keith P. Luria, "France: An Overview," in *A Companion to Multiconfessionalism in the Early Modern World*, ed. Thomas Max Safley (Leiden: Brill, 2011), 209–38; *La coexistence confessionnelle à l'épreuve: Études sur les relations entre protestants et catholiques dans la France moderne*, ed. Didier Boisson and Yves Krumenacker (Lyon: Université Jean Moulin III, 2009).

3 Judith Pollmann, *Memory in Early Modern Europe, 1500–1800* (Oxford: Oxford University Press, 2017), 1. See also Astrid Erll, *Memory in Culture*, trans. Sara B. Young (Palgrave: Basingstoke, 2011), 6–9.
4 Maurice Halbwachs, *On Collective Memory*, trans. Lewis A. Coser (Chicago: University of Chicago Press, 2003); Maurice Halbwachs, *The Collective Memory*, trans. Francis J. Ditter and Vida Yazdi Ditter (New York: Harper Collins, 1980). For a useful summary, see Erll, *Memory in Culture*, 14–6.
5 Jan Assmann, "Communicative and Cultural Memory," in *A Companion to Cultural Memory Studies*, ed. Astrid Erll and Ansgar Nünning (Berlin: De Gruyter, 2010), 109–18; Aleida Assmann, *Der lange Schatten der Vergangenheit: Erinnerungskultur und Geschichtspolitik* (Munich: C.H. Beck, 2006), 54–61; Erll, *Memory in Culture*, 27–37.
6 Ute Lotz-Heumann, "Confessionalization," in *The Ashgate Research Companion to the Counter-Reformation*, ed. Alexandra Bamji, Geert Janssen, and Mary Laven (Farnham, 2013), 33–53. On the application of this theory to France, see Philip Benedict, "Confessionalization in France? Critical Reflections and New Evidence," in *Society and Culture in the Huguenot World, 1559–1685*, ed. Raymond A. Mentzer and Andrew Spicer (Cambridge: Cambridge University Press, 2002), 44–61.
7 Edict of Nantes, article 1, in "L'édit de Nantes et ses antécédents."
8 Pollmann, *Memory in Early Modern Europe*, 140–58.
9 Edict of Amboise, article 9, in "L'édit de Nantes et ses antécédents." See also Olivier Christin, "Mémoire inscrite, oubli prescrit: La fin des troubles de religion en France," *Pariser Historischer Studien* 94 (2009), 73–4.
10 Jotham Parsons, "The Political Vision of Antoine Loisel," *Sixteenth Century Journal* 27, no. 2 (1996), 453–76; Mark Greengrass, "Amnistie et 'oubliance': Un discours politique autour des édits de pacification pendant les guerres de religion," in *Paix des armes, paix des âmes* (Paris: Imprimerie nationale, 2000), 113–23.
11 Antoine Loisel, *Amnestie ou de l'oubliance des maux faicts et receus pendant les troubles & à l'occasion d'iceux* (Paris: Abel l'Angelier, 1595), 29.
12 Paul-Alexis Mellet and Jérémie Foa, "Une 'politique de l'oubliance? Mémoire et oubli pendant les guerres de Religion (1550–1600)," *Astérion* 15 (2016), accessed July 7, 2021, https://journals.openedition.org/asterion/2829; Pollmann, *Memory in Early Modern Europe*, 140–54.
13 David van der Linden, "Archive Wars: Record Destruction and the Memory of the French Wars of Religion in Montpellier," *Sixteenth Century Journal* 51, no. 1 (2020), 129–49; and the special issue edited by David van der Linden and Tom Hamilton, "Remembering the French Wars of Religion," *French History* 34, no. 4 (2020).
14 Judith Pollmann, "Archiving the Present and Chronicling for the Future in Early Modern Europe," *Past & Present Supplement* 11 (2016), 231–52.
15 Allan Tulchin, "Massacres During the French Wars of Religion," *Past & Present Supplement* 7 (2012), 100–26; Laurent Ropp, "La violence des frères: Trois protestants méridionaux face aux massacres perpétrés par leurs coreligionnaires au temps des guerres de religion," *Revue d'histoire du protestantisme* 5, no. 4 (2020), 197–223.
16 Judith Pugh Meyer, *Reformation in La Rochelle: Tradition and Change in Early Modern Europe, 1500–1568* (Geneva: Droz, 1996), 82–103; Kevin C. Robbins, *City on the Ocean Sea: La Rochelle, 1530–1650: Urban Society, Religion, and Politics on the French Atlantic Frontier* (Leiden: Brill, 1997), 184–203.
17 Jean de La Haize, *Premier discours brief et veritable de ce qui s'est passé en la ville et gouvernement de la Rochelle, depuis l'an mil cinq cens soixante sept, jusques en l'année 1568*, 2nd ed. (La Rochelle: [Théophile Bouquet], 1575).

18 Médiathèque Michel Crépeau, La Rochelle [hereafter MLR], MS 46, Histoire de la Rochelle, ff. 979–80. On the authorship of this chronicle, see Léopold Gabriel Delayant, *Historiens de La Rochelle: Études lues à la Société littéraire de La Rochelle de 1853 à 1860* (La Rochelle: G. Maréchal, 1863), 59–67.

19 Armand-Désiré de La Fontenelle de Vaudoré, ed. "Chroniques Fontenaisiennes," *Archives historiques du Bas-Poitou* 1 (1841), 101.

20 Étienne Trocmé, "L'Église réformée de La Rochelle jusqu'en 1628," *Bulletin de la Société de l'histoire du protestantisme français* 29, no. 1 (1952), 138–41.

21 Kevin C. Robbins, "Rewriting Protestant History: Printing, Censorship by Pastors, and the Dimensions of Dissent among the Huguenots – the La Popelinière Case at La Rochelle, 1581–85," in *The Sixteenth-Century French Religious Book*, ed. Andrew Pettegree, Paul Nelles, and Philip Conner (Farnham: Ashgate, 2001), 239–55; George Wylie Sypher, "La Popelinière's *Histoire de France*: A Case of Historical Objectivity and Religious Censorship," *Journal of the History of Ideas* 24, no. 1 (1963), 41–54.

22 Simplicien Saint-Martin, *Histoire de la vie du glorieux pere S. Augustin religieux, docteur de l'eglise, evesque d'Hippone, et de plusieurs saincts et sainctes, et hommes illustres de son ordre des ermites* (Toulouse: Adrien Colomiez, 1641), 682. On Saint-Martin, see E. Ypma, "Les auteurs augustins français: Liste de leurs noms et de leurs ouvrages," *Augustiniana* 22, no. 3/4 (1972), 627–30.

23 Saint-Martin, *Histoire de la vie du glorieux pere S. Augustin*, 685.

24 Meyer, *Reformation in La Rochelle*, 77–82.

25 Ibid., 116; Pascal Rambeaud, *De la Rochelle vers l'Aunis: L'histoire des réformés et leurs églises dans une province française au XVIe siècle* (Paris: Honoré Champion, 2003), 222–3.

26 Meyer, *Reformation in La Rochelle*, 103.

27 Olivier Christin, *Une révolution symbolique: L'iconoclasme huguenot et la reconstruction catholique* (Paris: Éditions de Minuit, 1991), 55–60.

28 MLR, MS 46, Histoire de la Rochelle, f. 955.

29 Amos Barbot, "Histoire de La Rochelle," *Archives historiques de la Saintonge et de l'Aunis* 17 (1889), 172–3. On Barbot, see Delayant, *Historiens de la Rochelle*, 41–57.

30 Philippe Vincent, *Recherches sur les commencemens et les premiers progrés de la reformation en la ville de la Rochelle* (Rotterdam: Abraham Acher, 1693), 83. Vincent's career is outlined in Delayant, *Historiens de la Rochelle*, 181–201.

31 Vincent, *Recherches*, 109.

32 Francis Garrisson, *Essai sur les commissions d'application de l'Édit de Nantes* (Montpellier: Déhan, 1964), 93–5; Daniel Hickey, "Un mécanisme pour la résolution des conflits: Les Commissions pour l'exécution de l'édit de Nantes et leurs initiatives à La Rochelle, 1599–1617," in *Lendemains de guerre civile: Réconciliations et restaurations en France sous Henri IV*, ed. Michel De Waele (Paris: Hermann, 2015), 67–86.

33 MLR, MS 164, Procès-verbal of commissioners Parabère and Langlois, August 1599, ff. 24^r-25^v.

34 Ibid., ff. 31^v-33^r; Edict of Nantes, article 76, in "L'édit de Nantes et ses antécédents."

35 Hickey, "Un mécanisme pour la résolution des conflits," 80–1.

36 MLR, MS 165, Petition by the parishioners of St Barthélémy to Henry IV, December 7, 1603, ff. 34–5.

37 MLR, MS 165, Churchmasters of St Barthélémy vs. mayor of La Rochelle, November 18, 1603, ff. 1–16.

38 MLR, MS 165, Petition by the parishioners of St Barthélémy to Henry IV, December 7, 1603, f. 35^r; MLR, MS 165, Petition by the Catholic inhabitants of La Rochelle, 1617, articles 5 and 6, ff. 81^{r-v}.

39 David Parker, *La Rochelle and the French Monarchy: Conflict and Order in Seventeenth-Century France* (London: Royal Historical Society, 1980); Robbins, *City on the Ocean Sea*, 335–53. On the last war of religion, see Holt, *French Wars of Religion*, 178–94.

40 *Declaration du Roy, sur la reduction de la ville de La Rochelle en son obeissance, contenant l'ordre et police que Sa Maiesté veut y estre establie* (Le Mans: Veuve F. Olivier, 1628). See also Maïté Recasens, "Oubliance et commémorations du siège de La Rochelle (1628–1789)," in *Les Sources du Sacré: Nouvelles approches du fait religieux*, ed. Caroline Muller and Nicolas Guyard (Lyon: LARHRA, 2018), 167–86. For the Catholic reconstruction, see François Moisy, "Le rétablissement des structures catholiques après le siège de La Rochelle (1628–1648)," *Revue du Bas-Poitou et des Provinces de l'Ouest* 82 (1971), 345–75.

41 *Declaration du Roy*, 7. On the history of this monastery, see Bernard Coutant, *Les Minimes, pages d'histoire rochelaise* (La Rochelle: Rupella, 1968).

42 Service Historique de la Défense, Vincennes, MS 504, Claude Masse, Receuil des plans de La Rochelle, 1711, f. 86.

43 *Le banissement des Prestres de l'Oratoire, hors de la Rochelle* (Paris: Antoine Vitré, 1621), 8.

44 MLR, MS 148, Churchwarden accounts of Ste Marguerite, f. 1. See also Moisy, "Le rétablissement," 352; Thierry Lefrançois, *Peintures et dessins anciens des Musées d'art et d'histoire de La Rochelle* (La Rochelle: Édition des Musées d'art et d'histoire de La Rochelle, 2006), 25.

45 *Les remarques particulieres de tout ce qui s'est passé en la Reduction de la Rochelle & depuis l'entrée du Roy en icelle: Ensemble les ceremonies observées au restablissement de la Religion Catholique, Apostolique & Romaine* (Paris: Nicolas Rousset, 1628), 13–4.

46 *Declaration du Roy*, 7.

47 Philip Benedict, "Divided Memories? Historical Calendars, Commemorative Processions and the Recollection of the Wars of Religion during the Ancien Régime," *French History* 22, no. 4 (2008), 390–7; David van der Linden, "The Sound of Memory: Acoustic Conflict and the Legacy of the French Wars of Religion in Seventeenth-Century Montpellier," *Early Modern French Studies* 41, no. 1 (2019), 10–11.

48 Jacques Merlin, "Diaire de Jacques Merlin ou Recueil des choses [les] plus mémorables qui se sont passées en ceste ville [de la Rochelle] de 1589 à 1620," ed. Charles Dangibeaud, *Archives historiques de la Saintonge et de l'Aunis* 5 (1878), 107.

49 MLR, MS 164, Extract from the registers of the Conseil d'état, Paris, May 19, 1600, ff. 74–5; MLR, MS 165, Petition by the Catholic inhabitants of La Rochelle, 1617, articles 8 and 9, f. 82^r.

50 Archives municipales, La Rochelle (herafter AMLR), FF ARCHANC 12, Ordinance of June 25, 1631.

51 Archives départementales de la Charente-Maritime (hereafter ADCM), 300 J 40, Extracts from the Huguenot national synods at Charenton, 1631, and Alençon, 1637; AMLR, GG 737, Louis XIII to De Villemontée, Saint-Germain-en-Laye, February 18, 1638. See also Edict of Nantes, secret article 3, in "L'édit de Nantes et ses antécédents."

52 MLR, MS 148, Investigation by intendant d'Argenson, May 1645, ff. 26–33; ADCM, 300 J 177, Extract from the registers of the Conseil d'état, February 18, 1647.

Part III
Crossing Boundaries
Historiographic Introduction

As in any period of human history, so too in the early modern era both individuals and collectives of people sought to distinguish themselves from each other. Distinctions were made and articulated on the basis of many different characteristics, ranging from language, skin colour, and religious beliefs to place of birth or residence. Then and now, such processes of differentiation result in boundaries, lines of demarcation that divide human populations into different groups.

As is the case with "identity," the concept of boundaries has been embraced by scholars working in diverse fields, including anthropology, history, sociology, and the political sciences.[1] In general, scholars today emphasise that boundaries are human constructs and reflect the ways in which societies are classified, ordered, and organised (perhaps except for what we call natural boundaries, such as mountain ranges or seas, although these can also be imbued with symbolic meanings).[2] Because of their man-made nature, boundaries are likely to evolve over time as the circumstances in which they originated are themselves subjected to historical change.[3]

Scholars customarily make a distinction between various types of boundaries, including political, gender, class, and religious ones, each of them reflecting the salience of the particular differences dividing people in a given context. In addition, a useful distinction pertaining to the nature of boundaries is made. On the one hand, there are symbolic boundaries, such as those based on the conceptual distinctions between different religious groups in relation to their orthodoxy and orthopraxy. Social boundaries, on the other hand, are embodied in relationships and interactions between individuals and groups of people. Both types of boundaries "should be viewed as equally real" even though the domain in which they exist is different.[4] Furthermore, symbolic and social boundaries tend to be intimately related to each other, as the former are "often used to enforce, maintain, normalize, or rationalize" the latter.[5]

The process of boundary formation between religious groups and the extent to which they were respected or transgressed continues to be at the forefront of research on the practice of religious toleration because it informs us about the everyday relationships that existed between people divided by faith.

DOI: 10.4324/9781003030522-9

Whereas older research tended to emphasise the emergence of increasingly solid boundaries and the diminishing frequency of contact between religious groups over the course of the sixteenth and seventeenth centuries, nowadays it is generally held that the existence of boundaries did not necessarily hamper all forms of interaction.[6] For example, processes of cultural and intellectual exchange were capable of transcending the boundaries dividing groups.[7] Moreover, even seemingly solid religious boundaries were transgressed as people were motivated by a host of different incentives to do so and because not everyone accorded the same importance to these boundaries.[8] Whatever prompted the crossing of boundaries, doing so often destabilised the symbolic boundaries that underpinned the "hierarchy of differentiation."[9] And as scholars have noted, even the boundaries that were intended to prevent certain types of interaction between religious groups constituted "zone[s] of contact" where religious differences were articulated and experienced, and where identities were shaped and gained form.[10]

Although the categories and labels used by early modern people to differentiate between groups reflected symbolic boundaries and potentially social ones as well, their uncritical application can be reductionist in that they obscure the complexities of social life. In his chapter, Jesse Spohnholz argues that boundaries between groups were dynamic and complex, hence making a simple distinction between the "Dutch" migrants who fled the Low Countries and their "German" hosts often is impossible.[11] He arrives at this conclusion by examining 11 Dutch-speaking Reformed migrant communities in the sixteenth-century Holy Roman Empire. Due to the different interpretations of the Religious Peace of Augsburg by the authorities under whom these migrant communities resided, the confessional and constitutional boundaries between migrants and their hosts varied. The presence or absence of linguistic and social boundaries was also highly significant. In some cases, the linguistic and socio-economic profiles of the host society and migrant groups matched fairly closely, a situation that proved conducive to a higher degree of integration. Taken together, legal, linguistic, and socio-economic factors affected greatly the forms of coexistence that emerged locally. Hence Spohnholz's pertinent warning that we should be careful in applying labels, as they can misleadingly evoke an image of groups that were inherently different and separate.

When migrating from the Low Countries to the areas that were part of the Holy Roman Empire, a composite, polycentric political entity, the migrant communities studied by Spohnholz crossed a host of ecclesiastical, political, and spatial boundaries. Due to the surge in interest in topics such as globalisation, mobility, and migration, the spatial boundaries that demarcated geographical entities of various scales and sizes have received much attention in recent years.[12] Scholars interested in the history of religious toleration have studied the role of spatial boundaries in relations between religious groups, a fertile approach given the fragmented nature of political and religious authority in the early modern world.[13]

Spatial boundaries between religious groups were frequently embodied in physical objects such as walls and gates. Being hemmed in by walls was the fate that befell many Jewish communities, but not in the city of Livorno. This was rather remarkable given that across Italy over the course of the sixteenth century Jews were forced to reside in ghettos that were walled off from the rest of the city. Nicholas Terpstra argues that this was not necessary in Livorno: the city "*had* no ghetto because it *was* a ghetto." Apart from the fact that the whole city was surrounded by massive walls, the Jewish quarter and sizeable building in which Muslims were obliged to reside, known as the *Bagno*, were surrounded by churches and lay religious institutions, which marked the boundaries of these areas. At the same time, the soundscape of Catholicism, ever present in all corners of the city, left no doubts about Livorno's religious identity. Contrariwise, neither the Jewish nor the Muslim community of this city had a "real sensory presence," since the practice of their faiths was limited to the private sphere. In addition, certain types of interaction were strictly forbidden: Jews could not have sex with Christians or employ them in their homes or businesses. A combination, therefore, of social and sensory boundaries demarcated the religious groups living in Livorno and expressed the "spiritual hierarchy" of this city.

Planting a church in mission territory required the erection of boundaries as well. New religious identities were formed in no small part by the prohibition of certain forms of interaction with members of rival religious groups. Felicita Tramontana examines how the efforts of Catholic missionaries in the Syro-Palestinian region to erect boundaries between Catholics and other Christians took place within the existing legal and institutional framework devised by Ottoman authorities to govern interfaith relationships. The fact that Catholicism was not granted the status of a separate and legally recognised religious community (*ta'ifa*) influenced strongly the religious boundaries that were constructed. Given that a conversion to Catholicism was institutionally insignificant in that the convert would not become part of another *ta'ifa*, other boundaries had to be established in order to separate Catholics and non-Catholics. The resulting boundaries therefore "centered on a differentiation in behaviours and religious practices." The erection of these boundaries became a joint enterprise of the Catholic and Orthodox Churches as they feared each other's competition – in that sense, boundaries were thought of as effective defence mechanisms. These boundaries hindered well-established practices, such as the sharing of sacraments, that underpinned the form of religious coexistence in this region. Although the persistence of conversions and mixed marriages shows the difficulties involved in establishing religious boundaries, the latter did widen the distance between groups.

The three chapters in this section make clear that symbolic and social boundaries were important components of the different forms of coexistence that emerged in the early modern era. Resulting from processes of differentiation, boundaries comprised rules of engagement between different groups in society. As such, they could contribute to a degree of social stability and foster "regimes of coexistence."[14] At the same time, many boundaries remained porous, and acts of boundary-crossing destabilised the very classifications and categorisations on which these regimes rested.

Notes

1 Michèle Lamont and Marcel Fournier, "Introduction," in *Cultivating Differences: Symbolic Boundaries and the Making of Inequality*, ed. Michèle Lamont and Marcel Fournier (Chicago: University of Chicago Press, 1992), 1–20.

2 Ibid. Luca Scholz, *Borders and Freedom of Movement in the Holy Roman Empire* (Oxford: Oxford University Press, 2020), 87–8. For a work on confessional coexistence that finds itself in agreement, see Keith P. Luria, *Sacred Boundaries: Religious Coexistence and Conflict in Early-Modern France* (Washington, DC: Catholic University of America Press, 2005), esp. xxv: "boundaries create differences which aren't inherent."

3 For example, a change in the legal status of particular groups in society could affect the boundaries pertaining to them. E.g. Carys Brown, *Friends, Neighbours, Sinners. Religious Difference and English Society, 1689–1750* (Cambridge: Cambridge University Press, 2022).

4 Michèle Lamont and Virág Molnár, "The study of boundaries in the social sciences," *Annual Review of Sociology* 28 (2002), 168.

5 Ibid., 186.

6 Religious boundaries, for example, did not prevent interfaith interactions resulting from trade, another prominent field of research. See, e.g. Silvia Marzagalli, "Trade across Religious and Confessional Boundaries in Early Modern France," in *Religion and Trade: Cross-Cultural Exchanges in World History, 1000–1900*, ed. Francesca Trivellato, Leor Halevi, and Catia Antunes (Cambridge: Cambridge University Press, 2014), 169–91; Francesca Trivellato, *The Familiarity of Strangers: The Sephardic Diaspora, Livorno, and Cross-Cultural Trade in the Early Modern Period* (New Haven, CT: Yale University Press, 2009).

7 To offer but one example: the work of Miriam Bodian and Yosef Kaplan has shown how Sephardic Jewish communities in Amsterdam incorporated and continued to adhere to aspects of the Iberian Catholic culture in which they themselves or their ancestors were raised. Miriam Bodian, *Hebrews of the Portuguese Nation: Conversos and Community in Early Modern Amsterdam* (Bloomington: Indiana University Press, 1999); Yosef Kaplan, "Political Concepts in the World of the Portuguese Jews of Amsterdam during the Seventeenth Century. The Problem of Exclusion and the Boundaries of Self-Identity," in *Menasseh Ben Israel and His World*, ed. Yosef Kaplan, Henry Méchoulan, and Richard H. Popkin (Leiden: Brill, 1989), 45–62; Yosef Kaplan, "The Self-Definition of the Sephardi Jews of Western Europe and Their Relation to the Alien and the Stranger," in *An Alternative Path to Modernity. The Sephardi Diaspora in Western Europe*, ed. Yosef Kaplan (Leiden: Brill, 2000), 51–77.

8 For example, some people denounced the confessional type of early modern Christianity altogether, others were indifferent to religious differences, and still others wavered between different religions and/or were skeptical of their mutually exclusive truth-claims and adopted a more relativistic stance. See, e.g. Benjamin J. Kaplan, *Calvinists and Libertines: Confession and Community in Utrecht 1578–1620* (Oxford: Clarendon Press, 1995); Kaspar von Greyerz, "Konfessionelle Indifferenz in der Frühen Neuzeit," in *Konfessionelle Ambiguität: Uneindeutigkeit und Verstellung als religiöse Praxis in der Frühen Neuzeit*, ed. Andreas Pietsch and Barbara Stollberg-Rilinger (Gütersloh: Gütersloher Verl.-Haus, 2013); Nicholas Griffiths, "The Best of Both Faiths: The Boundaries of Religious Allegiance and

Opportunism in Early Eighteenth-Century Cuenca," *Bulletin of Hispanic Studies* 77 (2000), 13–39; Stuart B. Schwartz, *All Can Be Saved: Religious Toleration and Salvation in the Iberian Atlantic* World (New Haven, CT: Yale University Press, 2009).

9   Stuart B. Schwartz, *Blood and Boundaries: The Limits of Religious and Racial Exclusion in Early Modern Latin America* (Waltham: Brandeis University Press, 2020), 1.

10 Fredrik Barth, "Introduction," in *Ethnic Groups and Boundaries. The Social Organization of Cultural Difference*, ed. Fredrik Barth (London: Allen & Unwin, 1969), 9–38. Duane Corpis, *Crossing the Boundaries of Belief: Geographies of Religious Conversion in Southern Germany, 1648–1800* (Charlottesville, VA: University of Virginia Press, 2014), 8.

11 Spohnholz thus finds himself in agreement with scholars according to whom ethnic and cultural boundaries do not coincide and instead emphasise the role of people in the construction of boundaries and the formation of groups (through self-identification with particular groups). Frequently mentioned in this respect is the work of Norwegian anthropologist Frederick Barth, according to some because he pioneered the subjectivist approach, whereas others regard him as more a representative of this approach than a founder of it. Marek Jakoubek, "A Breakthrough of Ethnic Groups and Boundaries – Reality or a Myth? (On Amnesia in Ethnicity Studies)," *Ethnicities* 22, no. 2 (2022), 177–95.

12 See, e.g. Scholz, *Borders and Freedom of Movement*; Violet Soen et al., "How to Do Transregional History: A Concept, Method and Tool for Early Modern Border Research," *Journal of Early Modern History* 21 (2021), 343–64, and the literature cited in these publications.

13 E.g. Benjamin J. Kaplan, *Divided by Faith: Religious Conflict and the Practice of Toleration in Early Modern Europe* (Cambridge, MA: Harvard University Press, 2007), Ch. 6; Id., *Cunegonde's Kidnapping: A Story of Religious Conflict in the Age of Enlightenment* (New Haven, CT: Yale University Press, 2014); Jill Fehleison, *Boundaries of Faith: Catholics and Protestants in the Diocese of Geneva* (Kirksville, MO: Truman State University Press, 2010), esp. Ch. 4; Liesbeth Corens, "Seasonable Coexistence: Temporality, Health Care and Confessional Relations in Spa, c. 1648–1740," *Past & Present* 256, no. 1 (2022), 129–64.

14 For this term, see David M. Luebke, *Hometown Religion: Regimes of Coexistence in Early Modern Westphalia* (Charlottesville, VA: University of Virginia Press, 2016).

6 Constitutional Dynamism and Demographic Diversity in Early Modern Confessional Coexistence

Dutch Reformed Refugees in the Holy Roman Empire, 1554–1596

Jesse Spohnholz

Starting in the mid-sixteenth century, persecution and warfare drove tens of thousands of Dutch-speaking Protestants to flee to the Holy Roman Empire. As with so much scholarship on early modern toleration and coexistence in early modern Europe, research on how these migrants lived with their new neighbours has often treated the political, confessional, ethnic, and linguistic categories that distinguished migrants from hosts as relatively stable. Such works have examined "Dutch" "Calvinist" refugees fleeing to "Lutheran" and "Catholic" locations in "Germany."[1] Often inadvertently, such categorisations carry assumptions of morphological integrity of confessional or ethnic groups that, when used incautiously, might anachronistically imply that clear political and religious boundaries existed that mapped onto modern national or religious identities familiar to readers. Quite understandably, historians do this as a kind of shorthand so that they can get to their research methods without getting mired in fraught terminological explanations. So long as they explain their terms, there is nothing inherently problematic about this practice.

That said, this chapter argues that patterns of coexistence of these migrants and their hosts can be better understood when we develop more nuanced variations; in this case, by questioning the constitutional, confessional, ethnic, and sociocultural binaries that are usually deployed to examine these groups. Drawing on evidence from 11 Dutch-speaking Reformed migrant communities in three imperial cities (Cologne, Aachen, and Frankfurt), seven territorial cities in the duchy of Cleves (Wesel, Emmerich, Xanten, Kalkar, Goch, Rees, and Gennep), and one Dutch settlement in the Electoral Palatinate (Frankenthal), I argue that dynamism at the confessional, constitutional, and demographic levels allowed a wide variety of "regimes of coexistence," to borrow David M. Luebke's useful phrase.[2] Following anthropologists and historians before me, I suggest that rather than treating ethnic, religious, or political boundaries as static and autochthonous, we can better understand patterns of coexistence if we treat boundaries between groups as complex, and the maintenance and negotiation of those boundaries as generative of distinct and localised social outcomes.[3]

DOI: 10.4324/9781003030522-10

The first half of this chapter demonstrates that the negotiation of confessional boundaries and constitutional frameworks of cities and towns – particularly local authorities' application of the Peace of Augsburg as it pertained to Protestants – played a key role in how migrants managed within host communities. The second half highlights that the demographic diversity of these migrant communities – among themselves and compared to their hosts – helps us see that coexistence requiring building, crossing, or renegotiating locally distinct kinds of ethnic, linguistic, and sociocultural boundaries whose complexity and intersections belie any easy distinction between "Dutch" migrants and their "German" hosts. The study of Dutch Reformed migrants in the Holy Roman Empire offers us a case in which managing pluralism required finding local responses to navigate political, social, and confessional boundaries that were sometimes frustratingly ambiguous and sometimes painfully clear.

Boundaries in sixteenth-century Central Europe

Before getting to local variations, it's useful to make three observations about political and religious boundaries in this region of early modern Europe more generally. First, there was not a neat and tidy distinction between the Low Countries and the Holy Roman Empire, especially along the borderlands.[4] Politically, following the imperial constitutional reforms of the late fifteenth and early sixteenth centuries, the lands called the Low Countries, mostly (though not entirely) under the rule of the House of Burgundy, remained officially a part of the Burgundian Circle, an institutional subset of the Holy Roman Empire. In the early sixteenth century, through a series of wars and treaties, some areas of the Empire were integrated into the jurisdiction of this Netherlandish assembly of territories. From 1519 to 1555, Charles V, the "supreme lord of the Netherlands," also served as Holy Roman Emperor. When Charles abdicated his rule over the Empire to his brother and over the Netherlands to his son, the Netherlands formally remained part of the Empire. In practice, though, the Burgundian Circle operated largely independently from the rest of the empire. Still, Netherlandish delegates attended imperial diets. And during the unrest that would turn to outright civil war in the Netherlands, some nobles and magistrates (especially in the east) emphasised their status as imperial estates even through the 1570s.[5]

In addition, from a linguistic and cultural standpoint, the border was more fluid and the differences were gradual, so some migrations were far less dramatic than others. The linguistic borders did not match the political ones. Rather than forms of Dutch, forms of Lower Saxon German were spoken in parts of the eastern and northeastern Netherlands, while a form of Dutch was spoken along the Lower Rhine and Maas River regions in the Empire.[6] Moreover, no physical border actually existed between the two jurisdictions.[7] There were only a series of toll stations at towns along main roadways, which often paralleled the Maas, Rur/Roer, Niers, Rhein, and IJssel waterways.[8] If borderlines had been drawn, they only would have revealed a confusing array of exclaves, enclaves, and noncontiguous territories, such that princes and nobles in the Netherlands held territories within – or at least surrounded by – imperial territories, and vice versa.[9] Thus, while we can broadly distinguish between the Netherlands and the Holy Roman Empire as well as between Dutch and German cultural and linguistic arenas, when we get to the borderlands, where many of these host communities lay, these distinctions become pretty hard to maintain.

Second, for most of the period under consideration, the boundaries between different Protestant groups remained disputed and dynamic. Since 1530, the Augsburg Confession had been central in defining the emerging evangelical bloc in the Empire. However, disagreements about what this meant continued for decades because Philip Melanchthon had written multiple versions of the text as he worked to find a phrasing – especially on the Eucharist – that would help unify evangelicals. Early proposals to define the term were abandoned due to fears that more clarity might divide Protestants, leaving them vulnerable to Catholic stratagems.[10] The question was particularly important for Reformed Protestant migrants from the Netherlands because they were willing to sign Melanchthon's 1540 variation (*variata*), which offered more accommodating language on the Eucharist, but not the 1530 original (*invariata*), which was more explicit about Christ's Real Presence, which Lutherans preferred. In the Netherlands, too, some Reformed Protestants favoured signing the Augsburg Confession, especially since it might align them with powerful forces in the Empire. Meanwhile, both in the Empire and in the Netherlands, other Reformed Protestants rejected any version of the Augsburg Confession, proposing alternatives they hoped might find greater appeal. Even after a broad political consensus had formed around the *invariata* among Lutherans by about 1580, many Lutherans and all Reformed continued to embrace alternatives through the end of the century.[11] Thus, casually distinguishing between the categories of "Lutheran" and "Calvinist" presents a dynamic and contested set of religious debates and negotiations as both static and well-defined theologically.[12]

Third, imperial laws governing Protestantism were neither static nor were they consistently followed. For the purposes of this chapter, the most relevant law was the Peace of Augsburg (1555), which permitted imperial estates whose autonomy was only limited by their allegiance to the emperor – those with so-called *Reichsunmittelbarkeit* (in English, imperial immediacy) – to determine whether their territory would remain Catholic or adopt a church that conformed to the Augsburg Confession. However, no clear or uniform answer existed about how to apply the Peace, which did not define who counted as *Augsburger Konfessionsverwandten* (people who were akin or related – *Verwandt* – to the Augsburg Confession). As we will see later, there was not even an agreement about which *Reichunmittelbare* cities had the right to pick their church. Furthermore, an unpublished provision of the Peace granted nobles and some cities in ecclesiastical territories (who according to the main text would have to be Catholic) the right to continue adhering to the Augsburg Confession if they had already been doing so for several years. Disagreements arose immediately about the authenticity of that clause, since it had not been published or officially endorsed by the organs of imperial governance.[13] As we will see below, some people also invoked the Peace to legitimise claims to worship that it certainly did not permit. Thus, while the Peace of Augsburg provided a legal framework that successfully avoided large-scale warfare between Protestants and Catholics in the Empire for over 60 years, a key component of its success was in the malleability of its interpretation and implementation.

Constitutional and confessional boundaries for Netherlandish Reformed Protestants in the Empire

The ambiguities described above played out quite differently for Dutch-speaking Reformed Protestants depending on where they moved. In what follows, I consider the situation for Dutch Reformed migrants starting with places where their arrival was the most unambiguous from an imperial constitutional standpoint and moving to places where applying imperial law was more flexible. After the signing of the Peace, Catholics argued that only those imperial cities that had permitted Protestant worship before 1555 could choose to allow Protestantism after 1555. Cologne's Catholic magistrates followed that interpretation and thus accepted that they had no jurisdiction to permit Protestant worship. They repeatedly issued edicts against Protestantism and ordered the expulsion of Protestants.[14] And yet Dutch Reformed Protestants, who arrived in significant numbers in the 1560s, remained in Cologne through the rest of the century, worshipping at rotating locations in private houses. Keeping a low profile meant maintaining the trust of acquaintances – especially servants.[15] Dissenters also learned to prevaricate. In October 1571, Cologne's Reformed Protestants inquired at a synod held in Emden whether it was permissible to answer questions about whether they were Catholic with a simple "yes" and questions about whether they had disobeyed their king with a simple "no." They hoped that their casuistry about the meaning of the adjective "catholic" and their belief that King Philip could no longer claim obedience because he had broken his oath of office might provide them the safety they sought.[16] In 1570, the Reformed silversmith, Hubert van Coninxloo, from Brussels convinced officials that envious merchants had falsely accused him of heresy. Accused again three years later, Van Coninxloo brought in a local Catholic friend, Heinrich Faber, who explained that since Van Coninxloo lived with a number of Catholics, magistrates had no reason to worry about him.[17]

The survival of Dutch Reformed Protestants in Cologne was also due to the deliberate inaction of city officials, who often only took decisive steps due to external pressure. A raid of secret worship services in November 1571 followed insistence from Rome, Brussels, and the archbishopric of Cologne to take sharper action against Protestants.[18] Often, as long as religious minorities remained peaceable and quiet, city officials ignored them or were slow to act. Yet, given that Protestants made up some 10% of a city of about 40,000, roughly half of whom were Netherlanders, they must have remained a conspicuous presence.[19] A few Dutch Protestants even gained citizenship.[20] My point is not to paint a cheerful picture of a tolerant Cologne. Rather, it is to indicate that in a city where the constitutional situation was the least ambiguous – and the confessional boundaries the easiest to define – only lax enforcement of a clear law and careful discretion on the part of religious minorities allowed room for Dutch Reformed migrants to live there.

Dutch Reformed Protestants first arrived in the other leading imperial city of the northwestern empire – Aachen – in significant numbers by the early 1550s.[21] Like Cologne, Protestants living in Catholic Aachen worshipped underground before the Peace of Augsburg, and they did so after. However, unlike Cologne, Aachen's magistrates treated the decision to keep the city officially Catholic as theirs to make. In 1559, groups of non-Catholics requested permission to hold services according to the Augsburg Confession. Magistrates responded that they would not approve the request "at this time" (*noch zur Zeit*), implying that they might change their mind in the future.[22] It's not clear how many Reformed Netherlanders remained in Aachen after this, but the numbers rose again in 1567, to about 4,000 people, or roughly 15–20% of the population.[23] Pressure from Catholic princes from Brussels, Jülich-Cleves, and Liège convinced magistrates to order in April 1572 that all refugees from Brabant had to leave Aachen (and neighbouring Burtscheid, which was part of its jurisdiction).[24] But they never followed through on the order. Reformed Protestants were not even deterred from holding a synod in Burtscheid that November.[25]

Constitutionally speaking, matters grew more complex in 1574, when the government allowed *Augsburger Konfessionsverwandten* on the city council, effectively granting freedom of conscience for Protestants, if not freedom of worship. This decision sparked a question about the Peace of Augsburg: did cities that had been Catholic before 1555 possess the right to introduce Protestant worship? For Cologne, the answer had been "no". Aachen's magistrates seemed to say "yes". In 1581, the city council even permitted *Augsburger Konfessionsverwandten* to worship freely.[26] A furious Emperor Rudolf II named an imperial commission that ordered the expulsion of sectarians from Aachen. A legal case on this question wended its way through the empire's court system as Aachen now functioned as a triconfessional city.[27] Meanwhile, the city government treated Reformed Protestants as *Augsburger Konfessionsverwandten*, even though there also existed a different congregation that used the *invariata* (that is, Lutherans). Supporters of the new government denied that there were "Calvinists" in the city and insisted that Protestants only accepted ministers who followed the Augsburg Confession – without indicating which version.[28] Reformed Protestants continued to worship privately, though it is not clear whether they did so because of the unresolved legal questions making their way through the imperial court system, because they lacked funds, or because they feared military interference from an outside power.[29] But until a military occupation forced a Catholicisation of the city in 1614, Dutch Reformed migrants continued to live and worship in Aachen on the basis of both the city government's appeal to a contested imperial law and the ambiguity about whom that law applied to. In this case, the city did not recognise a legal boundary separating Lutherans from Reformed, but they did establish a clear ecclesiastical and congregational boundary.

The arrival of Netherlanders in Frankfurt posed different questions, since it had been officially Protestant since 1533. Initially, its pastors were more oriented towards Reformed brands of Protestantism. But in April 1536, the city joined the Schmalkaldic League, whose rules required adopting the Augsburg Confession. To comply, the city instead adopted the Wittenberg Concord, a confessional statement crafted that May to find a compromise between the two Protestant strands.[30] In 1542, Martin Bucer helped city officials produce the Frankfurt Concord (which was similar to the Wittenberg Concord, but now explicitly tied to the authority of the council), which city pastors signed that December. Thus, in Frankfurt the question was not whether the constitution gave the city council competency to make this decision as much as it was about defining what it meant to be "related" to the Augsburg Confession.

Within a year, Dutch-speaking Reformed Protestant migrants were permitted to live and worship in Frankfurt under the conditions that they would not interfere with local churches, that they would seek permission before appointing pastors, that they submit their doctrinal and liturgical standards to magistrates for approval, and that they accept the Frankfurt Concord.[31] The assumption was, then, that there were no constitutional hurdles to welcoming the newcomers because there was not a confessional distinction between them and their hosts. In September 1555, emboldened by the newly passed Peace of Augsburg, a couple of local pastors expressed scepticism that the newcomers were *Augsburger Konfessionsverwandten*. The foreign pastors explained that they would happily sign the Augsburg Confession, but did not clarify which version.[32] City clergy insisted that they follow the *invariata*. The council, however, only referred both groups to the Frankfurt Concord.[33] All sides were adopting different interpretations of what it meant to be *Augsburger Konfessionsverwandt*. Debates about what documents could be used to define *Augsburger Konfessionverwandtschaft* disturbed the city for the next six years.[34] By April 1561, magistrates decided that the only workable solution to this problem was to ask the migrants to sign the *invariata*. The pastor of the Dutch-speaking congregation, Petrus Dathenus, prepared a petition urging that "we are not fanatics [*Schwärmer*], nor violators of the sacrament, not even Calvinists or Zwinglians."[35] But members of the council would not be moved. Most foreign Protestants left the following spring. Some Dutch Reformed who stayed joined a French-speaking congregation that held services privately in a barn or a private house. In 1570, the Dutch again formed their own congregation, renting a separate house for services. However, they married and baptised in Frankfurt's city parishes and buried their dead in the city cemetery, though only dishonourable night burials. The situation had changed from religious concord to begrudging coexistence not because anyone's beliefs had changed, but because how they understood the boundaries between confessions relative to their beliefs had done so. In this case, the boundary dividing Reformed from Lutheran depended largely on one issue: The Real Presence of Christ in the Lord's Supper.

Over the following years, the migrants wrote repeated petitions requesting public worship. In these supplications, they underplayed religious differences with local clergy and stressed the importance of being able to worship in one's native language.[36] Meanwhile, city pastors complained about their illicit services and explained that the migrants spoke German perfectly well. But the council neither granted the strangers the right to worship nor made any effort to close their house churches. In 1577, Frankfurt's Dutch Reformed pastor, Werner Helmichius, wrote to a colleague in Delft that his congregation remained in the city by holding themselves quietly (*quiescimus*).[37] The size of Frankfurt's Dutch Reformed community stabilised and grew, climbing to 4,000 – roughly 20% of the city's population – by the 1590s.[38] In Frankfurt, religious diversity had shifted from a situation that looked more like Aachen's to one that looked more like Cologne's.

If constitutional questions prompted by the arrival of Dutch Reformed migrants could be confusing in imperial cities, they were even more so in Wesel, a territorial city in the duchy of Cleves. Even though *Reichsunmittelbarkeit* belonged to its Catholic prince, in 1552 Wesel's city council started establishing its own Protestant church, including adopting the Augsburg Confession.[39] When Dutch Reformed migrants arrived in 1553, the council's terms were standard: the newcomers had to accept the council's authority and conform to the local church.[40] In August 1555, as Peace negotiations in Augsburg were wrapping up, Wesel's city council stiffened its policy: anyone who would not adhere to the Augsburg Confession should leave within three days. As in Frankfurt, some local pastors expressed frustration that strangers did not conform to the *invariata* – especially on the Eucharist. Over the next few years, the council issued repeated rules requiring that migrants follow the Augsburg Confession. For four years – from 1561 to 1564 – magistrates required immigrants to sign another confessional statement, drawn up especially for their city, that closely followed the *invariata*, but they abandoned it when citizens urged them to back down after heated conflicts over this policy. After that, migrants still had to attend the local church and give lip service to 1530 Augsburg Confession, but no one pried too closely. Meanwhile, the Reformed strangers established a consistory that also helped them preserve the appearance of conformity.[41] Formally, the situation looked like Frankfurt. The key difference lay not so much in what public belief was permitted – the *invariata* was the standard in both – but how that rule was managed in practice. In Wesel, as long as the appearance of conformity was preserved, church attendance was robust and uneventful, social peace was maintained, and their own political authority was respected; magistrates mostly stayed out of people's business. Reformed Netherlanders came to make up about 50% of Wesel's population. In this hybrid form of coexistence, the boundaries between Lutheran and Reformed materialised rather differently than in Frankfurt: not so much around the Real Presence as around the consistory's practice of ecclesiastical discipline.

Wesel's solution depended not only on how magistrates enforced local law but also on how the duke of Cleves enforced imperial law. In a 1565 edict, Duke William I interpreted the Peace of Augsburg as banning non-Catholic worship but permitting *Augsburger Konfessionsverwandten* freedom of conscience. Until his death in 1592, Wilhelm never explicitly permitted non-Catholic worship, but he made no efforts to persecute those within Wesel's walls who adhered to the Augsburg Confession. In the late 1580s, magistrates still insisted to the duke that they "knew no one here who did not fully conform to the Augsburg Confession" and that "no Calvinists, but only Christians were baptised here."[42] Reformed Protestants also defended their rights to worship based on their adherence to the Augsburg Confession at meetings of the territorial estates in 1566, 1572, 1577, 1580, 1583, and 1592.[43] The duke never granted public worship for Protestants but instead decided – as he explained in 1580 – that he would "follow the religious peace to the letter."[44] And yet in practice, managing the arrival of Reformed migrants in Cleves usually did not require parsing the language of imperial law. At least within their civic jurisdictions, residents and migrants managed coexistence on their own.

This was also the case in smaller towns in the duchy of Cleves that hosted Dutch Reformed migrants where Catholics remained the majority. In Emmerich, Kalkar, Rees, and Xanten, Catholics also maintained a monopoly over public worship. Meanwhile, Goch and Gennep adopted accommodationist (or hybrid) liturgies in which Catholics and local *Augsburger Konfessionsverwandt*-Protestants (that is, Lutherans) worshipped together.[45] In all six towns, Reformed Protestants had private services in houses.[46] The Reformed congregations included some people who also periodically worshipped in the Catholic or mixed Lutheran-Catholic parishes. In some cases, this confessional fluidity resulted from the prerogative of individuals, but in others, it was enforced from above. In Goch, the town council required that members of the Reformed congregation attend sermons in the city's mixed churches periodically if they were to stay.[47] Reformed Protestants were most at risk when they travelled outside these towns because they might be stopped and arrested by ducal authorities. This was particularly a problem for pastors because cash-strapped congregations often shared ministers between them. In 1580, Goch's Reformed congregation fired its pastor, Nicholas Poncratius, because the elders deemed it too dangerous for him to be making such trips.[48] Sometimes entire congregations travelled to their pastor rather than him coming to them because that was the safer option.[49] Reformed Protestants from Xanten and Rees also appeared in Wesel to celebrate baptisms or marriages.[50] At the local level, the Peace of Augsburg usually did not play a central role. In January 1567, the Reformed pastor Bruno Bitter petitioned Xanten's city council for free worship according to the Augsburg Confession. When asked if he knew what that document said, he admitted his ignorance but said that he had heard that it was good and grounded in God's word.[51] Bitter seems to have been informed about the document's strategic value but not its content. The council did not accept his argument, nor did it close his church or arrest Bitter for heresy. As in Wesel, compromises at the local level were only possible because of the ambiguities of applying imperial law at the territorial level.

In Frankenthal, a Dutch Reformed settlement in the officially Reformed Electoral Palatinate, the newcomers' presence depended on how the Peace of Augsburg was applied, but in a wholly different way than the other cases. Starting in 1562 and 1563, Elector Palatine Frederick III stretched the limits of what it meant to be *Augsburger Konfessionsverwandt*, particularly because of his new Heidelberg Catechism's Reformed teaching on the Lord's Supper. Frederick argued that the Heidelberg Catechism agreed with *variata*, which he claimed constituted a legitimate interpretation of (rather than an alternative to) the *invariata*.[52] Frederick thereby concluded that his territory's church was permitted under the Peace, and Lutheran princes in the Empire – more concerned with external enemies (principally, the Ottoman Empire) and internal ones (Catholics) – could do little else but fume. When a group of Reformed Netherlanders who had abandoned Frankfurt in 1562 arrived in the Palatinate, Frederick granted them a tract of land at the former Frankenthal cloister, where they established a new Dutch settlement that followed Reformed norms without the secrecy or double-talk required elsewhere and banned all non-Reformed worship or belief.[53] Here confessional boundaries were defined tightly around the Heidelberg Catechism and the Palatine Church Ordinance and depended centrally on the patronage of a powerful prince to blur the limits of imperial law.

Clearly, the ambiguity of the Peace of Augsburg left diverse avenues for Reformed Protestants to find a home in the Empire. The variety of legal forms depended on not only how the Peace of Augsburg applied to a given polity but also how officials interpreted and enforced those rules and often how locals negotiated the boundaries between Lutheran and Reformed. Meanwhile, migrants also developed legal argumentation where they could, and cultivated political allies and patterns of discreet connivance where they couldn't, to develop local solutions to protect their stay. Thus far, we have identified two kinds of boundary management – confessional and constitutional. But as we will see, the situation gets even more diverse when we consider other forms as well.

Linguistic and social boundaries for Netherlandish Reformed Protestants in the Empire

A look at the linguistic and socio-economic profile of each of these Dutch Reformed communities also reveals considerable diversity that belies neat ethnic, sociocultural, or linguistic boundaries between "Dutch refugees" and "German hosts". Much of what follows draws on a demographic database of currently 19,530 individuals who lived in these communities. The database was produced by researchers for the project "The Rhineland Exiles and the Religious Landscape of the Dutch Republic, c.1550–1618," of which I am a co-director.[54] For this chapter, I used evidence from entries concerning the 2,236 individuals for whom researchers were able to ascertain the person's place of origin in the Dutch-speaking regions of the Low Countries *and* confirm their membership in one of these 11 Reformed congregations between 1550 and 1600.[55] Thus, while the first part of this chapter was organised around constitutional arrangements shaping regimes of coexistence, the second part begins with those host communities right along the border and then traces increasing social differentiation across linguistic and social boundaries between migrants and hosts as we move up the Rhine River watershed.

The surviving evidence suggests that, socially speaking, Dutch Reformed migrants travelling to Aachen shared a lot in common with their hosts. A large number (37%) of those whose territory of origin is known (*n* = 96) came from neighbouring Limburg. Of these, 54% came from Maastricht, only 30 km away, which had a long history of economic and cultural exchange with Aachen and throughout the Limburg-Liège-Aachen region.[56] In Aachen, many newcomers thus spoke a closely related dialect of *Rheinmaasländisch*, which allowed them to integrate readily.[57] In addition, 40% of the migrants came from Brabant, and only a few came from elsewhere in the Low Countries. Aachen's Dutch Reformed Protestants did not dramatically stand out in their socio-economic profiles either. The majority (57% of those whose occupation is known) were artisans and craftsmen that constituted an assortment of bakers, carpenters, locksmiths, tailors, cobblers, and cloth makers, similar to locals. The newcomers also joined local trade associations without sparking noticeable unease. Dutch Reformed merchants who moved to Aachen were largely tied to the same regional markets (especially of textiles, foods, and dry goods) that had long linked the city to Limburg and Brabant.[58] The immigrants did not stand out from their hosts for their wealth or their poverty, and there is no evidence of significant economic tensions between strangers and hosts. Neither did such linguistic and political divides define the ecclesiastical institutions that developed among Reformed Protestants in Aachen.[59] In 1567, one congregation moved – seemingly *en masse* – from nearby Maastricht and functioned separately from the other Reformed congregation, which included all other Reformed Protestants in the city, including many from the Netherlands. In 1579, the two congregations merged.[60] While confessional tensions shaped local social relations, German-Dutch linguistic, cultural, ethnic, or political boundaries did not form a significant part of this story.

The situation was similar in the small towns in Cleves that hosted Dutch Reformed migrants. Of the 66 migrants who left a record of their origin, over 70% came from across the border in Guelders, eastern Brabant, and Limburg.[61] The local Lower Franconian dialect in Cleves, called *Kleverlands*, was also linguistically closer to other Dutch dialects than to forms of High or Low German spoken further south and east.[62] Sometimes migrants also had family relations, and in the case of nobles, even property, in and around these towns, as was the case for the Van Randwijck family who moved from Nijmegen to Gennep – a "migration" of only 17 km.[63] Neither were the Dutch Reformed migrants in these Cleves' towns significantly distinguishable from their hosts in terms of their occupations. An astonishingly high percentage of those whose occupation can be identified were ministers (35%) – a result of the combination of unsafe road conditions in the Catholic duchy, which caused high turnover among Reformed pastors, combined with the fact that the congregations were small. Outside of that group, most of the migrants whose occupation is known do not present a distinct picture: they were an assortment of bakers, cobblers, clock makers, soldiers, cloth bleachers, and boat pilots. The Reformed congregations within these towns cannot be called "foreign" or "Dutch" churches in any straightforward sense. All of them constituted a mix between locals and migrants. At times, city leaders and other local elites joined these congregations.[64] Linguistic, social, and cultural boundaries were simply not central to these churches.

The situation was different in the duchy of Cleves' largest city, Wesel, where fleeing Netherlanders sparked a legitimate refugee crisis. From the 1540s, but especially after 1566, thousands of Reformed Protestants fled to Wesel, where a combination of extensive civic autonomy, widespread support for Protestantism, and an eagerness to bolster the local economy contributed to their mostly welcome reception. During the high point of immigration, refugees slept in the streets and camped outside the city gates.[65] Dutch migrants to Wesel were also more distinct demographically from locals than the migrants arriving in Aachen or smaller towns in Cleves. Among the 880 known Reformed Netherlanders in Wesel in the late sixteenth century, some 35% of whose origin is known came from Brabant (40% of whom came from Antwerp), while 21% came from Flanders. Significant numbers also came from Zeeland, Limburg, Guelders, and Overijssel. Basically, every region of the Low Countries was represented in Wesel. Linguistically, then, the Reformed migrants in Wesel spoke a diverse array of Dutch dialects among themselves, but also the Lower Saxon dialects of German spoken in northeastern parts of the Netherlands. There is little reason to think that most migrants arriving in Wesel imagined themselves as a single people.[66] However, the Dutch dialects spoken by most migrants were also intelligible to Wesel's Kleverlands speakers. There was enough of a difference that one married Dutch couple explained that they were travelling back to Leiden in August 1581 because "they could not understand the German language [*de Duytsche sprake*] of our church's ministers."[67] But the fact that they were the only Netherlanders to ever make this claim suggests that this was not a common problem. Mutual comprehensibility in Wesel made it realistic for officials to require that Dutch-speaking migrants attend the local church and difficult for migrants unsatisfied with this arrangement to argue that they should hold separate services because of language differences, as happened at Frankfurt.

In terms of wealth and status, Dutch migrants to Wesel looked neither especially richer nor poorer than long-time residents of Wesel. The dominant industries in Wesel were wool weaving, furriery, and armour making, while the city had an assortment of other artisans and craftsmen common in early modern cities. Roughly 43% of Dutch migrants to Wesel were also artisans and craftsmen, but the newcomers brought new areas of specialisation, especially production of the "new draperies," light, mixed cloths popular among northern Renaissance elites.[68] Merchants made up 24% of the Dutch Reformed population in the city – about twice the percentage of the local population. In Wesel, local traders brought wool, wine, and lumber to the Rhine River delta and returned with cured fish, salt, dry goods, and textiles.[69] Dutch merchants in Wesel mostly traded in higher value cloth goods, mostly "new draperies" produced locally. Meanwhile, educated professionals, such as ministers, schoolteachers, doctors, lawyers, and printers, made up another 28% of the Dutch Reformed migrants, roughly the same percentage as Wesel's population. Thus, Netherlanders fleeing to Wesel were not dramatically wealthier than the local population, but they definitely stood out. However, just as in Aachen and elsewhere in Cleves, Wesel's long-term economic, cultural, and linguistic connections with the Low Countries made worshipping together with their hosts possible.

Further up the Rhine River watershed, in the imperial cities of Cologne and Frankfurt, greater economic, linguistic, and cultural boundaries distinguished the Dutch migrants from their hosts. Researchers have identified the province of origin for 546 Dutch Reformed in Cologne and the city of origin for 520. Of these, 68% came from Brabant, with 90% of those coming from either Antwerp (70%) or Brussels (20%), and 18% came from Flanders (mostly Bruges, Ghent, and Oudenaarde). Only 14% came from all the other regions of the Netherlands combined. That is, Reformed Netherlanders in Cologne constituted a rather homogeneous population: these people largely came from the most densely populated and cosmopolitan parts of the Low Countries. And their Brabantine and Flemish dialects of sixteenth-century Dutch were further afield from the dialect of High German spoken in Cologne (called *Oberländisch*).[70] Communication between migrants and hosts depended on the high frequency of multilingualism among the migrants, not on a similarity between the two group's native tongues. This linguistic difference explains why this is the first location discussed here where Reformed Protestants segregated into distinct German- and Dutch-speaking congregations.[71]

Professionally, Cologne's Dutch Reformed community was dominated by a group of wealthy social elites. Of the 136 migrants for whom we have evidence of their occupation, 28% were educated professionals (doctors, ministers, schoolteachers, or government officials) or artists (engravers, painters, jewellers, and goldsmiths).[72] Merchants made up as much as 43% of Cologne's Reformed Netherlanders. Furthermore, these were among the wealthiest traders in Europe, most of whom had previously operated out of Antwerp, but who also had factors (agents) in Bremen, Hamburg, La Rochelle, Venice, Lisbon, Seville, London, and elsewhere, connecting them to vast global trade networks, giving them access to sugar from the Azores, as well as spices and diamonds from the Indian subcontinent.[73] They maintained a robust trade along the so-called Cologne Highway that ran along roads from Antwerp, via Liège and Jülich.[74] Cologne was the key transfer point for the trade in fancy clothes, spices, and sugar that were shipped further inland to Frankfurt and then on to places like Nuremberg, Augsburg, Venice, and Prague. Thus, for Protestant merchants fleeing persecution, Cologne presented an attractive location, despite its fame as a centre of Catholicism. Seven percent of Dutch Reformed in Cologne were servants or maids, mostly serving well-off Dutch migrant families. A relatively small proportion of the population whose occupation is known were ordinary craftsmen and artisans (15%). In all, Cologne's Dutch Reformed community looked in many ways like a foreign expatriate community common to large cities in sixteenth-century Europe, including Dutch communities in Hamburg and Venice.[75] The wealth of this foreign community also helps us understand local officials' occasional willingness to turn a blind eye to their religious dissent.

Frankfurt's Dutch Reformed community looked similar to Cologne's. This too was a group dominated by migrants from a few wealthy, cosmopolitan cities in the southern Netherlands. Of those whose territory of origin is known (536), 86% came from either Brabant (38%) or Flanders (48%). Of those from Brabant whose city of origin is also known, 78% came from Antwerp. Only 14% came from the rest of the Low Countries. That is, these people largely spoke the same dialect and largely came out of the same social circles back in the Netherlands. Many also operated within international networks of trade, information, and politics that included Nuremberg, Madrid, Lisbon, and Venice. While Frankfurt saw far fewer shipments from Antwerp than Cologne did, those shipments were over twice as valuable. Wagons arriving from Antwerp (transported through Cologne) brought sugar, spices, laces, embroidery, and belts to the wealthy Renaissance elites in Frankfurt and the surrounding region, and on to elsewhere in German-speaking lands up the Rhine and further east, as well as to Bohemia and Italy.[76]

In terms of its socio-economic profile, Frankfurt's Dutch Reformed population also resembled Cologne's. Educated professionals (like pastors, lawyers, printers, or doctors) or those involved in the arts (like jewellers, goldsmiths, and painters) made up 26% of the population. The 20% who were merchants were some of the wealthiest residents of the city.[77] Meanwhile, 26% of the Dutch Reformed population were servants, most of whom worked for wealthier members of their community. Frankfurt's Reformed Dutch community also had a bit higher proportion of craftsmen and artisans than Cologne (26% versus 15%), among whom most worked in the "new draperies." This profile meant that overall the Netherlanders were wealthier and more tied to lucrative trades than locals.[78] There also existed a significant linguistic gap between Brabantine or Flemish versions of Dutch spoken by the migrants and the Hessian-style German spoken in Frankfurt. Mutual incomprehensibility was taken for granted by Dutch and German speakers alike. This language difference had been the justification for permitting Dutch speakers to worship separately from locals in 1554.[79] In later years, Dutch Reformed migrants cited the language difference as the reason they could not worship in the local churches.[80]

Of all these migrant communities, Frankenthal's looked the most distinct from locals. Of course, this was because there was no host population – the Netherlanders were given a recently emptied tract of land where a cloister had once stood. Demographically, Frankenthal's residents looked like a pretty homogeneous enclave of settlers, distinct from the Germans in the nearby villages and towns in the Rhenish Palatinate. The vast majority (85%) came from Flanders (49%) and Brabant (36%). Many of those came from family networks in Bruges, Ghent, Ypres, Antwerp, Brussels, Steenwerk, and Oudenaarde. They also spoke a wholly different language than the Palatine dialect of High German used in the surrounding villages.[81] German- and French-speakers who later moved to Frankenthal were required to learn Dutch, the language of government into the seventeenth century. In 1582, German-speaking immigrants to Frankenthal petitioned the prince for a separate church, citing mutual incomprehensibility.[82] The occupational profile of migrants to Frankenthal was remarkably limited. Almost a third of the population whose occupation is known were goldsmiths, painters, and tapestry makers, often from Brussels and Oudenaarde.[83] About 10% were merchants, while 41% were ordinary artisans or craftsmen. Of those, most made fancy clothes for export. This was largely an outpost of Netherlandish artists, artisans, and educated urbanites building a Dutch Reformed settlement in the German countryside.

Conclusions

In considering the demographics of these immigrant communities next to their neighbours and alongside the diverse applications of imperial law, we can begin to discern distinct factors shaping the forms of coexistence they developed with their hosts. In places nearer to the Netherlands, coexistence was more easily built around cultural and linguistic similarities, which also permitted locals and migrants to worship together. That made it possible for Wesel to adopt a confessionally ambiguous public church that everyone was required to attend. It also made it possible for Reformed migrants in Aachen and the small towns of Cleves to find coreligionists in their new homes with whom they shared private or semi-private churches. Further afield, as in Cologne and Frankfurt, where migrants stood out socially and culturally, religious pluralism was instead built primarily on mutual economic interests, which convinced officials to look the other way at times and encouraged migrants to keep a low profile. Meanwhile, migrants only moved to Frankenthal as a result of failures of strategies of coexistence elsewhere. The migrants there look more like utopian settlers who avoided having to develop strategies for religious pluralism, but that was only because the Elector Palatine did this for them at the imperial level.

Of course, members of this Dutch Reformed diaspora understood themselves to be part of a transnational community of faith that was not only discrete and well-defined, but also connected to a universal, timeless, divine, and eternal spiritual community.[84] They exchanged letters frequently. They provided one another with financial and spiritual support. They met at regional assemblies to offer one another advice. As Dutch elders in Cologne wrote to coreligionists in Wesel enduring a terrifying siege by Spanish troops in November 1587:

> [W]e believe in a community of the Saints, who together are members of one body under one head, Jesus Christ, that calls to a common father in heaven, who are in one church, who are baptised with one baptism, who are governed with one spirit, like members of one body with one soul.[85]

Such bonds across the diaspora could prove powerful forces in holding an international Reformed movement together, which otherwise lacked political and ecclesiastical structures capable of doing so, as Ole Peter Grell and others have argued.[86] Examining such diasporic bonds and international networks can help us understand the nature and function of the Dutch Reformed diaspora whose members unambiguously defined themselves against others around them. But we should not stop at this emic perspective, centring on the views of church's pastors and elders, that treats Dutch Reformed refugees as an undifferentiated whole, with shared morphological characteristics across the diaspora, or parallel differences distinguishing them from their hosts. To understand the diverse forms of coexistence in which they participated, historians also need to adopt an etic perspective that seeks to understand diverse forms of boundary management among migrants themselves and between themselves and others. It was through the production, reproduction, and renegotiation of boundaries at the local level (within wider non-local frameworks) that regimes of coexistence between migrants and hosts formed. Admittedly, our understanding of how such regimes worked will always be incomplete, and there are many more contexts here I might have considered, including marriage patterns, the naming of children, clothing styles, and more. And there were more changes within these regimes of co-existence over time – as the result of new political pressures, new waves of migrants, and new economic opportunities – than I have space to describe. Still, it is clear to me that, even if individuals in the diaspora moved between these 11 communities (and others), the formal and informal rules governing their coexistence with their hosts were locally bounded. Those rules were also being ever redefined by dialogic interactions between various forms of boundary management, which generated and regenerated the distinctions between migrants and their hosts who did not *have* to learn to coexist, but seem to have done so anyway.

Notes

1 For example, Heinz Schilling, *Niederländische Exulanten im 16. Jahrhundert* (Gütersloh: Gütersloher Verlagshaus G. Mohn, 1972). Robert Roosbroeck, *Emigranten: Nederlandse vluchtelingen in Duitsland 1550–1600* (Leuven: Davidsfonds, 1968). In some ways, I did this myself in my first book. Jesse Spohnholz, *The Tactics of Toleration: A Refugee Community in the Age of Religious Wars* (Newark: University of Delaware Press, 2011).

2 David M. Luebke, *Hometown Religion: Regimes of Coexistence in Early Modern Westphalia* (Charlottesville, VA: University of Virginia Press, 2016), 203–13.

3 For historical accounts, Keith P. Luria, *Sacred Boundaries: Religious Coexistence and Conflict in Early-Modern France* (Washington, DC: Catholic University of America Press, 2005). Duane J. Corpis, *Crossing the Boundaries of Belief: Geographies of Religious Conversion in Southern Germany, 1648–1800* (Charlottesville: University of Virginia Press, 2014). For anthropological treatments, Frederik Barth, ed., *Ethnic Groups and Boundaries: The Social Organization of Cultural Difference* (Boston: Little, Brown and Company, 1969).

4 Johannes Arndt, *Das Heilige Römische Reich und die Niederlande 1566 bis 1648: Politisch-konfessionelle Verflechtung und Publizistik im Achtzigjährigen Krieg* (Cologne: Böhlau, 1998). Hugo de Schepper, "The Burgundian-Habsburg Netherlands," in *Handbook of European History, 1400–1600*, ed. Thomas A. Brady, Heiko Oberman, and James D. Tracy (Leiden: Brill, 1994), 501–4.

5 Maximilian Lanzinner, ed., *Der Reichstag zu Speyer 1570*, vol. 2 (Göttingen: Vandenhoeck & Ruprecht, 1988), 1001–3, 24, 33–4, 39–41. See also Rients Reitsma, *Centrifugal and Centripetal Forces in the Early Dutch Republic: The State of Overijssel, 1566–1600* (Amsterdam: Rodopi, 1982), 88, 220–1.

6 See below.

7 On early modern borders, see Bernard Vogler, "Borders and Boundaries in Early Modern Europe: Problems and Possibilities," in *Frontiers and the Writing of History, 1500–1800*, ed. Seven G. Ellis and Reingard Esser (Hanover: Wehrhahn Verlag, 2006), 20–38. Luca Scholz, *Borders and Freedom of Movement in the Holy Roman Empire* (Oxford: Oxford University Press, 2020).

8 Compare the locations of the toll stations to a regional street map. Herbert Münker, *Die Weseler Schiffahrt vornehmlich zur Zeit des spanisch-niederländischen Krieges* (Wesel: Carl Kühler, 1908), 45. Irmgard Hantsche, *Atlas zur Geschichte des Niederrheins* (Bottrop/Essen: Peter Pomp, 1999), 57.

9 See Hantsche, *Atlas*, 69. On political borders and religious coexistence more generally, see Benjamin J. Kaplan, *Divided by Faith: Religious Conflict and the Practice of Toleration in Early Modern Europe* (Cambridge, MA: Belknap Press, 2007), 144–71.

Constitutional Dynamism and Demographic Diversity 149

10 Matthias Pohlig, "Wahrheit als Lüge - oder: Schloss der Augsburger Religionsfrieden den Calvinsmus aus?," in *Konfessionelle Ambiguität: Uneindeutigkeit und Verstellung als religiöse Praxis in der Frühen Neuzeit*, ed. Andreas Pietsch and Barbara Stollberg-Rilinger (Gütersloh: Gütersloher Verlaghaus, 2013), 148–9.
11 Stefan Ehrenpreis and Ute Lotz-Heumann, *Reformation und konfessionelles Zeitalter* (Darmstadt: Wissenschaftliche Buchgesellschaft, 2002), 62–79.
12 On the pre-figuring of this divide onto the early Reformation, see Amy Nelson Burnett, *Debating the Sacraments: Print and Authority in the Early Reformation* (Oxford: Oxford University Press, 2019). On the continued ambiguity of this divide into the late Reformation, Pohlig, "Wahrheit als Lüge," 142–69.
13 Luebke, *Hometown Religion*, 39–42.
14 Hans-Wolfgang Bergerhausen, *Die Stadt Köln und die Reichsversammlungen im konfessionellen Zeitalter: Ein Beitrag zur korporativen reichsständischen Politik, 1555–1616* (Cologne: Kölnischer Geschichtsverein, 1990), 151–3.
15 Ute Langer, "Die konfessionelle Grenze in frühneuzeitlichen Köln: Das Zusammenleben von Reformierten und Katholiken zwischen Anpassung und Abgrenzung," *Geschichte in Köln: Zeitschrift für Stadt- und Regionalgeschichte* 53 (2015), 40.
16 Johan van Toorenenbergen, ed., *Brieven uit onderscheidene kerkelijke archieven* (Utrecht: Kemink, 1882), 14. F. L. Rutgers, ed., *Acta van de Nederlandsche synoden der zestiende eeuw* (Dordrecht: J.P. van den Tol, 1980), 90–6. On forms of dissimulation, see Johann P. Sommerville, "The 'New Art of Lyng': Equivocation, Mental Reservation, and Casuistry," in *Conscience and Casuistry in Early Modern Europe*, ed. Edmund Leites (Cambridge: Cambridge University Press, 1988), 159–84; Perez Zagorin, *Ways of Lying: Dissimulation, Persecution, & Conformity in Early Modern Europe* (Cambridge, MA: Harvard University Press, 1990).
17 Peter Gorter, *Gereformeerde migranten: De religieuze identiteit van Nederlandse gereformeerde migrantengemeenten in de rijksteden Frankfurt am Main, Aken en Keulen (1555–1600)* (Hilversum: Verloren, 2021), 74.
18 Gorter, *Gereformeerde migranten*, 75–6. For another instance, Gorter, *Gereformeerde migranten*, 83–4.
19 Bergerhausen, *Die Stadt Köln und die Reichsversammlungen*, 151.
20 Schilling, *Niederländische Exulanten*, 41.
21 Thomas Kirchner, *Katholiken, Lutheraner und Reformierte in Aachen, 1555–1618* (Tübingen: Mohr Siebeck, 2015), 51–3.
22 Walter Schmitz, *Verfassung und Bekenntnis: Die Aachener Wirren im Spiegel der kaiserlichen Politik (1550–1616)* (Frankfurt am Main: Lang, 1983), 46–7.
23 Arndt, *Das Heilige Römische Reich*, 196.
24 Schilling, *Niederländische Exulanten*, 32–3, 73–4. Kirchner, *Katholiken, Lutheraner und Reformierte*, 79, 96–9.
25 H. Q. Janssen and J. J. van Toorenenbergen, eds., *Acten van classicale en synodale vergaderingen der verstrooide gemeente in het land van Cleef, Sticht van Keulen en Aken, 1571–1589* (Utrecht: Kemink & Zoon, 1882), 22–4.
26 Schmitz, *Verfassung und Bekenntnis*, 122.
27 Kirchner, *Katholiken, Lutheraner und Reformierte*.
28 Kirchner, *Katholiken, Lutheraner und Reformierte*, 117.
29 Kirchner, *Katholiken, Lutheraner und Reformierte*, 277–8.
30 Anja Johann, *Kontrolle mit Konsens: Sozialdisziplinierung in der Reichsstadt Frankfurt am Main im 16. Jahrhundert* (Frankfurt am Main: Verlag Waldemar Kramer, 2001), 95–100.
31 Gustav Adolf Besser, *Geschichte der Frankfurter Flüchtlingsgemeinden, 1554–1558* (Halle: Druck von E. Karras, 1906), 9–10. Maximillian Miguel Scholz, *Strange Brethren: Refugees, Religious Bonds, and Reformation in Frankfurt, 1554–1608* (Charlottsville: University of Virginia Press, 2021), 44–103.

32 Tobias Schreiber, *Petrus Dathenus und der Heidelberger Katechismus: Eine traditionsgeschichtliche Untersuchung zum konfessionellen Wandel in der Kurpfalz um 1563* (Göttingen: Vandenhoeck & Ruprecht, 2017), 48.

33 Hermann Meinert, ed., *Die Eingliederung der niederländischen Glaubensflüchtlinge in die Frankfurter Bürgerschaft, 1554–1596: Auszüge aus den Frankfurter Ratsprotokollen* (Frankfurt am Main: W. Kramer, 1981), 18–20, 24–25.

34 These debates form a key focus of Scholz, *Strange Brethren*. Scholz looks at the French-, Dutch-, and English-speaking refugees together, while Peter Gorter compares the Dutch-speaking migrants in three imperial cities. Gorter, *Gereformeerde migranten*.

35 *Franckfurtischer Religions-Handlungen [...]*, vol. 1 (Frankfurt am Main: Franz Varrentrapp, 1735), Beylage XLII, 77.

36 Irene Dingel, "Religionssupplikationen der Französisch-Reformierten Gemeinde in Frankfurt am Main," in *Calvin und Calvinismus: Europäische Perspektiven*, ed. Irene Dingel and Herman J. Selderhuis (Göttingen: Vandenhoeck & Ruprecht, 2011), 281–96.

37 Gorter, *Gereformeerde migranten*, 47.

38 Schilling, *Niederländische Exulanten*, 52–3.

39 Spohnholz, *Tactics of Toleration*, 34–42.

40 Spohnholz, *Tactics of Toleration*, 42–51.

41 Spohnholz, *Tactics of Toleration*, 76–92.

42 Ludwig Keller, *Die Gegenreformation in Westfalen und am Niederrhein: Actenstücke und Erläuterungen*, vol. 2 (Leipzig: Hirzel, 1887), 188, 192.

43 Ingeborg Schipper, "Across the Borders of Belief: Netherlandish Reformed Migrants and Confessional Boundaries in the Duchy of Cleves, c. 1550–1600" (PhD diss., Vrije Universiteit Amsterdam, 2021), 111–21. Achim Dünnwald, *Konfessionsstreit und Verfassungskonflikt: Die Aufnahme der niederländischen Flüchtlinge im Hertzogtum Kleve, 1566–1585* (Bielefeld: Verlag für Regionalgeschichte, 1998), 251–7.

44 Ludwig Keller, ed., *Die Gegenreformation in Westfalen und am Niederrhein*, vol. 1 (Leipzig: S. Hirzel, 1881), 257.

45 Jan G.J. van Booma, *Communio clandestina: Archivalien der Konsistorien der heimlichen niederländischen reformierten Flüchtlingsgemeinden in Goch und Gennep im Herzogtum Kleve 1570–circa 1610*, vol. I (Bonn: Verlag Dr. Rudolf Habelt, 2010), 58–60. For similar situations in neighbouring Münsterland, Luebke, *Hometown Religion*.

46 Booma, *Communio clandestina*, 1:20, 215.

47 Booma, *Communio clandestina*, 1:176.

48 Schipper, "Across the Borders of Belief," 130–1.

49 Schipper, "Across the Borders of Belief," 88–9, 115.

50 Schipper, "Across the Borders of Belief," 142–3.

51 H. Kessel, "Reformation und Gegenreformation im Herzogtum Cleve (1517–1609)," *Düsseldorfer Jahrbuch* 30 (1920), 17.

52 Pohlig, "Wahrheit als Lüge," 154–7. Irene Dingel, "Augsburger Religionsfrieden und 'Augsburgerverwandtschaft' – konfessionelle Lesarten," in *Der Augsburger Religionsfrieden, 1555*, ed. Heinz Schilling and Heribert Smolinsky (Münster: Aschendorff, 2007), 160–1.

53 Elisabeth Bütfering, "Niederländische Exulanten in Frankenthal – Gründungsgeschichte, Bevölkerungsstruktur und Migrationsverhalten," in *Kunst, Kommerz, Glaubenskampf: Frankenthal um 1600*, ed. Edgard J. Hürkey (Worms: Wernersche Verlagsgesellschaft, 1995), 37–47. Judith Becker, "Kirchenordnung und Reformierte Identitätsbildung am Beispiel Frankenthals," in *Kommunikation und Transfer in Christentum*, ed. Irene Dingel and Wolf-Friedrich Schäufele (Mainz: Verlag Philipp von Zabern, 2007), 275–95.

54 The other co-director is Mirjam van Veen. Other researchers for this project, funded by the Dutch Research Council, were Inge Schipper, Peter Gorter, and Silke Muylaert. Researchers Daniel Herbert Fogt and Ana Barnes also contributed. For this chapter, people from the city of Mechelen are treated as coming from Brabant, though in the sixteenth century, the city belonged to a small enclave surrounded by Brabant.

55 Individuals who lived in multiple communities are counted separately for each place they lived.

56 Jean Lejeune, *Land zonder grens: Aken/Luik/Maastricht: Studie over de geschiedkundige ontwikkeling der drie steden* (Brussels: Charles Dessart, 1958).

57 For linguistic map, see Hantsche, *Atlas*, 67. Arent Mihm, "Rheinmaasländische Sprachgeschichte von 1500 bis 1650," in *Rheinische-Westfälische Sprachgeschichte*, ed. Jurgen Macha and Elber Neuss (Cologne: Böhlau, 2000), 139–54.

58 Donald Harreld, *High Germans in the Low Countries: German Merchants and Commerce in Golden Age Antwerp* (Leiden: Brill, 2004), 161.

59 Gorter, *Gereformeerde migranten*, 56–69.

60 Hansgeorg Molitor, "Reformation und Gegenreformation in der Reichsstadt Aachen," *Zeitschrift des Aachener Geschichtsvereins* 98/99, no. 1 (1992/1993), 190–1.

61 On cross-border allegiances in this area, Aart Noordzij, "Against Burgundy: The Appeal of Germany in the Duchy of Guelders," in *Networks, Regions and Nations: Shaping Identities in the Low Countries, 1300–1600*, ed. Robert Stein and Judith Pollmann (Leiden: Brill, 2009), 111–29.

62 Helmut Tervooren, "Sprache und Sprachen am Niederrhein (1550–1900)," in *Sprache an Rhein und Ruhr: Dialektologische und Soziolinguistische Studien zur Sprachlichen Situation im Rhein-Ruhr-Gebiet und ihrer Geschichte*, ed. Arent Mihm (Stuttgart: Franz Steiner Verlag, 1985), 30–47. Charlotte Giesbers, "Dialecten op de grens van twee talen: Een dialectologische en sociolinguistisch onderzoek in het Kleverlands dialectgebied" (PhD diss., Radbout University, 2008). Arent Mihm, "Spache und Geschichte am unterem Niederrhein," *Jahrbuch des Vereins für niederdeutsche Sprachforschung* (1992), 88–122.

63 Schipper, "Across the Borders of Belief," 42–7.

64 Kessel, "Reformation und Gegenreformation," 7–74. Schipper, "Across the Borders of Belief," 47–50.

65 Spohnholz, *Tactics of Toleration*, 71.

66 On political identities in the Netherlands, see A. C. Duke, "The Elusive Netherlands: The Question of National Identity in the Early Modern Low Countries on the Eve of the Revolt," *Bijdragen en Mededelingen betreffende de Geschiedenis der Nederlanden* 119, no. 1 (2004), 10–38.

67 Evangelisches Kirchenarchiv Wesel Gefach 72.2, f. 240^v.

68 These numbers are slightly different from those presented in Spohnholz, *Tactics of Toleration*, 186. The difference reflects both new prosopographical data added to the database since that original project and the fact that the earlier numbers included Lutheran and Anabaptist migrants, who are not considered here. On the "new draperies," see D.C. Coleman, "An Innovation and Its Diffusion: The 'New Draperies'," *The Economic History Review* 22, no. 3 (1969), 417–29.

69 Münker, *Die Weseler Schiffahrt*, 40–1.

70 Arend Mihm, "Sprachwandel in der frühen Neuzeit: Augsburg und Köln im Vergleich," in *Deutsch im 17. Jahrhundert: Studien zu Sprachkontakt, Sprachvariation und Sprachwandel: Gedenkschrift für Jürgen Macha*, ed. Markus Denkler et al. (Heidelberg: Universitätsverlag Winter, 2017), 265–319.

71 Gorter, *Gereformeerde migranten*, 77. In practice, they made the Maas River the border, though they made exceptions. Gorter, *Gereformeerde migranten*, 161–2.

72 This choice to categorise goldsmiths with these professions, rather than with artisans like weavers and smiths, resulted from the fact that most of Cologne's goldsmith

were masters who produced expensive artistic works, not middling journeymen. See J. G. C. A. Briels, "Zuidnederlandse goud- en zilversmeden in Noordnederland omstreeks, 1576–1625," *Bijdragen tot de Geschiedenis* 55 (1972), 89–112.

73 Before 1585, Dutch merchants in Cologne mostly engaged in Italian trade through deals with Italian merchants in the city. Gertrud Susanna Gramulla, *Handelsbeziehungen Kölner Kaufleute zwischen 1500 und 1650* (Cologne: Böhlau, 1972), 202–41.

74 Harreld, *High Germans in the Low Countries*, 29–32, 61, 106, 129–30. See also J. A. van Houtte, *Die Beziehungen zwischen Köln und den Niederlanden vom Hochmittelalter bis zum Beginn des Industriezietalters* (Cologne: Forschungsinstitut för Sozial- und Wirtschaftgeschichte an der Universität zu Köln, 1969), 6–14. Gramulla, *Handelsbeziehungen*, 219–22. Hermann Thimme, "Der Handel Kölns am Ende des 16. Jahrhunderts und die internationale Zusammensetzung der Kölner Kaufmannschaft," *Westdeutsche Zeitschrift für Geschichte und Kunst* 31 (1913), 389–473.

75 Maartje Van Gelder, *Trading Places: The Netherlandish Merchant Community in Venice, 1590–1650* (Leiden: Brill, 2009), 99–130. Jerun Poettering, *Migrating Merchants: Trade, Nation, and Religion in Seventeenth-Century Hamburg and Portugal*, trans. Kenneth Kronenberg (Berlin: De Gruyter, 2019), 194–6.

76 See Harreld, *High Germans in the Low Countries*, 129–30. Matthias Meyn, *Die Reichsstadt Frankfurt vor dem Bürgeraufstand von 1612 bis 1614: Stuktur und Krise* (Frankfurt am Main: Verlag Waldemar Kramer, 1980), 134–6.

77 Previous efforts to describe the occupational profile of Netherlanders in Frankfurt combined Walloons and Flemish, Lutherans and Reformed. See Anton Schindling, "Wachstum und Wandel von konfessionellen Zeitalter bis zum Zeitalter Ludwigs XIV: Frankfurt am Main 1555–1685," in *Frankfurt am Main: Die Geschichte der Stadt in neuen Beiträge* (Frankfurt am Main: Thorbecke, 1994), 226. Alexander Dietz, *Frankfurter Handelsgeschichte*, vol. 2 (Frankfurt: Gebrüder Knauer, 1921), 41. W. Brulez, "De diaspora der antwerpse kooplui op het einde van de 16e eeuw," *Bijdragen voor de geschiedenis der Nederlanden* 14 (1960/61), 292–3.

78 Only three percent of Frankfurt's population were merchants, while most were artisans and craftsmen who worked as cobblers, coopers, fishmongers, butchers, tailors, and the like. Robert Jütte, *Obrigkeitliche Armenfürsorge in Deutchen Reichsstädten der Frühen Neuzeit: Städtisches Armenwesen in Frankfurt am Main und Köln* (Cologne: Böhlau Verlag, 1984), 64–6.

79 Meinert, *Die Eingliederung*, 4. FRG, vol. 1, Beylage I, 2.

80 As for instance in 1592, *Franckfurtischer Religions-Handlungen [...]*, vol. 2 (Frankfurt am Main: Franz Varrentrapp, 1735), Beylage LXXIX, 121–2.

81 Meredith Hassall, "Dialect Focusing and Language Transfer in Sixteenth Century Germany" (PhD diss., University of Wisconsin-Madison, 2001).

82 Friedrich Cuno, *Geschichte der wallonisch-reformirten Gemeinde zu Frankenthal* (Magdeburg: Heinrichshofen, 1894), 11–2.

83 Erik Duverger, "Bildwerkerei in Oudenaarde und Frankenthal," in *Kunst, Kommerz und Glaubenskaumpf: Frankenthal um 1600*, ed. Edgard J. Hürkey (Worms: Wernerscher Verlagsgesellschaft, 1995), 86–96.

84 On this point, see Jesse Spohnholz, "Transnational Netherlandish Refugee Networks and the Politics of the Early Dutch Republic, 1568–1590," *Refugee Politics in Early Modern Europe*, ed. Geert Janssen and David de Boer (London: Routledge, forthcoming).

85 Toorenenbergen, *Brieven uit onderscheidene kerkelijke archieven*, WMV 3,5, 123.

86 Ole Peter Grell, *Brethren in Christ: A Calvinist Network in Reformation Europe* (Cambridge: Cambridge University Press, 2011). Mack Holt, "International Calvinism," in *John Calvin in Context*, ed. R. Ward Holder (Cambridge: Cambridge University Press, 2020), 375–82.

7 Ambivalent Neighbours
Sensory and Spatial Dynamics of Religious Exchange in Early Modern Tuscany*

Nicholas Terpstra

Early in July 1605, Bishop Antonio Grimani arrived in Florence as Papal Legate to the court of Medici Grand Duke Ferdinand I. Being among the first legates appointed by newly elected Pope Paul V shows how important the papacy considered his role. Some of his instructions were conventional, but Rome also ordered Grimani to observe everything that happens in Tuscany with regard to the Catholic religion.[1]

> You should have your eye principally on the two ports of Pisa and Livorno, where there is much traffic of foreigners, and from areas infected by heresy. And see that the Grand Duke does not fail to keep close watch on this with all diligence, since he is chiefly obligated to conserve and grow divine worship as much as possible, to maintain intact and to grow the Catholic Religion (*Religione Cattolica*).[2]

A short summary at the end of the letter underscored the point: "keep abreast of the Grand Duke's thinking on the point of what he will do with regard to Christianity (*Christianità*)."[3]

The letters went back and forth every week, instructions from Rome alternating with Legate Grimani's reports back. Grimani faithfully offered political and military intelligence, and Rome's replies sounded a consistent and anxious refrain: what are the Grand Duke's intentions with regard to *Christianity*? Why was Rome so worried? What was Grand Duke Ferdinand I doing or threatening, above all with regard to religious policy, that caused such anxiety at the papal court in 1605?

We can gain something of an idea of what may have been causing the Holy See to fret by looking at the Medici religious policy in the decades before and after 1605, particularly in relation to the leading cities of Florence and Siena and the new port town of Livorno. Florence and Siena had forced Jews into ghettos in 1570 and 1573, respectively, while Livorno was testing initiatives in cross-cultural coexistence that would gain it a reputation in the historiography as a place of unusual religious toleration. Was this reputation really deserved? Francesca Trivellato coined the term "communitarian cosmopolitanism" to describe the regime by which the Medici invited distinct "nations"

DOI: 10.4324/9781003030522-11

to settle in Livorno (chiefly Jews, Greeks, and Armenians) and granted them the right to organise themselves and gain limited representation in local government bodies. Ahead of its time in the seventeenth century, this would come to limit the "horizon of expectations" for members of these ethno-religious communities by the later eighteenth century and curb their broader political involvement in Livorno. Tuscan conservatism preferred to concede privileges to particular communities rather than recognise individual human rights. Francesca Bregoli has explored how this became an ever-greater drag on what Jews in particular could do and the roles they could play, and both she and Trivellato have noted that it contributed to the steady decline of the Jewish community through the Enlightenment period.[4]

Trivellato and Bregoli focus on the Jewish community and on trade as a critical component shaping its rights and relations, while Correy Tazzara has also emphasised economic relations as the key factor in expanding recognition for all non-Catholic communities in Livorno by the eighteenth century. This was a distant and unpredictable prospect in 1605. What were the forms and limits of toleration in late sixteenth- and early seventeenth-century Tuscany as "communitarian cosmopolitanism" was first taking shape in that new free port? And what were the Medici up to? Authorities in Rome seemed to think that the Grand Duke was on the verge of pitching out not only the Catholic religion, but Christianity itself. Was there anything to this? We can see that there was much in the immediate situation in 1605 to heighten Rome's anxieties. At the same time, the Medici were skilled politicians who, like the contemporary Venetians, were quite willing to give the impression of being open to radical religious Reformation, even when in practice they remained quite firmly and even traditionally Catholic. Their Catholicism was not Tridentine or Roman. If anything, it was a Catholicism shaped by earlier civic religious traditions and drawing heavily on confraternities.

Understanding the Medici policy requires moving beyond texts and trade to exploring spatial and sensory dynamics of inter-communal relations. Here we encounter a broader range of boundaries and limitations. Not all walls were made of brick, stone, or wood, and the absence of walls didn't necessarily translate into openness. When we aim to understand how communities lived in relation to each other, we certainly have to examine the legal and physical structures they built. Yet we also need to explore how they reinforced these with sounds, smells, sights, and touch. The senses gave an experiential structure to space.

Neighbours and neighbourhood were the critical building blocks of Renaissance Italian cities. But neighbours don't always get along. Renaissance Italians thought carefully about the relation of space and sense, about community and who was inside or outside it, about how some bodies might pollute particular spaces, and how to keep that from happening. In this chapter, I aim to search out how Tuscans lived with neighbours whom they *didn't really like*. A spatial and sensory approach to cross-cultural relations in early modern Florence, Siena, and Livorno allows us to explore the dynamics of their ambivalence by inviting us to sense the *sound* of a wall – or the smell, touch, or sight of it. We may then find that Tuscan ambivalence echoed Rome's anxiety and that *Christianità* – and indeed the *Religione Cattolica* – were in no danger of losing their primacy.

Three cities

The Grand Duchy of Tuscany in the sixteenth and seventeenth centuries provides many examples of how laws and the senses framed relations between Christians, Jews, and Muslims because it offers one of the very rare examples in Europe of a polity where these communities coexisted over many decades. That coexistence was marked by paradox. The Medici Duke Cosimo I (1537–74) heavily promoted Jewish migration from the 1540s to the mid-1560s before reversing himself and ordering almost all of Tuscany's Jews into walled ghettos in the two main cities of Florence and Siena in the years 1570–73. At roughly the same time, he was promoting the construction of a new port at Livorno since the duchy's main port at Pisa was silting up. The Jews who had settled in Pisa did not need to relocate to the ghettos of Florence and Siena, but in fact could live side by side with Christians without a ghetto. This more open coexistence with Jews would be amplified at Livorno under provisions adopted by Cosimo I's sons and successors Francesco I (1574–87) and Ferdinand I (1587–1609) to encourage the new port's economic development. Greek Orthodox, Armenian, and Maronite Catholics would also enjoy some limited open practice of religion. English and Dutch Protestants were winked at if discrete, and by the 1630s Muslims would be allowed to walk the streets openly and use some of the only designated Islamic prayer spaces on Italian soil until the twentieth century.

Religious diversity was nothing new in Italy. Sicily had a significant Muslim population from the ninth to thirteenth centuries, Jews had lived in Rome continually since the late republican period, and Waldensians had sheltered in alpine valleys for centuries. The Jews were the largest and most widely diffused among these minorities, in part since many of those expelled from modern-day Germany, France, Spain, and Portugal in the fifteenth century moved to Italy. Italian civic authorities aimed at that time to find a place for Jews with the legal structure of the *condotta* – the contract creating the fiction of belonging and allowing economic, religious, and legal privileges. Yet Catholic anxiety grew as the numbers of Jews increased, and there was always a strong reaction against Jewish settlement on the part of Observantist religious reformers in particular. Anti-Semitic sermons by preachers like Bernardino da Siena, Giacomo della Marca, Bernardino da Feltre, and Girolamo Savonarola triggered a series of restrictive moves that were often sensory or spatial. Jews were forced to wear visible public signs like hats or circles in yellow or red and some of the towns that had recruited Jews in the 1420s and 1430s began expelling them in the 1480s and 1490s (e.g., Perugia 1485, Parma 1488, Milan 1489, and Florence 1494).[5]

In 1516, the Republic of Venice implemented an influential spatial exercise in ambivalence by mandating a segregated and walled space for Jewish settlement. This *ghetto* (a new term based either on Venetian geography or Jewish language or both) was located geographically within the city while still separated from it socially and religiously by canals, gates, and laws that forbade all but public daylight exchanges. The Venetian model spread, particularly when Pope Pius IV mandated ghettos across the Papal State with the decree *Cum nimis absurdum* (14 July 1555) issued only two months after his election to the papacy. Rome, Ancona, Bologna, and Perugia all developed ghettos, though not all Italian ghettos were the same. While Venice's ghetto enclosed a relatively new and diasporic community of Jews from Iberia and transalpine Europe, Rome's ghetto of 1555 drew a wall around the oldest and most stable community of Jews in Europe, stretching back over 1500 years.[6]

Florence's first identifiable Jewish settlement had been in 1396 at the end of the Ponte Vecchio, and some preachers pushed repeatedly for their expulsion. Medici Duke Cosimo I invited and protected Jews (and particularly Sephardic merchants and bankers) when he was at odds with the papacy from 1548 to the late 1560s. He did an about-face after making peace with the papacy in the late 1560s, in part to receive the title of Grand Duke from Pope Pius V. Duke Cosimo required Jews to wear a distinctive badge (1567), denied migration of new families (1569), denied new lending permits (1570), and then ordered all of Tuscany's Jews into ghettos in Florence in 1571 and in Siena in 1573. Florence's ghetto was the larger. The city counted about 97 Jews in 19 households in a 1567 census, but took in 400 when the Jews were forced out of smaller towns across Tuscany, and grew to about 1000 as Iberian Jews also moved in. It had two synagogues, one following the Italian and the other the Levantine-Spanish rite. Siena's ghetto was expected to house seven families on opening in 1573, but almost immediately had 30 families and 132 people, and this number tripled over the next century.[7]

The ghettos came with further economic and legal restrictions: Jews could not trade in new goods, had their lending rights limited, and could not own property. They could not employ live-in Christian servants or use Christian wet nurses. Sexual relations between Christians and Jews were forbidden. These latter restrictions were harder to police, and later records demonstrate that the rules were violated regularly. Yet they were repeated and re-enforced in the 1670s and 1680s, and then again in the later eighteenth century.

Both ghettos were tiny – areas smaller than a modern city block housing many hundreds of residents behind walls and gates. In Siena, bricks closed off the windows and streets that might provide access to the rest of the city; Venice similarly walled up visual access points. In Florence, Christians did that work. Within the small urban block that the ghetto occupied, Christians had all of the outward looking apartments while Jews were limited to those which looked inwards to the restricted space of a small square and well. Only one shop, belonging to a Jewish butcher, had doors leading both into the ghetto square and out to the city. In Florence, the Medici themselves owned many of the properties within this block, so the ghetto also functioned as a real estate investment for the grand ducal family.[8]

Sensory barriers reinforced bricks and mortar. Both Tuscan ghettos were located next to brothels – in fact, both actually occupied some of the houses and spaces that had earlier been set aside for the civic brothels. This was a ritual humiliation by association that had immediate sonic implications, since what was to be the quietest day of the week in the ghetto was disturbed by the shouts and music of the busiest day of the week in the adjoining brothel. Both ghettos were adjacent to public markets as well – convenient on one level, but noisy and smelly. This also reduced the need or possibility for Jews to circulate on city streets and be visible on them. Both ghettos were adjacent to key civic and religious sites, the Cathedral and Palazzo della Signoria in Florence and the church of S. Martino and the Palazzo del Campo in Siena. This put them in the immediate sonic range of the most important sets of ecclesiastical and civic bells as they marked "Christian" time. Because of this, both ghettos were also where Christian processions converged, with crowds singing music and bearing banners. Siena's ghetto bordered the route taken by prisoners being led out of the city for execution in processions with loud public songs and prayers led by confraternities. When Ferdinand I threw butcher shops off the Ponte Vecchio in 1595, they were relocated to the precinct of the ghetto, ensuring that Jews would have the sounds of pigs being driven through the streets and the smell of blood running down them.

The sounds and smells of Christianity ringed both ghettos by design. Beyond that, we find numerous micro-aggressions that served to mark territory: verbal insults and petty violence on the streets were common (in spite of laws passed against this in 1567 and 1608), and neighbours regularly threw garbage over the ghetto walls. These weren't all equally major issues. Yet they reminded Jews hour by hour and step by step of religious limits, boundaries, and hierarchies. Walls enclose, but sounds carry, and in Florence and Siena they carried Christian rituals, calendars, and meanings over the ghetto walls.

At first glance, Livorno seemed to be something entirely different. A wholesale expansion of a small fishing village, it was planned in the 1570s as Tuscany's new military and commercial port. The architect was Bernardo Buontalenti, who had designed Florence's ghetto in 1570 and many of the Medici fortresses before and after that. Construction began in 1577, with thousands of forced labourers – prisoners and slaves – levelling the ground, digging the moat, building the port facilities and star-shaped fortress walls, and then constructing the houses, public buildings, churches, and other institutions.[9]

Construction was slow, and Buontalenti's plan was extensively adapted when construction accelerated under Ferdinand I in the 1590s. The building programme was carried out by the Customs authority (*Dogana*), using investment funds from individuals and three corporations: the civic hospital of the Ceppo in Prato, the military-religious Order of Santo Stefano, and the charitable pawn bank of the Monte di Pietà. All three were large, well-endowed, lay religious institutions with strong ties to the Medici. Like Florence's ghetto, Livorno was an enormous real estate investment.[10]

Livorno's growth spurt came after Ferdinand I issued decrees in 1591 and 1593, called the *Livornine*, that expanded Livorno's free port status, improved its legal and tax advantages, and allowed the free public exercise of religion by non-Catholics. Ferdinand wanted above all to attract Greeks, Armenians, and Sephardic Jews for their capital, mercantile networks, and maritime skills. But the Livornine decrees also overtly welcomed "Turks, Moors, and Persians." There were plenty of free ports around the Mediterranean offering tax advantages, but none offered the same promise of free public exercise of religion.[11]

The city grew rapidly with Greek, Armenian, Jewish, Dutch, German, English, and French merchants and workers. It counted only 1000 free residents when the Livornine decrees were issued in the early 1590s, but by 1609 it had 5800, rising to 9100 (1622), then 12,000 (1642), and reaching 30,000 by 1700, becoming the second largest city in Tuscany after Florence and a major European trading entrepôt.[12] The Livornine decrees expanded merchants' legal protections, ensuring that they would not be prosecuted here for debts incurred elsewhere; Livorno's Jewish community would not be prosecuted to cover the costs of fraud by dishonest Jewish merchants as happened elsewhere. The decrees also added extensive duty exemptions to promote international trade; goods in transit through Livorno could be warehoused tax free for up to a year.

The Greeks were among the earliest communities to settle in Livorno, and by 1626 there were roughly 30 families alongside a large but transient group of sailors. The Jewish population grew slowly: in 1601, there were 134. Over the next 50 years, this grew to about 1750 and then doubled to about 3500 by 1738.[13] Jews were free to buy property and live openly. They had their own synagogue on a public street and though initially under the control of the *parnassim* in Pisa, they gained local communal judicial autonomy under ducal oversight by 1628. Jews ended up living in four separate areas of the city, with the largest community clustered around the synagogue. Together with Hamburg, Amsterdam, and Venice, Livorno was one of the major sites of Jewish settlement in Europe.[14]

Yet in Livorno's first century, one other foreign population far outnumbered the Jews: these were Ottoman subjects, largely Muslim and mostly enslaved, originating from the Balkans, the Barbary Coast, and sub-Saharan Africa. The Medici had used slave labour to build or expand nine forts across the duchy from the 1550s to the 1590s, and they continued using convicts and enslaved oarsmen to power the galleys of their new fleet. Since Livorno was the new base of the Tuscan fleet, it had thousands of galley slaves who were housed in an enormous (6000 square metres over three stories around a central courtyard) secure enclosure called the *Bagno*.[15] There were many Muslim slaves in contemporary Italy, but elsewhere they lived on galleys – Livorno's Bagno was one of the only two purpose-built physical structures on land for Muslims in Italy, the other being Venice's merchant hostel for Ottoman traders, the *Fondaco dei Turchi*.

Between 2000 and 3000 Muslims from around the Mediterranean lived in Livorno in the seventeenth century, the number rising and falling with labour demand and seizures. Duke Cosimo I had initially purchased slaves, but by the time of Ferdinand I most were captives, taken either at sea or in North African coastal raids. One historian estimates that about 6000 were captured from 1600 until 1620, including 2000 Maghrebi Muslims from raids during the sieges of 1607 and 1610.[16] By the 1620s, ten times more Muslims than Jews lived in Livorno; about one third of the population was Muslim, and they would continue to far outnumber both Jews and Protestants for a century.[17] While their numbers were closely tallied, they fail to appear in official population counts, and so Livorno's actual population was far larger than the numbers given above. Nor were they an invisible presence in the Bagno. From about 1630, slaves could circulate through the city during the daylight hours when the fleet was in port (November to May), working as pedlars or scribes, or practising some trades like barbering. They were marked visually by shaved heads with topknots, and distinctive red breeches, and they were to return at night to the Bagno. There, three prayer rooms described initially as "churches for worship according to the Moorish law" functioned effectively as mosques and would be named as such both on a late seventeenth-century floor plan in the Florentine State Archive and in a 1698 account by French traveller Maximilien Misson.[18] These were the first identifiable mosques in Italy since the expulsion of the last Saracens and Moors from Sicily in 1300. It might be seen as a sign of Ferdinand I's ecumenism, and that was certainly how Rome took it.

Livorno was clearly a place of interracial, inter-religious coexistence: no ghetto; Jews, Muslims, Greeks, Armenians, Catholics, and Protestants walking the streets together; Islamic worship tolerated. In 1599, Pope Clement VIII threatened to excommunicate the Archbishop of Pisa if he did not enforce Catholic exclusivity. Was Livorno then a sign that Italians, or at least Tuscans, were moving beyond those impulses that created religious exiles and refugees in so many other parts of Europe at the very same time? This is certainly the way that it is presented in many histories.[19] Yet when we look at spaces and the senses, Livorno appears less as the violation of the rule than as the exception that proves it. And its exceptions to that rule are always partial and highly qualified.

Livorno *had* no ghetto because it *was* a ghetto. The star-shaped fortified settlement was in an isolated location surrounded by malarial swamps (Figure 7.1).[20] Its walls were among the first of the new urban construction projects, built in large part by 2500 Muslim slaves and Christian convicts. There were two fortresses within the circuit of walls and only one heavily guarded land gate, meaning that apart from the port itself, this city had fewer entry points than the ghettos of either Florence or Siena. All this gave Livorno the aspect of an open-air prison colony, and indeed through the early modern period,

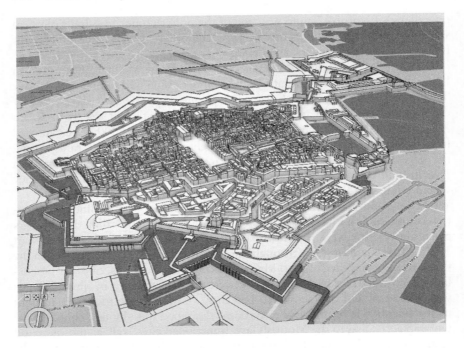

Figure 7.1 Livorno ca. 1750.
Courtesy of the DECIMA Project.

Tuscans guilty of minor crimes were banished to Livorno for periods of time while more serious crimes could earn them terms rowing on the state's galleys.

By 1604–5, the main religious sites were in place: its cathedral-style Collegiata was dedicated in 1604, the synagogue was built the same year, and the Bagno with its three Muslim prayer rooms opened in 1605.[21] This convergence may help explain Rome's anxiety conveyed to Legate Grimani that same year regarding Grand Duke Ferdinand's commitment to *Christianità*. It may have looked grim to some Catholics, though they need not have worried. Livorno's urbanistic layout and sensory regimes underscored the dominance of the Catholic faith. The Collegiata anchored the south end of the central piazza and its bell dominated the city acoustically. The baptistry adjoined the western transept where a door opened directly into the Jewish quarter. The synagogue was only 100 metres to the southwest of this door, bracketed four blocks to the west by the Barnabite Church of S. Sebastiano built after the 1630 plague. Immediately east of the Collegiata was the church dedicated to Livorno's patron saint Giulia (rebuilt 1603), and then four blocks northeast of these stood three "national" churches practically beside each other: the Greek Church of Annunciation (1606) and the Armenian Church of S. Gregory (1630s) flanking the Church of the Madonna (1607) where French, English, Germans, Dutch, Corsicans, and Portuguese all had altars. The Church of the Madonna offered a more latitudinarian low-church Catholicism meant to keep Protestants from being too unhappy. The Augustinian Church of S. Giovanni Battista flanked the Bagno while the Dominican Church of S. Caterina da Siena marked the Venezia Nuova warehouse district at the city's northern end. Confraternal chapels and hospitals clustered around the single land gate (Porta Pisana), and the fourteenth-century Marian shrine of Montenero overlooked Livorno from a hilltop south of the city and drew regular processions.[22] While thousands of Muslims and Jews might circulate around Livorno, what they saw and heard on its streets, squares, and entrances was decidedly Catholic.

Ferdinand I and Medici religious policy: ambivalence and the limits of diversity

Rome nonetheless saw Livorno as clear proof that Ferdinand I was dangerously open to Judaism, Islam, and Protestantism. It rejected the promises of open worship promised in the Livornine decrees as being beyond the competence or authority of a secular ruler. It was equally concerned that, beyond welcoming many non-Catholics, the Grand Duke seemed indifferent to prosecuting Iberian Conversos and Moriscos who were returning to their ancestral faiths. He had set up a press to publish Arabic texts, and in 1605, he sent a diplomatic mission to Persia to improve relations. Who was this man?

Ferdinand was the fifth son of Cosimo I and was already a Cardinal in Rome when his elder brother Francesco I died under suspicious circumstances in 1587, leaving Ferdinand the family's only legitimate male heir. He assumed the Grand Ducal title but did not relinquish the cardinalate until two years later on the eve of his marriage to Christine of Lorraine; he had never taken priestly orders. In Rome, he had been Cardinal protector of the Maronite church, Arab Catholics using Syriac liturgy in the Arab language, and had overseen the publication of the first Maronite missal in 1584. In Florence, his press the *Typographia Medicea* published religious and humanistic texts in Arabic for three decades in the period 1584–1614, including a gospel translation in 1591. Ferdinand I became a political ally of Henri de Navarre, encouraging his conversion to Catholicism, and also of the Druze Emir Fakhr al-din Ma'an II, an opponent of the Ottomans who would find political refuge in Livorno and Florence in 1613.[23]

In early 1605, things could not have looked better for Ferdinand I. In March, cousin Alessandro de Medici, a Cardinal and close ally who had also been Archbishop of Florence, was elected Pope, taking the title Leo XI in honour of the previous Medici pope, Leo X. But Leo XI fell sick and died in less than a month. He was succeeded by Paul V, the first of the series of Borghese popes who transformed Rome and the papacy in the seventeenth century. Does the ecumenical Ferdinand I give us some idea of what Catholicism and Italy might have become under Pope Leo XI? It's unlikely. Ferdinand's apparent ecumenism was not born out of freethinking convictions.

It was conservative and conventional, a practical *quid pro quo* coexistence carried out in very limited terms for economic advantage and justified by the hopes of converting Muslims and Jews.[24]

To begin with spatial arrangements: the Bagno was a healthier place to keep slaves and hence more cost-effective. The prayer rooms or mosques were a diplomatic concession, a reciprocation of the chapels for Christians found in the *bagnos* of the Barbary Coast. If Muslim slaves were mistreated in Livorno, then Christian slaves would be mistreated in Algiers and Tripoli. Even at that, Livorno's Bagno was more akin to a prison than to a merchant *fondaco* like that in Venice.[25] The public synagogue was more significant, as there were none in Italy outside of the walled ghettos of Venice, Rome, and other major cities. Yet this too was strategic and to some extent moot, since as noted earlier, Livorno *had* no ghetto because it *was* a ghetto. Among Christians, the range of public religious expression was tightly limited to those confessions which had been observed and practised for centuries around the Mediterranean basin, chiefly the Greek Orthodox, Armenian (church in 1701), Melchite (Arab Christians using Greek liturgy and language), and eventually also Maronite from 1712–13.[26] Non-Catholics were buried outside city walls in unconsecrated ground, and authorities resisted allowing walls to be erected around these burial grounds for fear that religious services might take place there. [27] Anglican baptisms could not even be conducted in the home of the English consul but had to take place offshore on board of a ship. As late as the eighteenth century, reports of this in the English press caused great controversy in Tuscany. There would be no public Protestant churches until the nineteenth century.[28]

The Medici retained close control over the local Catholic religious establishment. They kept Livorno as a single parish rather than a bishopric, leaving them with rights of nomination and tighter control over local clergy. This also left Tuscany's second largest city without a resident bishop at a time when many far smaller cities and towns boasted bishops and even archbishops. Much of the fabric of Livorno's religious life was handled outside the parochial system by confraternities, in a manner resembling that of the pre-Tridentine period. A network of over 40 confraternities oversaw the public cult, ritual life, and institutional charity following forms of civic religion familiar in Florence, and often imported directly from the capital. Many originated in mendicant churches, particularly S. Giovanni Battista of the Augustinians and S. Caterina da Siena of the Dominicans. In the absence of guilds, confraternities also organised the ritual life and mutual assistance of artisans, with distinct groups for fruit and vegetable sellers, cheese mongers, construction and foundry workers, hospitality workers, wine sellers, and tailors among others. In 1681, all Livorno's lay confraternities were formally put under the Grand Duke's control by a concordat with Pope Innocent XI.

We can distinguish three groups of confraternities by origin and function. First was a group of older brotherhoods led by the companies of *Sts. Cosmas and Damian* and of *S. Giulia*.[29] Cosmas and Damian were the Medici patron saints, and this confraternity emerged in 1572 to renovate a church that Cosimo I had established in 1559–60.[30] In 1607, a ship captain gave the brotherhood a wooden image of the Madonna del Carmine seized from a Barbary pirate ship off Corsica. They lent it to the Observant Franciscans when building a new oratory, but the Franciscans were unwilling later to return it. In 1631, another sea captain and *confratello* gave them another relic ostensibly recovered from Muslim pirates, the body of the second-century martyr S. Vigilia. In 1647, she was declared to be a co-patron of Livorno, with the Company of Sts. Cosmas and Damian responsible for her cult, including a procession of her relics through the city after Easter. The confraternity also oversaw the large hilltop shrine at the Madonna del Montenero south of the city. The Company of S. Giulia was one of the oldest confraternities in the city, named after the first patron saint, Giulia of Corsica (d. 439). It was also the most civic group among confraternities; its emblem included the arms of Livorno underneath an image of S. Giulia. Ferdinand I ceded to it the church of S. Giulia built next to the Collegiata and opened in 1603. These brothers oversaw taking the host to the sick, were the first to start the 40 hours devotion, and held a major annual procession with all city magistrates to the Montenero shrine. This group of older confraternities also included the *Compagnia della SS. Madonna della Piazza* or *Compagnia della Vergine*, which started meeting at a wall shrine in the old city in 1573 and by 1599 developed as a youth confraternity offering catechetical instruction. A matriculation list that year records 96 youths, all identified by reference to their fathers as an implicit confirmation of their legitimacy.[31]

A second group of confraternities included charitable groups established during the first period of real growth from the 1590s to 1620s as offshoots of major Florentine brotherhoods.[32] The most important of these was the *Misericordia*, established in 1595 and drawing its statutes and officers from Florence.[33] As in the capital, it functioned as Livorno's welfare service: burying the dead, clothing the poor, opening four hospitals for pilgrims, priests, and poor women, collecting foundlings, and running a home for unhappily married women and reformed prostitutes. It cared for prisoners and comforted those condemned to death, who in Livorno constituted a large community given the extensive use of prisoners (*sfortzati*) in construction and on galleys. The Misericordia passed Livornese foundlings on to the Trovatelli foundling home in Pisa, which in turn was controlled by Florence's foundling home of the Innocenti. This was efficient when Livorno was still quite small, but the practice continued even after Livorno's Misericordia got its own wheel (*ruota*) for anonymous abandonment in 1677. Shipping foundlings out of Livorno ensured that the city did not develop a large local population of those of mixed race and diverse religious backgrounds.[34] The Misericordia also organised processional and ritual theatre. Following the terrible plague of 1630, 32 of the confraternity's children marched barefoot with large wax candles, wearing crowns of thorns and the symbol of the Misericordia confraternity on their back, followed by 120 adult members, including some who carried a large silver image of the Madonna of Misericordia up to Montenero. In the mystery play that followed, one female youth played the Madonna, while four youths represented the city's male patron saints (Francesco, Giovanni Battista, Tobit, and Sebastiano).[35] The Misericordia gathered other brotherhoods under its wing, including the *Compagnia de SSti Crespino e Crespiniano*, a mutual assistance brotherhood of shoemakers meeting in the Augustinian Church of S. Giovanni Battista, and *S. Maria del Suffraggio* (1628), which built a church in the southern area of the city near the market and the main Jewish quarter.[36]

The third group of confraternities consisted of new brotherhoods established in the 1630s to perform a range of devotional activities for education and conversion, to organise and fund devotions at altars in different churches, and to organise mutual assistance for groups of artisans in place of guilds. These included the *Natività di Maria Vergine* (1631–32), the *Assunta di Maria* in Montenero (1637), the *Madonna di Loreto* (1638), and *SS Trinità* (1653) located in the new neighbourhood of Venezia Nuova and involved in ransoming Christian slaves in North Africa.[37]

Lay confraternities controlled much of the public fabric and practice of religion through chapels, charities, and processions. Religious orders were also present, particularly the Augustinians, Dominicans, Franciscans (Ferdinand had been their Protector), and Capuchins. The clerics who were conspicuously absent were those who represented Roman influence and control: there was no local Inquisitor, no Jesuits until 1708, and no bishop until 1806.[38]

The spaces and senses of religion

The spaces and senses of religious diversity in Livorno were tightly controlled. The Collegiata dominated the main square and the churches of confraternities, religious orders, and nations marked strategic intersections. The synagogue and Bagno were immediately to the west of the main square, the former just off the apse of the Collegiata at the south end and the latter just behind the Governor's quarters (*Palazzo del Pretorio*) and Customs office (*Dogana*) at the north end. Judaism and Islam had locations, but no real *sensory* presence in the city as you might get with calls to prayer, wedding and funeral processions, or open feasts. Both synagogue and mosque were surrounded physically and sonically by civic structures and Catholic churches whose bells and processions were reminders of Livorno's spiritual hierarchy. In contrast to these very public, mobile, and musical expressions of the Catholic faith, the silence and invisibility imposed on Jews and Muslims were much like the form of toleration that Catholics and Mennonites experienced in the contemporary Dutch Republic – no bell towers, no grand public structures that were overtly religious, and discretion was required. Their separate cemeteries were also outside the city walls.[39]

Conversion efforts also continued with formal Houses of Conversion. Jews were sent to Florence and Muslims to Rome (about 1000 of the latter). Unlike Muslim slave ports like Algiers or Tunis, conversion to the dominant

Figure 7.2 Giovanni Bandini and Pietro Tacca, *Ferdinando I e I Quattro Mori* (1597–99; 1617–26).

Image provided by author.

religion did *not* bring automatic release from slavery, or much opportunity for advancement. Some converts remained as slaves for years unless they were ransomed. Anyone arriving at Livorno's port encountered a monumental statue underscoring the local racial and religious hierarchy, with an over-life-sized Ferdinand I brandishing a staff (*bastone*) and elevated above four nearly naked Ottoman slaves who were clad only in breeches, with shaved heads and topknots, and straining at their chains (Figure 7.2). Sculptor Pietro Tacca was commissioned by Cosimo II to provide the decorative pedestal for an existing statue of his father Ferdinand I. While his early gesso studies (1617–26) depicted four males in classical form (Figure 7.3), the final version offered distinctly North African, Arabic, and Balkan slaves of startling verisimilitude, giving it the name of *Quattro Mori* and notoriety across Europe.[40]

The local Governor's orders opened with a statement that justified Livorno's variety of religious expression as both a mercantile necessity and an opportunity to convert aliens to the true Catholic faith. The Governor was to keep a close eye that these aliens not introduce "sects which would undermine our Holy Catholic faith" ("qualche setta in dispregio della nostra

Figure 7.3 Pietro Tacca, *Gesso study for Quattro Mori* (1617–26).
Courtesy of Museo Civico Giovanni Fattori di Livorno.

S. Religione Cattolica").[41] He was further ordered to protect the local confraternities and churches. He could not allow the Augustinian Church of S.
Giovanni, located immediately next to the Bagno, to become a refuge for
murderers and disturbers of the peace, as that would be a bad example for
those of foreign nations.[42] This toleration was forbearance, not acceptance.
Neither Ferdinand I nor his successors closed the crowded ghettos of Florence or Siena or their conversion houses.[43] In fact, Livorno gained a house of
conversion even as it became home to 3000 Jews, roughly 10% of the population. It may have had more mosques than anywhere else in Italy and one of
the most impressive synagogues in Europe, but there was little sign outside
either one as to their purpose.

There was certainly more freedom for non-Christians in Livorno than in
Florence and Siena. But we should not overlook the ongoing micro-aggressions vis-à-vis the Jews as found in Florence and Siena. Nor should we ignore
the fact that these actually increased in Livorno at just the time when other
European cities were gradually reducing restrictions on other communities.
As non-Catholic populations grew, the legal and sensory markers became
more important signs of the Catholic order. For 50 years, from 1663 to 1713,

the Grand Duke was the traditionally pious Catholic, Cosimo III, who was determined to curb the privileges and visibility of non-Catholics. He did not aim to expel them but did work to reduce their sensory presence. He installed the Capuchins – the order responsible for missions to Africa and Islam, and for their work with Christian slaves in North Africa – on the top floor of the slave Bagno as agents of surveillance. In the late 1670s and early 1680s, he renewed the traditional decrees prohibiting Jews from employing Catholics in their homes or businesses, forbidding any sexual contact (including with prostitutes), and forbidding Christian wet-nursing of Jewish babies. One third of the fines (and by far the largest fines) for Jewish-Christian sexual contact in the last record (1683–1774) were levied under his regime.[44]

Cosimo III also raised new visual and aural boundaries to cross-cultural coexistence elsewhere in Tuscany. In 1682, Siena's Christians were prohibited from putting a foot into a Jewish shop. Jews had to make themselves invisible and silent at certain times and places: they could not be in the main public square of the Campo when Mass was being celebrated in the chapel of the town hall (1682). During Corpus Domini and other special holidays, they had to be off the streets entirely, in the ghetto, with doors and windows closed (1687, 1691). They were not allowed on streets where a religious procession was scheduled to pass, under penalty of a large fine of 25 *scudi*.[45] While Jews in Livorno ostensibly had greater rights, they were under some of the same restrictions. They too had to make themselves invisible when religious processions passed by their homes, remaining inside with doors and windows closed.

These sensory, sexual, and social restrictions continued long after pious Cosimo III died, and indeed long after the Medici died out in 1737, to be replaced by the House of Lorraine. While this Austrian line is usually associated with promoting more secular Enlightenment values, there was ongoing prosecution of the laws against sexual contact. These actually increased from the 1750s, with most fines being charged against Jews from Livorno (over one third from 1750 to 1774). There were increasingly tense outbreaks of inter-communal violence in the later eighteenth century. New Jewish immigrants arriving from Ottoman North Africa (hence called "Turchi") in the 1750s were less willing to live by the invisibility laws. Some openly taunted Christian processions, sparking riots between Christians and Jews. Christians deliberately provoked encounters by sending torchlit processions down predominantly Jewish streets, and by 1764 the city's governor was considering isolating a single neighbourhood where only Jews could live and where Christians were excluded. Jewish leaders wanted this ghetto for their own security, though in the end it was not constructed. By this point, the Muslim population had almost disappeared. Always tied to galley slavery, the number of Muslims declined as galleys, and most of those remaining returned to the Ottoman Empire when a peace treaty was signed in 1747.

Florence and Siena unambiguously restricted Jewish spaces and gave no public space to any churches apart from those in the broader Mediterranean Orthodox tradition. When we scratch the surface of Livorno's "communitarian cosmopolitanism," we see some coexistence, along with sensory, spatial, and legal boundaries that underscored Catholic dominance.[46] Sensory regimes highlighted the continuing deep and broad ambivalence *about* coexistence. Politically, there was no effort made to use Livorno as a model for reorganising inter-communal relations in Tuscany's major cities. Muslims were a labour resource, expelled when no longer needed. Jews remained and advocated for their rights to the limit of the law, though Livorno's attraction for Sephardic merchants waned by the eighteenth century. Greek, Armenian, and Maronite Christians had their separate churches renewed in the early eighteenth century. Yet there were no public Protestant churches for another century, when Anglican (1840), Scots Presbyterian (1845), and Dutch (1864) churches opened. All were outside the city walls. Apart from the Protestants, most of these "national" communities supported the invisible boundaries that permitted functional and largely economic contacts while preserving cultural and religious distinctions and allowing communities to exercise social discipline on their own members.

Conclusions

The physical walls of ghettos – as fashioned in Florence and Siena – are clear, physical, and immediate. Yet there are other ways to raise boundaries and hem people in. The absence of physical boundaries did not mean the presence of toleration or even open coexistence, though we may have to bring in other sources and other senses in order to recognise this. The mundane elements of day-to-day interaction were the tissue of neighbourhood experience and paying attention to space and sense in daily life allows us to detect those walls which were no less real for being invisible. Studying *regimes* of sound and sense get us beyond occasional noise and pious hopes to the bones of society and the tissue of human experience.

Livorno's experiment in cross-cultural coexistence remained an exception, limited to largely transient populations, hemmed in by lay civic religious institutions, and hidden behind walls. Navigating religions in a free port meant, above all, keeping a close eye on where the wind was blowing, and continuing to use very traditional maps that plotted familiar routes close to the coast. Unlike larger cosmopolitan republics like Amsterdam and Venice, Livorno was a small working port under the tight control of absolutist rulers who kept one eye trained on Rome and another on the Barbary Coast. It was not a capital, there was no university, no active local cultural elite, and no active press outside the Jewish community. Its most diverse population grew at the intersection of piracy, crusade, and enslavement, and even if some were learned, there were few opportunities for intellectual exchange. The only diasporic community that developed a stronger local residential and intellectual life was the Jewish one, with a first press in the mid-seventeenth century and strong intellectual and commercial links to both Northern Europe and the Eastern Mediterranean. Yet there seems to have been little intellectual contact between Jews and Christians.

Legate Grimani and his anxious Vatican minders in 1605 need not have worried about Grand Duke Ferdinand I's intentions about Catholicism or Christianity. What religious coexistence or toleration could be found in Livorno was limited only to Abrahamic faiths in their most traditional expression, and even this was closely circumscribed by space, sense, and motion. The "new" religious settlement in Tuscany was deeply and traditionally Christian, less a departure from Catholicism than a reaffirmation of its pre-Tridentine, confraternal, and lay-directed forms.

Notes

* Versions of this chapter were originally presented as lectures at Fordham University, Monash University, the Free University of Amsterdam, and the University of Richmond; my thanks to the hosts who organised these lectures and the participants who joined in discussions. Abbreviations employed in the notes: ASF (Archivio di Stato Florence), ASLi (Archivio di Stato Livorno), ASP (Archivio di Stato Prato), ASPi (Archivio di Stato Pisa), ASV (Archivio Segreto Vaticano), and MP (Medici del Principato).

1 Antonio Grimani was bishop of Torcello from 1587 to 1618 when he resigned. He was Apostolic Nuncio to Florence from July 11, 1605 until his resignation on June 27, 1616. He became Patriarch of Aquileia on December 22, 1622 and died on January 26, 1628. See: http://www.catholic-hierarchy.org/bishop/bgrimaa. html [accessed July 4, 2019]. Pope Paul V (Camillo Borghese) was elected pope on May 16, 1605 and died on January 28, 1621.

2 "Et per far questo, e necessario che lei habbia l'occhio principalmente alle due Porti di Pisa, et di Livorno, dov/an occasioni/ del traffico concorre gente forastiere, et di parti anco infetti di heresia. Et se ben/ il Gr. Duca non manca di'invigiliar/ in questo con ogni studio, tuttavia per essere principal obligo delli Ecc/ il conservare et accrescere il culto divino dovra lei far il possibile, accio si mantenga intatta, et s'aumenta la Religione Cattolica." ASV, Segreteria dello Stato, Firenze, Armario I, 193, ff. 6ᵛ-7ʳ.

3 "quanto al pensiero, che tiene il Gr Duca di far quell servitio rilevato alla Christianità." ASV, Segreteria dello Stato, Firenze, Armario I, 193, ff. 9ʳ⁻ᵛ.

4 Francesca Trivellato, *The Familiarity of Strangers: The Sephardic Diaspora, Livorno, and Cross-Cultural Trade in the Early Modern Period* (New Haven: Yale University Press, 2009), 73–4. Francesca Bregoli, *Mediterranean Enlightenment: Livornese Jews, Tuscan Culture, and Eighteenth-Century Reforms* (Stanford: Stanford University Press, 2014), 2–14. Stephanie Nadalo describes Livorno's pluralistic regime as shaped by the "competing dynamics of segregation, integration, and assimilation" in "Constructing Pluralism in Seventeenth Century Livorno: Managing Religious Minorities in a Mediterranean Free Port (1537–1737)" (PhD diss., Northwestern University, 2013), 289. Correy Tazzara, *The Free Port of Livorno and the Transformation of the Mediterranean World, 1574–1790* (Oxford: Oxford University Press, 2017).

5 Flora Cassen, *Marking the Jews in Renaissance Italy: Politics, Religion, and the Power of Symbols* (Cambridge: Cambridge University Press, 2017), 20–49. Nicholas Terpstra, *Religious Refugees in the Early Modern World: An Alternative History of the Reformation* (Cambridge: Cambridge University Press, 2015), 74–132.

170   Nicholas Terpstra

6 Dana E. Katz, *The Jewish Ghetto and the Visual Imagination of Early Modern Venice* (Cambridge: Cambridge University Press, 2017), 21–47. Benjamin Ravid, *Studies on the Jews of Venice* (Aldershot: Ashgate, 2003). Kenneth Stow, *Theatre of Acculturation: The Roman Ghetto in the Sixteenth Century* (Seattle: University of Washington Press, 2003). Kenneth Stow, *Anna and Tranquillo: Catholic Anxiety and Jewish Protest in the Age of Revolutions* (New Haven: Yale University Press, 2016), 68–78.

7 On Cosimo's tense relations with the papacy from the late 1540s to 1560s: Nicholas Terpstra, *Lost Girls: Sex & Death in Renaissance Florence* (Baltimore: Johns Hopkins University Press, 2010), 133–5. On conditions before the ghetto: Justine Walden, "Before the Ghetto: Spatial Logics, Ritual Humiliation, and Jewish-Christian Relations in Early Modern Florence," in *Global Reformations: Transforming Early Modern Religions, Societies, and Cultures*, ed. Nicholas Terpstra (London: Routledge, 2019), 98–114. Siegmund minimises the influence of Cosimo's drive for an enhanced title and emphasises investment strategies. Stefanie B Siegmund, *The Medici State and the Ghetto of Florence: The Construction of an Early Modern Jewish Community* (Stanford: Stanford University Press, 2006), 51–73. On Siena's ghetto: Nicholas Terpstra, "Race, Gender, and the Politics of Enclosure in Early Modern Siena," in *La ghianda e la quercia*, ed. Wietse de Boer, Vincenzo Lavenia, and Giuseppe Marcocci (Roma: Viella, 2019), 190–5. Francesco Fusi and Patrizia Turrini, *Salicotto com'era: il plastico del quartiere e il risanimento negli anni '30* (Siena: il Leccio, 1999).

8 Piergabriele Mancuso of the Medici Archive Project (https://www.medici.org) has produced a digital reconstruction based on detailed archival research into property records. P. Mancuso, "The Politics of Segregation in Grand Ducal Florence: The Ghetto of Florence from Material Fall to Virtual Rebirth," in *Judisches Kuturerbe (re-)praesentieren - Judisches Kulturerbe - Band 2*, ed. Katrina Kessler, Martha Stellmacher, Alexander von Kienlin, and Ulrich Knufinke (Braunschweig: Selbstverlag, 2019), 45–66.

9 Lucia Frattarelli Fischer, *L'Arcano del mare: Un porto nella prima età globale: Livorno* (Pisa: Pacini Editore, 2018), 63–9, 113–34.

10 For some of the discussions on how to boost real estate values and investment in the 1570s: ASF MP 1181, Inserto 3, ff. 112^r-113^v. The Ceppo was an early investor, with 49 buildings by 1592 valued at 15,000 scudi. It invested a further 14,123 scudi in 24 properties in 1595 and 15,144 in 9 properties in 1599: ASP, Ceppi, ms 1929 (nf: febbraio 1592; gennaio 1595, gennaio 1599). A century later in 1691, it still had 55 properties in the Bacchettoni and S. Giulia districts and 4 large structures and 19 warehouses in the Venezia Nuova district: ASP, Ceppi, ms 1472 "1691 Catasto". M.L. Conforto and L. Frattarelli Fischer, "Dalla Livorno dei Granduchi alla Livorno dei mercanti: Città e proprietà immobiliare fra '500 e '600," *Bollettino Storico Pisano* 53 (1984), 211–34.

11 Paolo Castignoli and Lucia Frattarelli Fischer, eds., *Le Livornine del 1591 e 1593* (Livorno: Cooperative Edile Risorgimento, 1988). Cesare Santus, "Moreschi in Toscana: Progetti e tentativi di insediamento tra Livorno e la Maremma," *Quaderni Storici* 48 (2013), 745–78.

12 By the late seventeenth century, Florence had a population nearing 70,000, Livorno's was at 30,000, and Pisa's population had fallen to about 14,000.

13 1723 in 1644–45, 2397 in 1693, 3476 in 1738, 3687 in 1758: Trivellato, *Familiarity of Strangers*, 54–6, 71.

14 By the eighteenth century, its Jewish population was second only to Amsterdam in western Europe. Trivellato, *Familiarity of Strangers*, 43–101. Lucia Frattarelli Fischer, *Vivere fuori dal Ghetto*. Id., *L'arcano del mare*, 122. Bernard Cooperman, "From Pisa to Livorno: Ethnicity, Social Conflict, and the Birth of an Early Modern Jewish Community" (manuscript shared privately), 61–9.

15 Justine Walden, "Slave Labor in Grand Ducal Tuscany and the Dynamics of Migration in the Early Modern Mediterranean," *Scienze e politica* 11 (2020), 194–204. Lucia Frattarelli Fischer, "Il bagno delle galere in 'terra cristiana'. Schiavi a Livorno fra Cinque e Seicento," *Nuovi Studi Livornesi* 8 (2000), 69–94 (79–82). The forts were in Livorno (1534; 1590); Arezzo (1538), Portoferraia/Elba (1549–52), Piombino (1552–57), Cortona (1556), Siena (1563), S. Piero a Sieve (1569), Belvedere/Firenze (1590–95).

16 In 1618, there were 2172 male *schiavi* and 994 *forzati* and an unknown number of females. Nadalo estimates that by 1676 they still represented 8.5% of the population. Stefanie Nadalo, "Negotiating Slavery in a Tolerant Frontier: Livorno's Turkish *Bagno*," *Medievalia* 32 (2011), 278, 291–7, 314, n. 37.

17 Franco Angiolini, "Slaves and Slavery in Early Modern Tuscany (1500–1700)," *Italian History and Culture* 3 (1997), 71–3.

18 Frattarelli Fischer, "Il bagno delle galere," 80, 89. Nadalo, "Negotiating Slavery," 278.

19 Nadalo, "Negotiating Slavery," 276, 307, n.1.

20 This aerial view is based on a digital reconstruction of Livorno produced by the DECIMA (*Digitally Encoded Census Information and Mapping Archive*) Project in conjunction with Alessandro Merlo and Emanuela Ferretti of the Faculty of Architecture of the University of Florence. Digitisation of a scale model prepared by Lucia Frattarelli Fischer from a 1738 tax census, it is part of DECIMA's reconstruction of Livornese demography and social, sensory, and ritual geography based on seventeenth- and eighteenth-century archival records. See: https://decima-map.net and Lucia Frattarelli Fischer, *Livorno 1749: dai documenti al modello in scala* (Pisa: Casa di Risparmi di Pisa, 1990).

21 Lucia Frattarelli Fischer and Maria Teresa Lazzarini, *Chiese e luoghi di culto a Livorno: Dal medioevo a oggi* (Pisa: Pacini Editore, 2015), 27–71. The first plans for the *bagno* in 1598 had no mosque at all: Frattarelli Fischer, "Il bagno del gallere," 79–82.

22 Frattarelli Fischer and Lazzarini, *Chiese e luoghi di culto a Livorno*, 37–71, 56–103. Lucia Frattarelli Fischer and Stefano Villani, "'People of Every Mixture': Immigration, Tolerance, and Religious Conflicts in Early Modern Livorno," in *Immigration and Emigration in Historical Perspective*, ed. Ann Katherine Isaacs (Pisa: Edizioni Plus, 2007), 93–107.

23 Known by Tuscans as *il Faccardino*, the Emir was in Tuscany and Naples for five years from November 3, 1613 until September 1618. Returning then to Lebanon, he was captured in 1635 by the Ottomans and beheaded.

24 Alessandro de Medici was a strong supporter of Ippolito Galantini, founder of Congregation of Christian Doctrine (1603–4) whose Florentine establishment of S Francesco (1602) became the centre of the city's first Casa dei Catechumeni for the conversion of Jews. See note 44 below. Galantini was a controversial figure suspected of being a "Luterano" and schismatic heretic.

25 See report on the operation of the Constantinople *bagno*, produced on January 17, 1604 (sf), and compare with the report produced on December 24, 1604 on how to organise the Livorno *bagno*: ASF, MP, 1829, ff. 308ʳ–309ᵛ; 310ʳ⁻ᵛ. Frattarelli Fischer, "Il bagno delle galere," 79–82. Santus, "Crimini, violenza, e corruzione nel Bango di Livorno: gli schiavi 'turchi' in alcuni processi del XVII secolo," in *La città delle nazioni: Livorno e I limiti del cosmopolitanismo (1566-1834)*, ed. A. Addobbati and M. Aglietti (Pisa: Pisa University Press, 2015), 93–109.

26 All of these would gain a more public presence from the 1730s under the Lorraine regime. Guido Bellatti Ceccoli, *Tra Toscana e medioriente: La storia arabi cattolici a Livorno (secoli XXVII-XX)* (Livorno: Editasca, 2008), 45–70, 221–35, 305–12. See also Frattarelli Fischer and Lazzarini, *Chiese e luoghi di culto*, 91–128.

27 A London Protestant doctor and galley slave Wiliam Davies was imprisoned for participating in the burial of a Protestant sailor in Ferdinand's time. William Davies, *True relation of the Travails and most miserable captivitie of William Davies, Barber Surgion of London, under the Duke of Florence [...]* (London: Nicholas Bourne, 1614). Modern edition: Algerina Neri, ed., *Uno schiavo inglese nella Livorno dei Medici* (Pisa: Edizioni ETS, 2000), 92–6.

28 Frattarelli Fischer and Lazzarini, *Chiese e luoghi di culto*, 128–35. Frattarelli Fischer and Villani, "People of Every Mixture".

29 The group of older brotherhoods included the companies of S. Anna, S. Antonio, S. Barbara, S. Francesco d'Assisi, S. Martino in Salviano, S. Omobono, and S. Ma Vergine. ASLi, Confraternite 1599–1785, Inventory 21, 1–14, 16, 20, 42.

30 From January 14, 1595 to March 25, 1604 (sf), it gathered 175 male members from 16 different Italian cities, all noted by patronymics and toponyms rather than by occupation. On October 28, 1649, it approved a mass registration of 68 Tuscan soldiers in a group, the troop of Captain Vincente Gio Bochotti, suggesting that it may have been following the contemporary Venetian practice of enrolling state employees as a form of social support. ASLi, Confraternite 76, ff. 1^r-4^r, 53^r.

31 ASLi, Confraternite 350, ff. 1^r-10^v.

32 This group included the companies of S. Maria del Suffragio and the SS Nome di Gesu, ASLi, Confraternite 1599–1785, Inventory 21, pp. 37, 39, For the Misericordia, see: ASLi, Spedali Riuniti, 99.

33 The five founders included three Florentines, a Milanese, and a Pistoiese, and they aggregated with Florence's Misericordia immediately. ASLi, Spedali Riuniti 99, np [4, 5].

34 Nicholas Terpstra, "Found and Lost: Race and Demography in Early Modern Foundling Care," in *Lost and Found: Locating Foundlings in the Early Modern World*, ed. Nicholas Terpstra (Rome: Officina Libraria, 2023).

35 ASLi, Spedali Riuniti 99, np [9–12].

36 There were 22 members from 13 different towns in Italy, France, and Flanders. ASLi, Confraternite #116 [1616 statutes], ff. 2^r, 6^v.

37 ASLi, Confraternite 1599–1785, Inventory 21, 2–3, 18, 31, 41.

38 Frattarelli Fischer and Lazzarini, *Chiese e luoghi di culto*, 106–17.

39 See Nadalo's description of the 1680 funeral of a prominent rabbi: "Constructing Pluralism," 279–81.

40 The gesso studies can be found in the Museo Civico Giovanni Fattori. Three of the slaves appear Caucasian and one is Black, and all are generic; modern art historians believe that the final sculptures offer portrait-like representations of individual slaves in the *Bagno*. Steven F Ostrow, "Pietro Tacca and His Quattro Mori: The Beauty and Identity of the Slaves," *Artibus et Historiae* 71 (XXXVI) (2015), 145–80. M. Rosen, "Pietro Tacca's *Quattro Mori* and the Conditions of Slavery in Early Modern Tuscany," *Art Bulletin* 9, no. 1 (2015), 46–52.

41 ASF MP, 1814, f. 495^r [part of instructions to governor Giulio di Montauto, June 2, 1621 – cf. 493–8].

42 Clause 6 of the orders specified that the Governor had to uphold and defend the hospital of S. Antonio della Misericordia and to protect the quarters of the confraternities of S. Giulia, S. Cosimo, and S. Barbara, the church and convent of the Madonna, and the church of the Greek nation. Clause 7 specified that the Augustinian church of S. Giovanni across the street from the *bagno* was to be a place of prayer and sacraments and worship of God, and not a refuge for receiving homicides and those who had spilled human blood or other *malfattori* or *perturbatori* of public peace. It was not good to shelter them, and they should be removed so that there is no impeding the work of justice, which pleases God. ASF MP, 1814, f. 495^r.

43 Florence's conversion house (*casa dei catecumeni*) opened on June 14, 1636 after some decades of lobbying by the Carmelites. It actually occupied two houses next to the quarters of the Christian Doctrine confraternity of S. Francesco on Via Palazzuolo just west of modern Via Porcellana. Quarters were restricted and converts housed in private quarters across the city until a three-storey structure facing the monastery of S. Silvestro was acquired on Borgo Pinti. Samuela Marconcini, *Per amor del cielo: Farsi cristiani a Firenze tra Seicento e Settecento* (Florence: Firenze University Press, 2016), 19–20, 27–8, 40–68.

44 The eight-folio register of fines from 1683–1774 was compiled on June 6, 1775 from the Libri Mastri of the Spedale dei Trovatelli: ASPi, Ospedale dei Trovatelli, Ospedale. Riunite di S. Chiara, ms. 2388. Early targets include Jews from both Pisa and Livorno, but after 1750 all recorded fines were levied against Jews from Livorno. See also Trivellato, *Familiarity of Strangers*, 84–92.

45 Terpstra, "Race, Gender, and the Politics of Enclosure," 190–5.

46 Trivellato, *Familiarity of Strangers*, 70–101. Frattarelli Fischer and Villani, "People of Every Mixture," 10–3, 19. Frattarelli Fischer, *L'Arcano del mare*, 135–6.

8 Crossing Borders?

Conversions and Mixed Marriages in Ottoman *Bilād al-Shām* (Seventeenth and Eighteenth Centuries)*

Felicita Tramontana

In the last few decades, the study of the Reformation and Counter-Reformation has experienced a "Global Turn."[1] On the one hand, the "confessionalisation paradigm," increasingly questioned within the borders of Europe, has seen its fortunes rising on a global scale, with its applications in extra-European contexts and to the relationship between, and within, other faiths.[2] On the other hand, and in a somewhat different direction, research on the Reformations has increasingly begun to look beyond the borders of Europe and to explore how the concerns raised by the "Reformation movements" were translated into other parts of the world and influenced the relationship between the Christian churches and between Christianity and other faiths. This development runs in parallel with a recent approach within research on early modern Catholicism that questions the traditional division between Europe and the rest of the world, between a Tridentine and a missionary space. Thanks to this trend, the debate on the different outcomes of the implementation of the Counter Reformation and the plurality of early modern Catholicism, once confined to Europe, has recently acquired a global dimension.[3] Inspired by this research, this chapter explores the creation of confessional borders between Catholics and the other Christian communities in the seventeenth- and eighteenth-century Syro-Palestinian region and investigates how the Tridentine Church's commitment to strengthening Catholic identity and towards a greater uniformity was translated in the area.

In the aftermath of the Reformation, and consistent with the wider missionary impulse that characterised early modern Catholicism, the Church started to look towards the Middle East, at the time under Ottoman rule. Catholic missionaries arrived in Anatolia in the last decades of the sixteenth century and in the Syro-Palestinian region in the 1620s. Their objectives were the reconciliation of Eastern Christians with Rome and the establishment of local Catholic communities in a place where Catholics were mostly foreigners. The fact that in a Muslim area missionary activity was almost exclusively directed at the Christian minority was a consequence, on the one hand, of the Ottoman ban on apostasy from Islam and missionary activity among Muslims. On the other hand, it also fit in with a centuries-long story of attempts (and failures) to bring Eastern Christianity under the

DOI: 10.4324/9781003030522-12

authority of the Pope.[4] In the period under consideration, these efforts were fuelled by the competition between Catholics and Protestants, with both sides eager to gain the support of the Eastern churches. Rome in particular also feared the diffusion of Protestant ideas in the East.

Because of the presence of numerous Christian denominations in the region, the creation of a strong confessional identity – which was a cornerstone of early modern Catholicism vis-à-vis the Protestant churches – soon became equally important in the Ottoman Empire. The establishment of local Catholicism was, therefore, intertwined with a commitment to create borders that separated and distinguished Catholics from the members of the other churches. As in Europe, so too here, this was far from a linear process. In what follows I will reconstruct the tortuous development of local Catholicism through the analysis of conversions and mixed marriages between Catholics and other Christians.

Conversion and mixed marriages are closely connected one to the other insofar as mixed marriages frequently resulted in the conversion of one of the spouses. Within research on the Reformations, these two phenomena have attracted the attention of many scholars for a variety of reasons: both are ways to cross confessional boundaries and have also represented, for confessional churches, the possibility of gaining a member and at the same time the risk of losing one.[5] In this respect, as much as conversions, mixed marriages also had a demographic impact which was particularly important in the case of small religious communities. Some studies have focused on how the Catholic and Reformed churches tried to prevent and regulate both conversions and mixed marriages. Others have tended rather to focus, from a bottom-up perspective, on the difficulties faced in implementing these measures. Taking as their starting point the analysis of conversion and mixed marriages as moments of border crossing and transgression, the latter have highlighted the incompleteness of the process of social disciplining, the persistence of daily interactions, and the development of forms of coexistence and toleration.[6]

Similarly, the reconstruction of attempts, failures, and successes in disciplining conversion and mixed marriages in Ottoman *Bilād al-Shām* sheds light on the process of confessionalisation that the arrival of the missionaries precipitated in the area: its slow progress, the factors that influenced it, and the difficulties faced by the missionaries. The chapter tells this story and focuses on how this process was affected by the way relationships between faiths were organised in the Ottoman Empire.

In the territories ruled by the sultans, interfaith relationships were regulated through a set of norms that were the expression of a coherent policy. This policy also governed the establishment and maintenance of religious boundaries and their meaning. Whereas in many parts of Europe the confessionalisation process created a new division within the wider Christian population, when the missionaries arrived in the Middle East, Christianity was already subdivided into numerous denominations whose coexistence was regulated by rules that had been in place for centuries. This aspect has not always been accorded the importance it deserves; nonetheless, it serves to frame in a new and wider perspective the confessional borders created and also to draw a contrast with other ways of organising interfaith relationships. The specific case studied here raises important questions about the peculiarities of the borders that the missionaries sought to establish, first regarding how they fitted with the local organisation of interfaith relationships and, second, how that pre-existing organisation influenced the implementation of the guiding criteria of the Counter-Reformation and was influenced in its turn. While addressing these questions, in a wider perspective the chapter contributes to the current debate regarding the confessionalisation process, its links with social discipline, and the influence exercised in it from below.

The chapter is organised as follows: the first section provides an overview of how the relationships between faiths were organised in the Ottoman Empire and of the characteristics that defined religious conversions either to Islam or between the other religions. Taking the analysis of the passage to Catholicism as its starting point, the second section discusses its peculiarities and explores the differences between the interdenominational borders the missionaries were seeking to create and those that already existed. Section three describes the implications of the persisting phenomenon of mixed marriages not only for the construction of a Catholic identity, but also for the demography of newly established Catholic communities. Taking as its point of departure the decline in mixed marriages during the eighteenth century, section four reflects on the construction of confessional borders in the Syro-Palestinian region and the factors that influenced this process.

The Ottoman Empire: religious pluralism, toleration, and borders between communities

When the first Catholic missionaries arrived in the Syro-Palestinian region, Catholics in the Ottoman Middle East were few and mostly foreigners. The spread of Islam in the area had started in the seventh century, at the time of the Arab conquest, and in the seventeenth century most of the population was Muslim. Jews and Christians were religious minorities. The Christians were divided into various churches with their own rituals and liturgical languages. Besides the Greek Orthodox, which was the pre-eminent group and whose separation from Rome dates to the great schism in 1054, there were various Oriental churches, mostly established at the time of the doctrinal controversies in the fifth century. This was the case with the Armenian Church, which rejected the Chalcedonian doctrine.[7] Copts and Nestorians, to give two other examples, were followers of a theological tradition anathematised by the Orthodox mainstream in 431.

From an administrative point of view, religious minorities were organised into communities (*ṭā'ifa*, plural: *ṭawā'if*)[8] that were responsible for the education and welfare of their members and, most importantly in the eyes of Ottoman authorities, for the collection and payment of the taxes owed to Istanbul.

Matters of personal status, marriage, divorce, and inheritance, moreover, were regulated by religious laws. Religion shaped an individual's identity and their belonging to Islam or otherwise – together with the distinction between men and women, *askeri* (members of the military class) and *re'aya* (commoners), slaves and free persons – defined their legal and social status.

Following Islamic law, religious minorities were considered *ahl al-dhimmah* ("people of the covenant").[9] They enjoyed the right to own property, and to move and live wherever they chose, on condition that they paid the poll tax (*jizya*).[10] They were also free to practise their faith, albeit with certain restrictions: public display and religious ceremonies were banned and building new houses of worship was prohibited. Yet the differences between non-Muslims and Muslims, and the latter's privileged status, were asserted and constantly reinforced through a complex set of norms combining sumptuary laws and prohibitions of various sorts that regulated everyday conduct: for example, the ban on riding specific animals and the obligation to make way for Muslims. Despite these restrictions, life for religious minorities was easier in the Ottoman Empire than in Europe, as European travellers and intellectuals did not fail to notice. Jews and Christians participated in economic life, joined guilds, enjoyed a degree of social mobility, and were free to move, engage in business, and accumulate wealth, without being persecuted.

Istanbul's treatment of religious minorities has been the subject of many scholarly studies. Since the 1990s, Ottoman "toleration" has been increasingly viewed in the context of imperial politics. Toleration has, therefore, started to be seen as a means of rule and a way to accommodate diversity and enforce state power.[11] The absence of persecution and the wish to accommodate diversity, however, went in parallel with a readiness to maintain the separation between communities, which was another cornerstone of Ottoman policy towards religious minorities. Indeed, the above-mentioned prescriptions regarding the behaviour of religious minorities were aimed at defining and maintaining clear boundaries between religious communities. The same aim lay behind the autonomy granted in matters such as education, welfare, and conflict resolution, as far as non-Muslims were involved. This attitude is also reflected in the *fatāwā*[12] of Ebüssuûd Efendi, who held the office of *Shaykh al-Islām* (leader of the Ottoman religious scholars) during the reign of Suleiman I (1520–66) and Selim II (1566–74). In his *fatāwā*, he supported the jurisdiction of Christian and Jewish religious authorities on family matters and prevented Christians from adopting Muslim practices regarding marriage, such as polygamy.[13]

Non-Muslim religious authorities shared Istanbul's wish to maintain clear borders, being themselves concerned about not losing believers to the Muslim majority. However, religious boundaries were not the same in all directions. First of all, they were porous towards Islam but not the other way around. Conversion to Islam was permitted; indeed, various economic and social incentives encouraged it. Conversely, apostasy from Islam was punished with the death penalty. Marriages between Muslim men and Christian or Jewish women were allowed, but not the other way around, and children of mixed couples had to be raised as Muslims. If we leave Islam aside, borders between minorities were not policed by the Ottoman state. The battle against transgressions, conversions, and mixed marriages was left to religious leaders, who could count only on their moral authority.

Although split into different sects, from an administrative and fiscal standpoint, Jews were all part of the same community. Conversely, Christians were divided into various communities of Greeks, Armenians, et cetera. Notwithstanding the administrative and fiscal implications of this division, borders between communities were characterised by a certain fluidity, which resulted in the widespread practice of mixed marriages and sacramental sharing: Christians would often receive the sacraments from a priest of a different church, and followers of different denominations would routinely attend the same ceremonies. These behaviours were encouraged by a long tradition and by the use of the same church buildings, which was a consequence of the paucity of existing Christian places of worship and of the Ottoman ban on building new ones.

The importance that religion had in structuring the social hierarchy and regulating many aspects of everyday life determined what "crossing religious boundaries" and conversion meant in Ottoman lands. Due to the privileged status of the Muslim community, conversion to Islam enhanced social status and changed the convert's legal position. Since a Muslim could not owe money to non-Muslims, for example, conversion might result in the cancellation of debts. Conversion could also be a way to escape marriage. Becoming Muslim allowed a man to end his marriage by repudiation and a woman to initiate a divorce.[14] Furthermore, since Muslim women could not be married to non-Muslim men, if Jewish or Christian women were to convert, their marriages to a Christian or Jewish husband would immediately become invalid.[15]

A change of faith from one minority religion to another had administrative consequences too. It entailed entry into a new religious community with different rules relating to welfare and sometimes personal status. Converts would pay taxes with their new co-religionists and would be represented before Ottoman authorities by the leaders of their new community. What in this context were the peculiarities of conversion to Catholicism and, indeed, its intrinsic meaning? What were the differences between the existing inter-denominational borders and those the missionaries tried to establish between Catholics and other Christians?

The task of the missionaries: conversion and the creation of confessional borders

The spread of Catholicism in Ottoman lands was greatly helped by the increasing French interest in the region and the expansion of French trade. Indeed, the very arrival of Catholic missionaries in the last decades of the sixteenth century was made possible by the capitulation, or trade treaties, signed between

Istanbul and France. These allowed religious orders to enter the territories ruled by the sultans to provide spiritual succour to French merchants.[16]

The progress of missionary activity and the spread of Catholicism among Eastern Christians in the Middle East have been studied by numerous scholars.[17] Conversions to Catholicism were called "reconciliations" and consisted in the rejection of the dogmas of the former church and a confession. In most cases, the passage to Catholicism did not entail major changes in ritual and liturgy. In this respect, the instructions of Rome were clear: converts' adoption of the Latin rites[18] was prohibited. They had to keep their Oriental liturgies and rites, whose legitimacy was reaffirmed time and again by the Roman congregations. The newly established Catholic Eastern churches, therefore, retained their own liturgical tradition and were guided by local clergy.[19] An exception was represented by those who were reconciled by the Reformed Franciscans of the Custody of the Holy Land, as the friars actively promoted their adoption of the Latin rite[20] and integrated them into their parish system.

In order to gain followers, missionaries made generous use of their medical competences, offered economic incentives, and, setting out from their houses, which were mostly located in places inhabited by Christian merchants, would visit outlying villages. In some areas, Catholicism spread first among those who had daily contact with the missionaries and from them to their acquaintances. Scholars have comprehensively analysed the incentives that facilitated the spread of Catholicism, such as the affiliation with French merchants and the opportunity to enter western trade networks; economic incentives; and a good education for their children. In Eastern Catholicism, Mass could be in Arabic rather than Greek or Armenian, and rules regarding fasting and the degree of consanguinity allowed in marriage were less rigid than Orthodox prescriptions. Finally, the passage to Catholicism chimed with the existing centrifugal tendencies of the local Orthodox Church, which sought to gain autonomy from the Greek clergy in Istanbul.[21]

Despite the joy and pride with which reconciliations were reported by missionaries, conversion was just a first step in the long process by which Catholic identity was established. Indeed, an analysis of conversions to Catholicism in the period under consideration reveals the great complexity of this process, and the difficulty faced by missionaries when trying to create confessional borders. This is borne out by, for example, the frequency of returns to the former faith and secret conversions.

In early modern Europe, reconversions or relapses represented a serious problem for the Reformed and Catholic Churches alike. At a time when the churches struggled to establish clear confessional borders and strong confessional identities, returns to the former faith showed that borders were still porous and identities fluid.[22] This was also the case in the Middle East, where returns to the former churches also represented a challenge to the very existence of the newly established Catholic communities. During the entire seventeenth century and first decades of the eighteenth, the return of new Catholics to their former faith was a common occurrence in the region. The Reformed

Franciscans often complained about their flocks' lack of perseverance and expressed irritation at how returns to the Orthodox Church were used as a threat in order to obtain the friars' economic help.[23]

Reconversions were motivated by social and economic considerations or occurred in response to pressure from former co-religionists. In certain periods, they were also encouraged by the measures adopted by Ottoman authorities to prevent conversions between Christian denominations. Initially, Istanbul did not interfere with Catholic missionary activity directed at Eastern Christians. Later, however, this attitude changed following the increasing pressure exerted by Orthodox religious authorities, who tried hard to halt the drain of followers. In the region as a whole, conversion between Christian denominations was by no means a new phenomenon. Nonetheless, the passage to Catholicism represented an unprecedented challenge because of the number of people involved and the means at the disposal of the missionaries. Orthodox religious authorities, therefore, did their utmost to prevent their flocks' conversion to Catholicism. They also appealed to Ottoman authorities, suggesting that Catholics were subversive. As a result, during the eighteenth century, Istanbul periodically issued orders prohibiting conversion between Christian denominations and missionary activities among the Eastern Christians.

Conflicts with former co-religionists and the prescriptions of Ottoman authorities were also the reasons invoked by the missionaries to justify secret conversions. These were widespread in the Middle East during the seventeenth and the eighteenth century. Febe Armanios has described in great detail the persistence of the phenomenon in Egypt, where even Coptic clergymen secretly professed their allegiance to Rome but publicly continued to serve their former congregations.[24] In seventeenth-century Palestine, secret conversions were so common that the Reformed Franciscans supplying lists of their parishioners to De Propaganda Fide[25] regularly distinguished between those who had embraced Catholicism publicly and those who had done so secretly. To give just one example, the latter in 1664 represented more than 30% of the total number of Catholics in Bethlehem (30 out of 98).[26] And as in Egypt, so in Palestine, too, even some clergymen swore their allegiance to Rome secretly.

The validity of secret conversions was amply debated in the correspondence between Rome and the missionaries. The reasons why they were considered a necessary evil by the latter are well explained in a number of letters written in the 1630s by the Guardians of Reformed Franciscans and addressed to the Congregation De Propaganda Fide. In a letter dating to 1637, for example, Father Andrea d'Arco invoked the authority of St. Thomas Aquinas to claim that conversions could be kept secret if the convert's safety was in jeopardy. The Guardian further pointed out that the rejection of secret conversions would jeopardise the spread of Catholicism among local Christians,[27] an argument that, as we shall see, was also used to justify mixed marriages and sacramental sharing. Besides the problem of validity, these conversions also raised several other issues, such as whether converts could receive sacraments from non-Catholic priests and attend religious ceremonies with their former co-religionists, or whether clergymen who had converted to Catholicism secretly could administer sacraments in their former churches.[28]

As in Europe, so too in the Middle East, the abundance of relapses and secret conversions well into the eighteenth century testified to the persisting fluidity of the borders between Catholics and the other churches. It also put in doubt the post-Reformation model of conversion, which emphasises the sincerity and commitment of the convert and the transformative nature of conversion.

Even setting aside relapses and secret conversions, however, the passage to Catholicism in the seventeenth-century Middle East was far from a transformative event. On the contrary, it brought minimal changes in the life of new converts, reflecting in this regard the peculiarities of conversion to Catholicism. Whereas in the Middle East a change of faith entailed a change of *ṭā'ifa* with all the relevant administrative consequences, in the seventeenth and eighteenth centuries a Catholic *ṭā'ifa* did not exist and those who were reconciled with Rome remained officially part of the Armenian, Greek, or other *ṭā'ifa*. They would continue to pay taxes with their former co-religionists and would be represented before the Ottoman authorities by the same representatives. In certain matters, such as burials, they were also dependent on Orthodox religious leaders, if they were the legal heads of their *ṭā'ifa*.[29] The passage to Catholicism moreover, as already mentioned, did not imply a change in rituals. Converts would keep their traditional liturgy, feast days, and icons. In the seventeenth century and for the best part of the following one, Catholicism remained a private religion, as prayers and ceremonies were held in private houses. Confession and visits by occasional missionaries were the only elements that distinguished Catholics from their former co-religionists.[30]

When looked at from the point of view of the organisation of interdenominational relationships in the region, the spread of Catholicism created a fracture within Oriental Christianity and started a process of construction of confessional identities. The confessional borders that the Catholic Church sought to create, contrary to the existing ones, were not based on differences in rituals and liturgy, nor did they run along the administrative borders between religious communities. Rather, they created a division between Catholics and Orthodox within the existing Christian churches and associated communities. Moreover, whereas the pre-existing borders between Christian denominations were fluid enough to allow sacramental sharing and mixed marriages, such a porousness was incompatible with the confessional borders that, following the model elaborated in Western Europe, the Church sought to establish between Catholics and members of the other churches. Indeed, with the arrival of Catholicism, the very concepts of conversion and religious borders had to be recast.

This process, however, was slowed by numerous factors. As shown by missionaries' letters, the Church's tendency towards greater uniformity and discipline had to be balanced with its commitment to the global expansion of Catholicism and the wish to gain new souls. This was particularly problematic in a place like the Ottoman Empire, where the Church's ability to create and police confessional borders was affected by the indifference, if not open hostility, of the ruling power and by the competition represented by conversion to Islam, which in the seventeenth century represented an attractive option for religious minorities. These issues were often raised by missionaries and clergymen "on the ground" when trying to justify an attitude of forbearance towards converts' behaviour.

Scholarship has convincingly argued that missionaries often had a more pragmatic approach towards the enforcement of Tridentine prescriptions than did Roman authorities, and tried through their letters to soften the latter's position.[31] The correspondence between the Roman congregations and missionaries in the Ottoman Empire, especially during the seventeenth century, in general terms confirms this interpretation. Missionaries, in most cases, seemed to accept and justify forms of *communicatio in sacris*.[32] Consistent with this, they opposed the decrees of Propaganda aimed at fighting this practice.[33] That said, one should avoid drawing a dichotomy between the congregations' and missionaries' positions. In practice, the attitude of missionaries and clergymen who resided in Palestine often varied on a case-by-case basis, with forbearance towards sacramental sharing being among the accusations most frequently exchanged between members of different religious orders. Conversely, the positions expressed by different congregations did not always coincide, and even the Propaganda itself adopted a variety of positions, which generally became stricter during the eighteenth century.[34]

To return to the factors that slowed the development of a Catholic identity: the fact that converts retained their liturgical traditions, feast days, and icons, on the one hand, might have encouraged their passage to Catholicism by allowing them to keep what they wanted from the old religion without renouncing the opportunities offered by conversion to Catholicism. On the other hand, the retention of the old liturgical traditions might have also affected the converts' very understanding of the passage to Catholicism. Indeed, one cannot help but wonder how converts, for whom theological differences were difficult to grasp, perceived a conversion that did not imply a change in rituals, liturgy or community.

As a result, during the seventeenth and eighteenth centuries, the persistent fluidity of interdenominational borders and the difficulties involved in disciplining converts' behaviours were manifested not only by the frequency of secret conversions and returns to the former faith; sacramental sharing and mixed marriages also remained common: Catholics continued to attend ceremonies with former co-religionists, receive sacraments from priests of other churches, and, as we shall see, marry members of other denominations.[35]

Mixed marriages

Converts' marriages have always raised concerns and doubts among both missionaries and Catholic authorities.[36] Issues surrounding the form of marriage, its validity, and interfaith marriages have been the subject of numerous debates, both between the Roman congregations and between them and the religious "on the ground." The Ottoman Empire does not represent an exception in this regard. Missionaries' letters raised questions regarding polygamy, the validity of marriages celebrated by Orthodox priests or Muslim judges, repudiations, and interfaith marriages.[37] In this respect, unions between Catholics and members of other denominations were problematic for the Catholic Church, for a number of reasons. Just as reconversions and sacramental sharing did, they challenged the construction of borders between communities and testified to their persistent fluidity. Furthermore, because of their link with conversions, mixed marriages also represented a demographic problem for the establishment of Catholic communities. Finally, mixed marriages and sacramental sharing were also in conflict with the importance that participation in rites, especially weddings and baptisms, had for confessional churches in Europe.[38]

The Catholic Church, like all the other churches, had prohibited these mixed unions, yet it did not question their validity. According to the decree "Tametsi," a marriage celebrated without a priest was not valid; therefore, by forbidding priests to attend such weddings, the Church aimed to combat these unions. This, however, was possible only in those places where the decree had been published and which were predominantly Catholic.[39] Missionaries in many parts of Northern Europe complained that if a priest refused to bless these unions, the spouses would turn instead to Protestant ministers.

Similarly, letters sent by missionaries in the Ottoman Empire clearly show the difficulties they faced in enforcing Rome's prohibitions well into the eighteenth century. The parish books that were kept in some of the Latin parishes managed by the Reformed Franciscans yield some information on the phenomenon. In the town of Bethlehem, for example, mixed marriages celebrated by the Franciscans alone represented 20% of the 76 marriages recorded in the *Liber Coniugatorum* between 1669 and 1699.[40] These numbers do not take into account mixed marriages celebrated by Orthodox priests.[41] It is also likely that in the Latin parishes mixed marriages were far less numerous than in those places where Catholics had retained their rites and sacraments, which were mostly administered by local Catholic clergy. Consisting for the most part of clergy from the Eastern churches who had converted to Catholicism, the latter were in fact usually willing to celebrate mixed marriages.[42]

As missionaries explained, within the small and newly established Catholic communities, mixed marriages were a necessity because of the sheer narrowness of the marriage market, a narrowness exacerbated by the ban on marriages within a certain degree of consanguinity and by preferences regarding social status. As the letters of the Franciscans indicate, in many cases mixed marriages could not be avoided: for a girl who was already 26 and had no Catholic suitors, or when the higher social status of Catholic women would make the match unsuitable.[43] The point is confirmed by the presence in the above-mentioned *Liber Coniugatorum* of Bethlehem of numerous dispensations granted by the Guardian of the Holy Land from the Catholic rules regarding consanguinity and of records of out-of-town weddings. Even exogamous marriages were sometimes not between Catholics.[44]

When justifying their attitude of forbearance towards mixed marriages, missionaries often claimed that the latter represented an opportunity to gain new followers. Indeed, the first conversions recorded in Bethlehem were those of the Greek wives of the Catholic dragoman of the Franciscan convent. During the 1620s and 1630s, according to Franciscan documents, in both Jerusalem and Bethlehem conversions of Greek wives in mixed marriages were numerous.[45] The higher number of conversions by women is consistent with the fact that in most of the recorded cases Catholic men married non-Catholic, Greek wives.

Not all the interdenominational marriages, however, had such a positive outcome and not all the Orthodox wives converted to Catholicism. This also affected the faith in which the children from these marriages would be raised, an issue of great concern to religious authorities here as in Europe.[46] In 1633, the Franciscan Vincenzo Gallicano explained that in mixed families boys were baptised as Catholic, following the father's religion, and girls were raised in the Orthodox faith of the mother,[47] a practice that was also common in some parts of Europe.[48]

The consequences of mixed marriages could, from the perspective of the Catholic Church, be even worse. Parish books and registers of conversions, by their very nature, do not provide much evidence of the passage of Catholic spouses to another denomination nor do they list the unions celebrated by Orthodox priests. The *Register Coniugatorum* of the parish of Bethlehem, however, provides some interesting evidence in this respect. At the end of the list of marriages celebrated in the year 1699, there is a section entitled "Notes (*Note* in Italian)" where the friars recorded mixed marriages, six cases in total. The reason why these marriages were recorded in a separate section is that they had not been celebrated by the parish priest, but by a Greek one. All these unions were celebrated between 1697 and 1700, and all were followed by the conversion of the Catholic spouse and sometimes part of his or her family as well. The Catholic "Ioannes," son of "Giorgius" and "Oliva,"[49] for example, married a Greek girl and became Orthodox, shortly followed by his father and mother. The latter, however, the records inform us, was later secretly reconciled to Catholicism.[50] Other similar cases were recorded on the same page. Two Catholic women thus married Greek men before an Orthodox priest and became Orthodox themselves, one of whom was even followed by her father and brothers.[51] That these were not isolated cases is attested by the fact that the friars not only wrote down when the spouses' relatives converted, but also whether they remained Catholic.[52] This is also consistent with the way Catholicism spread in Bethlehem and Jerusalem, where those who embraced Catholicism were often followed by their family members.[53]

These records also corroborate the concern, often voiced by the missionaries, that if they refused to celebrate mixed unions, the latter would be blessed by Greek priests and that their refusal would prompt Catholic converts' return to their former faith. In the above-mentioned cases, the records suggest that the spouses turned to the Orthodox priests because the Guardian of the Holy Land had refused to bless their nuptials. His stance, however, was not due to any opposition on his part to mixed marriages, but rather to his fear of the reaction of Greek religious authorities, backed by a recently issued Ottoman decree in their favour.[54]

As in the case of secret conversions and returns to the former faith, in the seventeenth and part of the eighteenth centuries, missionaries' letters regarding mixed marriages show an attitude of forbearance. From the 1730s, however, and with the evident advance of Catholicism in the region, such attitudes started to change. The Church's opposition to this practice intensified, as attested by the ban on *communicatio in sacris* issued by Rome in 1729.[55]

Mixed marriages, conversion, and the creation of confessional borders

Studies on early modern Europe have seen mixed marriages as evidence of the persisting fluidity of confessional borders that characterised "the first generation of the Reformation," when these unions were socially accepted and familial solidarities prevailed.[56] This first phase was followed by a tightening of confessional borders. In the northern Netherlands, opposition to mixed unions grew over the seventeenth century and led in the 1650s to the adoption of measures against them by both Catholic and Reformed churches. The same process can be discerned later in the Syro-Palestinian region, where the number of mixed marriages, which were common in the seventeenth century, steadily decreased over the eighteenth century. The different timelines of the two processes are particularly evident in the mid-eighteenth century.

In 1741, Pope Benedict XIV issued the *Declaratio Benedictina* for the northern and southern Netherlands. By affirming the validity of nuptials celebrated without following the prescriptions of the Tametsi decree, the *Declaratio* rendered interfaith marriages *de facto* easier. Initially, an extension of this document to the Ottoman territories was contemplated, and in 1769 a commission was established by Pope Clement XIII to consider the issue. The idea, however, was rejected on the grounds that in a region characterised by the coexistence of many different Christian denominations, the application of the *Declaratio* would nullify the efforts of missionaries and increase the number of mixed marriages. And this at a time when, despite the prohibitions, the number of such marriages was still high and the creation of a Catholic identity separated from the other churches was yet to be achieved.[57] The decision not to apply the *Declaratio* in Ottoman land not only affected marriages between Catholics and Orthodox, but also those between Catholics and Protestants in the region, in contrast to the contemporary relaxation of rules on the matter in Protestant Europe.[58]

The analysis of mixed marriages in the Syro-Palestinian region also highlights the importance of local differences. In Bethlehem, already in the first decade of the seventeenth century, Greek religious authorities strongly opposed nuptials between members of their flock and Catholics. As a result, mixed marriages had to be celebrated in private houses and without bans, or even in nearby Jerusalem. Such a situation might have been connected to the conflicts between the Reformed Franciscans and Orthodox Greeks over control of the Holy Shrines in both Jerusalem and Bethlehem. There is, however, no reason to question the existence of a general pattern that signifies a strengthening of confessional identities over the course of the eighteenth century.

Even though the number of mixed marriages still aroused Catholic fears as late as 1769, since the 1730s the construction of more rigid borders had slowly progressed. This is attested towards the end of the eighteenth century by the decreasing number of conversions and by the fact that most of the issues raised by the missionaries were related to the passage between Catholic rites, rather than between Catholicism and Orthodoxy.[59]

Because of the Catholic presence in the former *ṭā'ifa* and the sharing of sacred spaces, the distinction between Catholics and other Christians, even more than in other contexts, had to be based on differentiation in behaviours and religious practices. If on Italian soil the Church's intolerant attitude towards Orthodox minorities could be translated into prescriptions aimed at their assimilation or at maintaining the separation between them and the Catholic majority,[60] this was not the case in Ottoman lands. Here, the lack of political support – and therefore the fact that control of the behaviour of the faithful was not part of a wider process of social discipline – and the subordinate position in which Catholic clergy often found themselves within the *ṭā'ifa* enhanced the importance of a process of interiorisation of the differences between Catholics and their former co-religionists: only the casting of the latter as heretics could prevent mixed marriages and sacramental sharing.

The same can be said regarding the disciplining of Catholics' everyday behaviours, from the consumption of tobacco to women's and girls' conduct in public.[61] A cornerstone of the Reformations in Europe, the Church's efforts in this direction were even more important and challenging in the Ottoman Empire, whose inhabitants, whether they were Christians, Jews, or Muslims, shared habits, customs, and even places of worship. In this respect, however, differentiation of behaviours and religious practices had already been pursued by the Orthodox churches, which in the sixteenth century, for example, had started to push for a Christianisation of marriage ceremonies.[62]

Even though for centuries interdenominational relationships in the region had been characterised by porous borders, the arrival of the missionaries and the process of confessionalisation they started precipitated a reaction from the Orthodox Church which soon became an essential ally in the construction of confessional churches. In the eighteenth century, the interiorisation of Church teaching, the quest for uniformity, and the drawing of sharp contrasts and oppositions between Christian churches were promoted by the clergy of both sides.[63] This is attested by the large number of controversies whose principal aim was to explain each church's defining characteristics to its own flock.[64] Equally important were the Orthodox churches' attempts to ban sacramental sharing, which culminated in 1755, during the Synod of Constantinople, in the Orthodox decision to consider Catholic baptism invalid, a decision that broke with a centuries-long tradition of mutual recognition of baptism among Christian churches.

The establishment of confessional borders and the creation of a Catholic identity were also promoted, especially towards the end of the eighteenth century and during the nineteenth, by the cooperation of the faithful. Its role of active collaboration has been highlighted by recent research on early modern Europe. While questioning the traditional understanding of social discipline as a top-down process, these works have rather seen it as "the appropriation of religious differences within a specific social and cultural setting."[65] The case of the Syro-Palestinian region corroborates this finding and emphasises the importance of geopolitical circumstances. Indeed, the spread of Catholicism and the construction of a Catholic identity were intertwined with the emergence of a Catholic and Christian bourgeoisie in the eighteenth and nineteenth centuries.[66] The association between Catholicism and French power and the perception of the growing influence of the latter, especially in the nineteenth century, served to enhance the appeal of conversion. The prestige that was increasingly associated with belonging to the Catholic community encouraged its members to differentiate themselves from other Christians.

The increase in the number of Catholics and the greater differentiation between them and their Orthodox counterparts were preconditions for the creation of communities that were separate from an administrative point of view. During the eighteenth century, the coexistence of Catholics and Orthodox Christians within the same *tai'fa* led to numerous conflicts over the use of places of worship, the division of the tax burden, and the elections of leaders. Even Ottoman courts were sometimes involved in these conflicts.[67] This situation came to an end in the nineteenth century with the establishment by the Sultan of the communities (*milletler*, singular *millet*) of the Uniates.[68] This outcome was, however, the result of broader changes in the organisation of religious minorities, linked to the emergence of the policy of the *millet* in the eighteenth century.[69] Initially promoted by the Greek patriarch of Constantinople, this process entailed the centralisation of all the affairs of religious minorities under the political and ecclesiastical authority of their respective leaders – a patriarch or chief rabbi – located in Istanbul. The first *millet* to be established by the Sultan was the Orthodox one in the eighteenth century, followed shortly by the Armenian one. In the course of the following century, all the other Christian churches would be allowed to establish their own *millet* as well.[70]

The implementation in the Middle East of a model of Christianity elaborated in post-Reformation Western Europe met with local resistance and the results were by no means uniform across the region. Among the factors impinging upon the process, Bernard Heyberger mentions the weakness of ecclesiastical institutions, the variety of religious practices (an aspect exacerbated by migration and mixed settlement), lack of political support, and the failure of "the humanist and post-Reformation idea that standardisation could be achieved through the historical investigation of sources."[71] Differences between city and countryside, for example, remained. Again, some issues raised by mixed marriages shed light on the meaning that the former borders between denominations might continue to have. In the second half of the eighteenth century, the Maronite Church, for example, would still try to prevent marriages with Catholics from another *tai'fa.*[72]

Conclusions

Relying on the analysis of conversions and mixed marriages, this chapter has described the construction of a Catholic identity, a process intertwined with the spread of Catholicism, in the Syro-Palestinian region. The frequency of mixed marriages, reconversions, and secret conversions well into the eighteenth century testifies to the difficulty of establishing borders between Catholics and the members of other churches.

In the Middle East, the development of local Catholicism was influenced by the way interreligious relationships were organised in the region when missionaries arrived and by geopolitical circumstances. The development of a Catholic identity implied the creation of a new form of division within Christianity that was not consistent with the way interfaith relationships were organised locally, but rather followed a model elaborated in Western Europe. The spread of Catholicism did not result for a very long time in the creation of a new *ṭā'ifa* but served to create a division within the existing ones between those who converted to Catholicism and those who did not. The nature of the new confessional borders disrupted the long-standing coexistence between denominations by banning well-established practices of mixed marriage and sacramental sharing.

The fundamental differences between the new borders missionaries tried to establish and the old ones explain why the pre-existing division between Christian denominations did not result in the drawing of confessional boundaries around the newly established Catholic communities. On the contrary, those differences may even have slowed down the process by making it more difficult for converts to understand the meaning of a passage of faith that had no administrative consequences and did not result in a change in rituals and liturgy. As a result, the confessionalisation process started by the missionaries changed permanently the face of Eastern Christianity and, in a place where interreligious relationships were dominated by the distinction between Islam and the other faiths, introduced a dichotomy within Christianity between Catholics and Orthodox.

When seen within the framework of research on the Counter Reformation, the analysis of the confessionalisation process in the Syro-Palestinian region corroborates those research findings that have questioned the link between state support and confessionalisation and the latter's allegedly top-down nature, and rather depict it as the result of a negotiation between the faithful, Rome, and the missionaries. As in many parts of Europe, so too in the Ottoman lands the lack of political support and fierce competition between faiths slowed the construction of a Catholic identity but did not prevent it from succeeding. Moreover, despite the fluidity of borders that for centuries had characterised the relationships between Christian churches in the region, Orthodox churches soon became important allies in the creation of confessional borders, similarly to how Reformed churches in northern Europe did. The case of the Syro-Palestinian region also highlights the importance of socio-economic and geopolitical circumstances since the emergence of a Catholic identity in the region is inextricably linked with the emergence of a Christian (and Catholic) bourgeoisie and the entrance of the Ottoman Empire into a world market economy dominated by Europe.[73]

Notes

* This research has been funded by the Greggs Well Small Research Award, awarded by the Centre for the Study of the Renaissance, University of Warwick, and by the Italian Ministry of University and Research, Programme FARE 2020, research project: "MISGLOB – Catholic missions and the global circulation of people and goods in the early modern period (1500–1800)."

The area referred to as *Bilād al-Shām* encompasses modern Syria, Lebanon, Jordan Palestine, and Israel.

1 Nicholas Terpstra, ed., *Global Reformations: Transforming Early Modern Religions, Societies, and Cultures* (London: Routledge 2019), esp. 1–12.

2 On the Ottoman Empire, see Tijana Krstić, *Contested Conversions to Islam: Narratives of Religious Change in the Early Modern Ottoman Empire* (Stanford: Stanford University Press, 2011), 12–6. Derin Terzioğlu, "Where ʻİlm-i Ḥāl Meets Catechism: Islamic Manuals of Religious Instruction in the Ottoman Empire in the Age of Confessionalization," *Past and Present* 220 (2013), 79–114.

3 Simon Ditchfield, "De-centering the Catholic Reformation: Papacy and Peoples in the Early Modern World," *Archiv für Reformationsgeschichte* 101 (2010), 186–208; Karen Melvin, "Globalization of Reform," in *The Ashgate Research Companion to the Counter-Reformation*, eds. Alexandra Bamji, Geert H. Janssen, and Mary Laven (Ashgate, 2013), 391–405. On the implementation of Tridentine Catholicism in Persia, see Christian Windler, *Missionare in Persien: Kulturelle Diversität und Normenkonkurrenz im globalen Katholizismus (17.–18. Jahrhundert)* (Cologne: Böhlau, 2018); Id., "Ambiguous Belongings: How Catholic Missionaries in Persia and the Roman Curia Dealt with *Communicatio in Sacris*," in *A Companion to Early Modern Catholic Global Missions*, ed. Ronnie Po-Chia Hsia (Leiden-Boston: Brill, 2018), 205–34. On the Ottoman Empire, see: Bernard Heyberger, *Les Chrétiens du Proche-Orient au temps de la Réforme catholique* (Rome: École française de Rome, 1984); Id., "Catholicisme et construction des frontières confessionnelles dans l'Orient ottoman," in *Frontières religieuses à l'époque moderne*, eds. Francisco Bethencourt and Denis Crouzet (Paris: Presses Universitaires de la Sorbonne, 2013), 123–142; Id., "Fasting: The Limits of Catholic Confessionalization in Eastern Christianity in the Eighteenth Century," in *Scholarship between Europe and the Levant. Essays in Honour of Professor Alastair Hamilton*, ed. Jan Loop and Jill Kraye (Leiden: Brill, 2020), 217–35; Cesare Santus, *Trasgressioni Necessarie: Communicatio in Sacris, Coesistenza e Conflitti Tra Le Comunità Cristiane Orientali* (Rome: École française de Rome, 2019).

4 M.-H. Blanchet, "La question de l'Union des Églises (13e-15e siècle): historiographie et perspectives," *Revue des études byzantines* 61 (2003), 5–48.

5 Benjamin J. Kaplan, *Divided by Faith: Religious Conflict and the Practice of Toleration in Early Modern Europe* (Cambridge, MA: Harvard University Press, 2007), 268.

6 Kaplan, *Divided by Faith*. See also Bertrand Forclaz, *Catholiques au défi de la Réforme. La coexistence confessionnelle à Utrecht au XVIIe siècle* (Paris: Honoré Champion, 2014). Among the numerous enquiries into marriage in post-reformation Europe, see Dagmar Freist, "One Body, Two Confessions: Mixed Marriages in Germany," in *Gender in Early Modern German History*, ed. Ulinka Rublack (Cambridge: Cambridge University Press, 2002), 275–304; Benjamin J. Kaplan, "Intimate Negotiations: Husbands and Wives of Opposing Faiths in Eighteenth-Century Holland," in *Living with Religious Diversity in Early-Modern Europe*, eds. C. Scott Dixon, Dagmar Freist, and Mark Greengrass (Farnham: Ashgate, 2009) and the bibliography mentioned in the footnotes below.

7 The Chalcedonian Council (451) condemned the belief regarding the one incarnate nature of Christ (monophysis).

8 "Group" or "party" – in Ottoman documents the term referred to a variety of collective social or economic groups, such as tribal groups, merchants, or foreigners.

9 The term indicates Jews, Christians, and Samaritans (People of the Book or *Ahl al-Kitāb*) who lived under Muslim rule and enjoyed the state's legal protection (*dhimmah*) on condition of paying the poll tax (see below).

10 A tax levied on non-Muslim men living in Muslim-ruled territories.

11 Karen Barkey, *Empire of Difference: The Ottomans in Comparative Perspective* (Cambridge: Cambridge University Press, 2008), 110. On the historiography of interfaith relationships in the Ottoman Empire, see Eleni Gara, "Conceptualizing Inter-religious Relations in the Ottoman Empire: The Early Modern Centuries," *Acta Poloniae Historica* 116 (2015), 57–91.

12 Legal opinions based on the Islamic law.

13 See Kermeli, Eugenia, "Ebussuud Efendi," in *Christian-Muslim Relations 1500–1900*, eds. David Thomas, John Chesworth et al., vol. 7 (Leiden: Brill, 2015), 715–723, at 719–20.

14 Al-khul is a procedure through which women can initiate a divorce.

15 Marc D. Baer, "Islamic Conversion Narratives of Women: Social Change and Gendered Religious Hierarchy in Early Modern Ottoman Istanbul," *Gender and History* 16 (2004), 425–58; Maya Shatzmiller, "Marriage, Family, and the Faith: Women's Conversion to Islam," *Journal of Family History* 21 (1996), 235–66.

16 Charles A. Frazee, *Catholics and Sultans: The Church and the Ottoman Empire 1453–1923* (Cambridge: Cambridge University Press, 1983), 73.

17 On Catholic missions in the seventeenth-century Middle East: Bernard Heyberger, *Les Chrétiens du Proche-Orient*; Id., "Frontières confessionnelles et conversions chez les chrétiens orientaux (xviie-xviiie siècles)," in *Conversions islamiques*, ed. Mercedes García-Arenal (Paris: Maisonneuve et Larose, 2001), 245–58; Frazee, *Catholics and sultans*, 67–150; Bruce Masters, *Christians and Jews in the Ottoman Arab World* (Cambridge: Cambridge University Press, 2001), 68–97; Robert M. Haddad, "Conversion of the Eastern Orthodox Christians to the Unia in the Seventeenth and Eighteenth Centuries," in *Conversion and Continuity: Indigenous Christian Communities in Islamic lands, Eighth to Eighteenth Centuries*, eds. Michael Gervers and Ramzi J. Bikhazi (Toronto: Pontifical Institute of Mediaeval Studies, 1990), 449–59; Lucette Valensi, "Inter-communal Relations and Changes in Religious Affiliation in the Middle East (Seventeenth to Nineteenth Centuries)," *Comparative Studies in Society and History* 39, no. 2 (1997), 251–69; Felicita Tramontana, *Passages of Faith. Conversions in Palestinian Villages* (Wiesbaden: Harrassovitz Verlag, 2014). On Egypt: Febe Armanios, *Coptic Christianity in Ottoman Egypt* (Oxford: Oxford University Press, 2011) and

Alastair Hamilton, *The Copts and the West, 1439–1822: The European discovery of the Egyptian Church* (Oxford: Oxford University Press, 2006).
18 Forms of worship and liturgies employed by the Catholic Church in Western Europe.
19 Heyberger, *Les Chrétiens du Proche-Orient*, 235. Eastern Catholic Churches are formed of Eastern Christians who have left their mother Church to join the Catholic communion. They are in full communion with Rome but have retained their own liturgy and organisation.
20 On Franciscan parishes in Palestine, see Beat Kümin and Felicita Tramontana, "Catholicism Decentralized: Local Religion in the Early Modern Periphery," *Church History* 89, no. 2 (2020), 268–87.
21 Masters, *Christians and Jews*, 80–8; Haddad, "Conversion," 454; Bernard Heyberger, "Les chrétiens d'Alep (Syrie) à travers les récits des conversions des missionnaires Carmes déchaux (1657–1681)," *Mélanges de l'Ecole française de Rome* 100, no. 1 (1988), 461–99.
22 Luria, *Sacred Boundaries*, 252–3.
23 Archivio della Sacra Congregazione De Propaganda Fide, Rome [hereafter ASCPF], Scritture originali riferite ai congressi generali [hereafter SOCG], vol. 135, f. 237.
24 Armanios, *Coptic Christianity*, 123; Frazee, *Catholics and Sultans*, 219.
25 The Roman Congregation that since 1622 had been in charge of missionary activities in those places where a Church hierarchy was yet to be established. On Propaganda Fide, see Giovanni Pizzorusso, *Governare le missioni, conoscere il mondo nel XVII secolo. La congregazione pontificia de Propaganda Fide* (Viterbo: Sette Città, 2018).
26 SOCG vol. 242, f. 63^v. On secret conversions in Bethlehem, see Tramontana, *Passages of Faith*, 100–1.
27 SOCG vol. 106, f. 179^v.
28 See, for example, SOCG vol. 565, ff. 127–131. On the issue of secret conversions in Palestine, see also Archive of the Congregation for the Doctrine of Faith (ACDF), Rome, St. St. (Stanza Storica), UV 50.
29 On burials, see Heyberger, *Les Chrétiens du Proche-Orient*, 389.
30 Ibid.
31 Bernard Dompnier, "L'administration des sacrements en terre protestante à la lumière des facultates et des dubia des missionnaires (XVIIe-XVIIIe siècles)," *Mélanges de l'Ecole française de Rome* 121, no. 1 (2009), 23–38, at 30.
32 See, for example, the letter of the Custos Andrea d'Arco, mentioned above SOCG, 106, f. 179. See also SOCG, 470, f.7, the letter of the Jesuit father Michel Nau. See also *infra*.
33 Heyberger, *Les Chrétiens du Proche-Orient*, 387–8 and *passim*.
34 I reached a similar conclusion when analysing the correspondence between Rome and the missionaries regarding the interactions between Protestants and Catholics in the Ottoman Empire. Felicita Tramontana, "'Né si potevano castigare per la libertà del loco e il dominio che vi è': cattolici e protestanti nell'Impero ottomano attraverso i dubia e le facultates," *Mélanges de l'École française de Rome - Italie et Méditerranée modernes et contemporaines* 129, no. 1 (2017), 215–27, at 222–3.
35 On sacramental sharing, see Cesare Santus, *Trasgressioni necessarie: communicatio in sacris, coesistenza e conflitti tra le comunità cristiane orientali (Levante e Impero ottomano, XVII–XVIII secolo)* (Rome: École française de Rome, 2019).
36 See Charlotte de Castelnau L'Estoile, "Le mariage des infidèles au XVIe siècle: doutes missionnaires et autorité pontificale" and Paolo Scarramela, "I dubbi sul sacramento del matrimonio e la questione dei matrimoni misti nella casistica delle

congregazioni romane (secc. XVI-XVIII)," both in *Mélanges del'Ecole Française de Rome. Italie et Méditerranée* 121, no. 1 (2009), 95–121 and 1–20.

37 Marina Caffiero, "Lorenzo Ganganelli consultore del Sant'Uffizio. I pareri sui battesimi di infedeli e sui matrimoni dei cattolici in terra ottomana," in *L'Inquisizione e l'eresia in Italia: Medioevo ed età moderna*, eds. Giuliana Ancona and Dario Visintin (Montereale Valcellina: Menocchio, 2013), 253–70.

38 Ute Lotz-Heumann, "Imposing Church and Social Discipline," in *The Cambridge History of Christianity*, ed. Ronnie Po-chia Hsia (Cambridge: Cambridge University Press, 2007), 244–60, at 246.

39 See Cecilia Cristellon, "The Roman Congregations and the Application of the Tametsi as an Instrument of Their Policies towards Mixed Marriages in Europe (1563–1798)," *Rechtsgeschichte–Legal History* 27 (2019), 163–71.

40 Archivio Storico della Custodia di Terra Santa (thereafter ASCTS) Jerusalem, Parrocchie, Betlemme Santa Caterina. Sacramenti, Registrazioni miste, vol. 2, *Registrum coniugatorum* (11/05/1669-08/21/1721); missing years: 1674, 1675, 1688, 1689, 1696.

41 See below.

42 See, for example, Francesco Da Serino, *Chroniche o Annali di Terra Santa*, vol. 2, eds. G. Golubovich OFM and T. Cavallon, in Golubovich, *Biblioteca bio-bibliografica di Terra Santa [...]*, vol. 7 (Firenze: Quaracchi 1939), 183; Heyberger, *Les Chrétiens du Proche-Orient*, 77, 79, 386.

43 See SOCG, vol. 104, f. 118v. On similar problems in the Netherlands, see Kaplan, *Divided by Faith*, 285.

44 See Felicita Tramontana, "Geographical Mobility and Community-Building in Seventeenth-century Palestine: Insights from the Records of Bethlehem's Catholic Parish," *Continuity and Change* 35, no. 2 (2020), 163–85.

45 See Tramontana, *Passages of Faith*, 93–5.

46 Kaplan, *Divided by Faith*, 287; Id., "Intimate Negotiations," 238–9; Dagmar Freist, "One Body Two Confessions," 294–322.

47 SOCG, vol. 104, f. 118.

48 Kaplan, *Divided by Faith*, 287–8.

49 I have kept the spelling of the original Franciscan documents.

50 ASCTS, Parrocchie, Betlemme Santa Caterina. Sacramenti, Registrazioni miste, vol. 2, *Registrum coniugatorum* (11/05/1669-08/21/1721), 19.

51 Ibid.

52 ASCTS, Parrocchie, Betlemme Santa Caterina. Sacramenti, Registrazioni miste, vol. 2, *Registrum coniugatorum* (11/05/1669-08/21/1721), 20.

53 On the diffusion of Catholicism in Bethlehem and the surrounding area, see Tramontana, "The Spread of Catholicism in Palestinian Villages," in *Space and Conversion*, eds. Giuseppe Marcocci et al. (Leiden: Brill, 2015), 81–102.

54 Ibid., "causa comandamenti imperatorii turcarum datum in favorem grecorum et alias hereticorum et scismaticorum."

55 Timothy K. Ware, "Orthodox and Catholics in the Seventeenth Century: Schism or Intercommunion?," in *Schism, Heresy and Religious Protest*, ed. D. Baker (Cambridge: Cambridge University Press, 1972), 259–76.

56 Bertand Ferclaz, "The Emergence of Confessional Identities," in *Living with Religious Diversity*, 250. See also Luria, *Sacred Boundaries*, 147.

57 Archivio della Congregazione della dottrina della fede (ACDF), St. St., UU 25, folder 1. Caffiero, *Lorenzo Ganganelli*, 253–70.

58 Tramontana, "'Né si potevano castigare per la libertà del loco e il dominio che vi è'."

59 Heyberger, *Les Chrétiens du Proche-Orient*, 403.

60 See Benjamin Arbel, "Roman Catholics and Greek Orthodox in Venetian Overseas Colonies, (Mid-Fifteenth to Mid-Seventeenth Century)," in *Religious Interactions in Europe and the Mediterranean World. Coexistence and Dialogue from*

the 12th to the 20th Centuries, eds. Katsumi Fukasawa, Pierre-Yves Beaurepaire, and Benjamin J. Kaplan (London: Routledge, 2017), 245–60, at 250–2.

61 Bernard Heyberger, "Missionaries and Women. Domestic Catholicism in the Middle East," in *Catholic Missionaries in Early Modern Asia: Patterns of Localization*, eds. Nadine Amsler, Andreea Badea, Bernard Heyberger, and Christian Windler (London: Routledge, 2020), 190–203. On the impact of the confessionalisation of individual behaviours and community's life, see also Id., "Catholicisme et construction des frontières confessionnelles dans l'Orient ottoman," 123–42.

62 Heyberger, *Les Chrétiens du Proche-Orient*, 537.

63 On the condemnation of mixed marriages by Copt clergy, see, for example, Armanios, *Coptic Christianity*, 137–8.

64 Heyberger, *Les Chrétiens du Proche-Orient*, 399.

65 See Freist, "Crossing Religious Borders," 207. Marc Forster, *The Counter-Reformation in the Villages* (Ithaca: Cornell University, 1992), esp. 20–41, 200–13; C. Scott Dixon, *The Reformation and Rural Society: The Parishes of Brandenburg-Ansbach-Kulmbach 1528–1603* (Cambridge: Cambridge University Press, 1996). For general reassessments, Ute Lotz-Heumann, "Imposing Church and Social Discipline," 244–60.

66 Masters, *Christians and Jews*, 95–6, 115–7.

67 See Masters, *Christians and Jews*, 63.

68 Masters, *Christians and Jews*, 106–9. On the Uniate Churches – formed by Eastern Christians who left their mother Church to join the Catholic communion – see Robert J. Taft, "Between East and West: The Eastern Catholic ('Uniate') Churches," in *The Cambridge History of Christianity*, eds. Sheridan Gilley et al. (Cambridge: Cambridge University Press, 2006), 412–25.

69 Millets are "hierarchically organized religious bodies with a decided political function." Masters, *Christians and Jews*, 61–2. See also pp. 98–111. On the historiographic debate about the millet system, see Gara, "Conceptualizing Inter-religious Relations," 66–72.

70 The Catholic Armenian millet was established in 1831. Masters, *Christians and Jews*, 98–108.

71 Heyberger, "Fasting: The Limits of Catholic Confessionalization," 217–8.

72 Heyberger, *Les Chrétiens du Proche-Orient*, 548. The Maronite Church is an eastern-rite church in full communion with the Roman Catholic one. The largest part of its members resides in Lebanon.

73 Masters, *Christians and Jews*, 115–6.

Part IV

Interacting and Engaging

Historiographic Introduction

Between around 1990 and 2010, how historians conceived of relations between religious groups in the early modern world underwent a sea-change. Whether they had focused on rival Christian churches in Europe, Christians and non-Christians in Europe's expanding empires and commercial networks, or indeed any two religions around the globe, most historians had previously represented such relations as dominated by conflict. A legacy partly of the Enlightenment, they had tended to see early modern religions as absolutist and irreconcilable in their claims to truth. They presumed that people committed to one such religion could only be intolerant of people who adhered to other religions. As a result, histories of relations between groups tended to focus on manifestations of intolerance: religious wars, missionary offensives, theological disputes, and of course persecutions. When the confessionalisation paradigm emerged in the 1970s and 1980s, it too encouraged scholars to regard religious groups – at least, maturely "confessionalised" ones – as ideologically infused, mutually antagonistic blocks. As late as the 1990s, the work of Bernard Lewis and Samuel Huntington's "clash of civilisations" thesis likewise posited a fundamental irreconcilability between Christianity and Islam, and with it the inevitability of conflict.[1]

Of course, specialists had always recognised that in practice, people of different faiths coexisted in some parts of the early modern world. Peaceful coexistence, though, was generally presented as the exception to the rule, and few of its dimensions were the subject of extensive investigation. In some of the best known cases, such as those of the Ottoman Empire (a Muslim polity with major Jewish and massive Christian minorities) and of Italy, where Jews were confined to ghettos, most scholars satisfied themselves with an understanding of the formal arrangements laid down in law, ignoring the gap between law and practice. Only in the 1990s did historians begin to reconsider the exceptionality of coexistence and to inquire more deeply into how it worked in the day-to-day life of mixed communities. When they did, one of their first concerns was to examine patterns of interaction and forms of engagement between people of different religions. Interaction and engagement thus became one of the first themes to be treated in the new histories of religious toleration that began to be written. To tackle this theme, historians

DOI: 10.4324/9781003030522-13

applied research methods developed in preceding decades by social historians intent on studying society "from the bottom up." What they produced was a kind of social history focused on mixed communities and the religious groups that comprised them.

One of the historians to pioneer this new approach was Étienne François, whose book *Die unsichtbare Grenze* (the invisible border) first appeared in 1991. Examining Protestants and Catholics in the German city of Augsburg, François investigated the changing demographic characteristics of the two groups, their patterns of mobility, the structure of their families, their occupational profiles and wealth, the geographic distribution of their homes, whether they employed or did business with one another, what books and arts they produced and consumed, what festive holidays and anniversaries they celebrated, what names they gave their children, what clothing they wore, how they decorated their homes, whether they intermarried, and how often they converted to the other faith.[2] François' book remains an exemplary study, setting an ambitious agenda for historians studying relations between religious groups in other locales. To the agenda laid down by François, historians have subsequently added topics such as education, charity, civic rituals, friendship, burial arrangements, and the various rites of passage. They have also broadened the range of methods they apply, drawing on ones derived from cultural anthropology, human geography, and the new institutional economics as well as sociology and demography. Locales have continued often to serve as the primary unit of investigation, not least because early modern societies were so intensely localistic, with cities, towns, and villages functioning arguably as the most basic unit of community after the family. Even within a single polity, mixed communities also varied enormously in their composition and in the tenor of relations between groups. While therefore it has grown since the 1990s, our understanding of how religious groups interacted and engaged with each other remains piecemeal: for each community or region where the subject has been analysed, more remain unstudied.[3]

One of the important findings to emerge from the new histories of toleration is that early modern religious groups were anything but homogeneous blocks. Although members of a group often shared certain non-religious characteristics – Augsburg's Catholics, for example, tended to have larger families than Protestants, while Jews in most places had a different occupational profile from that of Christians – every group consisted of people of different ranks, occupations, families, ages, and genders, while they might differ also in civic status, geographic origins, social networks, and other attributes. Individuals invariably had multiple memberships, allegiances, and sources of identity, which might overlap with and reinforce religious ones but could equally cut across and complicate the latter, especially in larger, more complex communities. How different subgroups interacted and engaged with people of other faiths varied. As an alternative, then, or supplement to locale, a small but growing number of historians have taken as their unit of analysis a social subgroup within a religious group.[4]

This is what Giada Pizzoni does in her contribution to this volume. Inspired partly by the work of Francesca Trivellato on Sephardi Jewish merchants, Pizzoni examines English Catholic merchants around the turn of the eighteenth century and their relationships with Protestant merchants.[5] Focusing on Catholic trading families based in London, she finds that the latter forged numerous business partnerships with Protestants. These families formed "a community tightly bound by ties of marriage and ethnicity," yet when it came to business, they chose partners for their trustworthiness, acumen, and profit potential, not their religion. Their Protestant counterparts did likewise. Not that religious affiliation was irrelevant: it played a role in determining the economic functions a group performed. The ties Catholic merchants had to co-religionists in France, Spain, and elsewhere gave them access to ports and markets on the European continent from which Protestants, during times of war, were shut out. That made Catholic merchants particularly attractive partners to Protestant merchants. Together, Catholic and Protestant merchants engaged in smuggling and privateering and, as one war succeeded another, kept trade flowing between England and the continent. Pizzoni's study makes an important contribution to debates as to whether early modern religious minorities formed economic networks closed to outsiders, whether people of different religions could establish bonds of trust with one another, and whether commercial capitalism tended to undermine the social cohesion of religious groups.

For all its lacunas, the study of how religious groups interacted and engaged with one another in Europe has advanced further than the study of the same topic for other parts of the world. The gap is perhaps the smallest for the Ottoman Empire, whose study has been influenced in recent years by methods and paradigms developed in the European context. One finds in recent Ottoman historiography an appreciation for the density of interconnections between religious groups, the difference between legal structures and lived realities, the porousness of boundaries, and the agency exercised by individuals.[6] Studies focusing on zones of encounter between Christians and Muslims, such as Eric Dursteler's on Istanbul and Molly Greene's on Crete, have gone a long way towards refuting the formerly dominant conflict-model.[7] By contrast, many studies of Asia continue to follow a traditional storyline, recounting the efforts by western missionaries to spread Christianity. In the Asian context, historiographic innovation has come from two developments. The first is a more sophisticated understanding of early modern intercultural interactions, with religion conceived as part of culture. Instead of seeing a one-way process of westernisation, modernisation, or Christianisation, scholars have come to recognise the complex dynamics and reciprocal influences exercised in encounters between European and non-European cultures.[8] The second development is captured by the term "global Reformations": a reconceptualisation of the movements for religious reform in the sixteenth and seventeenth centuries as global rather than European phenomena. Such movements were global in scale and ambition, aiming to "reform" not only Christians in Europe but also non-Christians overseas. They were global too in forming an intrinsic part of Europeans' colonial and imperial endeavours.[9]

This last aspect of the global is what concerns Hendrik Niemeijer in his contribution to this volume. Focusing on the Moluccas, once known as the "Spice Islands," now part of Indonesia, Niemeijer shows how the efforts of Calvinist missionaries to Christianise natives can only be understood properly if put in their colonial political context. Eager to gain a monopoly over the valuable spices produced on the islands, the Dutch East India Company (VOC) signed treaties with native rulers in the North Moluccas, whose centre was Ternate. These treaties allowed the Dutch to establish churches and schools, but entailed a commitment on their part to tolerate Islam. In the Central Moluccas, whose centre was Ambon, many local rajas converted to Calvinism and themselves took the lead in promoting the religion among their subjects. In the long run, this enabled missionaries to achieve success by peaceful means. In the Banda Islands, the Dutch resorted to violent conquest. Mass resistance by the native populations ended with mass emigration, European settlement, import of slaves, outlawing of Islam, and strict enforcement of Calvinist norms by ministers and VOC officials working in cooperation. The Moluccas thus offer a study in contrasts, with three different colonial contexts resulting in three different religious outcomes. Relations between Christians and Muslims on the islands varied accordingly.

The chapters in this section thus exemplify two of the approaches taken by recent historians to investigate how people of different religions interacted and engaged with one another in the early modern world. Although this theme was one of the first to be explored by the new histories of toleration, it continues to invite further research, as our knowledge of it remains fragmentary.

Notes

1 See i.a. Bernard Lewis, *Cultures in Conflict: Christians, Muslims, and Jews in the Age of Discovery* (New York: Oxford University Press, 1995); Samuel P. Huntington, *The Clash of Civilizations and the Remaking of World Order* (New York: Simon & Schuster, 1996). For a work of synthesis contesting the conflict-model of relations between religious groups, see David Cannadine, *The Undivided Past: History Beyond Our Differences* (London: Allen Lane, 2013).

2 Étienne François, *Die unsichtbare Grenze: Protestanten und Katholiken in Augsburg 1648–1806* (Sigmaringen: Jan Thorbecke Verlag, 1991), published subsequently in French as *Protestants et catholiques en Allemagne: identités et pluralisme, Augsbourg, 1648–1806* (Paris: Albin Michel, 1993).

3 The study of cities in particular was encouraged also by the emergence of the genre of urban case studies of the Protestant Reformation. Examples of local studies include Gregory Hanlon, *Confession and Community in Seventeenth-Century France: Catholic and Protestant Coexistence in Aquitaine* (Philadelphia: University of Pennsylvania Press, 1993); Benjamin J. Kaplan, *Calvinists and Libertines: Confession and Community in Utrecht, 1578–1620* (Oxford: Oxford University Press, 1995); Muriel C. McClendon, *The Quiet Reformation: Magistrates and the Emergence of Protestantism in Tudor Norwich* (Stanford: Stanford University Press, 1999); Frauke Volkland, *Konfession und Selbstverständnis: reformierte Rituale in*

der gemischtkonfessionellen Kleinstadt Bischofszell im 17. Jahrhundert, Veröffentlichungen des Max-Planck-Instituts für Geschichte (Göttingen: Vandenhoeck & Ruprecht, 2005); Jesse Spohnholz, *The Tactics of Toleration: A Refugee Community in the Age of Religious Wars* (Newark: University of Delaware Press, 2010); David Frick, *Kith, Kin, & Neighbors: Communities & Confessions in Seventeenth-Century Wilno* (Ithaca: Cornell University Press, 2013); Victoria Christman, *Pragmatic Toleration: The Politics of Religious Heterodoxy in Early Reformation Antwerp, 1515–1555* (Rochester: University of Rochester Press, 2015); David Martin Luebke, *Hometown Religion: Regimes of Coexistence in Early Modern Westphalia* (Charlottesville: University of Virginia Press, 2016); Martin Christ, *Biographies of a Reformation: Religious Change and Confessional Coexistence in Upper Lusatia, 1520–1635* (Oxford: Oxford University Press, 2021).

4 Subgroups studied include nobles, merchants, scholars, musicians, and women. For examples see Jaap Geraerts, *Patrons of the Old Faith: The Catholic Nobility in Utrecht and Guelders, c. 1580–1702* (Leiden: Brill, 2019); Francesca Trivellato, Leor Halevi, and Catia Antunes, eds., *Religion and Trade: Cross-Cultural Exchanges in World History, 1000-1900* (New York: Oxford University Press, 2014); Jeanine de Landtsheer and Henk Nellen, eds., *Between Scylla and Charybdis: Learned Letter Writers Navigating the Reefs of Religious and Political Controversy in Early Modern Europe* (Leiden: Brill, 2011); Claudio Bacciagaluppi, *Artistic Disobedience: Music and Confession in Switzerland, 1648–1762* (Leiden: Brill, 2017); Carys Brown, "Women and Religious Coexistence in Eighteenth-Century England," in *Negotiating Exclusion in Early Modern England, 1550–1800*, ed. Naomi Pullin and Kathryn Woods (New York: Routledge, 2021), 68–87.

5 Francesca Trivellato, *The Familiarity of Strangers: The Sephardic Diaspora, Livorno, and Cross-Cultural Trade in the Early Modern Period* (New Haven, CT: Yale University Press, 2009).

6 For historiographic overview and bibliography, see Eleni Gara, "Conceptualizing Interreligious Relations in the Ottoman Empire: The Early Modern Centuries," *Acta Poloniae Historica* 116 (2017), 57–91.

7 E.R. Dursteler, *Venetians in Constantinople: Nation, Identity, and Coexistence in the Early Modern Mediterranean* (Baltimore: Johns Hopkins University Press, 2006); Molly Greene, *A Shared World: Christians and Muslims in the Early Modern Mediterranean* (Princeton: Princeton University Press, 2000); Noel Malcolm, *Agents of Empire: Knights, Corsairs, Jesuits and Spies in the Sixteenth-Century Mediterranean World* (London: Allen Lane, 2015); Catherine Wendy Bracewell, *The Uskoks of Senj: Piracy, Banditry, and Holy War in the Sixteenth-Centruy Adriatic* (Ithaca: Cornell University Press, 1992); Cemal Kafadar, ed., *Between Two Worlds: The Construction of the Ottoman State* (Berkeley: University of California Press, 1995).

8 E.g. William Dalrymple, *White Mughals: Love and Betrayal in Eighteenth-Century India* (London: Harper Perennial, 2003); Sanjay Subrahmanyam, *Courtly Encounters: Translating Courtliness and Violence in Early Modern Eurasia* (Cambridge, MA: Harvard University Press, 2012); Anand Amaladass and Ines G. Zupanov, eds., *Intercultural Encounter and the Jesuit Mission in South Asia (16th-18th Centuries)* (Bangalore: Asian Trading Corporation, 2014); Nadine Amsler et al., eds., *Catholic Missionaries in Early Modern Asia: Patterns of Localization* (New York: Routledge, 2019).

9 See, e.g. Nicholas Terpstra, ed., *Global Reformations: Transforming Early Modern Religions, Societies, and Cultures* (New York: Routledge, 2019); Charles H. Parker, *Global Calvinism: Conversion and Commerce in the Dutch Empire, 1600–1800* (New Haven, CT: Yale University Press, 2022).

9 Catholic Merchants in British Commerce in the Age of Mercantilism

Giada Pizzoni

Narratives of the early modern centuries do not usually associate Catholicism and trade. Influenced by the famous "Weber thesis" about the rise of capitalism, historians traditionally represented early modern Catholics as idle, risk-averse, and focused on the other world, while they associated Protestantism with entrepreneurship, thriving commerce and industry, and successful empires.[1] Weber's arguments about a work ethic and "this-worldly asceticism" distinctive to certain Protestant groups have long been subject, however, to criticism, and scholars have shown that other groups too were successful in business, including ones with profound religious lives.[2] England has always been taken as one of the lands where Protestantism left a deep mark on economic behaviour as well as national identity. Yet England also had a Catholic community that survived the Protestant Reformation and endured over the following centuries. This community included wealthy mercantile as well as aristocratic and gentry families. Just as historians have come to reconsider the exclusively Protestant nature of English – and in the eighteenth century, British – identity, so they need to take a fresh look at the English, later British, economy in light of Catholic participation.

The mercantile community of London offers a valuable case study. In the late seventeenth and early eighteenth centuries, London merchants showed themselves willing to work with anyone who could provide the skills and resources needed for a given endeavour. Collaboration was based on reputation, and an individual's religion never acted as an impairment. Protestant merchants relied on Catholic contacts to maintain a foothold in continental and imperial markets, and this collaboration ensured the continuity of British trade even as war raged between Britain, Spain, and France for over 20 years between 1688 and 1714. Catholic merchants from Britain coordinated smuggling operations and secured the supply of provisions such as fruit, wine, wheat, and, more importantly, the Spanish colonial dyes that were essential for the British manufacturing sector. In exchange, Britain re-exported tobacco, cod, and fabrics to the continent. When direct trading routes between the British Isles and Spain or France were interrupted, Catholics tapped their contacts in Portugal, Italy, and the Netherlands to keep international trade cycles spinning. British Catholics forged those links for their co-nationals and

DOI: 10.4324/9781003030522-14

ultimately for their country. Interfaith relations thus contributed a great deal to Britain's prosperity.

History of Catholicism and trade

In a recent analysis of mercantile communities, historians have paid limited attention to the links between religion and trade, and even less to the role of Catholics.[3] Recent literature has either disregarded or denied any possible connection between Catholics and the Atlantic-Mediterranean trade. We know that Protestant minority groups such as Huguenots and Quakers defined themselves through strong family relationships and shared faith,[4] and that merchants of these religions often conducted business with co-religionists across national borders. Their economic partnerships were based on their religious beliefs. By contrast, Catholicism often has no presence in analyses of the mercantile world in the seventeenth and eighteenth centuries.[5] Yet the vastness of Atlantic trading made acting exclusively within a single religious group unprofitable, and with the multiple exchanges required and involvement of so many agents, it was often impossible even to know everyone's religion. Among the most fruitful contributions made in recent years to the study of interfaith relations is Francesca Trivellato's *The Familiarity of Strangers*.[6] This analysis of the western Sephardi diaspora revealed that Jewish merchants worked not only with different circles of co-religionists but also with non-Jews. Part of a broader historiography on trade across cultures, in particular between Christians and other religious groups, Trivellato's work inspired my line of inquiry into the trading rationale of British Catholics. While the literature on mercantile communities has, to a great extent, neglected Catholics, the London Catholic community fits perfectly into the various analyses offered by recent historiography: London's Catholic merchants worked in transatlantic and European trade and tapped into the communities of British expatriates based in Spain, France, and Netherlandish territories. They worked with Protestants and moved outside their religious group as the new global economy expanded, requiring wider networks in order to be profitable. Their dynamics and strategies were not very different from those of other merchants of the time. Prospering in a largely Protestant commercial world, they acted for profit and their commercial endeavours were not restricted by their religion; they were citizens of the world who based themselves in London, the epicentre of Atlantic commerce at the beginning of the eighteenth century.

Catholic context

The Glorious Revolution of 1688 was a watershed moment for English Catholics as it was for England as a whole and for all the British Isles. Long suspected of disloyalty to the Protestant nation and subject to penal laws, English Catholics found themselves associated with the political cause known as Jacobitism – with calls for the restoration to the throne of deposed Catholic monarch James II, and after his death, that of his Catholic son, the would-be James III. Under William III (1689–1702), penal legislation against Catholics was revived and amplified, while under the following reign of Anne, James II's Protestant daughter, anti-Catholicism played a key role in the negotiations that led to the formation in 1707 of a British state. Following Anne's death in 1714, power passed to the Hanoverians, possibly the most profoundly non-Catholic dynasty in British history.[7] Jacobitism reached one climax in the Jacobite rebellion of 1715, which appeared to many Protestants as a Catholic crusade. Retaliation for it was harsh but not equal across the country,[8] with levels mostly depending on the relationship between local Protestants and Catholics and on local politics. In mercantile communities and trading centres generally, support for the Jacobite cause was always lukewarm because of its association with insurrection and disruption.[9] Only after the battle of Culloden in 1746 did Jacobitism suffer a decisive blow, which reduced its perceived threat and created a context in which anti-Catholic legislation could grow more lax.[10]

In the 1690s, Jacobitism functioned as an ideology of opposition to the government. It was seen as treasonous, but it was also inconsistent, incoherent, and not clearly identifiable with a political party. Gradually, however, it became a sort of nostalgia or fantastical solution to the nation's ills, a force that expressed dissatisfaction with the policies of William III, who was perceived as a foreign monarch more interested in commerce and overseas affairs than in the country he was meant to rule. In social terms, Jacobitism was not strong among all Catholics, and support for it did not correspond neatly with social class. In fact, the Catholic community was torn between allegiance to the crown and support for the Stuart cause.

In England, some Catholic merchants supported the Stuarts, and indeed, Catholic traders exchanged merchandise and seditious information across the Channel in support of James III.[11] Most members, though, of the vast network of London merchants involved in Channel contraband were Protestants; their interest lay in continuing economic exchanges disrupted by the war, not supporting a deposed king. Whether Catholic or Protestant, merchants were concerned to avoid civil unrest, which would have a negative impact on trade.[12] It was feared that a Stuart restoration would lead to the adoption of commercial policies favourable to France, which would have considerably weakened British interests. As a group, therefore, Catholic merchants were not at all fervent Jacobites. Rather, as Linda Colley has suggested, their stance was ambiguous, especially during wartime, when Catholic merchants defied many national policies and remained crucial in keeping the wheels of British commerce spinning.

Meanwhile, English society was undergoing profound changes. While the landed classes came under new pressures, the expansion of commerce swelled the numbers and prosperity of the "middling sort."[13] Persecution and penal laws added to the difficulties experienced by Catholic aristocrats and gentry,[14] some of whom adapted by moving away from landowning and into commerce. Penal legislation had always focused on landowners and of-fice-holders, whereas there was no precise legislation on the emerging new economic and financial activities. To be sure, the Catholic Church forbade lending money at interest. Potential profits, though, outweighed for Catho-lics the proscription by their church of usury, and a lack of legal restrictions allowed them to seize the new financial opportunities. Transforming them-selves into merchants, Catholic landowners avoided taxation and imprison-ment while their money ensured integration within the economy. Thus the social profile of the Catholic community changed, and the Catholic com-munity took on a new role in English society. It did this while integrating with Protestants to a greater degree than ever before.[15] Catholics were able to answer the fiscal needs of the newly born British state and this ability opened a path into the core of British society.

Catholic-Protestant partnerships and their commercial strategies

An analysis of economic activity among the most important Catholic trad-ing families of the seventeenth and eighteenth centuries shows that they did not favour business partners of their own religion. While they sometimes resorted to family and friends, their most profitable deals were with Prot-estants. These were astute merchants whose economic rationality made in-terfaith interactions normal. Through the London group, it is also possible to reconstruct Catholic mercantile groups abroad. Their extensive networks operated in Atlantic and Mediterranean trade from the 1570s well into the nineteenth century, as testified by the literature on Catholic expatriates in various European ports.[16]

The late seventeenth century was the age of mercantilism, in which English foreign trade boomed and global trading exchanges emerged. Like their gov-ernments, the merchants of the time believed in a national commercial policy that pursued wealth while exploiting other countries in what was understood as a zero-sum game.[17] As Atlantic trade boomed, London became one of Europe's premier places for doing business. With its busy counting-houses, hectic docks, and bustling streets, London became one of the largest cities in Europe where the majority of the British population lived and thrived.[18] The opportunities the city had to offer attracted people from near and far, and merchants were drawn by the lure of high profits. Almost all the commodities being traded around the world, from West Indian products to Persian silks, passed through London before being either re-exported or sold domestically. The city was also becoming the financial heart of Europe, with its financial and legal institutions providing a firm basis for commerce to flourish. Lon-don offered opportunities to develop commercial skills and gain professional training, as well as to tap into far-flung trading networks.[19]

The Catholic presence in London's mercantile community was substan-tial, consisting of a varied group of Irish immigrants, English Catholics, and mixed Anglo-Irish families. This was a community tightly bound by ties of marriage and ethnicity, but with trading networks that connected them with the wider mercantile world.[20] Through these networks, and through the geographic movement of individuals, members of the community forged enduring global connections from the south Mediterranean, via the Atlantic, to Jamaica. Among the most prominent Catholics operating in the port of London were the Fitzgeralds, the Frenches, the Lynchs, the Arthurs, the Blakes, the Browns, and the Aylwards. They had close ties to British Catholic exiles who had settled in ports across the European continent and had retained important positions in both British commerce and Jacobite activism. The partners of London's Catholic merchants were in some cases non-Catholic, and many of the merchants' most significant deals came through collaboration with Protestant merchants. Particularly during times of warfare, Protestant-Catholic partnerships secured the survival of Britain's trade through smuggling and privateering.

Due to clashing political and colonial interests, Europe found itself in the throes of almost 20 years of warfare: the Nine Years' War (1688–1697) and the War of the Spanish Succession (1701–1713). During these decades, Catholic merchants were able to move goods to and from England by resorting to a variety of strategies. When France and England were at war, it was safer to export French goods first to Spain before sending them on to England. During the War of the Spanish Succession, when both France and Spain were English rivals, the most feasible option for importing was to co-ordinate the smuggling of French and Spanish goods into Portugal, from whence they were shipped on to London. During those times, British Catholics needed – and were able – to devise strategies that worked around the obstacles to trade, succeeding by tapping into wider communities.[21]

With the landing of William of Orange in England in 1688, hostilities began that had immediate repercussions for international trade. As France supported the deposed Stuart king, its products were soon banned in England. Yet they remained highly sought after; France provided not only fabrics but also fruit, wine, and imperial goods coming from France's north Atlantic possessions. In the early 1690s, merchants devised a variety of strategies to bring French goods into English ports. Each transaction required a different strategy and partners mapped out all the possibilities available to them. They would countenance any trade, legal or illegal, and resorting to privateering was one of the safest options. Privateering is often confused with piracy, and it was certainly difficult to distinguish between the two since both involved assaults on, and seizures of, commercial vessels. Officially they both targeted the cargo of ships belonging to the enemy, but in times of war any vessel and crew might become prey. The main centres for privateering during the Nine Years War were ports facing the Channel: Dunkirk, St Malo, and Brest on the continent; and on the English side, coastal hubs such as Falmouth, Dartmouth, Weymouth, and the Channel Islands of Guernsey and Jersey.[22] Precisely because of the great risks involved, business during the first years of hostilities was extremely lucrative.

It was at this time that Protestant partners first proved vital for London's Catholic merchants, who worked closely with prominent Protestant merchants such as Charles Horde and Thomas Brailsford. In fact, it was with the Glorious Revolution that each community came to realise fully the importance of interfaith partnerships for bringing French goods to London. Initially thanks to privateers, merchants were able to fake seizures, or to send French linens via Dutch ports such as Amsterdam and Rotterdam before going on to London. It was the Aylward-Brailsford firm, though, that adopted the most diverse and interesting strategies, being so confident in their success that they insured all cargoes they carried.[23] Initially, Brailsford found it impossible to obtain passes for French goods. As Catholics, however, the Aylwards were able to procure licences for the movement of French goods thanks to the good offices of their co-religionists in France. Once the licences were obtained, merchants in St Malo would rename the vessels being used and inform their partners in London of the ships' new details and how many men would be covered to travel. Thanks to the licences, the ships would be left untouched by French privateers in the Channel. Another strategy was to send goods from France to Faro in Portugal, where they were unloaded onto fishing boats and directed on to Spain. This strategy assured the safety of the goods from English assaults as well as from the French.

Having trustworthy partners was important for merchants at all times. In periods of warfare, though, it was essential, as exchanges were far riskier; accuracy and attention to detail could make the difference between success and failure. To be sure, Catholic merchants in London built business networks with family and co-religionists, but they did not find fellow Catholics, even their own family members, necessarily more trustworthy than other partners.[24] Despite being at the base of most mercantile partnerships in the early modern era, family relationships sometimes caused problems when it came to distant overseas trade. While it was perhaps easier to reconcile some conflicts within the family,[25] feuds between relatives could significantly strain commercial relations and it was not unusual for family members to be financially unreliable, fail to meet expectations, or fight over management. Because the environment for mercantile activity was largely unregulated, merchants had to be able to depend on partners to behave honourably and not spend too much money. Reputation and trustworthiness were built on universal rules that combined self-interest with religion, reason, and honour. Firms could worry for weeks about how to manage transactions, and agents whose attitudes or actions delayed transactions caused enormous concern. Firms, therefore, placed a very high value on reliable partnerships with merchants chosen above all for their reputation and business abilities. Such partnerships sometimes lasted for decades. Among the most important Protestant partners with whom Catholic firms worked was the Londoner Charles Peers.[26]

During the Nine Years' War, Protestant merchants in Britain often profited from the ability of Catholics to move undisturbed in continental ports. During the War of the Spanish Succession, such merchants relied even more on partnerships with Catholics.[27] This second decade of the international conflict saw Protestant-Catholic commercial collaborations grow even stronger. With England at war with both France and Spain, London's Catholic traders feared not only for their businesses, but for their safety too. They adapted by deploying more targeted strategies, using their business networks to maximum advantage. During these years, the London associates worked mainly with non-Catholic partners in Portugal and with family and co-religionists in Spain and France. Agents based in Portugal played a key role, suggesting strategies and choosing factors. In the Portuguese ports of Faro and Lisbon, merchants could buy English goods in exchange for French and Spanish products. Indeed, between 1706 and 1710 English goods flooded into these ports, helping British Catholics to secure strong partnerships there. Via these ports, British merchants supplied the transatlantic vessels that harboured in Cadiz, while from Lisbon they had wine, fruit, and dyes smuggled into England. The investments required to establish these flows of trade proved highly profitable.

During the Nine Years' War, only French imports were banned from England, but from 1701 Spanish products were too. English merchants engaged in international trade, therefore, needed to devise more elaborate strategies than ever.[28] In actuality, their strategies were simple. Portugal was the only gateway to England that remained open, so the merchants knew that all goods had to be diverted there. To this end, they first moved French goods to Spain. There, French commodities would join Spanish and other Mediterranean provisions coming from Livorno and Genoa. Finally, all merchandise would be shipped to Portugal, where non-Catholic partners would send them on to England. These transactions were only made possible by extensive networks that included partners of other faiths as well as co-religionists and relatives. Only the best, most tested contacts were utilised. The Catholic community, though, remained essential, providing access to Catholic ports. London Catholics could tap their fellow co-religionists and kinsmen in France and Spain, notably those in Rouen, St Malo, Bordeaux, Paris, Antequera, Port St Mary, Malaga, Cadiz, Faro, and Lisbon. In Cadiz, the prominent Catholic firms of Woulfe & Trublet and Power & Hill supervised many commercial transactions, including those of established trading families such as the Comerfords, the Creaghs, and the Arthurs. These associates had worked together since the 1680s, and despite relying largely on a few trusted partners, in Spain they resorted also to family who, thanks to their religion, could move freely in the Spanish and French ports. Their interests extended to Italy and the Netherlands as well as Spain and France, and ultimately they always managed to supply the transatlantic vessels in Cadiz before returning colonial goods to London. These firms were renowned for planning carefully and securing the best deals. In 1699, they coordinated exchanges between France, Spain, and England on French boats, consigning merchandise to French partners so as to avoid the charges pressed upon the English by the French consul in Spain. In French ports, particularly St Malo and Marseilles, the London associates relied on family and local merchants to supply fish coming from French imperial possessions. These inter-imperial exchanges were facilitated by privateers in the Channel, including the White family, who operated in those waters for years. In addition to Woulfe & Trublet, another of the most prominent firms was Aldrington & Bowles. Associates of these two firms moved constantly between the Iberian commercial cities, Livorno, Genoa, and Marseilles as they sought out the best deals and goods. Thanks to the partners' organisational skills, goods would arrive in Portugal before landing in England.

Many Catholics worked also in Amsterdam, Rotterdam, and especially Ostend, which hosted a very large community of British Catholics.[29] Until 1713, Ostend was under Spanish rule, thus fostering secure links with merchant communities in Spain – Cadiz and Seville in particular. Privateers and smugglers thrived in Ostend, partly due to its proximity to French Dunkirk, a hub of contraband. Many families in the area, in particular the Brownes and the Creaghs in Ostend and Bruges and the Cloots in Amsterdam, worked regularly with Catholic merchants in London. Of English origin, the Brownes family continued for centuries to adhere to the Catholic faith. Never hiding their Jacobite sympathies, the family financed contraband in the Channel. They were related to the Aylwards. The Creagh family had fled Ireland after the Cromwellian War and become prominent in the economic and political life of the region. They were part of the Catholic diaspora but not necessarily Jacobite exiles. During the warfare of the late seventeenth and early eighteenth centuries, the Creagh family arranged exchanges between the Netherlands and the Spanish ports via privateers, whose use they found considerably less costly than financing an organised fleet. England made use of privateers against French and Spanish vessels, while France used the same against English shipping.

By this time, the Brownes and the Creaghs had become renowned smugglers. From their base in the Dutch territories, they always tried to protect the interest of the London merchants they worked with; this protection was all the more valuable when French troops initially entered that country. The associates in London with whom these families worked most were the Peers. Dutch commerce complemented British trade by providing a selection of manufactured goods and Baltic grain to be re-exchanged for provisions from southern Europe. The Catholic agents in the Dutch Republic worried particularly about hostile fleets in the Mediterranean south of Spain. As Anglo-Spanish transactions were prohibited by the British government and hindered by Spanish authorities, Catholic merchants became even more creative in their tactics. Merchant letters from Spain were diverted to either Portugal or the Netherlands, and nicknames were used in them. Merchants' marks on transport barrels were hidden or redrawn. In all these exchanges, British Catholics played a crucial role, showing good business knowledge and shrewdness in organising their cargoes. They tapped their Catholic networks to secure the goods they needed and to import merchandise into Portuguese docks. They then relied on their British nationality and their partners in the

London mercantile community to ship products to England – though not necessarily London, as the cargoes frequently landed in Sussex, Kent, Portsmouth, Bristol, or even the ports of Yarmouth and Falmouth. The latter two were, unsurprisingly, the ports mostly affected by contraband, since they were in a position to control the movement of shipping in the Channel and were relatively close to London.

These same ports, used so successfully in peacetime, remained important during the War of Spanish Succession, when London Catholics had to tap into different networks. London's Catholic merchants continued procuring French commodities thanks to the contacts – a vast network of Catholic merchants and family relations – that they established in France during their residence in St Malo. Letters were constantly exchanged between London, St Malo, Rouen, Nantes, and Paris; French imperial goods were moved from Marseilles to Spain and Portugal, while from St Malo, Brest, and Dunkirk, they would reach England or Spain. In the Iberian ports, a circle of partners was constantly juggling transactions between Malaga, Cadiz, Bilbao, Madrid, and Cartagena, keeping the London merchants informed of political developments as well as of market demand. In Italy, British merchants relied on contacts in Livorno and Genoa and also in Naples and Sicily, from whence they accessed the Levantine markets of currants, silk, and pepper. From the Netherlands, they secured supplies of manufactured goods via their network of co-religionists in Ostend, Rotterdam, and Amsterdam – all with the aim of sending cargoes to Cadiz before returning them to London. During the War, religion, the use of skilled partners, and shrewd tactics allowed British Catholics to close many lucrative deals. They established partnerships through trust and common values; once an associate proved reliable, they counted on him constantly, disregarding faith or nationality. In this way, the Catholic community developed trading strategies that worked despite all the impediments created by war, allowing British traders to survive and prosper.

In general, Catholic merchants moved within both family circles and wider networks of commercial relations. During the Nine Years' War and the War of the Spanish Succession, however, they worked mainly with non-Catholic partners. The Catholic community and various relatives remained involved in the deals struck but played lesser roles. Catholic and Protestant merchants associated with one another to retain their business, basing their partnerships on trust and selecting only the best, most tested contacts they had in the various markets. The religious factor, however, was key, providing Catholic merchants with a competitive edge in accessing continental ports. The merchants involved, both Protestant and Catholic, were well aware of the advantage of joint enterprise. By working together, they were able to sustain and indeed expand Britain's international commerce even during wartime.[30]

British Catholic merchants worked in the Atlantic and Mediterranean markets for almost two centuries. From the early English incursions in the Mediterranean in the late sixteenth century to the emergence of the empire in the eighteenth, Catholics' interests extended to ports in Spain, France, Italy, and the Netherlands, tapping into trading networks that were slowly becoming global. Continental commerce remained always essential for viable international exchanges, as the Mediterranean gave access to colonial markets as well as to the east-trading routes.[31] That is why British Catholic merchants always cherished their contacts with the Spanish, French, and Italian ports. Even after the British empire fully expanded, tapping into continental markets remained crucial. Britain became one of the most important markets in the world by re-exporting American products across Europe and beyond. But, again, the balance of trade relied upon the continent, and non-European trade was profitable only because of existing continental demand.

An instrumental use of religious contacts and national ties enabled merchant houses in the late seventeenth and early eighteenth centuries to thrive commercially. Catholic merchants in London deftly used various networks and partnerships based on mutual trust and common interests. Interfaith cooperation was crucial in creating the smuggling schemes that gave merchants a competitive edge in times of war. British Catholics survived in trade thanks partly to their religious identity, but they looked beyond their own religious community to trade with anyone they deemed reliable and trustworthy. Protestant merchants in London needed partners able to anticipate what the south European markets wanted while also providing merchandise. Ultimately, what the accounts of these traders suggest is how crucial a role Catholic merchants played in the late seventeenth and early eighteenth centuries. Without their involvement, British commerce would have certainly been more difficult. By furthering the economic interests of their nation, Britain's Catholic merchants laid a foundation for the Catholic relief acts that came later.

The record of Catholic merchants certainly suggests the pragmatic and pluralistic nature of British trade with the continent and the Atlantic. It further suggests economic and religious integration at a time when the British Isles were undergoing profound changes. The new commercial and financial economy was creating a more pragmatic society, with new values and social classes undermining the traditional bases of land and faith as means to political power and wealth. Perhaps it was this uncertainty that allowed Catholics to become a vital point of connection between Britain, the Mediterranean, and the Americas. London Catholics were close to all the institutions and people that counted in commerce and they traded from a privileged position. By the beginning of the eighteenth century, they had accumulated vast capital and, to their Protestant associates, they offered the advantage of dealing with Britain's Catholic enemies overseas. To be sure, Catholicism was not yet undergoing any rehabilitation in Britain, but Catholics in the London mercantile community experienced toleration. When they smuggled, it was because this was one of the few options available to traders and their dealings had no other aim than profit. As in previous decades, their work suggests a tale of social and economic integration. The commercial world was too vast to be controlled and it was impossible to supervise all the agents involved or to know their personal circumstances or beliefs. Catholics worked with non-Catholic merchants as this was in both parties' interests; it was essential for British products to be sold in the colonial markets and it was important to access provisions that northern Europe needed but could not produce. Collaboration among merchants of different denominations served both groups well. Thus Catholics played a fundamental role in British trade in times of peace and even more in times of war.

As a result of these Protestant-Catholic partnerships, an attitude of tolerance developed towards Catholicism. The economic policies that characterised the age of mercantilism offered Catholics opportunities for inclusion. The late seventeenth century saw the birth of imperialism and a revolution in fiscal-military policies. It was a period of transformation in which the emerging economy offered openings to non-conformists. Catholics served the needs of the new British state. The period that followed, after 1714, was characterised by a more stable and secure political environment. After the Seven Years' War (1756–1763), France and Spain were no longer a threat, having tacitly acknowledged British naval superiority.[32] Nationally, the scare of Jacobitism faded. Needing support, Hanoverian Britain officially rehabilitated the Catholic community. The first Catholic Relief Act was granted in 1778, interestingly close to what historians see as the end of the mercantilist age in the 1780s.[33] Catholics had successfully seized the opportunities of a changing economic landscape, embracing risk and rightly earning their place within the nation.

Conclusions

The late seventeenth and early eighteenth centuries were a crucial period for English Catholics; Bossy characterises it as a period of transition. In 1685, the accession to the English throne of the Catholic James II had seemed almost a vindication for Catholics, who suddenly became protagonists again in national affairs. But this enthusiasm was short-lived, ending with the revolution of 1688, which had both a political and an emotional impact on the community, as many Catholic aristocrats fled to the continent or organised rebellions at home. The Jacobite threat that ensued was real, but not all Catholics wanted a Stuart restoration, especially those merchants worried about the potential of civil war to disrupt commerce.[34] As Glickman has shown, English Catholics were not like foreigners in their own land. He disagrees with Bossy's argument that Catholics' patriotism was undercut by their religious allegiance. Not all Catholics were supportive of the religious policies of James II or of the struggle to restore him to the throne. Many simply objected to a Dutch ruler. Ultimately, being Catholic did not necessarily mean being Jacobite.[35] The principal objection Catholics had in the 1710s to taking an oath of obedience to George I was not that it declared loyalty to the Hanoverians, but that it rejected Catholic doctrine as superstitious. Despite this source of tension, many Catholics believed that Catholicism was compatible with the English constitution and wanted to assert their obedience to the sovereign. Glickman concludes that British national identity was not, and could not be, exclusively Protestant. The Catholic merchants examined in this chapter were not Jacobites, nor did they necessarily participate in local politics. They were informed about political events, but simply as dictated by the necessities of their profession. They thought of themselves as British, working with Protestants for a common goal and, despite living in various countries, always pursuing British interests.

Britain has a largely Protestant identity, or so it has been construed over the centuries, constructed against a Catholic and continental other. National history in Britain has been told in providential terms as an unfolding of events that would free the country from popery and draw together the various kingdoms into a composite nation, with parliament as the embodiment of national unity. For centuries, recurrent wars with France, or the fear of them, fostered unity at home. International politics played a role especially in times of war, when propaganda fuelled anti-Catholic sentiments. Catholicism was widely perceived as a foreign and suspect belief system, responsible for some of the darkest episodes in the British past. Being British meant being different from Catholic Europe, whose religion was considered despotic and its practices obscure. The British nation was defined, to a considerable extent, in negative terms, shaping its idea of itself in opposition to "something else," whether that was the Catholic French, the Irish, or colonial subjects. Between 1689 and 1815, the impact of more than a hundred years of war with the French and of imperial competition fostered a united Britain. Increasingly, the British defined themselves in contrast not only to continental Catholicism but also to the native subjects of their empire, a domain developing in the east where people did not practise Christianity or speak English and were not white-skinned. This contrasting image helped British colonists perceive themselves as different and as part of a unique and providential whole. This was a self-image that unfortunately has shown its flaws, with its centrifugal forces re-emerging when the empire ended and peace with the continent was secure.

Catholic merchants played an important role in strengthening the British economy, first with its continental partners and ultimately on the global stage. Their economic success implied Protestant collaboration and from this collaboration ensued political integration. Ultimately, both Catholic and Protestant merchants were entrepreneurs, each with their own agenda but both pursuing British interests. Catholics felt themselves part of the British nation, tapping into continental networks only to provide the supplies needed as they leveraged their competitive edge economically to obtain political inclusion. In the final analysis, Catholic merchants contributed to the construction of a concept of Britain that was not exclusively English and non-continental. Among the different kingdoms and cultures that forged the nation, they played a significant role. Now more than ever, the British nation is rethinking itself. Hopefully, as it did in the age of mercantilism, it will still act out of pragmatism and cherish its continental links.

Notes

1 Giancarlo Poggi, *Calvinism and the Capitalist Spirit: Max Weber's Protestant Ethic* (London: MacMillian Press, 1983), 40–78; Max Weber, *The Protestant Ethic and the Spirit of Capitalism* (London: Routledge, 1992), 3–50.
2 Francesca Trivellato, *The Familiarity of Strangers: The Sephardic Diaspora, Livorno and Cross-Cultural Trade in the Early Modern Period* (New Haven, CT: Yale University Press, 2009). Holly Snyder, "'Under the Shado of Your Wings': Religiosity in the Mental World of an Eighteenth-Century Jewish Merchant," *Early American Studies: An Interdisciplinary Journal* 8 (2010), 581–622.
3 Nuala Zahedieh, "Making Mercantilism Work: London Merchants and Atlantic Trade in the Seventeenth Century," *Transactions of the Royal Historical Society* 6th Series (1999), 143–60; Nuala Zahedieh, "Overseas Expansion and Trade in the Seventeenth Century," in *The Oxford History of the British Empire: the Origins of Empire*, vol. I, eds. Nicholas Canny et al. (Oxford: Oxford University Press, 2011), 398–421; R.C. Nash, "Irish-Atlantic Trade in the Seventeenth and Eighteenth Centuries," *The William and Mary Quarterly Journal* 42 (1985): 329–56; Xabier Lamikiz, *Trade and Trust in the Eighteenth Century Atlantic World: Spanish Merchants and Their Overseas Networks* (Woodbridge: Boydell Press, 2010); Nuala Zahedieh, *The Capital and the Colonies, London and the Atlantic Economy, 1660–1700* (Cambridge: Cambridge University Press, 2010); Perry Gauci, *The Politics of Trade: The Overseas Merchant in State and Society, 1660–1720* (Oxford: Oxford University Press, 2010); Stanley Chapman, *Merchant and Enterprise in Britain from the Industrial Revolution to World War I* (New York: Cambridge University Press, 1992); Sheryllynne Haggerty, *"Merely for Money"? Business Culture in the British Atlantic, 1750–1815* (Liverpool: Liverpool University Press, 2012); David Hancock, *Citizens of the World, London Merchants and the Integration of the British Atlantic Community, 1735–1785* (Cambridge: Cambridge University Press, 1995); Sheryllynne Haggerty, *The British Atlantic Trading Community, 1760–1810: Men, Women and the Distribution of Goods* (Leiden: Boydell Press, 2006).
4 Bosher, "Huguenots Merchants and the Protestant International in the Seventeenth Century," 99–100; Frederick B. Tolles, *Meeting House and Counting House, The Quaker Merchants of Colonial Philadelphia, 1682–1763* (New York: Norton & Co., 1963).
5 Zahedieh, *The Capital and the Colonies*; Id., "Making Mercantilism Work," 143–60; Id., "The Merchants of Port Royal, Jamaica, and the Spanish Contraband Trade, 1655–1692," *The William and Mary Quarterly* 43 (1986); Hancock, *Citizens of the World*; Haggerty, *"Merely for Money."*
6 Trivellato, *The Familiarity of Strangers*.
7 David Matthew, *Catholicism in England 1535–1935, Portrait of a Minority: Its Culture and Tradition* (London: Catholic Book Club Edition, 1938). J.C.H. Aveling, *The Handle and the Axe. The Catholic Recusants in England from Reformation to Emancipation* (London: Blond & Briggs, 1976), 180–238.
8 Colin Haydon, *Anti-Catholicism in Eighteenth-Century England, c. 1714–80: A Political and Social Study* (Manchester: Manchester University Press, 1993), 81.
9 J. S. Bromley, "The Jacobite Privateers in the Nine Years War," in his *Corsairs and Navies, 1660–1760* (London: Hambledon Press, 1987), 139–66.
10 Brian Magee, *The English Recusants: A Study of the Post-Reformation Catholic Survival and the Operation of the Recusancy Laws* (London: Burns, Oates and Washbourne, 1938), 176. Aveling, *The Handle and the Axe*, 366.
11 Paul Monod, "Dangerous Merchandise: Smuggling, Jacobitism, and Commercial Culture in Southeast England, 1690–1760," *The Journal of British Studies* 30 (1991), 150–82.

12 David Parrish, *Jacobitism and Anti-Jacobitism in the British Atlantic World, 1688–1727* (Woodbridge: Boydell & Brewer, 2017), 38–65. Linda Colley, *Britons: Forging the Nation, 1707–1837* (New Haven: Yale University Press, 2014).

13 Jonathan Barry and Christopher Brooks, eds., *The Middling Sort of People. Culture, Society and Politics in England, 1550–1800* (London: MacMillian, 1994).

14 Bossy, *The English Catholic Community*; Aveling, *The Handle and the Axe*; Tony Claydon and Ian McBride, eds., *Protestantism and National Identity, Britain and Ireland, c. 1650–1850* (Cambridge: Cambridge University Press, 1998); Peter Marshall and Geoffrey Scott, eds., *Catholic Gentry in English Society: The Throckmortons of Coughton from Reformation to Emancipation* (Burlington: Ashgate, 2009); Haydon, *Anti-Catholicism in Eighteenth-Century England*; Gabriel Glickman, *The English Catholic Community, 1688–1745: Politics, Culture and Ideology* (Woodbridge: Boydell Press, 2009).

15 Glickman, *The English Catholic Community*, 59–64. Marshall and Scott, *Catholic Gentry in English Society*, 1–30.

16 John Bergin, "Irish Catholics and their Networks in Eighteenth-Century London," *Eighteenth-Century Life* 39, no. 1 (2015), 66–102; Thomas Truxes, *Irish American Trade, 1660–1783* (Cambridge: Cambridge University Press, 1988), 84; Craig Bailey, *Irish London: Middle-Class Migration in the Global Eighteenth Century* (Liverpool: Liverpool University Press, 2013); L.M. Cullen, "The two Fitzgeralds of London, 1718–1759," in *Irish and Scottish Mercantile Networks in Europe and Overseas in the Seventeenth and Eighteenth Centuries*, eds. David Dickson et al. (Gent: Academia Press, 2006), 251–70.

17 Steve Pincus, "Rethinking Mercantilism: Political Economy, the British Empire, and the Atlantic World in the Seventeenth and Eighteenth Centuries," *The William and Mary Quarterly* 69, no. 1 (2012), 3–34; Id., *1688: The First Modern Revolution* (New Haven: Yale University Press, 2009).

18 E.A. Wrigley, "British Population during the Long Eighteenth Century, 1680–1840," in *The Cambridge Economic History of Modern Britain, Industrialisation 1700–1860*, vol 1, eds. R. Floud and P. Johnson (Cambridge: Cambridge University Press, 2008), 57–95. In 1680, the population of Britain was roughly 6.5 million people; Perry Gauci, *Emporium of the World: The Merchants of London, 1660–1800* (London: Hambledon Continuum, 2007).

19 Hancock, *Citizens of the World*, 85–8.

20 Bergin, "Irish Catholics and Their Networks in Eighteenth-Century London"; Truxes, *Irish American Trade*, 84; Bailey, *Irish London*; Cullen, "The Two Fitzgeralds of London."

21 J.S. Bromley, "The North Sea in Wartime," in *Corsairs and Navies, 1660–1760* (London: Hambledon Press, 1987), 53.

22 David Starkey, *British Privateering Enterprise in the Eighteenth Century* (Exeter: Exeter University Press, 1990), 85–110; W.R. Meyer, "English Privateering in the War of the Spanish Succession 1702–1713," *Mariner's Mirror* 69 (1983), 435–46.

23 For a thorough analysis of the strategies and the source material, see my *British Catholic Merchants and Their Trading Networks in the Commercial Age (1670–1714)* (Woodbridge: Boydell & Brewer, 2020).

24 Zahedieh, *The Capital and the Colonies*; Haggerty, *"Merely for Money,"* 17, 198–236. Trivellato, *The Familiarity of Strangers*; Richard Grassby, *Kinship and Capitalism, Marriage, Family and Business in the English-Speaking World, 1580–1740* (Cambridge: Cambridge University Press, 2001); S.D. Aslanian, *From the Indian Ocean to the Mediterranean: The Global Trade Networks of Armenian Merchants from New Julfa* (London: California University Press, 2011)

25 Grassby, *Kinship and Capitalism*, 269–311.

26 In the London Metropolitan archives, it is possible to consult MS 10137, *Day Book of Charles Peers*.

27 For an extensive analysis of the trading strategies, see Pizzoni, *British Catholic Merchants*, Ch. 5.
28 T.C. Barker, "Smuggling in the Eighteenth Century. The Evidence of the Scottish Tobacco Trade," *The Virginia Magazine of History and Biography* 62, no. 4 (1954), 387–8; L.M. Cullen, "The Smuggling Trade in Ireland in the Eighteenth Century," *Proceedings of the Royal Irish Academy. Section C: Archaeology, Celtic Studies, History, Linguistics, Literature* 67 (1968/1969), 151.
29 Jan Parmentier, "The Sweets of Commerce: The Hennessys of Ostend and Their Networks in the Eighteenth Century," in *Irish and Scottish Mercantile Networks in Europe and Overseas in the Seventeenth and Eighteenth Centuries*, eds. David Dickson et al. (Gent: Academia Press, 2006), 70; Id., "The Irish Connection: The Irish Merchant Community in Ostend and Bruges during the late Seventeenth and Eighteenth Centuries," *Eighteenth Century Ireland* 20 (2005), 31–54.
30 Pizzoni, *British Catholic Merchants and their Trading Networks*, Ch. 3.
31 Giada Pizzoni, "Britain's long history of trying – and failing – to gain independence from European trade partners," theconversation.com, last modified February 5, 2019, https://theconversation.com/britains-long-history-of-trying-and-failing-to-gain-independence-from-european-trade-partners-110679.
32 Colin Haydon, *Anti-Catholicism in Eighteenth Century England* (Manchester: Manchester University Press, 1993), 170–6, 227. Haydon argues that the Seven Years' War was seen as a religious war, when Britain and Prussia fought Austria, France, and Spain. See his "Eighteenth Century English Anti-Catholicism: Contexts, Continuity and Diminution," in *Protestant-Catholic Conflict from the Reformation to the 21st Century. The Dynamics of Religious Difference*, ed. John Wolffe (London: Palgrave Macmillan, 2013), 49; C. Johnson, *Developments in the Roman Catholic Church in Scotland 1789–1829* (Edinburgh: Donald J. Ltd, 1983).
33 Pincus, "Rethinking Mercantilism."
34 Colley, *Britons: Forging the Nation.*
35 Glickman, *The English Catholic Community.* Id., "A British Catholic Community? Ethnicity, Identity and Recusant Politics, 1660–1750," in *Early Modern English Catholicism, Identity, Memory and Counter-Reformation*, eds. J.E. Kelly and S. Royal (Leiden: Brill, 2017), 60–81; J. Sommerville, "Papalist Political Thought and the Controversy over the Jacobean Oath of Allegiance," in *Catholics and the Protestant Nation, Religious Politics and Identity in Early Modern England*, ed. Ethan H. Shagan (Manchester University Press, 2005), 162–84.

10 Conquest, Colonialism, and Religious Conflict in the Moluccas in the Early Seventeenth Century

Hendrik E. Niemeijer

Introduction

This chapter focuses on the problem of tolerance and intolerance in the famous Spice Islands, which were once a principal target of early modern European colonial expansion. During the sixteenth and early seventeenth centuries, the traditional local village communities (*soa*), villages (*negeri*), and village federations (*uli*) in the Moluccas went through a dramatic and often disruptive process of conquest, political and military submission, economic exploitation, and religious transformation. This process was imposed first by the Portuguese (from Goa and Malacca) and the Spanish (from Manila), and then by the Dutch East India Company (VOC), founded in 1602. Following the conquest of the Portuguese city of Ambon in 1605, the VOC established three governments in the Spice Islands, on Ambon, Ternate, and Banda, each governing an extensive region. From the outset, these governments were also centres for the propagation of Calvinism (also known as Reformed Protestantism), the official faith of the Dutch Republic. The city of Batavia, established on the island of Java in 1619, functioned as the VOC's headquarters in Asia and also as its religious centre. Starting in the 1620s, the VOC administration and Reformed church in Batavia actively promoted the establishment of Reformed churches in the Moluccas under the protection of the three VOC governments.

Our knowledge of the history of religious transformations and confrontations in the Moluccas has been greatly increased in recent decades by the recovery of primary source materials. For the sixteenth century, H. Jacobs' *Documenta Malucensia* is essential to understand the beginnings of the Catholic missions under Francis Xavier and others.[1] Based on meticulous research in the VOC archives, G.J. Knaap's book offers the most detailed analysis of Ambonese society in the second half of the seventeenth century.[2] My dissertation focused on religious tolerance and toleration in the city of Batavia and examined the effects of Calvinist church discipline and poor relief on colonial (slave) society. One of its conclusions is that Calvinist officials working in the VOC headquarters and for the city's institutions were more tolerant towards the religious practices of the local Muslim community than towards those of the (mostly mestizo) Catholics

DOI: 10.4324/9781003030522-15

and Chinese Buddhists.[3] Was this also the case in the Moluccas? My research in the rich minutes of the governing body, known as the consistory, of the Reformed church in Batavia led to the further disclosure of hitherto unknown correspondence between this consistory and the three consistories in the Moluccas. Several discoveries were made in the late 1990s in the formerly inaccessible consistorial archive of Batavia in the National Archives of the Republic of Indonesia (ANRI) in Jakarta.[4] In the end, 957 ecclesiastical documents from the Moluccas (1605–1791) were collected and published in six volumes.[5] Further research on the history of the nineteenth-century Moluccas resulted in source publications by M. van Selm[6] and Chr. G.F. de Jong.[7]

Charles H. Parker's recent study *Global Calvinism* follows an earlier limited attempt by Gerrit J. Schutte to create an overview of the most important politico-religious developments in the Dutch parts of the Indonesian archipelago (and beyond).[8] Parker's analysis is quite right that "conversion" in the Dutch Empire was largely a matter of community formation via baptism and admission to the Lord's Supper. It also included an active policy of poor relief.[9] In this chapter, I would like to focus on a crucial phenomenon that preceded the stage of community formation: the making of political and religious contracts. This usually involved the signing of treaties with local rajas, within or outside the VOC's conquered territories. Without political appeasement, either by means of a treaty (which tended to include religious articles) or through conquest and direct submission, it was impossible to establish schools and churches and Christianise local island societies. Therefore, in order to understand the possibilities and limitations of spreading Christianity in local societies, we need to examine the process of political appeasement or subjugation first. In the next sections, we will do so for each of the three VOC governments in the Moluccas: Ternate, Ambon, and Banda.

Ternate: a fortification by contract

The political contexts of the three regions mentioned above, involving indigenous power centres, colonial collaborations, intrusions, and conquests, were markedly different. With the spread of Islam in the sixteenth century, the volcanic clove islands of Ternate, Tidore, and Bacan in the north Moluccas developed into influential Islamic kingdoms. They enjoyed close connections to Chinese overseas trading networks and to maritime networks leading via Malacca to the Indian Ocean. Many Malay, Javanese, Indian, Persian, and Arab traders were familiar with the spice trade.

With the coming of the Portuguese and the Spanish (combined since 1580), the Moluccan kingdoms became more closely connected than ever before to the global economy. Tracing the complex history of European expansions in the Moluccas is not our main concern here. The famous early eighteenth-century work *Oud en Nieuw Oost-Indiën* by François Valentijn (a Reformed minister serving in Ambon in the periods 1686–1694 and 1706–1712) still offers the most extensive historical coverage of events.[10] One pivotal moment in the history of Ternate, however, deserves highlighting: the Portuguese surrender on December 26, 1575 to the Ternate Sultan Babullah. The Portuguese left Ternate, moving to Ambon, and the old fortress in Ternate became the sultan's palace. In the last quarter of the sixteenth century, the Portuguese expanded the clove forests on Ambon and adjacent islands and promoted Catholic missionary efforts.[11] Spanish attacks on Ternate eventually forced Sultan Saidi Berkat in 1606 to surrender his fortresses and sign a treaty that made Ternate a vassal of the Spanish king. All the leaders of the islands of Ternate, Tidore, and the further islands of Bacan and Siau took an oath of allegiance and swore not to admit any Dutch traders to buy cloves. Two months later, Sultan Saidi and 24 nobles were taken away to Manila. In this victory, the Spaniards saw the hand of God, as "Maluku" had been restored "to our ministers and preachers, and the Evangelical Voice [was] once again heard in the furthest ends of the earth."[12]

In the following year (1607), Dutch Admiral Cornelis Matelief arrived in Ternate in response to a request from Ternaten diplomats in the port of Banten (West Java). It was the perfect moment for the Dutch to sign a favourable contract with the remaining leadership of Ternate, who were in dire need of support. Both the contract with Ternate (May 26, 1607)[13] and the VOC's capture in 1609 of the Spanish-Portuguese fortress in the small port town of Labuha on the island (and Sultanate) of Bacan were strategic moves, made with the impending start in the mind of the Twelve Years' Truce between the Dutch Republic and Spain (1609–1621). In two years, the Dutch built 11 fortifications on the islands of Ternate, Makian, Moti, Bacan, Jailolo (Halmahera), and Tidore. The most important was at Malayu on Ternate, within walking distance of the Spanish fortress of Gammalamo. The people of Ternate quickly began to resettle around the Dutch compound.[14] In the newly built Fort Orange, both a government and a church were established, which had to compete with the Catholic church in Gammalamo. Ministers of the church of Ternate, together with "visitors of the sick" (*ziekentroosters*), had responsibility for the pastoral care of the people living in the scattered 11 Dutch fortresses and military posts in the region. They also provided pastoral care for the community of Asiatic and the "Mardecas"[15] families under the direct control of Fort Orange.[16]

Ambon: a territorial takeover

After being expelled from Ternate in 1575, the Portuguese founded the town of Ambon on the island of Ambon (Figure 10.1). They held this town for 30 years, until in 1605 VOC Admiral Steven van der Haghen took the Portuguese fortress there. This takeover of Portuguese territory was accomplished with the help of a fleet of warships belonging to the raja of Hitu, a small Islamic kingdom and port town on the other side of Ambon. This anti-Portuguese alliance between Dutch traders and Hitu Muslims was forged five years earlier when Hitu decided to sell all its cloves to the Dutch in return for military aid. Van der Haghen's report on the 1605 conquest[17] states that

Figure 10.1 The island of Ambon.

From François Valentijn, *Oud en Nieuw Oost-Indiën [...]*, vol. 2 (Dordrecht-Amsterdam: Joannes van Braam, Gerard Onder de Linden, 1724), between pp. 124–5. Taken from the facsimile edition published by Van Wijnen (Franeker, 2002–2004).

the VOC promised to ensure peace between Muslims and Catholics and to protect Ambonese converts to Catholicism. Economically, it was crucial for the VOC to obtain the exclusive right to buy the cloves. In the early years of the VOC, the Company's directors in the Dutch Republic, known as the Gentlemen XVII, preferred to achieve this monopoly not through conquest but by signing exclusive contracts and building fortifications with the permission of local rulers. The capture of Ambon, although strategically important, had not been anticipated and came as a surprise to the Gentlemen XVII. Under the circumstances, however, the arrangement suited the local Muslim rulers of Hitu and Ternate well – for the time being.

Threatened by the raja of Hitu, the Catholic clergy and heads of two dozen Catholic villages in Ambon-Leitimor and on the adjacent Lease Islands (Haruku, Saparua, and Nusa Laut) quickly submitted themselves to the VOC and agreed to convert to Protestantism. The Catholic missionaries perhaps hoped it was a matter of time before aid came from Portuguese Malacca. That never happened, however. After five Ambonese wars and a final pacification in 1656, the second half of the seventeenth century saw a decades-long process of Calvinist missionary activity that resulted in stamping these islands with a firm Calvinist identity. Over the following centuries, the Calvinist identity of this centre of spice production became increasingly entrenched; nowadays, it still is one of the most Protestant areas in Indonesia.

Banda: a violent conquest

The small nutmeg islands to the southeast of Ambon represent a third, different case. The Banda Islands mainly consist of Pulau (Mal., island) Banda-Neira, Pulau Lontor, Pulau Ai, Pulau Run, and Pulau Rozengain (Figure 10.2). On March 15, 1599, Jacob van Heemskerck reached the Banda Islands with

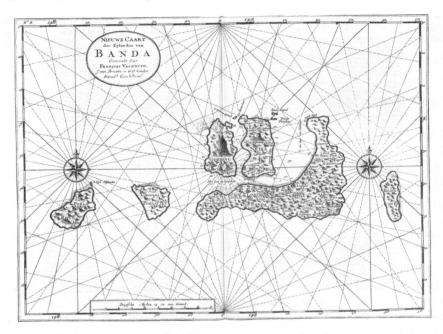

Figure 10.2 Map of the Banda Islands.

From François Valentijn, *Oud en Nieuw Oost-Indiën [...]*, vol. 3 (Dordrecht-Amsterdam: Joannes van Braam, Gerard Onder de Linden, 1726), between pp. 6–7. Taken from the facsimile edition published by Van Wijnen (Franeker, 2002–2004).

two Dutch ships. At the time, Banda was the world's main production area of the "fragrant gold": nutmeg and its by-product, mace. Initially, the Bandanese leadership (the *orang kaya* or wealthy trading elite) saw the Dutch as allies in their resistance to the Portuguese. To obtain a monopoly over nutmeg, the VOC made contracts with local leaders. After the departure of the Company's ships, though, the local producers usually returned to the custom of selling freely to any of their old-time trading partners: the Javanese, Makassarese, Malays, Arabs, Indians, and Chinese. This behaviour made the Bandanese, in the eyes of the Dutch, untrustworthy business partners. The Gentlemen XVII saw the conquest of Banda as an essential part of a grand scheme whose ultimate goals were Dutch independence from Spain and control of the European spice market. Without such control, they feared, the VOC would not survive.[18] As Martine J. van Ittersum has shown, between 1609 and 1621 "a toxic combination of warfare and treaty-making stripped the Bandanese of their liberty and independence." European powers never conceived the treaties they made with native populations as agreements between equals.[19]

The conquest of Banda started in 1609, when a VOC fleet was led by Commander Pieter Willemsz Verhoeff captured the site on Neira where the

Portuguese had attempted to build a fort. The Bandanese retaliated by killing Verhoeff and several of his men, which in turn triggered counter-attacks by VOC soldiers. After these clashes, a peace treaty was concluded by which the Bandanese agreed to the construction of a fortress (Fort Nassau). This was a turning point. Subsequently, Commander Simon Janszoon Hoen claimed, based on the right of conquest, to have an agreement with "the honourable orangkayas of all the islands, towns of the entire Banda Islands."[20] For their part, the Gentlemen XVII concluded that they had acquired rights over the whole of Banda, and in 1614 they reconsidered the strategy of small punitive expeditions and decided to use large-scale force to achieve the final submission of all the islands. The Dutch conquered the island of Pulau Ai in 1616. Having been "conquered by the sword in a just war," the Bandanese leadership of Banda-Neira, Pulau Ai, Pulau Run, and Pulau Rozengain were compelled to sign a contract that entailed their complete submission to the Dutch. In order to finally subdue the largest island, Great Banda or Lonthoir, in 1621 Governor-General Jan Pieterszoon Coen (1617–1623, 1627–1629) sent an expeditionary force to Banda from Batavia.[21] After the Dutch conquest and an ensuing exodus, of the estimated 13,000 to 15,000 original inhabitants of Banda, only about 1,500 remained.

Despite the ongoing English claim to Pulau Run, Dutch control of Banda was virtually complete after 1621. The VOC effort now focused entirely on the production and shipping of nutmeg and mace. This could not be done without the formation of a new society, including the settlement of relocated people and slaves. The cultivation of nutmeg on Pulau Ai had started in 1616 with people from Siau (captured by the Company in 1614) and by making use of prisoners and slaves, necessary because Banda was almost completely depopulated. To make settlement attractive to Europeans, the forestry area was divided into "perks" and leased to European settlers, the *perkeniers*. They formed the core of the new colony, supported by Company staff and a military garrison. Slaves were transferred to Banda from various parts of Asia, including the slave markets located on the South-Asian coasts of Malabar, Coromandel, and Bengal. Together with the remaining original inhabitants, they provided the necessary labour for the cultivation, harvesting, processing, packing, and harbouring of the nutmeg. The *perkeniers* supervised an efficient production system and supplied the VOC at a fixed price. Here the Company had a firm grip on the lives of all inhabitants – free citizens, native population, and slaves. This firm grip also included a strict religious policy.

From the perspective of the Bandanese leadership and its regional political network (Hitu and Ternate and Makassar), the struggle with the Dutch was not only about the defence of their property and the right to continue to trade spices with their centuries-old partners. Islam, which seems to have been more militant in Banda than in other areas of the Spice Islands, provided the ultimate justification for the use of force against the VOC. The conflict in Banda was both a clash between European powers and a confrontation between two conflicting monotheistic worldviews.[22]

Contracts as a mechanism of dominion, intolerance, and toleration

Despite the conflict in Banda, traditional and Islamised island societies tended elsewhere to respond pragmatically to the VOC's presence, at least initially. Although firmly Islamic, the leaders of Ternate and Hitu welcomed the Dutch, partly because the latter seemed not to pose a threat to the religious status quo. Only in cases of territorial subjugation and occupation (Ambon and Banda) were western colonial norms and values imposed on formerly Catholicised villages or newly established colonial settlements. Where contracts were agreed upon that guaranteed that local rulers would retain political and religious spheres of influence, what generally emerged were situations characterised by a certain level of mutual toleration. Although in general the VOC favoured this last principle, the initial phase of colonising Ambon and Banda showed that its support for toleration was highly contingent.

Of all the parts of Asia where the VOC was active, the Moluccas saw the greatest number of political contracts made.[23] The religious articles in these political contracts aimed to avoid potential religious conflicts. This aim had already been visible in earlier contracts made by the Portuguese. Commercial considerations played an important role, as it was feared that intolerance would decrease or even destroy business opportunities. Like the earliest contracts signed on Banda, Ambon, and Ternate, many subsequent ones also involved confirmation of the religious status quo.

The first treaty with Banda dates from as early as 1602. In it, Dutch traders acknowledged the commitment of the Bandanese leadership to Islam. Made between Wolphert Harmensz and the *orang kaya* of the villages of Selama, Labataka, Dender, and (Pulau) Rozengain, the contract stipulated that the Dutch could leave some people there. This was only possible, however, on condition that "each shall serve his God according to his own faith, without the one hating the other or giving cause for issues to arise from it." The Dutch were not allowed to interfere in internal conflicts on Banda. If a Company servant ran away, he had to be brought back and could not convert to Islam. On the other hand, a free Dutchman was allowed to become a Muslim on condition that his conversion took place without coercion and fear of punishment and that he remained a Dutch subject. In return for these concessions, the village heads promised to sell their spices exclusively to the Dutch.[24] Conversely, if a free Bandanese citizen wanted to become a Christian, he should not be prevented from doing so. The Bandanese Muslim leadership were probably not happy with this, but the contract with the *orang kaya* of Pulau Ai of June 17 of that year contained the same clause.[25] In later contracts such a permissive clause was unthinkable.

After the conquest of Ambon in 1605, and after an incident in which some Dutchmen who had converted to Islam were killed by their countrymen in

Figure 10.3 The island of Nera with Fort Nassau.

From François Valentijn, *Oud en Nieuw Oost-Indiën [...]*, vol. 3 (Dordrecht-Amsterdam: Joannes van Braam, Gerard Onder de Linden, 1726), between pp. 4–5. Taken from the facsimile edition published by Van Wijnen (Franeker, 2002–2004).

the house of a Muslim preacher, Van der Haghen sailed to Banda to conclude a new contract that would be valid for all the Banda islands. This contract devotes considerable space to the strict regulation of religious matters. Conversions were not permitted anymore, and the Dutch were (again) not permitted to interfere in internal Bandanese political affairs. At the same time, the Bandanese were obliged, after negotiating a price, to sell all their nutmeg to the Dutch. This contract was considered permanent, and those who breached the contract would be punished.[26]

The next contract, made in 1616 by Jan Dirckz. Lam, stipulated that converts to both Islam and Christianity should be reported to Fort Nassau (Figure 10.3).[27] After the final conquest of Lonthoir in 1621, Coen signed a treaty with the *orang kaya* of Pulau Run to arrange the island's final submission to the highest authority of the Dutch Republic, the States General. Greatly dissatisfied with the content of these contracts, the heads of Pulai Ai and Run came to Neira with an alternative text, the so-called Eight Articles. In these, the remaining islanders urgently requested protection from molestation and forced labour. More importantly, they asked "that they [the Dutch] do not inconvenience us in our religion, but that we may live according to our religion and that the Dutch may do so according to their religion." Muslim citizens insisted on being able to live in their own kampongs (*kampung*) while enjoying freedom of conscience.[28] In the event, as we will see, they were subsequently subjected to religious restrictions.

Religious arrangements for Ambon were agreed upon immediately after its fall in 1605. Van der Haghen concluded a treaty with his ally there, the raja of Hitu, to consolidate their business interests. Hitu, it stipulated, would deliver spices only to the Company and would assist in future conflicts. Although Hitu became a subject of the Dutch States General, the third article of the treaty stated: "Everyone lives in his faith, as God convinces him in his heart, or as he thinks he will be saved."[29] The same applied to the Islamic villages that were in the territories seized from Portugal, which also became part of the VOC's *pax religionis*. The four Islamic *negeri* on the island of Haruku (Hatuhaha, Kabauw, Kailolo, and Halaliu) and Rumahkai on Seram "will stay in their [Islamic] faith, without those of the castle or the Dutch being allowed to harm them, or drive them out because of their faith." The Muslims of these villages, however, were forbidden to disturb the nearby Christian *negeri* by reading the Koran or by proselytising and recruiting members for their mosques according to the "Moorish faith." Such acts would be punished by the governor of Ambon.[30]

Vis-à-vis Ternate, the contract that Admiral Cornelis Matelieff signed in 1607 at the invitation of the Sultan of Ternate stipulated that the VOC would build a bulwark in the village of Malayu and leave some ships at the anchorage in front. In addition, more troops would be sent "to chase the Castilians out of Ternate" at Ternate's own expense and, most importantly for the Dutch, cloves would not be sold to anyone but the VOC. Only the brief twelfth article concerned religion: "As for religion, no one should mock or hinder the other, but each will live as he can justify himself before God."[31]

All these early contracts included a limitation on Dutch missionary activities: according to them, Christianity was not to be propagated in a local ruler's territories. The kingdoms of Ternate and Hitu are examples of this rule; the earliest churches in the sultanates of Ternate (Malayu) and Bacan (Labuha) were planted in small extraterritorial enclaves or places. Within the VOC's territories, the religious status quo was maintained in order to avoid religious clashes and disruption to the production of cloves. Only in the second half of the seventeenth century did Reformed Protestantism begin to be propagated, and then only in those places where local rulers had contractually agreed with the VOC governors and consistories to establish a school and a church. The decision to adopt a particular religion was usually made by the local ruler and elites, who often sent their sons to one of the Dutch ministers to be educated in the Christian faith.

By contrast, in conquered territories such as Ambon and Banda, the VOC applied the laws of the Dutch Republic: only the Reformed Church could have a public presence, while other religions were restricted to the private sphere.[32] In these territories, the VOC followed the dominant norms of Christian governments in Europe, employing its political power to prevent ungodly behaviour and prohibiting the practices of rival confessions and religions. Governmental support for the Reformed Church was vital, given that the newly established consistories encountered great resistance to their efforts to inculcate Calvinist moral and social norms.

The establishment of three Calvinist consistories

The means by which ministers and company servants tried to impose Calvinist norms, attitudes, and beliefs on native populations were based on the means that the government and church had at their disposal in the Dutch Republic. The most powerful one was the establishment of consistories.

The first consistory in the Dutch East Indies was the one established in Batavia in January 1621. In the more limited but still vast area of the Spice Islands, 20 years passed between the formal arrival of a Reformed visitor-of-the-sick in 1605, when Van der Haghen conquered Ambon, and the establishment of the first consistory there in 1625. This lay pastor said a prayer of thanksgiving in Fort *Nossa Senhora da Anunciada* (henceforth: Fort Victoria) immediately after the fall. Over the following weeks, the Catholic villages on Ambon-Leitimor and the nearby Lease Islands formally converted to Protestantism – a political choice made by the local rajas. Seven years later, in 1612, Casparus Wiltens, the first Reformed minister, preached and baptised further north in the conquered small port of Labuha, on the island of Bacan, and the work of establishing congregations slowly started. The establishment of a consistory in Ternate and election (with governmental approval) of members to it was an equally slow process and only took place in 1626, that is, 19 years after the first contract there was signed. Only in the case of Banda was a consistory elected immediately after the island's conquest, in April 1622. Apart from the lack of suitable ministers, the authorities were of the opinion that a consistory could only be established in an orderly society that was ready for it.

The three consistories in the Moluccas covered an enormous area. Ambon's consistory had jurisdiction over the churches in the Central Moluccas, including Southwestern Seram. The consistory of Banda followed the territorial expansion (through contracts with local rajas) of the Company into the so-called Southwestern and Southeastern Islands, from the island of Wetar in the southwest to the large island of Aru in the east. The Ternate consistory initially had jurisdiction over the churches established on the clove islands of Ternate, Makian, and Bacan with its capital Labuha, but saw its territory expanded significantly to North Sulawesi (capital Manado) and the Sangihe-Talaud archipelago after the departure of the Spaniards from the island of Tidore and from Manado in 1663.

Amboina: conquest and Reformation

To the frustration of native Christians waiting to be baptised or married, it took the Company several years before the first Protestant ministers were sent to the Moluccas. Casparus Wiltens (1612–1619) and Sebastianus Danckaerts (1618–1622) were the most prominent first-generation Dutch ministers in the Moluccas. Their treatises are quite revealing of their European and Calvinist outlook on, and prejudices towards, other religious traditions and customs.

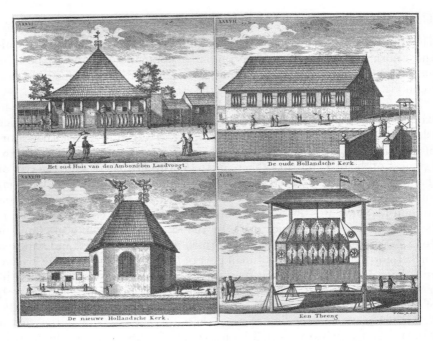

Figure 10.4 Four buildings on the island of Ambon, including two Dutch Reformed churches.

From François Valentijn, *Oud en Nieuw Oost-Indiën [...]*, vol. 2 (Dordrecht-Amsterdam: Joannes van Braam, Gerard Onder de Linden, 1724), between pp. 132–3. Taken from the facsimile edition published by Van Wijnen (Franeker, 2002–2004).

Their first – recently recovered – letters were all aimed at informing administrators and churches in the Dutch Republic about the true state of affairs of Moluccan "nominal" Christianity and reflect the mindset of the earliest Calvinist colonists.

Wiltens initially worked in the small Catholic (mestizo) community based in Labuha. After being placed in Ambon (Figure 10.4), he wrote to the classis of Amsterdam in 1616 that "one can see in [the Ambonese] a peculiar profanity and irreligiosity, yea so that they even do not labour to serve their devils unless they are haunted by them." In all "heathen" nations, one cannot find "such profanity and irreligiosity, [the people] making so little effort or content of religion." The nature of the people was not easy to change: "the more the people are inclined to a bestial life, the slower they are to change their nature."[33]

The opinions of Wiltens and Danckaerts mattered. Danckaerts corresponded directly with the Gentlemen XVII in the Dutch Republic and Governor-General Coen in Batavia. Sent by the classis of Hoorn in Holland, the young preacher arrived in Ambon in January 1618, where he served until May 1622. Upon his arrival in Amboina, the two lay preachers already present asked him whether he had come to serve. When Danckaerts confirmed this, the preachers responded that he might as well "present his service to dogs and pigs," based on what Wiltens, "who had been so diligent," had said.[34]

After a few frustrating years, in 1621 the 29-year-old Danckaerts wrote a lengthy treatise in which he expressed his negative judgement of the Ambonese people. Danckaerts's frustration about the overly optimistic oral and written messages being sent from the East Indies to the Republic was so great that he returned to the Netherlands, explaining the real situation, as he saw it, in a pamphlet published in The Hague in 1621 entitled *Historical and thorough relation of the state of Christianity in the quarter of Amboina, and the hope and appearance of a Reformation and improvement.*[35]

The religious classification of the Moluccans used by these clergymen was fixed from the start, consisting only of pagans, Muslims, and Christians. In the correspondence of Wiltens, however, this classification was complicated by a custom that Europeans found odious: whether Muslim or Christian, the Ambonese were also cannibals. Moreover, they were true servants of the devil: "The Ambonese do not serve the devil as an idol that is indeed the devil, or in which the devil is, but they serve the devil as the devil."[36]

Danckaerts's description of traditional Ambonese animist folk religion, circumcision rites, and marriage practices was the earliest and also most negative of its kind. He dismissed the religion as "devil's service" and superstition. At least as important was his description of the national character of the Ambonese. He characterised them as "faithless, fearful, small-hearted, blunt, indocile" and further, in contrast to other Asiatic peoples, as "not curious or inquisitive to learn or investigate anything." Furthermore, they were uncreative and unable to produce artistic crafts or art. They had no chronology and no script, as did the Malays, Javanese, and Chinese. They hardly knew any trade other than the clove trade and led a very frugal existence. In short, he concluded, though human nature is known to be corrupt, of all the heathen nations, the most profanity is found in the Ambonese, who are even lazy in the devil's service. Among the Muslim Ambonese as well, Danckaerts found more superstition than true religion. Islamic rituals, according to him, were purely external formalities. He found among Muslims on their deathbeds "not one jot or tittle of repentance for sins, nor any repentance or prayer for forgiveness or the like [...] which would be points of religion." He concluded that there was no hope whatsoever for the Ambonese pagans or Muslims. Among the former, one could not detect curiosity or inquisitiveness; among the latter, one could find only stubbornness.

Concerning the Christians in Amboina, Danckaerts was positive about the inhabitants of the village of Hative, close to Fort Victoria, because they had been allies of the Portuguese and enemies of the Muslims of Hitu. The Portuguese had used coercion and authority to bring about the conversion of the Hativese to Catholicism. Under the Dutch, "devil-service" was strictly forbidden and attendance at church and prayer meetings was made obligatory. Nevertheless, the Hativese continued their secret "devil-services" in their homes, fields, and forests. Danckaerts was most positive about the "Mardecas," the free Asiatic or Indo-European citizens.[37] Ever since these Christians came under the authority of the Company, however, "it was all hypocrisy," as Wiltens wrote.

What, then, was the best way of achieving a "reformation," according to Danckaerts? Based on the experience of the Portuguese with the pagans, Hativese, and Mardecas, he asserted that Christianisation took place only as a result of "authority, fear and awe rather than inquisitiveness and curiosity." That meant compulsory church attendance, catechism classes, and prayer meetings. Danckaerts, however, did not specify exactly what form the compulsion should take; this he regarded as a "political matter." Religious compulsion, he wrote, could be justified by the fact that the Ambonese did not display the normal signs of "faith, hope, love, mercy, gratitude, sincerity, piety, godliness, long-suffering, forgiveness of sins, and other such Christian virtues and duties [...] And they also have not as many affections and [spiritual] sentiments as we have." Normally God's Spirit worked through the preaching of the Word, but this instrument was missing. "The indicators of God's Grace are still so small and so few, that one can scarcely see it; on the contrary, there seems to be a special curse from God upon that people, the signs of which abound." The central point of both Wiltens's and Danckaerts's remarks and perceptions was that the Ambonese people could neither be influenced nor "civilised." In fact, developments in the second half of the seventeenth century proved them wrong.[38]

Although Danckaerts's successors in the Moluccas wrote about the native population and their religious customs in a more nuanced way, Danckaerts's assessment set the tone: Christianisation could only succeed with the help of government legislation and regulations. That assessment was reflected in Article 20 of the first Church Ordinance (1625): "Given the great slowness of the Ambonese to hear God's Word, the authorities are requested to fine anyone who goes into the woods or stays at home on Sunday and does not come to church, so that the Lord may have His glory."[39]

To legitimise a conquest like the one of Ambon by making a local alliance and citing the maritime and international law of the time is one thing. To justify a long-term colonisation scheme, establish a permanent government, and initiate a religious transformation is another. While in the Dutch case, overseas conquest tended to be predominantly motivated by economic prospects and the desire to establish a monopoly, such conquest required more than the stealing of land and dispossession of local inhabitants. As David Day explains in his book *Conquest*, "supplanting the savages" is a common justification for colonisation. The natives of a conquered land are portrayed by the conqueror "as barbarian or savage and thereby having a lesser claim, or even no claim at all, to lands that may have been theirs for centuries but which were now coveted by the invaders."[40] In a similar fashion, the conquest of the Moluccan islands was justified by portraying the inhabitants as barbaric, immoral, wild, primitive, stupid, and living in complete religious

darkness. In this regard, Calvinist ministers played a significant role in justifying Dutch colonial rule. Moreover, the toleration of other religious traditions, native religious customs in particular, was minimal as such traditions
formed a major obstacle to the civilising process envisaged by Dutch secular
and ecclesiastic authorities.

The control of morals in Ternate and Labuha

The inhabitants of Malayu on the island of Ternate interacted with the Catholic community in and around Gammalamo on the western part of the island. In the first decades of the Dutch presence, pastoral care was limited to
the soldiers occupying the newly built Fort Orange. In Labuha, on the island
of Bacan, Fort Barnevelt (1609) had a Catholic community that, in addition
to the European occupation force of the VOC, consisted of slaves, Catholic
Mardecas, and a few Christian Chinese. Unlike in Ambonese villages, where
rajas took the lead, in Malayu and Labuha the success of church and school
and the maintenance of Christian morality (particularly regarding marriage)
depended on political and administrative enforcement.

The earliest records of the Protestant church on Ternate, dating from
1626, reveal immediate tension between minister Georgius Candidius (1626),
a strict Calvinist of German descent, and Governor Jacques Le Febvre (in
office: 1623–1627). Their conflict focused on the implementation of strict
marriage laws among the Mardecas and Chinese under the Company's
authority. Le Febvre believed that cohabiting couples should be urged to
marry with "civil admonition and not threats." If Asiatic citizens were put
under too much pressure, he feared, they would defect to the Spaniards in
Gammalamo where the "papists" were much more tolerant. That was not
in the interest of the Company, which needed workers for the fortifications
and tradespeople to build up the small colony. Candidius, on the other hand,
advocated stricter measures and started to exercise his authority immediately
upon his arrival in April 1626. The consistory of Batavia had sent him with
specific orders to establish a consistory and introduce Calvinist social norms.
Behind this initiative were the ministers Danckaerts and Justus Heurnius.
Danckaerts, who after his period in Ambon (1618–1622) had travelled to
the Netherlands, returned to Batavia in 1624, where he remained a minister
until his death in 1634. Heurnius (Batavia 1624–1632, Ambon 1633–1638),
who had attended the first *Seminarium Indicum* in Leiden with Candidius,
also arrived in Batavia in 1624. Together they were responsible for writing
the first Church Ordinance for the Dutch East Indies, which was established
in August-October 1624.

Under pressure from Batavia, Candidius had to maintain a hard line or
risk losing authority. Since he and the Governor encountered one another
regularly at the dinner table in the Governor's Hall, it was not long before
the dispute between them got out of hand. During a discussion, Candidius
"beat his hand on the table [and said]: 'Lord, nay, Le Febvre, or Governor,

whatever we decide in our consistory shall stand and we will carry it out,' patting his hand on his chest, 'even if it costs life and body'." According to Daniel Otten, the castle's secretary, and others, there were Mardecas who had already packed their goods and intended to flee because the clergy had threatened to "drown the concubines in a pipe of water," which was the usual punishment for sodomy.[41]

The surviving sources enable us to follow the religious policy of the first generation of Reformed ministers further south in Labuha as well. Labuha was the first place conquered by the Company where a minister was employed: Casparus Wiltens. He wrote to the classis of Amsterdam that upon his arrival in 1612 he found about 50 Christian families living in dispersed clove forests. They rarely came to the fort. The rest of the island was subject to the Muslim raja of Bacan. It is striking that the consistory of Batavia in 1624 drew up a separate church ordinance for the Christian congregation in Labuha, different from the first Church Ordinance of the Dutch Indies. The Labuha ordinance was intended to steer the mostly Asiatic Christian community back towards church and school attendance, to prohibit conversion to Islam, and to implement Calvinist rules regarding marriage. Article 1 stated that anyone living "in whoredom" and "concubinage" was to be married immediately or pay a fine of 20 reales of eight. Divorce was no longer allowed. The fourth article stipulated that everyone had to leave their clove garden on Sundays to hear God's Word or pay a fine of a quarter real. Children were required to attend school – the families of those who did were to be rewarded with four pounds of rice per week (Article 7) – and further conversions to Islam were barred in Article 9. Anyone who converted to Islam for minor reasons to the detriment of Christianity and "oppression of their conscience" committed a serious offence punishable by a fine of 300 reales and "arbitral correction" (corporal punishment). Anyone who heard any rumour about someone wanting to convert to Islam was supposed to report it immediately to the fort. If the rumour proved to be correct, the informant would receive 12 reales in reward. The proceeds of the fines were to be distributed among the poor, the *sengaji* (village chief) of Labuha, and the *marinjo* (slave overseer).

Such laws clearly did nothing but increase the inhabitants' aversion to the Dutch. In 1626, the Catholic Labuhaese even planned an attack on Fort Barnevelt. However, this "treason" was discovered, and the instigators were convicted in Fort Orange (in Malayu). Lay pastor Jan Gerritsz. Block, who arrived in April 1627 to perform church services in Labuha, reported to the consistory of Batavia that he found the church building dilapidated. Schoolmaster Hendrick van Hengel wrote in 1628 that for the first two years after the rebellion only about three or four children came to the school. The inhabitants mocked him when he exhorted them to send their children. There were also people who resented that he "occasionally gave their children a blow with the wooden slat," as was customary in Dutch schools.

Despite these setbacks, a small Christian congregation continued to exist in Labuha. In 1634, minister Petrus Schotte (Ternate 1627–1633, Batavia 1633–1634) reported that he baptised children every year and that the school was running reasonably well. The list of names that pastor Harmen Jansz. sent to Batavia in 1635 has been preserved and gives an impression of the mixed Portuguese-Spanish-Asiatic Christian community of Labuha. This included 92 Mardecas with their families; 47 free burghers with their families; married Company soldiers with their families; and 16 Chinese with their families – a total of 283 persons.[42]

Banda: Christianisation and intolerance

After the conquest of Banda, the Dutch built an entirely new multi-ethnic colonial plantation society – one underpinned by religion.[43] The most important sources for an analysis of religious tolerance in the early years are the minutes of the Banda consistory, various sets of correspondence, and the registers of baptisms and marriages compiled by one of the first ministers, Wouter Melchiorsz. Vitriarius (Banda 1622–1625, Ambon 1628–1632). Like Danckaerts before him, Vitriarius also travelled back to the Netherlands (1626–1627) to present his findings to his church. He handed over a carefully handwritten copy of documents in a beautiful leather binding to the classis of Amsterdam. This "Copy-boeck," which is preserved in the Amsterdam City Archives, is the oldest complete compilation of church documents from the early seventeenth-century Moluccas.[44]

The "Copy-boeck" of Vitriarius reveals further traces of colonial intolerance. Unlike Governor Le Febvre in Ternate, the Governor of Banda, Martinus Sonck, was a Calvinist hardliner and proponent of strict marriage laws. In 1622, he issued a placard to "prevent fornication and adultery, which was very common here in this place, and was hardly counted as a sin among the people." The earliest marriage registers and minutes of the Banda consistory show that church and government acted in unison in attempting to establish an orderly society "because a disorderly society would bring God's wrath upon the church." The "Copy-boeck" is full of concrete cases and disputes with (mostly Asiatic) Christians, and over a period of nine years (1616–1625), a total of 196 couples were urged to marry officially in the churches of Pulai Ai and Neira.

Sonck and Vitrarius established an educational system that, together with a campaign to promote baptism, was intended to foster conversions. In 1621, a school on Pulau Ai was used to give catechism lessons in Malay to some 150 children, two-thirds of whom were from Muslim families that had been killed or had fled Pulau Run or Pulau Rozengain. Visitor-of-the-sick Adriaan de Keersemaker from Amsterdam settled in late 1622 on Run as the site for another school for native children and orphans. In addition, there was a school on Lonthoir with 100 children while a school on Rozengain was established as well. But the compulsory education of Muslim children was doomed to fail, even when the Company offered 20 pounds of rice per child every month. The consistory attributed high levels of school absenteeism to the fact that the Bandanese adults "obstinately persisted in Mahometan teaching." As of 1631, the Company was paying between 5000 and 6000 guilders per year to attract 208 children of Mardecas families and 63 Bandanese children to the schools. In the end, though, the experiment was halted. Many Muslim youths escaped from Banda to Seram, where they were united with small groups of Bandanese refugees.

Compared to the situation in other VOC territories, the one on Banda was atypical. On Banda, relations with the Muslims were fraught from the beginning. This may have been due to a greater religious fervour among Muslims there, whose main concern was defending Islam as the true religion, a stance that ruled out submission to the European "unbelievers" at any cost. The Dutch conquest of 1621 by no means spelled the end of Islam in the Banda Islands. A year later, the small Muslim community on Neira still held its "public Moorish exercises, as a result of which not only many Bandanese and other Moors are strengthened in their opinion, but also some women and children are lost to Christianity through marriage or otherwise." In the same year, a few imams continued to reside on Pulau Run, "to the considerable disadvantage, and to the dishonor of reputation and dignity, of our Christians, under whose rightful authority it pleased God to subject the lands of Banda and its islands." On Lonthoir as well, the relocated Runese people remained faithful to Islam. Both because of natural population growth and "the company of the 'papists' [i.e. imams], who are still among the Moors," the number of Muslims may even have increased.

Greatly disturbed by the continuation of Islamic practices, in 1625 the consistory asked the governor whether "the Moorish or Mahometan exercise, namely, the manner of marriage, and circumcision, with all the usual external superstition," could be prohibited. "In no Christian Republic can such a diminution of the glory of God be permitted or tolerated." The Calvinist preachers also proposed that observance of the Christian Sabbath be enforced. The government agreed to these proposals and appointed *marinjos*, or watchmen, who were paid by the Company. These *marinjos* supervised the baptism of newborn children and prevented Islamic gatherings or rituals. They also urged people to go to church and observe the Sabbath.

The Runese deported to Lonthoir were considered a particular problem. Reportedly, they had promised to send all their children to the school. However, a mission by church elders Joost Cornelisz. and Jan Michielsz. to the Runese in the "Moorish street" on Lonthoir was unsuccessful. The Runese denied they had made such a promise and argued that they had already sent some of their children to the school on Ai. Since Islam was now formally forbidden, the elders asked the Muslims: "How will you educate your children, without religion or any acquaintance with God? Do you want to let them live as unclean and unholy? Do you not know that God is greatly displeased by evil and ungodly people, and that on the day of judgement he will cast them into the abyss of hell?" But the Runese accepted the alternative of not following any religious ritual in public and firmly replied "that it was their destiny then, and that they were the devil's children and wanted to remain so."

The consistory of Batavia reported in 1644 to Amsterdam that the situation on Lonthoir was still the same and "that the devil caused the fragile Christianity there to decline, and that the Moors became bolder and braver every day." A few years later, the ministers on Banda sighed with relief: "As for Moordom, which no longer increases but decreases, we hope that the Lord God will remove it from our midst." Further research on Banda's annual population statistics should clarify just how large the Muslim group remained during the seventeenth and eighteenth centuries, and how they managed to live on the margins of colonial society.

Conclusions

The colonisation of former Portuguese territories in Amboina and the Lease islands, the emergence of small enclaves on Ternate (Malayu) and Bacan (Labuha), and the conquest of the Banda islands reveal different political situations and circumstances: a territorial takeover, a fortification by contract, and a violent conquest. The VOC's territorial expansion was followed by contracts with local rulers. These contracts included various religious articles, in particular relating to conversions. A political contract was a necessary precondition for the establishment of a school and church, two important means for the spread of Reformed Protestantism and the creation of Protestant communities. On the basis of the political contracts, one may conclude that the VOC officials followed in the Moluccas the same political pragmatism towards Islam as in Batavia.

The early seventeenth-century VOC governments tasked the first generation of Calvinist ministers in the Dutch East Indies with the organisation and regulation of a Christian society and, ultimately, the creation of a "Christian Republic." The ministers used the tools at their disposal: marriage laws, baptism, education, church attendance, and church discipline. All these means were modified so as to make them more efficacious in a colonial society based on forced or contracted labour. Under the direction of the consistory of Batavia, several strict local church ordinances were formulated and implemented by the newly established consistories.

In their writings, Dutch Reformed ministers demonstrated intolerant opinions towards native populations, whether pagan, Catholic, or Muslim. They advocated and defended an intolerant version of religious reform and conversion which quickly became part of an overall colonisation scheme in which western norms and values were propagated and imposed. The degree of intolerance was the highest in Banda, resulting in a permanent relationship between the Dutch and the Muslim Bandanese of mutual intolerance. Where the Muslim leadership on Ternate and Hitu initially showed more tolerance towards the Dutch for political reasons, the relationship between Protestant-ism and Islam in Banda was highly problematic from the start.[45]

Taken together, the different case studies analysed in this chapter show the links between political power and authority on the one hand and reli-gious (in)tolerance on the other. Whereas in some cases the balance of power forced the Dutch to accommodate religious differences, when their political dominance was on a surer footing, as it was on Banda, more intolerant poli-cies were rolled out. This was done under the pressure of Protestant minis-ters. In addition, then, to the religious outlook and convictions of Protestant ministers as well as government and Company officials, the political situa-tion on the ground significantly influenced both the policies espoused by the Dutch secular and ecclesiastical authorities and the interaction between the different religious groups that inhabited the Spice Islands.

Notes

1 Hubert Jacobs, ed., *Documenta Malucensia*, 3 vols. (Rome: Institutum Histori-cum Societatis Iesu, 1974–1984).

2 Gerrit Knaap, *Kruidnagelen en christenen: De VOC en de bevolking van Ambon 1656–1696*, 2nd ed. (Leiden: KITLV, 2004).

3 Hendrik E. Niemeijer, "Calvinisme en koloniale stadscultuur. Batavia 1619–1725" (PhD diss., Vrije Universiteit Amsterdam, 1996). Hendrik E. Niemeijer, *Batavia. Een koloniale samenleving in de zeventiende eeuw* (Amsterdam: Balans, 2005). About consistorial discipline in Batavia: Hendrik E. Niemeijer, "Consisto-ries," in *Judging Faith, Punishing Sin. Inquisitions and Consistories in the Early Modern World*, eds. Charles H. Parker and Gretchen Starr-LeBeau (Cambridge: Cambridge University Press, 2017), 279–92.

4 The inventory of the VOC archives in ANRI is published and accessible online: Frans van Dijk and Louisa Balk, et al, eds., *The Archives of the Dutch East India Company and the Local Institutions in Batavia* (Leiden: Brill, 2007), 531–45 (in-coming letters from Ambon en Banda on page 533). See for the introduction to this inventory by Hendrik E. Niemeijer, pp. 128–32. For the digital version, see www.sejarah-nusantara.anri.go.id/inventory/.

5 Hendrik E. Niemeijer and Thomas van den End, eds., *Bronnen betreffende Kerk en School in de gouvernementen Ambon, Ternate en Banda ten tijde van de Ver-enigde Oost-Indische Compagnie (VOC) 1605–1791*, 6 vols. (The Hague: Huy-gens ING (KNAW), 2015). Henceforth: *Bronnen*. Digitally available at: http://resources.huygens.knaw.nl/retroboeken/molukse_kerk/#page=0&accessor=toc&view=homePane [accessed June 7, 2022].

6 Mariëtte van Selm, ed., *De Protestantse kerk op de Banda-eilanden 1795–1923* (Zoetermeer: Boekencentrum, 2004).

7 Christiaan G.F. de Jong, ed., *De Protestantse Kerk in de Midden-Molukken 1803–1900. Een bronnenpublicatie*, vol. 1 (1803–1854); vol. 2 (1854–1900) (Leiden: KITLV, 2006).

8 Charles H. Parker, *Global Calvinism. Conversion and Commerce in the Dutch Empire, 1600–1800* (New Haven, CT: Yale University Press, 2022); G.J. Schutte, ed., *Het Indisch Sion. De Gereformeerde kerk onder de Verenigde Oost-Indische Compagnie* (Hilversum: Verloren, 2002).

9 Parker, *Global Calvinism*, Ch. 3, in particular 113–24.

10 François Valentijn, *Oud en Nieuw Oost-Indiën, vervattende een naaukeurige en uitvoerige verhandelinge van Nederlands Mogentheyd in die gewesten [...]*

(Dordrecht-Amsterdam: Joannes van Braam, Gerard Onder de Linden, 1724–26), five volumes in nine books. One of the rare modern studies is L. Andaya, *The World of Maluku. Eastern Indonesia in the Early Modern Period* (Honolulu: University of Hawaii Press, 1993).

11 Knaap, *Kruidnagelen en christenen*, 21.

12 Knaap, *Kruidnagelen en christenen*, 42–143.

13 Jan Ernst Heeres, *Corpus Diplomaticum Neerlando-Indicum* (The Hague: Martinus Nijhoff, 1907), vol. 1, 50–3.

14 Andaya, *The World of Maluku*, 153–4.

15 Or Dutch: "Mardijkers." Partly former slaves, partly born free Asiatic, or Indo-European settlers and small traders who were transported or came from other Portuguese colonies.

16 Hendrik E. Niemeijer, "Political Rivalry and Early Dutch Reformed Missions in Seventeenth-Century North Sulawesi (Celebes)," in *Missions and Missionaries*, eds. Pieter N. Holtrop and Hugh McLeod (Suffolk: The Boydell Press, 2000), 32–50. Id., "Agama Kumpeni? Ternate en de protestantisering van de Noord-Molukken en Noord-Sulwesi 1626–1795," in *Het Indisch Sion*, ed. G.J. Schutte, 147–75.

17 Van der Hagen's description of Amboina is published in: *Memories van overgave van gouverneurs van Ambon in de zeventiende en achttiende eeuw*, ed. G.J. Knaap (The Hague: Martinus Nijhoff, 1987) doc. II, 1–11.

18 Jurrien van Goor, *Jan Pieterszoon Coen 1587–1629. Koopman-koning in Azië* (Amsterdam: Boom, 2015), 435.

19 Martine Julia van Ittersum, "Debating Natural Law in the Banda Islands: A Case Study in Anglo-Dutch Imperial Competition in the East Indies, 1609–1621," *History of European Ideas* 42, no. 4 (2016), 459–501.

20 Van Ittersum, "Debating Natural Law," 466.

21 Van Goor, *Jan Pieterszoon Coen*, 433–67.

22 Van Ittersum, "Debating Natural Law in the Banda Islands."

23 Jan Ernst Heeres, *Corpus Diplomaticum Neerlando-Indicum*, 6 vols. (The Hague: Martinus Nijhoff, 1907–1955). Also published at https://sejarah-nusantara.anri.go.id/corpusdiplomaticum/

24 Heeres, *Corpus Diplomaticum*, vol. 1 (May 23, 1602), 23–5.

25 Heeres, *Corpus Diplomaticum*, vol. 1 (June 17, 1602), 25–6.

26 Ibid., 36–41.

27 Heeres, *Corpus Diplomaticum*, vol. 1 (May 3, 1616), 123.

28 Ibid., 163–6.

29 Ibid., 31–3.

30 Ibid., 58–61.

31 Ibid., 50–3.

32 Willem Frijhoff, "Religious Toleration in the United Provinces: From 'Case' to 'Model'," in *Calvinism and Religious Toleration in the Dutch Golden Age*, eds. R. Po-Chia Hsia and H.F.K. van Nierop (Cambridge: Cambridge University Press, 2009), 27–52.

33 Niemeijer and Van den End, *Bronnen*, vol. 1, part 1, 27 (doc. 10, C. Wiltens to Amsterdam [1616]).

34 *Bronnen*, vol. 1, part 1, doc. 11, 30 (Danckaerts to A. Hulsebos in Batavia, June 4, 1618).

35 Danckaerts's pamphlet is published in *Bronnen*, vol. 1, part 1, doc. 21, 49–66.

36 *Bronnen*, vol. 1, part 1, doc. 9, 18 (letter from Wiltens to the classis of Amsterdam, May 31, 1615).

37 See Note 14.

38 Knaap, *Kruidnagelen en Christenen*; Hendrik E. Niemeijer, "Orang Nasrani. Protestants Ambon in de zeventiende eeuw," in *Het Indisch Sion*, ed. G.J. Schutte, 127–47.
39 *Bronnen*, vol. 1, part 1, doc. 31, 83 (Article 20 of the consistory minutes, 1625).
40 David Day, *Conquest. How Societies Overwhelm Others* (Oxford: Oxford University Press, 2008), 69–83.
41 Valentijn also tells the story and defended Candidius. Valentijn, *Oud en Nieuw Oost-Indiën*, 1, *Uitvoerige beschryving der vijf Moluccos*, part 1, 387–9.
42 *Bronnen*, vol. 2, part 1, doc. 36, 89–92 (name list of the Christian congregation in Labuha on Bacan, prepared by lay pastor Harmen Jansz., July 20, 1635).
43 This paragraph is based on Hendrik E. Niemeijer, "Als een Lelye onder de doornen. Kerk, kolonisatie en christianisering op de Banda-eilanden, 1616–1635," *Documentatieblad voor de Geschiedenis van de Nederlandse Zending en Overzeese Kerken* 1, no. 1 (1994), 2–24.
44 A selection of documents is published in *Bronnen*, vol. 3, Banda, docs. 1–35.
45 See also Hendrik E. Niemeijer, "Dividing the Islands: The Dutch Spice Monopoly and Religious Change in 17th-Century Maluku," in *The Propagation of Islam in the Indonesian-Malay Archipelago*, ed. Alijah Gordon (Kuala Lumpur: Malaysian Sociological Research Institute, 2001), 251–83.

Part V

Sharing Space

Historiographic Introduction

On first consideration, it seems difficult to imagine that religious groups who reject and condemn each other's beliefs and practices could possibly worship in the same building or share the use of any site they both deem sacred. Yet instances of such sharing have long been known. In early modern Europe, the use of a single church by two or more Christian confessions was called "Simultaneum."[1] The churches so used were called in German, the language of the regions where most were located, "Simultankirchen." In the wake of the Protestant Reformation, Protestants and Catholics began to share the use of certain churches in Augsburg and several other cities of the Holy Roman Empire, while the practice became common in some religiously mixed parts of the Swiss Confederation, most notably Thurgau. In the seventeenth and eighteenth centuries, the arrangement proliferated in Alsace, the Electoral Palatinate, the Dutch-ruled Lands of Overmaas, and elsewhere. In some of these regions, Catholics and Protestants shared cemeteries and other resources as well as church buildings. Churches shared by two or more Protestant confessions existed at one time or another in Poland and Ireland, among other places, but paradoxically, since the groups were much closer to one another in doctrine and liturgy than were Catholics and Protestants, such churches were much rarer.[2]

Simultaneum began to attract the interest of scholars in the eighteenth century and continued to do so in the nineteenth and twentieth.[3] Generally, it was understood as a curiosity or aberration, the product of peculiar political and legal circumstances that overrode Christian norms. Louis XIV's demand, after his annexation of Alsace, that the Lutheran population there share the use of their churches with his Catholic co-religionists exemplifies the sort of political circumstance identified by scholars. The exercise of sovereignty jointly by Catholic and Reformed cantons over some of the Swiss Mandated Territories (an arrangement known as "condominium") exemplifies the sort of legal circumstance. Scholars conceived Simultaneum as a last resort, adopted reluctantly by secular rulers when circumstances made religious uniformity impossible. In this interpretation, Simultaneum was imposed "from above" by secular rulers upon unwilling Christian groups who were locked in conflict with one another.

DOI: 10.4324/9781003030522-16

In his contribution to this volume, David Luebke challenges this traditional interpretation. Using the cathedrals of Bautzen and Wetzlar as case studies, Luebke shows that Simultaneum was sometimes a product of cooperation as much as conflict, an expression of positive values such as "neighbourly goodwill" and "Christian neighbourly unity" that were shared by the inhabitants of these cities. Far from being imposed from above, the arrangement resulted from efforts on the local level through which parishes and civic communities sought to preserve their unity and peace. Luebke also shows how Simultaneum developed out of other arrangements by which Christians of different confessional inclinations accommodated one another. Over a period of decades, spatial arrangements within the cathedrals were negotiated and renegotiated; liturgical accommodations that made it possible for groups to worship together as a single congregation eventually gave way to a clearly demarcated partition of the cathedrals' interiors into separate Catholic and Protestant zones, "each with its own personnel, ritual objects, and hours reserved for public worship."[4]

In recent decades, new approaches to the study of religious toleration have generated renewed interest in the sharing of sacred spaces, both within Europe and outside it. Recognising that the peaceful coexistence of opposing religious groups is not as rare as once thought, historians and anthropologists have come to regard the sharing of sites less as an aberration than as one among a variety of arrangements that, at certain times and places, has helped to make such coexistence possible. With their new focus on the practice of toleration, scholars have turned their attention to how sharing worked in practice in daily life.[5] As exemplified in Luebke's chapter, some work that belongs to this new wave recognises the agency of non-elites as well as of rulers, tracing the interactions and dynamic negotiations that took place between a variety of parties, not least the rank-and-file members of opposing religious groups, in the course of sharing places of worship or other sites. Sharing a theme with earlier chapters in this volume, some of this new historiography has begun to consider the sensory dimensions of sharing sites; for example, what groups could see of each other's ritual accoutrements, and how they engaged with each other through the sounds they made.[6]

Scholars have also extended the subject of sharing space beyond places of worship to consider more widely the spatial configurations of religiously mixed communities. Where did religious groups encounter one another? What sorts of interactions did they have in different spaces? To what extent were religious boundaries articulated or reinforced through spatial ones? The sharing of sacred space has thus gained recognition as one of several ways toleration could be practised through the configuration of space. Other examples include drawing a distinction between public and private spaces, the relegation of minorities to peripheries, travel to attend services outside the boundaries of one's community ("Auslaufen"), and the invention of the ghetto.

In her chapter, Anat Vaturi examines the complex, changing religious topography of Cracow between mid-fifteenth and late sixteenth centuries.

Contrasting the spatial arrangements by which Protestants and Jews were accommodated in this officially Catholic city, Vaturi reminds us that sacred space could include private homes, communal facilities, and residential areas such as the "eruv" created by Jews for their sabbath. Vaturi's contrast between Protestants and Jews highlights the distinctiveness of strict residential segregation, reserved in the European context for Jews and Muslims.[7] Vaturi shows how relations between religious groups operated in more than one dimension, as it were, with different spatial configurations for religious, social, and economic relations. Her chapter ends by showing how Catholics eventually transformed the formerly contested space of the city into a "sacred topography" marked by Catholic symbols and rites. Such a transformation was a characteristic goal of Catholic reformers and missionaries in the early modern world.

Of course, scholars of religion have long had a powerful interest in space. Mircea Eliade, one of the most influential interpreters of religious experience, argued that all religions conceive of space in a similar way, as structured with openings, centres, thresholds, interconnected levels, and other recurring features that he found manifested in rituals, myths, and doctrines. As for Émile Durkheim before him, so for Eliade the distinction between sacred and secular, or "profane," space was fundamental. On a detailed, empirical level, though, recent historians have questioned whether the two are always sharply distinguished and separated.[8] Max Weber argued that the Protestant Reformation desacralised space as part of a wider "disenchantment" of the world. He had in mind phenomena such as Protestant iconoclasm, whose perpetrators repudiated the Catholic belief that divine and other supernatural forces were particularly present at certain sites. This interpretation of Protestantism has likewise been subjected to a great deal of revision.[9]

Recent decades have seen interest in space increase markedly across the humanities and social sciences generally. This heightened interest is sometimes referred to as the "spatial turn." Influenced by postmodernism, it brings with it a particular way of conceiving of space, not – or at least, not just – as a natural given or container within which history transpires. Instead, it regards space as a human construct that is produced by human activity, imagination, and representation and that in turn exercises agency of its own. Inspired by the work of geographers such as Henri Lefebvre, Doreen Massey, and Edward Soja, the spatial turn directs our attention to how people move through and use space; how they represent space, for example, in maps; and how the experience of space is shaped by the symbolic associations people attach to it.[10]

The chapter in this section by Susanne Lachenicht demonstrates how the spatial turn can deepen our understanding of relations between early modern religious groups. Lachenicht uses the term "transconfessional" for sacred spaces shared by different Christian confessions, and for the practices performed in those spaces by the members of those confessions together. Such spaces are constructed by clergy who moved between confessions and congregations to perform rituals and by lay people who attended services in different churches or joined more than one congregation. Lachenicht finds that the colonial context of British North America, with its shortage of personnel and infrastructure, led to the construction of many transconfessional spaces. Focusing on New York and South Carolina, she argues that the construction of these spaces in turn "aided the process of colonisation and empire-building." Lachenicht reminds us again that sharing sacred space was a more common phenomenon in the early modern world than once realised, that it took multiple forms, and that non-elites played important roles in the configuration of religious space.

Notes

1 In the early eighteenth century, jurists began to use the term "Simultaneum crudum" to distinguish this, the more common kind of Simultaneum from another in which religious groups used separate churches. See Helmut Neumaier, "Simultaneum und Religionsfrieden im Alten Reich: Zu Phänomenologie und Typologie eines umkämpften Rechtsinstituts," *Historisches Jahrbuch* 128 (2008), 137–76.
2 For overviews of locations where Simultaneum was practised, see Ute Lotz-Heumann et al., "Shared Churches in Early Modern Europe," https://shared-churches.arizona.edu/ [accessed July 27, 2022]; Benjamin J. Kaplan, *Divided by Faith: Religious Conflict and the Practice of Toleration in Early Modern Europe* (Cambridge, MA: Harvard University Press, 2007), 211–17; H. Henke, *Wohngemeinschaften unter deutschen Kirchendächern: die simultanen Kirchenverhältnisse in Deutschland—eine Bestandsaufnahme* (Leipzig: Engelsdorfer Verlag, 2008) surveys *Simultankirchen* in Germany that have survived to the present day.
3 Among the early treatments of the subject that are still useful are Burcard Gotthelf Struve, *Ausführlicher Bericht von der Pfältzischen Kirchen-Historie, in sich fassend die verschiedenen Religions-Veränderungen und den Kirchen-Staat in der Chur-Pfaltz [...] mit nöthigen Anmerckungen, [...] Documenten und publiquen Acten erläutert, etc.* (Frankfurt: J.B. Hartung, 1721); Conrad Straub, *Rechtsgeschichte der Evangelischen Kirchgemeinden der Landschaft Thurgau unter den eidgenössischen Landfrieden (1529–1792)* (Frauenfeld: Huber, 1902).
4 For similar changes over time in Westphalia, see David Martin Luebke, *Hometown Religion: Regimes of Coexistence in Early Modern Westphalia* (Charlottesville: University of Virginia Press, 2016), esp. Ch. 4. For the prevalence of liturgical accommodation in shared churches in Upper Lusatia, see Martin Christ, *Biographies of a Reformation: Religious Change and Confessional Coexistence in Upper Lusatia, 1520–1635* (Oxford: Oxford University Press, 2021).
5 Among anthropologists, see esp. Robert M. Hayden et al., *Antagonistic Tolerance: Competitive Sharing of Religious Sites and Spaces* (London: Routledge, 2016).
6 Martin Christ, "Sensing Multiconfessionality in Early Modern Germany," *German History* 20 (2022); Roísín Watson, "Decorating a Shared Church in Early Modern Württemberg," in *Sharing Sacred Space in Early Modern Europe*, ed. David M. Luebke, Marjorie Elizabeth Plummer, and Andrew Spicer (forthcoming).
7 Revisionist historiography, though, much of it focusing on Italy, where ghettos proliferated in the sixteenth century, has shown that residential segregation did not always lead to as much social segregation between Jews and Christians as was intended by authorities. See, e.g. Mark R. Cohen, ed., *The Autobiography of a Seventeenth-Century Venetian Rabbi: Leon Modena's Life of Judah* (Princeton: Princeton University Press, 1988); Robert Bonfil, *Jewish Life in Renaissance Italy* (Berkeley: University of California Press, 1994).

8 Mircea Eliade, *The Sacred and the Profane: The Nature of Religion*, trans. Willard R. Trask (New York: Harcourt Brace Jovanovich, 1957); Emile Durkheim, *The Elementary Forms of the Religious Life*, trans. Joseph Ward Swain (London: Collier Macmillan, 1915); critique in Will Coster and Andrew Spicer, *Sacred Space in Early Modern Europe* (Cambridge: Cambridge University Press, 2005).

9 Max Weber, *Economy and Society: An Outline of Interpretive Sociology*, trans. Guenther Roth and Claus Wittich, 2 vols. (Berkeley: University of California Press, 1978); critique i.a. by Robert W. Scribner, "The Reformation, Popular Magic, and the 'Disenchantment of the World'," *Journal of Interdisciplinary History* 23 (1993), 475–94; Alexandra Walsham, *The Reformation of the Landscape: Religion, Identity, & Memory in Early Modern Britain & Ireland* (Oxford: Oxford University Press, 2011).

10 Henri Lefebvre, *The Production of Space*, trans. Donald Nicholson-Smith (Oxford: Blackwell, 1991); Doreen Massey, *For Space* (London: Sage, 2005); Edward W. Soja, *Postmodern Geographies: The Reassertion of Space in Critical Social Theory* (London: Verso, 2010); for an overview, see Barney Warf and Santa Arias, eds., *The Spatial Turn: Interdisciplinary Perspectives* (London: Routledge, 2009).

11 A Middle Path to Toleration?
Sharing Sacred Spaces in Bautzen and Wetzlar, 1523–1625

David M. Luebke

On October 6, 1568, the mayor and council of Wetzlar, a medium-sized town in the hilly country north of Frankfurt, reached an agreement with the dean and chapter of the St. Mary's cathedral that divided its interior spaces into Catholic and Protestant spheres, each with its own clergy, rites, and liturgical equipment. The canons surrendered two chalices, for evangelical preachers (*Praedicanten*) to use in their administration of the Lord's Supper.[1] A little more than 30 years later, in 1599, a similar agreement was reached between the council and the cathedral chapter in Bautzen, the administrative seat of Upper Lusatia, an appendage of the Bohemian Crown. Like Wetzlar's treaty, it codified the subdivision of St. Peter's cathedral into clearly demarcated Catholic and Protestant zones, each with its own personnel, ritual objects, and hours reserved for public worship (Figure 11.1).[2] Both treaties proclaimed a common goal, "to plant and nurture Christian neighbourly unity," as Wetzlar's accord put it. To that end, Bautzen's agreement admonished clergy on both sides to "refrain entirely from all injury or slander toward any and all lawful religion," for the preservation of "peace, rest, [and] the unity of neighbourly goodwill." Finally, both treaties extended recognition and guarantees of security to both sides. Neither pact was the first attempt to regulate relations between Catholic and Protestant parishioners, and neither would be the last. But both achieved something new: a negotiated, formal, and full sorting of time, space, objects, and people between two confessions under one roof. Both agreements, in other words, codified *simultaneum* – the reciprocally guaranteed sharing of sacred spaces between peers.

The *simultanea* in both towns have survived to the present day and become a point of local pride. The citizens of Bautzen boast that theirs is "the oldest ecumenical congregation in Germany"; for the biconfessional clergy of Wetzlar, similarly, the *simultaneum* in St. Mary's cathedral symbolises a long "tradition of ecumenicism."[3] Such enthusiasms, however, while laudable, flatten a complex past as mere preambles to their modern, civic embrace of religious diversity. Historians, by contrast, cannot be accused of extolling *simultanea* as beacons of pluriconfessional conviviality in an age of dark intolerance. On the contrary, they have often judged *simultanea* harshly, as wellsprings not of peaceful coexistence but of acrimony and communal

DOI: 10.4324/9781003030522-17

Figure 11.1 The interior of St. Peter's Cathedral in Bautzen. Oil on copper, 58 × 51.5 cm. Museum Bautzen. Alamy image ID: MW9XJ3.

discord. One nineteenth-century Protestant historian sputtered that *simultanea* established in the Palatinate around 1700 were nothing less than "ecclesiastical terrorism" against his coreligionists.[4]

The judgements of more recent historians have been subtler and more generous, although a tendency persists to present *simultanea* as the products either of weakness or political equipoise, the sort of deal that could emerge only if no single confessional party were strong enough to overpower its competitors.[5] Bob Scribner, for example, suggested that ecclesial sharing arrangements could take shape either "as an interim strategy because the balance of contending groups allowed nothing else" or "by dint of too few resources to enforce wider conformity."[6] Much the same goes for religious toleration, a "loser's creed," as Andrew Pettegree quipped, demanded only by those in no position to grant it.[7] Certainly, this view is more amenable to the dominant early modern definition of *tolerantia* – the willingness of those in power to endure dissenters, whether as a political necessity or as the price of peace.[8] As Alexandra Walsham notes, such caution reflects an understandable scepticism towards triumphalist narratives that link "the Reformation with the rise of toleration." She warns, though, that our "postmodern disillusionment" may induce us to overlook the reasons why new attitudes towards religious plurality arose at all, let alone changed over time.[9]

There is another hazard. Embedded in that early modern definition of toleration is a conceit of sharp differences, self-evident hierarchies, and crystal-clear choices, as if the options had been obvious all along, as if every interaction were a struggle for supremacy in which victory were the only outcome that any party could actively desire. As I hope to show, the magistrates, clergy, and parishioners of both Wetzlar and Bautzen had more affirmative reasons than exhaustion or sullen resignation to accept the sharing of sacred spaces as a solution to the challenges posed to civic peace by the pluralisation of religion. Furthermore, disagreements over the Wittenberg reforms did not neatly pit cathedral clergy against magistrates and the laity. In neither town, finally, was there a single, discernible moment of decision, when the community chose between one or another alternative, between sharing on equal terms, say, or the active repression and the expulsion of dissenters.

The following chapter compares the experiences of both towns, showing how ecclesial sharing arrangements first emerged in the tumult of the 1520s and 1530s, then consolidated in both towns around appeals to good neighbourliness and civic unity. At first, both towns experimented with solutions that might properly be described as "middle-paths," in the sense that they were meant to accommodate a variety of liturgical demands, in part by blurring distinctions among them, in order to preserve the ritual unity of the parish. To that end, both towns recruited clergy who advocated explicitly the value of accommodation and of transcending differences that distracted the parish and its members from shared norms and beliefs. At issue during this intermediate phase was a question of hierarchy: whether and in what way the cathedral chapter would occupy a superordinate position towards the *Praedicanten* whom civic authorities engaged to serve the needs of evangelical parishioners, and how those relationships would play out in the arrangement of sacred spaces, times, and objects of devotion. Eventually, after many years of often-contentious negotiation, both towns veered off the middle path towards a regime based on sharper divisions of sacred space, time, and objects and founded on mutual guarantees of security between adherents of the two lawful confessions. But the ultimate goal remained the same: to secure Christian unity, civic concord, and "good neighbourliness." Neither the accommodation of difference nor *simultaneum*, in other words, were merely the least-worst option in an array of bad choices, but the product of an attenuated process, spanning many decades, in which the form and function of ecclesial sharing evolved in tandem with the very fissures that we too easily assume had been present all along.

Narrating origins

When Bautzeners claim that theirs is the oldest continuously operating *simultaneum* in Europe, they are usually referring to a decision in 1523 to appoint one Michael Arnold to preach in St. Peter's.[10] Not much is known about him. He had been a deacon in the Lusatian town of Görlitz but was expelled for his advocacy of the Wittenberg reforms. Once installed as preacher in

Bautzen, predictably, Arnold began "distributing the Holy Lord's Supper in both kinds" and, as one Catholic noted, preached "terrible things about monks, priests, and nuns."[11] According to historians who promoted 1523 as the inaugural year of Bautzen's *simultaneum*, Arnold's sermons made the interior of St. Peter's cathedral a blended space – still Catholic in obedience and liturgy, but with evangelical elements added in. Their story also pitted an evangelically inclined town council and laity squarely against a cathedral chapter that was determined to preserve the old ways.

But their narrative is marred by anachronism. For one thing, Arnold didn't last: his sermons proved to be so divisive that within a year of his appointment, the canons had restricted him to reading passages from scripture in front of the high altar, then dismissed him altogether in 1526.[12] More fundamentally, the idea that *simultaneum* commenced in Bautzen as early as 1523 elevates occurrences that were in fact widespread to high significance as the earliest plausible instance of relationships that in fact took much longer to form. This is to read history backwards, from outcomes to origins, heedless of context, as if the results had always been prefigured from some mythic beginning. If one were to list all the cities that in the 1520s responded to intramural pressures for church reform by hiring a pro-Wittenberg cleric to preach within an otherwise Roman Catholic liturgical setting, the result would be an illustrious catalogue of incipient *simultanea* that did not pan out in the long run. It would include such citadels of European Protestantism as Augsburg, Constance, Frankfurt, Hamburg, Nuremberg, Strasbourg, and Zurich.[13] Indeed, by this criterion, a hypothetical map showing cities that introduced *simultaneum* would have to include almost every city that introduced evangelical preaching during the 1520s and 1530s. The narrative of early origins, in other words, obscures as much as it reveals, imposing linear inevitability on developments that remained open-ended for years, even decades. In Bautzen, that process consumed nearly all of the sixteenth century.

We would do far better to abandon the assumption that confessional divisions hardened early or that the controversy over religion ruled out the accommodation of pluralising liturgical needs. Such an approach would make better sense of the earliest phases of reform in Wetzlar and Bautzen, as well as both towns' first experiments with sharing sacred objects and interior spaces. In neither town, for example, were cathedral clergy reflexively opposed to reforms that were consonant, at least, with the proposals emanating from Wittenberg. Some canons openly embraced Luther's theology, among them Petrus Laup, who in 1535 slandered Wetzlar's traditional Catholic parishioners as "evil papists" (*böse pfäffische*).[14] According to some accounts, the first person in Bautzen to preach "in a Lutheran manner" was not Michael Arnold but one Paul Cosel, a chaplain in St. Peter's.[15] By the mid-1520s, according to the eighteenth-century Catholic chronicler, Joseph Vitzk, "a majority of the [cathedral] clergy" had become "infected by the Lutheran heresy."[16] His characterisation smacks of anachronism and hyperbole, but other, more credible evidence suggests an early openness among the cathedral clergy to liturgical reforms that would accommodate the demands of evangelically inclined parishioners without breaking with Rome or rupturing the existing hierarchy of spiritual authority. According to a seventeenth-century Lutheran chronicler, the Dean of St. Peter's, Paul Küchler, delivered a sermon in 1524 or 1525 in which he argued that Bautzen's citizens should receive communion in both kinds, on the grounds that Upper Lusatia, as a dependency of the Bohemian crown, should enjoy the same concessions that had been granted to utraquist Hussites in the fifteenth century.[17]

Assuming the veracity of this account, Dean Küchler was not alone. Another member of Bautzen's cathedral clergy – Christoph von Haugwitz – published a tract that enjoined his fellow canons to devote themselves to serving the spiritual needs of their parishioners (Figure 11.2).[18] Haugwitz's publisher was none other than Nickel Schirlentz, a Wittenberg printer who, over the course of his career, produced no fewer than 143 of Luther's works.[19] The Wittenberg reformer Johannes Bugenhagen considered Haugwitz an ally and

Figure 11.2 The title page of Christoph von Haugwitz, *Woher Thumherrn Canonici heissen/unnd was ir und etlicher anderer jrer Thumpfaffen ursprüngliche Aempter/gewesen sind [...]* (Wittenberg: Nickel Schirlentz, 1536).

applauded his efforts "to ensure/that the beloved gospel be preached [...] in Bautzen/and that the holy sacraments/are given out according to Christ's command" – that is, in both kinds, bread and wine.[20] Haugwitz hoped that a "pious Emperor" would bring about a "strong Christian reformation" that would purge the church of "error and false doctrine," but his vision was fundamentally restorative: deans and canons should rededicate themselves to the spiritual care of parishioners and to the education of the young.[21] In sum, the canons of St. Peter's were not all averse to accommodations that would have yielded liturgical concessions to an increasingly evangelical citizenry, while preserving the basic structure of Catholic worship and hierarchy.

Much the same could be said of the governing councils in both towns. In their dealings with the cathedral chapter, Bautzen's magistrates presented themselves, increasingly, as the advocates of a presumptively evangelical lay population. Indeed, the weight of evidence suggests that by the 1530s, Bautzen's magistrates and lay population were more squarely in favour of the Wittenberg reforms than were the magistrates and burghers of Wetzlar. The chroniclers of sixteenth-century Bautzen recorded a series of attention-grabbing incidents in which layfolk tried to prevent canons from entering the church or subjected them to derision, even injury.[22] In 1525, for example, the evangelical parishioners of Bautzen removed Easter candles from St. Peter's, "as thick as a man and eleven cubits tall," then put the wax to better use.[23] Three years later, someone hurled a stone through a window of St. Peter's when Dean Küchler was about to perform a baptism, narrowly missing his head and puncturing the copper bowl in the baptismal font.[24] Then in August of 1528, Bautzen's evangelical parishioners drowned out the inaugural sermon of one Johannes Böhler, a Catholic preacher whom the chapter engaged to replace Michael Arnold, with singing the Lutheran hymn "God the Father, dwell with us."[25]

The magistrates' responses to these outbursts suggest that there was more to their stance than advocacy in the cause of evangelical reform. Rather than exploit such disruptions, Bautzen's magistrates tended to respond cautiously and for good reason: the volatility of religious differences posed real threats to the tranquillity of a town subject to a Catholic and (after 1526) Habsburg king. Like the ruling elites of most sixteenth-century towns, Bautzen's magistrates were caught between the demands of evangelically inclined layfolk, on the one hand, and on the other a well-connected cathedral chapter that, however amenable its members might have been to modest reforms, drew a line at fundamental challenges to its authority over St. Peter's. As the collective churchwarden for St. Peter's, moreover, the magistrates held a stake in that authority: the council was responsible for maintaining the cathedral, which it continued to do right through the turmoil of the early Reformation.[26] Indeed, Michael Arnold arrived in Bautzen in the midst of a major renovation project, begun in the 1490s and administered jointly by the council and cathedral chapter, that, among other things, gave St. Peter's a new roof and a steeple over its transept.[27] The council's interests in sustaining its cooperative relationship with the chapter were many and compelling – even in the face of impatience among the laity.

The religious alignments of Wetzlar's governing elite were, by comparison, far less clear.[28] As in Bautzen, however, institutional bonds between council and chapter favoured restraint. The two bodies had a long history of collaboration: since 1291, for example, they had shared equally in the choice of a parish priest for St. Mary's.[29] Familial ties between the council and the cathedral clergy were dense as well: prominent Wetzlar clans, such as the Scholer, Wacker, and Bicken families, strove to vest their sons with the cathedral's 22 vicarages and the incomes they generated.[30] For their part, almost all of St. Mary's ten canons lived in quasi-marital, concubinary unions, most likely with local women. One of them – the cathedral cantor Jakob Pistoris – married publicly in 1532 but retained his office, despite the statutory requirement that every cantor be a celibate priest.[31] Perhaps, the conflation of institutional and familial bonds blunted the edge of religious division. Be that as it may, the council's failure to take a firm and decisive stand on reform prompted one frustrated Protestant to demand in 1565 that the council finally "commit itself publicly to one of the two [religions], the Papist or the Evangelical, [...] and either to retain the Papist religion and Mass or defect (*abdretten*) to the Gospel (*Evangelio*) as it was proclaimed [...] in Augsburg."[32]

Whatever the explanation, the relations between council and chapter in both towns hovered between pressures for reform and long-standing cooperation, a field of tension that also shaped the early phases of ecclesial sharing. In both towns, for example, the decision to hire an evangelical preacher was arrived at jointly, between the two bodies. In Wetzlar, the first evangelical preacher, Konrad Diepel, was hired by joint agreement in 1532; he continued to preach in St. Mary's until the tumult over Petrus Laup's slanders prompted the chapter and council to join forces in expelling them both, in 1535.[33] In Bautzen, after a brief and abortive reaction against accommodation following Arnold's departure, the cathedral and council agreed in 1530 to hire a new preacher, Benedict Fischer, who would minister to the needs of evangelical parishioners.[34] The deal was likely brokered by the royal bailiff of Upper Lusatia, who provided political cover for the arrangement despite a royal prohibition against hiring evangelical preachers.[35]

The hiring of both Diepel and Fischer also initiated the first, tentative steps towards the differentiation of interior spaces. In Wetzlar, for example, Diepel preached in the Lutheran manner and administered the sacraments in both kinds, although it is not clear where in St. Mary's he performed the rite.[36] As we will see, communion in both kinds remained available in St. Mary's without interruption from 1535 on. In Bautzen, the continuous and regular celebration of "the holy most worthy Lord's Supper" – that is, communion in both kinds – likely dates to Fischer's inauguration in 1530.[37] The altar that Fischer and his successors used, however, was not located in the sanctuary, but at the eastern end of the southern side-aisle that had been added onto the nave of St. Peter's in the mid-fifteenth century.[38] From the 1530s on, in other words, the separation of Eucharistic celebrations underscored the sanctuary's character as a primarily Catholic space; the focus of evangelical observance lay *outside* the choir and *away from* the high altar at its head.[39]

Reasons to share

For people unaccustomed to the idea that *two* forms of Christianity could coexist under a single roof, these arrangements must have seemed awkward. Civic authorities in both towns were eager to contain their disruptive potential. Beginning in the 1540s, both towns negotiated agreements that regulated the character and use of sacred interiors and the objects inside them. Like the two treaties described at the head of this chapter, all of these agreements were couched in a normative language that stressed the precedence of values that sustained peace and unity, as well as norms of conduct such as "good neighbourliness" (*gute Nachbarschaft*) that preserved community against the injuries that slander and defamation could inflict. In 1556, for example, the authors of a deal that removed evangelical worship from the choir in St. Peter's described their agreement as one that promoted a "neighbourly, friendly, and Christian union" (*nachbarlicher freindtlicher undt Christlicher Vereinigung*).[40] Twenty years later, the council and the cathedral chapter in Bautzen pledged themselves to a formal procedure for resolving differences by "friendly and equitable agreement" (*freundliche nachbarliche vergleichung*).[41] This innovation elevated negotiation itself to a positive virtue that both chapter and council could invoke in self-defence, to charge foul against the other, and to justify their eventual agreements. As these adjectival strings also suggest, their culmination was unity – *Einigkeit* – as well as the suppression of all that negated it, especially slander and other verbal attacks across the religious divide.[42] Hence a paradox: the stated aim of regulating access to and use of sacred interiors and objects was not intended to terminate parochial unity but to *preserve* it, not to tear the community apart, but to *hold it together*.

It would be easy to dismiss such a language as little more than rhetorical damage control, meant to obscure the reality of division behind a fog of communalist jibber-jabber. But that judgement would repeat the local enthusiasts' error: to regard a certain outcome as predetermined, substituting a teleology of toleration with the inevitability of confessional strife. By ruling out the possibility of deliberate accommodation, moreover, it would also take sides in a complex debate that was ongoing in both towns, throughout the central decades of the sixteenth century, over the possibility and scope of religious toleration. Finally, it would reduce all discussions of religious difference to a binary confrontation between Protestants and Catholics.

In fact, both towns produced advocates of accommodation, churchmen who, for pragmatic and pastoral reasons, promoted liturgically inclusive solutions to the challenge of religious pluralisation. We have already met one of them: Paul Küchler, who served as dean of the cathedral in Bautzen, from 1524 until his death in 1546. Another was Johann Leisentrit, who

Non poſſumus quæ uidimus & audiuimus non
loqui. Aĉtorum. IIII.

Idcircò ab auditione mala non timebimus Pſal: CXL.

Figure 11.3 Portrait of Johannes Leisentrit (1527–1586), from his *Constitutio veteris, apostolicae et orthodoxae ecclesiae [...]* (Bautzen: Wolrab, 1572).

Courtesy of Bayerische Staatsbibliothek München, 4 J.can.p. 487, p. 4, urn:nbn:de:bvb:12-bsb10162511-0.

served in the same capacity from 1559 until his death in 1586 (Figure 11.3). Each in their way, both deans promoted liturgical accommodation. To be sure, Küchler renounced his flirtation with evangelical preaching not long after the expulsion of Michael Arnold in 1526.[43] And yet from 1530 until the end of his long tenure, Küchler cooperated with the town council to employ a series of evangelical chaplains, paid out of the cathedral's resources, and an evangelical *pedagogus* for the upbringing of evangelical children.[44] In 1542, he allowed the council to build a separate school for educating the children of evangelically inclined parents.[45]

Thanks to the work of Martin Christ, we are much better informed about the religious leanings and pragmatism of Johann Leisentrit.[46] Leisentrit never broke with Catholic doctrines of transubstantiation or concomitance – the idea of the whole and entire presence of Christ in each element of the communion rite.[47] As the dean of the cathedral, however, Leisentrit allowed baptisms to be performed in the vernacular; he permitted evangelically inclined parishioners to receive communion in both kinds; he incorporated Lutheran songs into a

252 David M. Luebke

Catholic hymnal for his diocese; and he allowed those who had received pastoral care from an evangelical minister to be buried in the Lutheran manner.[48]

These compromises reflected an acute understanding of local liturgical demands: by absorbing Lutheran ritualistic elements into an otherwise Catholic liturgical order, Leisentrit met his evangelically-inclined parishioners halfway while preserving the chapter's monopoly over initiations into the Christian community. Regarding communion, similarly, Leisentrit was at pains to underscore commonalities between Catholic and Lutheran doctrines of real presence, both to preserve Catholic observance in St. Peter's and to accommodate the demand for double communion among the evangelically-inclined parishioners.[49] Leisentrit thus managed to fuse doctrinal orthodoxy with a pragmatic syncretism, in a manner that would both preserve Catholic observance and accommodate demands for communion in both kinds. Like Küchler before him, Leisentrit's motive was to preserve the peace between Catholics and Lutherans, both in Bautzen and in Lusatia generally.

Even more than Küchler or Leisentrit, Gerhard Lorich epitomises the middle-path quest for accommodation and compromise. Hired in 1536 as the principal priest at St. Mary's in Wetzlar, Lorich was an enthusiastic advocate of the lay chalice.[50] In his inaugural sermon, he explained why both the bread and the wine should be distributed, in accordance with Christ's words of institution, to the laity as well as the clergy.[51] But Lorich was no champion of the Protestant cause. Despite some youthful enthusiasm for the Wittenberg reforms, Lorich had matured into a follower of Erasmus of Rotterdam and, like many other travellers on the middle path, he strove to cleanse Christian religion "of all old superstitions and abuses" while clinging to the sacrificial nature of communion and to the doctrines of transubstantiation and concomitance (Figure 11.4).[52] But he did not insist that parishioners share these doctrines, let alone pledge their adherence to them as a precondition for participating in the communion rite. Like Leisentrit, Lorich excluded only those who *denied* any concept of physical presence – a criterion for admission to the Eucharistic rite that any theologically aware follower of Luther's could meet.[53] All this, Lorich believed, was more consistent with the example of the early church than the positions taken by either the "Papists" or the "Evangelici."[54]

Lorich, in short, strove to accommodate the beliefs and liturgical tastes both of traditional Catholics and Luther's followers and to keep the peace between them by organising devotional life around moral upbringing and pastoral nurture towards redemption. This, presumably, had been the point of hiring him in the first place: to keep traditional Catholics and adherents of the Augsburg Confession together, in a single rite, under one roof. This, too, was consistent with Lorich's Eucharistic theology. The communion rite was, in his view, first and foremost a "sacrament of community (*eyn Sacrament der gemeynschafft*) given to all of us, so that all who eat the food and drink the fluid become one body with Jesus Christ," irrespective of wealth or estate, a "sign [...] of peace and unity whereby we are made one body with Christ our Lord."[55]

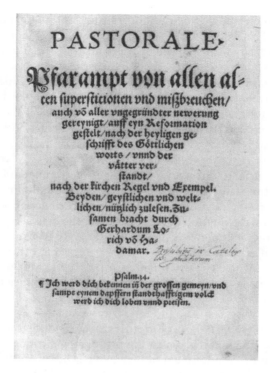

Figure 11.4 Title page of Gerhard Lorich (1485–1553), *Pastorale: Pfarampt von allen alten superstitionen und mißbreuchen/auch von aller ungegründter newerung gereynigt [...]* (Frankfurt: Egenolf, 1537).

Courtesy of Bayerische Staatsbibliothek München, 4 Polem. 3205#Beibd.7, cover, urn:nbn:de: bvb:12-bsb00024111-0.

Sharing, hierarchy, and toleration

All three churchmen – Küchler, Leisentritt, and Lorich – held in common a desire to accommodate the liturgical demands of their evangelically-inclined parishioners, as far as possible, within a Catholic framework, in the interest of preserving both the ritual unity of parish and the peace of the community. It was a tolerant stance, though not in the sense of an embrace of diversity as a positive moral value. Rather, middle-path solutions best fit the predominant early modern meaning, to indicate a lenient forbearance with otherwise objectionable beliefs or practices in the interest of promoting tranquillity and concord.[56] Such a position did not require the recognition of its object as valid or morally equivalent. On the contrary, for those in possession of legitimate authority, sixteenth-century *tolerantia* typically meant indulging beliefs they considered both dangerous and wrong.[57] In this sense, toleration was, as Alexandra Walsham aptly put it, a "charitable hatred" that served the common good.[58] There was no contradiction, in other words, between Johann Leisentrit's insistence that the Catholic doctrines of transubstantiation and concomitance were correct and his willingness to indulge the provision of communion in both kinds to evangelically inclined laity. It was something he was willing to allow in the interest of unity and peace, despite the risk of censure.[59] Hence also his insistence that communicants must not "disdain, still less slander or condemn" their fellow parishioners for receiving the Host in one kind or both.[60]

It is difficult to imagine how sharing regimes might have emerged organically in the absence of such forbearance. Unless Küchler and Leisentritt had allowed liturgical accommodations in the interest of peace, it is unlikely that any *simultaneum* could have taken shape without heavy external pressure. That said, it is crucial to distinguish between the accommodations that characterised this intermediate phase in both towns and the full-blown *simultaneum* that eventually resulted from it. Unlike mere accommodation, *simultaneum* was predicated on the division of spaces and objects between parties that were equal functionally, if not always *de jure*.[61] As Wendy Brown argues, the "posture of indulgence" embedded in premodern concepts of toleration cloaked a discourse of power. Toleration in this sense entailed magnanimous superordination, not parity; hierarchy, not equality.[62] The treaties that established *simultaneum*, by contrast, transformed liturgical accommodations into sequestrations of rites, objects, space, and time between effectively coequal peers.

This distinction shaped the evolution of sharing in both towns. At St. Peter's in Bautzen, the boundary between confessionally distinct spaces remained blurry long after the appointment of Benedict Fischer in 1530 and the concession of a side-aisle altar to the evangelically inclined. Until 1556, for example, evangelical ministers appear to have preached "in front of the [high] altar" (*vor dem Altar*), inside the sanctuary, and in full view of the entire congregation. According to an agreement drafted in that year, evangelical ministers would henceforth preach "from the pulpit" (*von dem predigtstuhl*), located in the nave.[63] As Martin Christ emphasises, it is not clear whether this agreement was ratified.[64] But a memorandum in the cathedral archive suggests that several of its provisions were put in place – including, most importantly, the division of sacred time and evangelical preaching from the pulpit.[65] And the construction of a latticework barrier (*Gitter*) between the choir and the nave in 1566 suggests that if nothing else, the 1556 deal hastened the process of spatial sequestration.[66] So too did the construction, in 1582, of a permanent pulpit in the increasingly Protestant nave.[67] These innovations lay the groundwork for a sequestration of sacred space along a demarcation line that ran between choir and nave – a pattern of subdivision that would eventually be replicated in hundreds of *simultanea* throughout the Empire.

That said, the relationship between cathedral clergy and evangelical ministers in Bautzen remained unequal and hierarchical. Benedict Fischer and the evangelical ministers who succeeded him in Bautzen remained subject to the cathedral chapter's moral discipline – including the requirement of celibacy, which in practice meant that marriage could trigger expulsion from office. Indeed, two of Fischer's successors – Johann Cellarius (1532–1538) and Georg Roschitz (1538–1540) – were dismissed soon after marrying local women, presumably because they no longer met the celibacy requirement. Another, Nikolaus Behem (1545–1579), likely owed his long tenure in office in part to the fact that he remained unmarried.[68] Politically, too, their positions remained precarious. In 1544, for example, evangelical preachers were expelled from Bautzen by a decree of the Holy Roman Emperor, Ferdinand – only to be readmitted a year later, with the chapter's connivance.[69]

Crucially, the cathedral chapter in Bautzen preserved its superordinate position by enforcing a monopoly over the administration of rites of passage – rituals that marked an individual's admission to the human community and transit through the stages of life. All marriages, for example, were officiated by Catholic clergy – until 1544, that is, when Protestant couples started celebrating their nuptials in the new, evangelical school.[70] Perhaps most important, the cathedral reserved the right to perform public baptisms in Bautzen "for the children of the entire citizenry and inhabitants [...] without distinction and in an orderly manner."[71] As long as the chapter was able to make good on that claim, Protestant parents would be obliged to present their infants for baptism before a Catholic priest, a gesture of recognition and ritual subordination that many evangelical parents experienced as an intolerable burden on conscience (*gewissens zwangk*).[72] Thanks to Leisentrit's liturgical adaptations, as Martin Christ has shown, that rite included many elements borrowed from Lutheran liturgy.[73] But many old-church elements remained, and for parents who wanted none of that there was little alternative but to baptise their infants secretly, in private dwellings. Prior to 1599, quite a few Protestant parents had done exactly that – much to the chagrin of cathedral canons, who considered each secret baptism that was performed "without [consecrated] baptismal water" to be a "violation of [their] lawful rights and privileges."[74]

In Bautzen, this was the nub of distinction between accommodation and *simultaneum*: as long as the cathedral clergy monopolised the rite of admission into the human community and the superordinate position it entailed, there could be no parity between the two groups, Catholics and the evangelically inclined. Here, too, lay the significance of that treaty, inked in 1599: in its aftermath, Catholics and Protestants would constitute distinct and roughly equal partners in the use of St. Peter's cathedral, each occupying its own sphere, each with its own clergy, rites, and sacred objects. On March 7, 1599, two unnamed girls, perhaps twins, were the first to receive baptism lawfully under the new regime.[75] Equality and parity had been achieved in word and deed.

The contrast between middle-path accommodation and full-blown *simultaneum* was even sharper at St. Mary's in Wetzlar. As long as Gerhard Lorich remained in charge of lay worship, there would be no differentiation of liturgies, still less a division of interior spaces into Catholic and Protestant spheres. On the contrary, the thrust of his pastoral theology was to smother such differences under a blanket of Erasmian accommodation and moral catechisation. Anyone could receive the Eucharistic elements in both kinds, if they so desired. As for preaching, Lorich offered a catechetical agenda organised around the concepts of sin, grace, and salvation that were at least compatible with Protestant teachings.[76] He would teach, for example, that "merit (*verdienst*) must be ascribed not to human powers, but to the true grace of God," which "Christ has won for us."[77] His sermons should emphasise the three virtues that weighed most in the judgement of God – faith, hope, and love – which, though distinct, must remain together "for the redemption of men" (*so sie den mentschen sollen selig machen*).[78]

Lorich's regime remained in place after his departure in 1540, albeit with the difference that Wetzlar's governing council soon began hiring openly evangelical *Praedicanten* to assist the Erasmian priests it recruited jointly with the cathedral chapter. The chapter accepted this innovation on the condition that the office of parish priest remained in the hands of "an upstanding priest of the old religion" – a condition that the chapter defined with enough elasticity to include Anthonius Wedensis, whom the chapter and the council hired jointly to replace Lorich. Wedensis, according to one account, was yet another Erasmian "hermaphrodite [*Zwitter*] who is neither Papist nor Evangelical."[79] Over the next 20 years, give or take, worship services in St. Mary's remained Catholic in their basic structure, with no clear differentiation of sacred spaces along confessional lines. Instead, the choir remained a zone for canonical hours, as it had always been, shut off from the rest of the church by an ornate, fourteenth-century rood screen. The nave remained an Erasmian domain, in which chalice-seekers of all confessional inclinations could find satisfaction, if they could endure the "papist" trappings.[80] Until the early 1560s, the cathedral clergy in Wetzlar, like their colleagues in Bautzen, also sustained a monopoly over the rites of passage, including baptism.[81]

In both towns, then, the fundamental line of confrontation was not simply between Catholic and Protestant, but between those who were content with accommodation and hierarchy as means to preserve parochial unity and those who wanted a sharper, more choreographed differentiation of objects, spaces, time, and people. In both towns also, the former yielded to the latter when evangelically inclined parishioners and their ministers laid claim to a portion of the church interior and control over the rites and ceremonies that would transpire within it. In both towns, these interventions by the laity provoked a change of course. In Wetzlar, the point of transformation arrived in 1565, when a Protestant minister named Johannes Hell launched a campaign to seize the nave of St. Mary's and to introduce a regime based on credal exclusion, in which parishioners would be entitled to partake in the rites of the Augsburg Confession only if they acknowledged that the Catholic sacraments "profaned, adulterated, and are opposed to the command and institution of Christ."[82] In contrast to the 1540s, the council now intervened decisively on the Protestants' side, seizing the nave of St. Mary's in April 1567 and establishing Johannes Hell as the principal pastor (*Pfarrherr*) in the now-uniformly evangelical portion of the church's interior, the nave. The agreement reached in 1568 codified this arrangement. More tumult lay ahead – in September 1571, for example, Protestants briefly occupied the entire church, driving the canons out.[83] But with intervention by the Archbishop of Trier, the status quo was soon restored; henceforth, Catholic observance was confined to the sanctuary, behind the old rood screen, and (with the archbishop's acquiescence) Protestants would have to make do with only the nave. Wetzlar's *simultaneum* would remain in place.

Conclusions

In a 1595 petition to the Bautzen city council, Protestant "citizens and artisans" invoked a long history of peaceful cohabitation with the cathedral chapter and adherents of the Roman creed. "Every time the exercise of the Augsburg Confession and its attendant ceremonies have come into the fray," they recalled, the chapter has transacted in such a manner that "both religions remain beside one another [...] without detriment, so that such unity is called upon as an example to others, not only by foreigners but by crowned heads [*hohe heupter*]."[84] Their aim in presenting the petition was to break the chapter's monopoly over the administration of baptism, and with the council's help, they won – against the wishes of the cathedral chapter. But what is most significant about their petition is that it deployed an ideal of unity, conjoined with peaceful coexistence between the confessions, as a rhetorical tool to secure parity with the chapter. It was effective not least because, by 1597, all parties could look back on six decades of peaceable negotiation towards the accommodation of religious difference. Unity could be achieved without uniformity, either of belief or worship.

Ultimately, both Bautzen and Wetzlar arrived at similar distributions of space, time, people, and objects in the name of preserving unity and civic concord. In both towns, the process of division was punctuated by moments of turmoil as well as long phases of tranquil collaboration. Despite their growing differences over doctrine and observance, canons and magistrates in both towns often collaborated in the quest for ministers and in the regulation of disputes between the emerging religious factions. Both towns experimented with middle-path solutions that were structured to accommodate difference while preserving the nominally Catholic status of both cathedrals. In time, the negotiation itself was elevated to a normative good. In the name of good neighbourliness and Christian unity, finally, both towns eventually found a path to secure peaceful coexistence between the confessions on a basis of sequestration, mutual recognition, and parity.

None of these solutions were especially tolerant by modern standards – if by that we mean a regime of coexistence predicated on the embrace of religious diversity as a positive good. Neither did they conform precisely to a negative definition of toleration as principled non-interference between religious groups: in crucial respects, after all, both Catholics and the evangelically inclined remained members of a *single* religious community.[85] During their middle-path phases, especially, the lynchpin of coexistence in both towns was the preservation of a hierarchy that both obscured difference and indulged unwanted irritants. In that sense, their middle-path phases more strongly resembled the early modern understanding of *tolerantia* as the endurance of pain for some higher good. Symbolically, the evangelically inclined parishioners of both towns recognised the chapter's superordinate position, whether by presenting their infant offspring for baptism in the Catholic rite or by receiving communion in both kinds from a Catholic priest. The sharing arrangements that emerged *after* the middle-path phase kept the ends but changed the means: as before, "Christian unity" and "good neighbourliness" remained the lodestar of negotiation. But the means to achieve those ends had changed: now less dependent on the preservation of hierarchy, the regimes in both towns now involved a parity aimed at concord, even in the face of demographic imbalances between the two sides.

It is difficult to imagine how any of these relationships could have arisen, let alone endured, without the pragmatic, everyday tolerance towards religious differences that enabled people in both towns to get along peaceably in everyday life.[86] The "ecumenicity of everyday life," as Willem Frijhoff called it, surely blunted the edge of antagonisms that might otherwise have ruptured "good neighbourliness" and "Christian unity."[87] By the same token, however, it would also be misleading to portray coexistence and antagonism as if they excluded one another. The formation of *simultaneum* in both towns, after all, reflected the gradual consolidation of boundaries between religious groups sharing a common space. As the identities underlying those boundaries evolved, so too did the duality, the "two-ness" of their relations become more pronounced. Indeed, one could argue that ultimately, any durable *simultaneum* needed clear distinctions; inclusion, after all, presupposes difference. In both towns, maintaining unity and concord against the threat of violence inspired by religion involved constant negotiation, contestation, and compromise.[88] In Bautzen and Wetzlar, more often than not, antagonism promoted coexistence.

In that sense, both towns contained in microcosm the solutions towards which the Empire as a whole had been struggling since the late 1520s, a process that would culminate in the peace settlements reached at Augsburg in 1555 and at Münster and Osnabrück in 1648: the coexistence, first of two, then three lawful forms of Christian observance, founded on reciprocal obligation and regulated through permanent negotiation. They also anticipated the sharing arrangements that would proliferate throughout the Empire, especially after 1648: the regulated subdivision of sacred spaces between two or more lawful forms of public Christian observance. In a word: *simultaneum*.

Notes

1 "Copia Vertrags zwischen Bürgermeister und Rath der Stadt Wetzflar an einem / und Dechant samt Capitul des Stiffts daselbst / vor Fürstl. Heßischen Statthalter und Räthen zu Marburg geschehen / Anno 1568," in Georg Melchior Ludolf, *Historische Nachricht Alter und neuer Sachen von des Heiligen Römischen Reichs Stadt Wetzflar, wie auch dem nahe beygelegenen Adelichen Jungfrauen Closter Altenburg, Praemonstratenser Ordens [...]* (Wetzlar: Nicolaus Ludwig Winckler, 1732), no. VII, 106–9.

2 Diözesanarchiv des Bistums Dresden-Meißen / Domstiftsarchiv Bautzen (hereafter cited as DAB) A1 0028, ff. 155ʳ-158ᵛ, "Compactata zwischen V.C.B. und dem Rath zu Budißin," March 6, 1599; Stadtarchiv Görlitz [hereafter StAG] XIVa N5, vol. 1 [n.p.]; and XIVa NS vol. 2, 23ʳ-33ʳ, "Tauff Recess zu Budeßin 1599"; and Stadtarchiv Bautzen [hereafter StAB] 68002 Handschriftensammlung U III, nr. 188, 1–3, *Budissinische Chronologium* (also known as the "Klahre-Wahren-Chronik; hereafter as KWC) 3: 39ʳ-42ᵛ. I am grateful to Martin Christ for making copies housed in the Stadtarchiv Görlitz available to me.

3 Karin Wollschläger, "Sachsen startet Reformationsgedenken in Simultankirche: Älteste ökumenische 'Kirchen-WG' bundesweit," *Domradio.de*, 4 January 2017; Michael Hollenbach, "Eine Kirche, zwei Altäre, drei Stromrechnungen," *Deutschlandfunk*, January 11, 2016.

4 Ludwig Häusser, *Geschichte der rheinischen Pfalz nach ihren politischen, kirchlichen, und literarischen Verhältnissen*, 2 vols. (Heidelberg: Mohr, 1845–1856), 2: 711.

5 For one example among many, see Norbert Kersken, "Konfessionelle Behauptung und Koexistenz: Simultankirchen im 16. Jahrhundert," in *Konfessionelle Pluralität als Herausforderung: Koexistenz und Konflikt im Spätmittelalter und Früher Neuzeit*, eds. Joachim Bahlcke et al. (Leipzig: Universitätsverlag, 2006), 287–302.

6 Bob Scribner, "Preconditions of Tolerance and Intolerance in Sixteenth-Century Germany," in *Tolerance and Intolerance in the European Reformation*, eds. Ole Peter Grell and Bob Scribner (Cambridge: Cambridge University Press, 1996), 32–47, here 36, 37.

7 Andrew Pettegree, "The Politics of Toleration in the Free Netherlands, 1572–1620," in *Tolerance and Intolerance*, eds. Grell and Scribner, 182–98, here 198.

8 Wendy Brown, *Regulating Aversion: Tolerance in the Age of Identity and Empire* (Princeton: Princeton University Press, 2006), 2–47. The most thorough analysis of early modern definitions of *tolerantia* remains Klaus Schreiner, "Toleranz," in *Geschichtliche Grundbegriffe: Historisches Lexikon zur politisch-sozialen Sprache in Deutschland*, eds. Reinhart Koselleck et al., rev. ed. (Stuttgart: Klett-Cotta, 2004), 445–605.

9 Alexandra Walsham, "Toleration, Pluralism, and Coexistence: The Ambivalent Legacies of the Reformation," *Archive of Reformation History / Archiv für Reformationsgeschichte* 108 (2017), 181–190; here 182–3.

10 The first to make this claim was Richard Võtig, *Die simultankirchlichen Beziehungen zwischen Katholiken und Protestanten zu St. Peter in Bautzen* (Leipzig: Noske, 1911).

11 The authoritative account of Arnold is Martin Christ, "Biographies of a Reformation: Religious Change and Confessional Coexistence in Upper Lusatia, c. 1520–1635" (PhD diss., Oxford University, 2017), 57–84. The characterisation of his preaching comes from StAB 68002 Handschriftensammlung U III, nr. 200/3, Christian Gottlieb Platz, *Lusatica specialiter, seu annuatim uit in manus pervenerunt collecta* (1694) [hereafter cited as *Lusatica*], 4: 508–9, entry for 1525; and from DAB A1 0145, "Versuch einer Stiftschronik" [1763], Heft 4, n.p. On Arnold's sacramental practice, see Hermann Kinne, *Das Kollegiatsstift St. Petri von der Gründung bis 1569* (Berlin: De Gruyter, 2014), 115 and Wilhelm Tischer, "Die Reformation in Bautzen," in *Die Einführung der Reformation in der sächsischen Oberlausitz nach Diözesen dargestellet*, ed. Hugo Friedrich Rosenkranz (Leipzig: Strauch, 1917), 28–62, here 37.

12 *Lusatica* 4: 508. See also Christ, "Biographies," 57–8.

13 From the voluminous literature on urban reformations, see Bernd Hamm, *Bürgertum und Glaube: Konturen der städtischen Reformation* (Göttingen: Vandenhoeck & Ruprecht, 1996), 77–103; Thomas A. Brady, Jr., *German Histories in the Age of Reformation, 1400–1650* (Cambridge: Cambridge University Press,

2009), 166–83. See also Euan Cameron's comparative overview of urban reformations in *The European Reformation* (Oxford: Clarendon, 1991), 213–63.

14 This emerges from an oath that Laup was obliged to give in a settlement that resolved the dispute, to refrain from seeking revenge against his attackers; Franz Schulten, *Das Wetzlarer Marienstift im 16. Jahrhundert: Versuch einer Zusammenfassung der Urkunden und Akten aus dem Archiv des ehemaligen Marienstifts zu Wetzlar und sonstiger Quellen* (Wetzlar: Stadt Wetzlar, 1991), 111–2.

15 On Cosel's preaching, see DAB A1 0146, Heft 4 [n.p.], entry for 1526.

16 Matthäus Joseph Vitzk, "Chronicon venerandi capituli et collegiatae ecclesiae Budissinensis auctore Matth. Jos. Vitzk Decano nec non Administratore Ecclesiastico utramque per Lusaticam [c. 1712]," *Neues Laustzisches Magazin* 33 (1857), 186–231 [hereafter Chronicon Vitzk], 203.

17 DAB A1 0146, Heft 4 [n.p.], entry for 1526: "Paulus Küchler...[sagte] in einer gehaltenen predigt: es könnt denen leyen hier auch vermöge des Baßler Consilii den Lausitzern gestattet werden unter beyder gestalt die Communion geniessen, wie es denen Böhmen gestellet worden." On Küchler, see Kinne, *Kollegiatstift*, 115–8, 834–6; and a biographical sketch inserted between the entries for 1559 and 1560 in DAB A1 0416, Heft 4 [n.p.].

18 Christoph von Haugwitz, *Woher Thumherrn Canonici heissen / unnd was ir und etlicher anderer jrer Thumpfaffen ursprüngliche Aempter / gewesen sind [...]* (Wittenberg: Nickel Schirlentz, 1536). On Haugwitz, see Kinne, *Kollegiatstift*, 991–2 and Kai Wenzel et al., *Der Dom St. Petri zu Bautzen* (Bautzen: Lusatia Verlag, 2016), 91.

19 Andrew Pettegree, *Brand Luther: 1517, Printing, and the Making of the Reformation* (New York: Penguin, 2015), 270–1.

20 See Bugenhagen's preface to Haugwitz, *Woher Thumherrn Canonici heissen*, Aii^r.

21 Haugwitz, *Woher Thumherren Canonici heissen*, Div^r.

22 *Lusatica* 4: 576–7, entry for 1528.

23 KWC 2: 539, entry for 1525.

24 KWC 2: 556.

25 Johannes Böhler delivered his inaugural sermon on August 1, 1528 and departed during Advent of the same year; *Lusatica* 4: 577; KWC 1: 180–1.

26 Since 1388, Bautzen's city council had elected a board of church elders (*vitrici ecclesiae*) who were responsible for the physical upkeep of St. Peter's; see Kinne, *Kollegiatstift*, 445–8.

27 KWC 2: 309, 311, 548–9. On the renovation project, see Wenzel et al., *Der Dom St. Petri zu Bautzen*, 51–90.

28 Schulten, *Wetzlarer Marienstift*, 95–106.

29 "Copia des alten Compromiss-Spruchs zwischen dem Stift B.M.V. und Innwohnern zu Wetzflar über verschiedene Kirchen-Sachen Anno 1291," in Ludolf, *Historische Nachricht*, 263–6.

30 Schulten, *Wetzlarer Marienstift*, 28–30, 38–42.

31 Schulten, *Wetzlarer Marienstift*, 36–8.

32 Franz Schulten, "Anthonius Wedensis und Gerhard Lorich-Hadamar: Zwei Gestalten der Wetzlarer Reformationsgeschichte," *Mitteilungen des Wetzlarer Geschichtsvereins* 32 (1987), 43–53, here 51.

33 Konrad Diepel's presence in Wetzlar is attested already in February 1533; Franz Schulten, "'...zwo religionen beyeinander unter eynem dach...': Die Geschichte der simultanen Nutzung des Wetzlarer Domes nach Akten des ehemaligen Marienstifts," *Mitteilungen des Wetzlarer Geschichtsvereins* 42 (2004), 85–142, 97; Id., *Wetzlarer Marienstift*, 75; Id., "Anthonius Wedensis," 47.

34 *Lusatica* 4: 551; KWC 1: 179–85. Fischer's inaugural sermon took place on February 27, 1530 – Estomihi Sunday.

35 Vötig, *Die simultankirchlichen Verhältnisse*, 8. For the royal bailiff's role, see DAB A1 0146, Heft 4 [n.p.], entry for 1530.

36 This according to an attempt to mediate conflicts between Diepel, on one side, and the council and chapter on the other in January 1535; reprinted in Schulten, *Marienstift*, 77–8.

37 DAB A1 0028, 52ʳ-61ᵛ, "Gemeine Bürgerschaft und Handwerker zu Budissin an E[inen] E[hrbaren] Rath daselbst, die Taufe durch ihre Geistlichen betr[effend]," August 22, 1597. See also StAG XIVa NS, vol. II, 15ʳ-22ᵛ, "Orgel vertrag zwischen einem Ehrw: Dom Capitulo St. Petri zu Budißin undt E[inem] E[hrbaren] Rathe daselbst," May 17, 1583, §1.

38 Wenzel et al., *Der Dom St. Petri zu Bautzen*, 53–9.

39 DAB A1 0027, 1ʳ-2ᵛ, "Memoriale unter welcher Bedingunge VCB d. Rath d. Alten BVM in der Thumbkirche cediren wolle" [undated].

40 StAG Rep. I, 756, vol. 2, 2ʳ-8ʳ, October 2, 1556.

41 DAB A1 3525, n.p. "Vierfache Copey eines Vereins zwischen dem Domcapitt. u dem Rathe die enstnandenen Irrugne güttlich beizulegen, d. Budiß. d. April 14, 1575.

42 DAB A1 3235, "Einig[e] E. Capitels grauamina" [c. 1555].

43 Kinne, *Kollegiatstift*, 834.

44 DAB A1 3525, n.p. "Einig. E. Capitels grauamina wieder ein E. Rat zu Budissin" [c. 1555]; Vötig, *Simultankirchliche Beziehungen*, 4, 13. On the *pedagogus*, see *Lusatica* 4: 528, entry for 1526.

45 Construction was completed in 1544. See *Lusatica* 4: 1052, 1100; KWC 2: 567–8, 574–5; and Chronicon Vitzk 203.

46 Martin Christ, *Biographies of Reformation: Religious Change and Confessional Coexistence in Upper Lusatia (1520-1635)* (Oxford: Oxford University Press, 2021), 115–52; Id., "Catholic Cultures of Lutheranism? Confessional Ambiguity and Syncretism in Sixteenth-Century Upper Lusatia," in *Cultures of Lutheranism: Reformation Repertoires in Early Modern Germany*, ed. Kat Hill (Oxford: Oxford University Press, 2017), 166–88.

47 Johann Leisentrit, *Catholisch Pfarbuch Oder Form und Weise, wie die Catholischen Seelsorger in Ober und Niederlausitz [...] jhre Krancken eingefarten ohne vnterscheidt besuechen [...] sollen mit Nachfolung einer Catholischen Protestantion wider alle Ketzereyen unnd angehafftem außführlichem Bericht, wo die ware Catholische Christliche Kyrche [...] anzutreffen, zu glauben und zu halten* (Cologne: Maternus Cholinus, 1578), 65–102.

48 Christ, *Biographies*, 118–20, 125–37.

49 Christ, *Biographies*, 120–5.

50 For the best biographical sketch of Lorich, see Michael Kunzler, *Die Eucharistietheologie des Hadamarer Pfarrers und Humanisten Gerhard Lorich: Eine Untersuchung der Frage nach einer erasmischen Meß- und Eucharistietheologie im Deutschland des 16. Jahrhunderts* (Münster: Aschendorff, 1981), 57–68.

51 Gerhard Lorich, *Von der euangelischen Vollkommenheit und was ursach, meynung und weise, das Heilig Sacrament des Fronleichnams Christi, in beider Gestalt, nach der Heiligen Kirchen Regel und Exempel [...]* (Frankfurt: Egenolff, 1536).

52 On Lorich's pastorate in Hadamar, see Walter Michel, "Gerhard Lorich und seine Theologie: Ein Beitrag zur Reformationsgeschichte im Lahrgebiet," *Nassauische Annalen* 81 (1970), 160–72, here 161.

53 Kunzler, *Eucharistietheologie*, 160–83.

54 Lorich uses both descriptors in his *Pastorale: Pfarampt von allen alten superstitionen und mißbreuchen / auch von aller ungegründter newerung gereynigt / auff eyn Reformation gestalt / nach der heyligen geschrifft des Göttlichen worts / unnd

der vätter verstand (Frankfurt: n.p., 1537), iii^r. See also Kunzler, Eucharistietheologie, 110–3.

55 Lorich, Pastorale, liiir^{r-v}. See also Lorich, Vollkommenheit, [10].

56 Schreiner, "Toleranz," 472–94.

57 To paraphrase Jesse Spohnholz, The Tactics of Toleration: A Refugee Community in the Age of Religious Wars (Newark: University of Delaware Press, 2011), 13.

58 Alexandra Walsham, Charitable Hatred: Tolerance and Intolerance in England, 1500–1700 (Manchester: Manchester University Press, 2006).

59 Those risks were considerable; see Christ, Biographies, 148–51.

60 Leisentrit, Catholisch Pfarbuch, 75.

61 The cathedral chapter continued to claim ownership of the entire church against the magistrates' claims in the late seventeenth century to own the nave; see Matthias Göbeln, "Deductio brevis, daß der Evangelische Theil der Kirchen S. Petri zu Budißin nicht dem Capitulo, sondern dem Rathe und der Bürgerschafft daselbst eigenthümlich zuständig [...]," Singularia historico-literaria lusatica 12 (1736), 765–91.

62 Brown, Regulating Aversion, 25–7.

63 StAG Rep. I, 756, vol. 2, 2^r-8^r, October 2, 1556.

64 Christ, Biographies, 197.

65 DAB A1 0027, 21^r-22^v, "Artigkel welcher ein Erbar Rath zu Budißin zu erlangung des begereten Chores Schrifftlich vol ziehen solle, solche für sich unnd ihre nach kommende künfftiger Zeit [...] zu halten" [1556].

66 Chronicon Vitzk, 207.

67 Friedrich Hermann Baumgärtel, Die kirchlichen Zustände Bautzens im 16. und 17. Jahrhundert (Bautzen: E.M. Monse, 1889), 35 and Cornelius Gurlitt, Bautzen (Stadt) [Beschreibende Darstellungen der älteren Bau- und Kunstdenkmäler des Königreichs Sachsen, vol. 33] (Dresden: Meinhold, 1909), 18.

68 Karl Gottlieb Dietmann, Die gesamte der ungeänderten Augsb. Confession zugethane Priesterschaft in dem Marggrafthum Oberlausitz (Lauban: Johann Christoph Wirthgens, 1897), 1: 25–9; Baumgärtel, Die kirchlichen Zustände, 17–8.

69 Vötig, Die simultankirchlichen Verhältnisse, 18.

70 DAB A1 0027, 21^r-22^v, "Artigkel welcher ein Erbar Rath zu Budißin [...] zu halten" [1556], § 5. On the construction of a separate school for evangelical children, see Lusatica 4: 1052, 1100; KWC 2: 567–8, 574–5; and Chronicon Vitzk, 203.

71 DAB A1 0028, 23^r-24^v, "V.C.B. Gravamina an den Kaiser," November 8, 1595.

72 DAB A1 0028, 52^r-61^v, "Gemeine Bürgerschaft und Handwerker zu Budissin an E.E. Rath daselbst, die Taufe durch ihre Geistlichen betr[effend]," August 22, 1597.

73 Christ, Biographies, 119.

74 For an enumeration of the clergy's objections, see DAB A1 3525, "Einig E. Capitels grauamina wieder einen erbarn Rath der Stadt Budissin" [c. 1555].

75 KWC 3: 32^v.

76 Lorich, Pastorale, C ii^r-[Civ^r].

77 Lorich, Pastorale, C ii^r.

78 Lorich, Pastorale, C ii^r.

79 Schulten, "Anthonius Wedensis," 45; Id., "zwo religionen beyeinander," 49. The first two clergy to serve as evangelical predicant were Johann Thoen (1543–1549) and Johann Diemar (1543–1554), both adherents of the Augsburg Confession.

80 Schulten, "zwo religionen beyeinander," 98.

81 This emerges from a judgement by the theology faculty at the newly founded university in Marburg on whether it is permissible for Catholics to stand as godparents at baptisms performed in a Lutheran manner; see "Die Theologen zu Marburg an die Geistlichkeit zu Wetzlar [1564]," in Heinrich Leuchter, Antiqua Hessorum fides Christiana et vera Das ist: bericht vom alten und wahren Christlichen Glauben oder Religion der Hessen (Darmstadt: Balthasar Hofmann, 1607), 181–2.

82 "Die Theologen zu Marburg an die Geistlichkeit zu Wetzlar [1564]," in Leuchter, *Antiqua Hessorum fides Christiana*, 181–2.

83 Schulten, "zwo religionen beyeinander," 103.

84 DAB A1 0028, 52ʳ-61ᵛ, "Gemeine Bürgerschaft und Handwerker zu Budissin an E.E. Rath daselbst, die Taufe durch die ihre Geistlichen betr.," August 22, 1597.

85 For the negative definition of toleration as "non-interference," see Michael Walzer, *On Toleration* (New Haven, CT: Yale University Press, 1997), 2.

86 See Benjamin J. Kaplan, *Divided by Faith: Religious Conflict and the Practice of Toleration in Early Modern Europe* (Cambridge, MA: Harvard University Press, 2007), 10–1; Scribner, "Preconditions," 38.

87 Willem Frijhoff, "The Threshold of Toleration: Interconfessional Conviviality in Holland during the Early Modern Period," in his *Embodied Belief: Ten Essays on Religious Culture in Dutch History* (Hilversum: Verloren, 2002), 39–66.

88 Robert M. Hayden's concepts of "antagonistic tolerance" and "competitive sharing" capture this distinction well; see his "Antagonistic Tolerance: Competitive Sharing of Religious Sites in South Asia and the Balkans," *Current Anthropology* 43 (2002), 205–31 and Id. et al., *Antagonistic Tolerance: Competitive Sharing of Religious Sites and Spaces* (London: Routledge, 2016), 1–24.

12 From Contested Space to Sacred Topography

Jews, Protestants, and Catholics in Reformation Cracow

Anat Vaturi

Throughout the sixteenth and into the start of the seventeenth century, a time when England was satirically considered a "Hell of Horses [...] and the Paradice of Weomen,"[1] Poland was described as a paradise for Jews (*paradisus Judaeorum*) and refuge for heretics (*asylum haereticorum*).[2] Indeed, in a Europe fraught with religious wars, Poland – in its "golden and silver age"[3] – accommodated a multicultural, multiethnic, and multireligious mosaic that attracted members of persecuted denominations from outside the country and empowered the development of local religious groups.[4] The unification with Lithuania (1569) and the resulting territorial expansion from the Baltic Sea almost all the way up to the Black Sea coincided with economic prosperity as Poland became the "wheat barn of Europe" and experienced a cultural and intellectual boom. Concurrently, the aristocracy's increased power in relation to the church and monarchy led to the emergence of a "democracy of nobles," able to legislate limited religious pluralism. All these factors, along with a pronounced fear of religious war, resulted in the coexistence of Catholics, Orthodox Christians, Armenians, Muslims, Jews, and Protestants of different denominations in sixteenth-century Poland, with minimal religious coercion from the state.[5] This situation encouraged the development of everyday practical toleration among neighbours of different religions or confessions and facilitated the development of a number of arrangements that allowed different ethnic or religious groups to share urban spaces. The shared churches of Catholics and Protestants, or of Lutherans and Calvinists, mosques in the outskirts of Vilna, multiple Jewish communities, and a multidimensional coexistence between the followers of various confessions were a source of Polish pride at the time and attracted the attention of foreign travellers and emissaries, such as the papal nuncio Niccolo Stoppio, who was astounded by the power of Protestants during his visit of Cracow in 1564:

> So powerful are the heretics, that they dare take arms and wreak havoc on the royal city.[6]

What puzzled Stoppio was not the sheer existence of Protestants in Cracow, which at that time was the most ethnically diverse metropolis in Poland, with

DOI: 10.4324/9781003030522-18

a large immigrant population.[7] Rather, the papal nuncio was astounded by Protestants' status and their ability to publicly express religious diversity and exercise power in a city known for its Catholic religiosity. This chapter seeks to shed some light on the character of the religious diversity that surprised the papal legate. Concentrating on the Jewish and Evangelical communities,[8] it traces the dynamics of interreligious coexistence and discusses the local arrangements that helped establish and constantly redefined the experience of a shared city centre in the period immediately prior to the triumph of the Catholic confessionalisation in the second half of the seventeenth century.[9]

The Jewish challenge

Late medieval Cracow was known as Poland's principal metropolis, a university town, and a flourishing commercial, cultural, and political centre with extensive ties to other states and a substantial number of foreign residents.[10] It was also a Catholic spiritual centre with a growing number of churches, convents, and relics attracting pilgrims, as well as home to the most influential Jewish community in the Polish Crown. Until 1469, Jewish communal institutions and houses of most community members were centrally located on and near today's *Jagiellońska Street*,[11] and *Judengasse*, or Jewish street, otherwise known as St. Anne Street (Figure 12.1, #27). This street ran from the main market square to the city walls and the so-called Jewish Gate (*portula Iudaeorum*) leading to the main Jewish graveyard outside the city walls (Figure 12.1, #1).[12] There were no walls or gates to indicate spatial segregation and Christians lived adjacent to Jews. Nonetheless, the city corner marked with an old synagogue (built before 1356) with an adjoining cemetery located on a parcel in front of the Church of St. Anne (Figure 12.1, #7) was recognised as a Jewish space.[13] In contemporary documents, the location of this church and of the first university buildings was designated as *in Judea* or *inter Judeos*.

During the fifteenth century, Jews were very active in the Cracovian real estate market. Some sold their houses to Christians, while prominent Jewish community members purchased properties for themselves and for the entire community in another part of the city centre, near the Szczepańskiego Square, behind the Church of Saint Stephen (Figure 12.1, #8).[14] A new synagogue was established close by on St. Mark Street. In 1469, an exchange agreement was signed between the representatives of the Jewish community and the Dlugosz brothers, who negotiated the terms on behalf of the Academy of Cracow which had its first buildings located *inter Judaeos*.[15] According to the contract, the Jews left their old neighbourhood and moved to the northern part of the city (Figure 12.1, #2). Although the rules of Jewish residence and the legal status exempting Jews from municipal jurisdiction did not change, the new location was not only more remote from the main road to the city as well as from the city scale and the town hall, but also distanced Jewish homes from the upscale first row of city square houses. In exchange for a less central location, the communal authorities maintained Jewish residences inside the city.

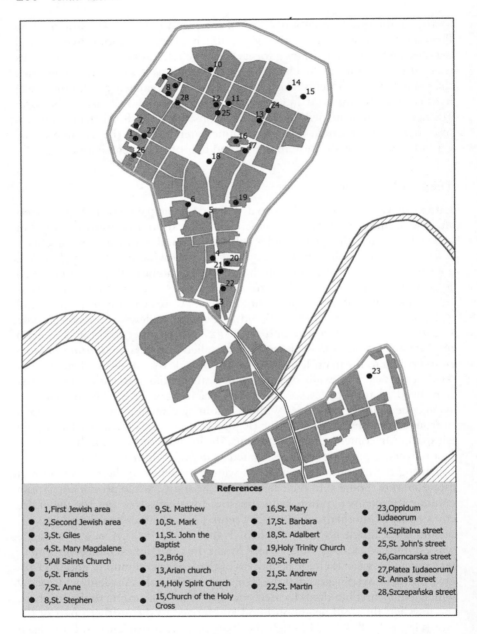

Figure 12.1 Religious topography of Cracow in the fifteenth and sixteenth centuries.
Created by Oded Naidik, licensed surveyor.

The Jewish community quickly managed to re-establish a quite consolidated new neighbourhood. Although the new location wasn't physically defined with a wall or limited to Jewish residents, and its formal religious space centred around a single synagogue, Jewish domestic practices and rituals rendered it a distinct sanctified urban area in which urban reality was mixed with imaginary halachic cartography in order to symbolically establish a space in which one was permitted to carry items on Sabbath, known as an Eruv.[16] On Fridays, after the candle-lighting time was reckoned in the synagogue, the Jews wearing Sabbath clothes returned to houses marked with mezuzuot, in which the "table [was] set and bed made" to receive the blessing of good angels for the Sabbath.[17] Although its official name had not been changed, very soon Szpiglarska Street became known as Jewish Street in everyday topography, thus challenging the sacred landscape and municipal jurisdiction of the Catholic capital. This source of contention was part of the wider context of the final attack on the new Jewish neighbourhood in 1494 and the ensuing lawsuit. While in the streets the crowd used fire as an opportunity to plunder Jewish houses and shops, the city council, strongly supported by the high clergy, including the king's brother Cardinal Frederick Jagiellon, blamed the Jews for burning the streets of the capital and demanded their punishment: expulsion.

The land exchange agreement of 1469 between the Jews and the Dlugosz brothers, thus moving the Jewish challenge to the city's Christian image further away from the city centre, did mitigate the spatial conflict. Although significant, this change of residential area did not ease the more pressing tension resulting from the Jewish share in the urban economic sphere and their physical and economic omnipresence in the central market square. This issue led to the 1485 agreement between the Cracovian magistrate and the elders of the Jewish community.[18] This rather constrained compromise, which aimed at limiting Jewish competition in trade and sales, actually divided the contested economic sphere between Christian and Jewish merchants. To preserve their share in the city's urban economy, the Jewish community agreed:

> To abstain from trade and cease from dealing with merchandise. Likewise, not to take various commodities or merchandise and sell with our own hands to other Christians, except for our unredeemed pledges by which we lost in usury and which we can sell in our houses at any time and opportunity. We may not dare to convey and bring these pledges to sell them in the streets or markets in the city, except for two specific days of the week, that is on Tuesday and Friday, restricted for markets, as well as on the fair-days [...] Likewise we shall sell only the pledges we can swear on the Torah to be ours. [...] Likewise, poor Jewesses have the right to sell on all days headdresses and neck jewels made by their own hands and craft. [19]

For local authorities, struggling with Jewish exemption from municipal jurisdiction, this arrangement was a way to subject the Jewish community to their authority. For Christian merchants, this agreement sought to deprive Jews of the full economic rights enjoyed by city residents and reduce their market activity at least to the limited level of other foreign merchants (*extranei*),[20] who were allowed to sell their products at fairs and were subject to the city's staple rights.[21] From the perspective of sacred topography, this arrangement reflected the church's policy to strengthen the Catholic identity of urban streets by limiting Jewish economic activity on Sundays and Christian holidays. From the Jewish perspective, this agreement limited community members' share of retail and wholesale activity. Yet at the same time, it officially secured Jewish presence in the urban economy and created an opportunity for Jews to increase their activity in pawnbroking and trade in unredeemed pledges (so-called lapsed bonds – *obligatio sub lapsu*). It forced Jewish merchants to develop marketing methods that would overcome the urban mercantile cartel, such as the employment of mercantile agents who worked on percentage and flooded the city streets and markets or the enrollment of family members and especially women as free help to increase the sales of handicraft products. Thus, while fewer Jews probably appeared at the city scale, Jewish peddlers and agents enticing customers became an omnipresent feature of the city squares. The economic interreligious rivalry continued growing[22] and, together with the aforementioned spatial challenge and increasing jurisdictional tension, this necessitated new arrangements limiting the Jewish share in Cracow's religious landscape and economy to a tolerable level.

Redefining the Jewish share in contested space

While searching for ways to overcome the economic limitations imposed on them, some of the affluent Cracovian Jews purchased properties in the adjacent independent royal city of Kazimierz, south of the northern branch of the Vistula (*Wisła*) river.[23] In 1495, following a great fire and several anti-Jewish riots, the entire Cracovian Jewish community, amounting probably to 500–700 individuals at the time, was transferred from Cracow to Kazimierz, where they joined a small Jewish community that had been present there since the fourteenth century.[24] The nature of this resettlement and the interreligious tensions behind it were interpreted differently not only by modern historians but by contemporaries as well.[25]

However, when analysing the sociopolitical and economic forces at play and perceiving physical space as a "contested ground," it seems that the Jewish community consciously agreed to move to a designated quarter of the royal city of Kazimierz, which, although independent, was still a part of Cracow urban economy under royal jurisdiction. By settling a mere half-hour walk from the Cracovian city market, Jewish authorities gained a higher degree of communal autonomy and congruence. Moreover, they also acquired more freedom pertaining to the economic activities of Jewish merchants and craftsmen in the capital, and all without losing the jurisdictional protection assigned to Jews residing in royal domains under the supervision of the administrator of royal estates (*wielkorządca*).

Whatever the circumstances were behind the move to Kazimierz, the significance of this change remains undisputed. The Jewish community and its institutions were erased from the sacral topography of Cracow. With the exception of very distinguished individuals who had royal permits to reside in the capital,[26] no Jews permanently dwelled in the city or remained there after the town watch announced evening curfew. If any Jews did reside in the city, or in its enclaves owned by nobles, they still needed to walk to Kazimierz to attend religious services or receive communal assistance. Hence, the mode of Jewish residence itself was altered and the jurisdictional and social environment changed. Although socio-economic, confessional, and political tensions similar to those occurring in Cracow could emerge in Kazimierz, the situation and dynamics in this town on the main city's outskirts were different.

Whereas in the case of other urban centres forbidding Jewish residence (*de non tolerandis Iudaeis*), Jewish communities were usually established in smaller, private towns nearby and their members lived on designated streets.[27] In Kazimierz, two separate "sacred areas" were gradually established – a Christian town and a Jewish quarter called "the city of Jews" (*Oppidum Iudaeorum*) (Figure 12.1, #23). This rare arrangement reduced the frequency, amplitude, and resonance of conflicts. Around 1530, after settling the stormy quarrels with new emigrants from Bohemian lands, the size of the Jewish population in Kazimierz was more or less the same as that of the Christian population (circa 2000),[28] and the Kazimierz community was on the cusp of the period known as its golden age. The community soon had a number of functioning synagogues[29] and turned into a fast-developing "big urban community" managed by an autonomous self-government in a corporation-like manner and ready to adapt itself to the evolving surroundings.[30] The community secured the needs of its members not only in the spiritual realm but in everyday life as well. After the king officially forbade Jews to live in the Christian part of Kazimierz (1566),[31] the community received the first of what were probably three privileges *de non tolerandis Christianis* (to not tolerate Christians) ever granted on Polish Crown lands (1568).[32]

Following their relocation to Kazimierz, the negotiations between Jews and the Cracovian magistrate continued. Yet, their character and orientation changed. The recurring conflicts had economic roots and although some religious rhetoric was gradually added to the opposition against renting city shops and storage to the Jews or against Jewish economic activity on Sundays and Christian holidays, the negotiations focused on the contested urban market and the new Jewish position in the metropolitan economic constellation. While Cracovian burghers insisted on treating Jews as foreign merchants and constantly returned to the aforementioned agreement of 1485,[33] the Jewish merchants and craftsmen sought to utilise their "in between" position. On the one hand, they claimed that the restrictions of the 1485 pact could not be imposed on them as they were no longer city residents. On the other hand, the community continued to refer to itself as the Holy Community of Kroke (Cracow in Yiddish) and emphasised its location within the co-urban economic triangle of Cracow–Kazimierz–Kleparz and therefore demanded a fair Jewish share in the urban economy.[34] Since Christian inhabitants of Kazimierz enjoyed some special trade rights in the capital, including the permission to freely sell their products and purchase materials necessary for their craft,[35] Jews insisted on equal treatment.[36] They appeared in Cracow on every possible occasion, selling various commodities around the city, attracting Christian buyers, taking an active part in local bazaars and fairs, and making use of the small city weighing scale not only for measurements and taxes but also for closing deals.[37] Following Jewish merchants' requests, the king allowed them to rent a number of stores and warehouses in the centre of the capital:

> Jews are allowed to rent shops and storage spaces, display merchandise at the market of Cracow; the magistrate and custom officials should not charge them with high or special payments, different to those required of the citizens of Cracow or Kazimierz.[38]

While small merchants opposed renting shops to the Jews, other groups in the Cracovian society supported doing so. The Cracovian elite sought to continue to rent spaces to Jews for substantial sums,[39] while the municipality enjoyed the taxes collected from Jewish merchants. Even the poorer strata of Cracovians supported Jewish peddlers for their provision of cheaper products:

> If only Jews were allowed to sell goods and roots, we would get them for much cheaper; [Christian merchants] are worse vendors than Jews, that is why they hate Jews [...].[40]

The royal interventions did not always manage to ease the conflict between the negotiating sides and at times, when the city council could not appease guild members or Christian merchants claiming exclusive trade rights, the conflict escalated and even before they reached the city the competition over agricultural products included confiscation of merchandise or violent excesses.[41] In times of crisis, not only merchants but the city magistrate took extreme measures, such as the temporary closing of the city gates for Jews.[42] Using the excuse of epidemics brought by Jews as outsiders entering the city, the municipality sought to end the cycle of multiple litigations and antagonism and redefine the market division anew, emphasising the residential separation of the parties.

Throughout the sixteenth century, the existence of separate religious spheres in the Cracovian conurbation diminished the importance of religious topography in determining Christian-Jewish relations and as a root of reoccurring conflicts. The sacral character of capital was not the key argument used by anti-Jewish opposition fighting for their everyday income. Following the Jews' relocation to Kazimierz, economics constituted a framework for *convivencia* and religious diversity while it simultaneously fuelled the market rivalry and supported the management of crises and reconciliation. In this new arrangement, unusual for Eastern Europe, Jews and Christians saw themselves as physically separated from one another. Although Jews no longer lived in unifying *intramuros* space, they cohabited in the same economic and administrative environment. Both sides understood the inevitability of economic tides and encounters and negotiated – albeit not always peacefully – their character, frequency, and scale. They imposed limits on interreligious ties and economic activity that could lead to overexposure to another way of life or challenge the sacredness of religiously demarcated space. As long as they posed no religious threat and agreed to limitations, Jews were interwoven into the symbiotic metropolitan economic structure. The residential separation was the product of a complex multifaith reality and it supported economic relations, which in turn reinforced religious diversity and grassroots practical toleration in the shared market space, even when the Protestant Reformation posed a new challenge to the religious topography of Cracow.

The rise of the Protestant challenge

Cracow, as a heterogenic city with a large German-origin population, and as a university town with a thriving publishing and cultural scene that also served as a centre of international trade, was exposed to the ideas of the Reformation at an early stage. Many members of Cracow's academia[43] had a keen interest in Luther's ideas and read and discussed his publicly sold works. Despite the papal bull and a number of anti-Reformation decrees issued by the king,[44] Lutheranism continued to spread across Cracow with every passing day, not only among humanists and intellectuals but also among urban nobles and wealthy city dwellers.[45] In an attempt to quell the spread of the Reformation in this early stage, the church launched a series of public sermons and began prosecuting city residents accused of Lutheran errors and the desecration of Catholic sacraments (1525–1531). Public interest in Luther's teachings brought to Cracow a former student of its academia and a zealous preacher, Jakub of Iłża. In 1528, he was put on trial for supporting Lutheran doctrine, but received only a warning. Jakub continued to propagate Lutheran ideas, this time from the pulpit in St. Stephen's (Figure 12.1, #8), and became the first preacher to build a following in Cracow. He was put on trial again (1534); this time, after the church authorities understood the threat of losing a parish church to a new confession, he was forced to escape into exile.

The rising presence of Lutheranism in the city and the threat of losing parish churches were also behind the church authorities' recommendation to move German sermons from St. Mary's – the largest, most prominent, and centrally located parish church in town (Figure 12.1, #16) – to the smaller one of St. Barbara's in St. Mary's churchyard (1536) (Figure 12.1, #17).[46]

In response to the church's clampdown, the Reformation movement in Cracow went underground, with supporters convening clandestinely in private residences. Between 1542 and 1547, the royal librarian Andrzej Trzecieski, known in modern historiography as "the first hero of the Polish Reformation,"[47] hosted what were to become the most famous Protestant private gatherings in his home. Gradually, many Reformation supporters began abandoning the Catholic Church and officially accepting the Protestant faith. Consequently, even before the death of King Sigismund I the Old (1548), who was a strident opponent of the Reformation, the movement resurfaced. Public Lutheran sermons could be heard in several of Cracow's Catholic churches that became contested spaces and budding sites of Protestant sacred topography. The Catholic response, at that stage, was focused on providing pastoral care and strengthening doctrinal understanding.

At that time, Cracow was the beating heart and soul of Poland, and although it differed from other towns in size, population, and character, the winds blowing in the capital could be felt around the whole country. Thus, every religion strove to have its stronghold in the capital. The Reformation began truly to thrive in Cracow with the enthronement of young Sigismund II Augustus, "inclined to pragmatic compromise" in matters both political and religious.[48] As of 1552, the minister Grzegorz Paweł of Brzezin, one the most prominent leaders and theologians of the Polish Reformation movement, began conducting Protestant services in private homes near Cracow. These were attended "by masses of people arriving on foot from Cracow with the utmost enthusiasm […] in good times and bad times, and without fear of the threats or insults levelled at them along the way at the incitement of the church."[49]

In the 1550s, many Poles who had previously been interested in Lutheranism turned towards Calvinism, which was better tailored to the needs of wealthy city dwellers and nobles. Calvinist congregations were quick to emerge. On August 17, 1557, the first public Protestant mass was held in Cracow, at the court of the burgrave and senator Jan Boner.[50] This event marked the official beginning of the Cracovian Evangelical community. At the request of its followers, Grzegorz Paweł was appointed as the first permanent chief Protestant minister in Cracow, serving in this position for ten years.[51] In addition to continuous attempts to introduce Protestant preachers to parish churches,[52] Protestant services were held at the private homes of nobleman Marcjan Chełmski next to the Church of St. Francis (Figure 12.1, #6)[53] and of Jan Tarło on St. John Street (Figure 12.1, #25). Although not ecclesiastical, these buildings became acknowledged sites of religious practice and of the fast-developing alternative sacred topography. Their appearance in the midst of the city centre and next to ecclesiastical buildings giving expression to and shaping Catholic religious life introduced Protestantism to the official public sphere and made it more pluralistic, to the obvious dismay of Catholic Church authorities.

The difference between Lutherans and Calvinists was not the only division in the Polish Protestant community. Calvinist doctrine as it was adopted in

Poland gave no room to social ideals that would appeal to city commoners or members of the lower classes and after some theological disputes, many residents left the Calvinist Church in favour of even more radical sects. The Calvinist denomination split into the larger Reformed Church and the anti-Trinitarian minor church (*Ecclesia Minor*), referred to by its rivals as Arian (after the ancient Christian sect) and by its supporters as the Polish Brethren.[54] Grzegorz Paweł became a leader of the Polish Brethren in Cracow. In the capital, members of the more radical denomination held their services at a residential building on 14 Szpitalna Street, at the corner of St. Thomas Street, which had been donated to the Polish Brethren Church by Stanisław Cikowski.[55] Cracow quickly became the most important centre of this radical denomination (alongside Lublin), up until the establishment of the ani-Trinitarian centre in Raków (1567). This division did not impede the rapid growth of the Calvinist community in Cracow. According to the clearly not objective account of the Protestant minister Wiśniowiecki, there were approximately 1000 Protestants in the Cracow metropolitan area in 1556.[56] Based on Urban's likely inflated estimates, there were 2,000–3,000 Protestants of different faiths and sects in the Cracow metropolitan area already in 1568. That amounts to roughly 10% of the local population,[57] most of them Calvinists.[58]

Despite their growing numbers, the impact of Protestants on the city's religious outlook was still insignificant. Their domestic space had no visible sacred character and their daily urban life did not greatly differ from that of their Catholic neighbours. Protestants gathered in private residences and ceased their missionary activities. As Janusz Tazbir accurately summarised, in Poland "the transition to the Protestant faith did not involve lifestyle changes; nobles who changed their faith did not sever ties with Catholics and vice versa."[59] Research shows that Calvinist communities in Poland were dissimilar to those in Western Europe, as the Polish Protestant nobility did not change its ways or make efforts to propagate the new faith, nor were they secluded from their Catholic neighbours.[60] The fact that the Calvinist Synod called upon believers to change their ways, to avoid "gluttony, drunkenness, and immodest dancing [...] and extravagant dress,"[61] likely points to the lack of any significant behavioural change among Polish followers of Geneva. Some burghers and nobles who converted to Calvinism did become more earnest and righteous, and more inclined to live modestly or abstain from luxury.[62] Otherwise, religious differences had very little influence over the day-to-day lives of believers and thus posed but a minor challenge to the city's religious outlook. Despite the opposition of religious authorities on both sides, on a grassroots level intermarriage was not uncommon, and Christians of different denominations gathered in assemblies and accommodated each other as guests. Catholics discussed religion with Protestants and attended Protestant funerals. Wealthy owners employed Protestant servants and clerks. The atmosphere as a whole encouraged the development of pragmatic approaches to interfaith interaction, which existed alongside a prejudice and religious animosity that was promoted by Catholic ecclesiastical authorities. This period of relative status quo, observed by the papal nuncio Stoppio, was temporary, and it changed when Protestants' achievements started to threaten the sacred topography of Cracow.

In 1564, the first Protestant gymnasium was founded, attracting students from all over Poland and establishing Cracow as one of the centres for reformist education.[63] In 1569, "thanks to the influence of the Protestant magnates,"[64] King Sigismund II Augustus permitted the establishment of an Evangelical cemetery in an ancient garden outside one of the city gates (*Brama Mikołajska*).[65] On May 2, 1572, after years of praying in private homes, proclaiming Protestant ideas in contested parish churches, and following continuous effort and fundraising, the community managed to obtain a permit from the king to open a Protestant church (*zbór*) in the city, on 6 St. John Street (Figure 12.1, #12).[66] Due to the unique structure of the roof, reminiscent of a movable structure used to cover hay barracks (Figure 12.2), the church was nicknamed "Bróg" (the Haystack).[67] This was the so-called "shared church," in which members of both the Augsburg Evangelical (Lutheran) Church and the Evangelical Reformed (Calvinist) Church held their services separately according to the common Evangelical confession, formulated in 1570 and

Figure 12.2 Demolition of Evangelical Church Bróg (drawing from 1574).

Wikimedia, Creative Commons License.

known as *Consensus Sandomirensis*.[68] German services were held in a separate hall on the uppermost floor, while the German-Lutheran minister was subordinate to the Polish minister.[69]

Besides those local achievements, the Protestants in the capital benefitted also from the state-wide political successes of their leaders. For example, owing to the annotation to the legislation of King Casimir IV Jagiellon, they could hold titles and positions "as long as they were members of the Christian faith," and not necessarily "members of the Christian faith who answer to the Roman Church."[70] Moreover, the Warsaw Confederation (1573) reinforced their legal status and did not permit state interference in conscientious matters, thus strengthening the Evangelical Protestants' legal status within the Polish-Lithuanian Commonwealth. Following the Evangelicals' series of triumphs in the regional and "national" political arena, the Cracovian congregation began to attract opposition from the Catholic Church. Markedly, while anti-Protestant excesses had both religio-political and socio-economic grounds, the most resented Evangelical actions were those that influenced the religious topography of Cracow's city centre. Although Catholic authorities tolerated Protestants in the city council and market square,[71] it was a rather antagonistic tolerance, based on Catholics enduring the modest presence of Evangelicals without embracing it. It was a very delicate equilibrium which lasted as long as the sacred landscape of the capital was preserved. Collective use of public space for processions and the establishment of new sites of religious practice shook the balance. However, since the church authorities had their hands tied by political agreements, anti-Protestant opposition, instigated by the same authorities, moved to "the streets." Of all the cities in Poland, Cracow, as the spiritual centre through which one could influence interconfessional and interreligious relations in the entire country, became the site of exceedingly frequent albeit not deadly religious riots.

Beginning in the late 1550s, the Polish Catholic Church, inspired by the Council of Trent and the Counter-Reformation, disseminated anti-Protestant propaganda with the help of charismatic preachers like Piotr Skarga and later the Jesuit Order. Susceptible to its influence, crowds of commoners and students targeted public displays of Protestant worship. They attacked Protestant funerals (1557, 1578, 1581, 1597), demolished the Evangelical cemetery (1574, 1577, 1578, 1585) and the Evangelical hospital (1607), and assaulted Protestant clerics and community members, breaking into their homes or setting them on fire (1577, 1578, 1581, 1610). The Brog church building was demolished twice (1574 and 1587) (Figure 12.2). On May 26, 1591, it was burned to the ground along with the city's Polish Brethren church building (Figure 12.1, #13). During the first attacks, Protestants sought to retaliate against their Catholic aggressors. Protestant violence usually took the form of individual attacks against students or clerics. Examples include the assaults carried out by Piotr Tomicki in 1576 and by Jan Stadnicki in 1577 and 1581. In addition, a student was murdered by Mikołaj Dłuski's servant in 1582.[72] There were also isolated cases of group attacks by Protestants, such as an ambush on a group of passersby who had approached the Bróg in 1578, an attack on worshippers during a Catholic mass by a group of soldiers in 1587, or an attack on the Carmelite church in 1588. However, in the face of the escalating pressure of the Counter-Reformation and the arrival of the Jesuits in Cracow (1564), the Protestant leadership ceased its displays of power and assumed a defensive position instead. They sought above all to maintain their existing achievements by using the political power of congregation members, and to ensure the safety of their co-religionists by relying on help from local authorities, who were often reluctant to provide it.

Redefining the Protestant share in urban space

After the complete destruction of the Protestant church building, the Catholics adopted the far-reaching objective of securing the monopoly of Catholic topography in the centre of Cracow: "we should strive with all our power, so that no other synagogue of Satan is erected in place of the destroyed Bróg."[73] Fearful of building it anew, the Protestant community moved its services away from Cracow, and the urban public sphere was purged of Evangelical institutions. The community now gathered in the village of Aleksandrowice, owned by Stanisław Iwan Kamiński, one of the community elders. In this village, 10 km away from Cracow, Polish Protestants – whose numbers were now falling across the country – prayed and assembled together with members of German descent who had remained Lutheran. The community continued as yet another small and local community, while its influence beyond the region gradually eroded.

The Counter-Reformation re-established the Catholic sacred topography of Cracow while limiting Protestant worship to the private sphere. Polish Evangelicals, who unlike the Jews did not create visible signs of their religious affiliation around their domestic space, were allowed to live in the city centre. They were permitted to use public space while refraining from public expressions of their religion, which were viewed as challenging the sacred topography of the city. Furthermore, as the Counter-Reformation conquered the urban space, the Catholic Church sought to transform the central public sphere from contested or shared to sanctified. Setting an example for other towns in the Polish Crown, Cracow's Catholic authorities set about retaking former Protestant buildings and re-establishing them as manifestly Catholic ecclesiastical spaces. In this way, they used urban space as part of their narrative of victory over dissidents and religious diversity. For example, they convinced the king to hand the Bróg's ruins over to Stanisław Lubomirski, a pious Catholic and sponsor of many churches, who then gave them to the Cistercian Order. The Protestants voiced opposition to this move in the 1627 General Assembly, but to no avail. In the 1630s, the construction of a new Catholic church of Saint Mary of the Crib began atop the ruins of the Bróg. In addition to retaking Protestant churches, the Counter-Reformation movements included rebuilding existing churches and establishing new religious sites in central city areas. As in many other places in central Europe, non-Catholic symbolic markers were erased from the contested city centre and the urban landscape reverted to being an overwhelmingly Catholic topography.

In 1613, students from Cracow attacked the Protestant congregation in Aleksandrowice. Following the incident, a new place for the congregation was agreed upon: Wielkanoc, not far from Łuczanowice. As it was 16 km away from Cracow, services could be held there only on holidays, special occasions, and funerals. Services for the elderly, sickly, and children, as well as christenings, were held in Łuczanowice, somewhat closer to the capital. As an alternative to the often-desecrated cemetery in Wesoła, a new Evangelical cemetery was also established in Łuczanowice in 1626. In 1655, a mob attacked the Protestant church and minister's abode on the Wielkanoc.

Conclusions

On March 18, 1596, King Sigismund III Vasa decided to move his residence from Cracow to Warsaw. Although this change contributed significantly to the decline of Cracow's political and economic importance, it did not influence the prominence of Cracow as a religious centre. In the same year, Giovanni Paolo Mucante, the secretary of the papal legate Enrico Caetani, visited Poland and wrote in his diary that Cracow was indeed a spiritual centre worthy of the old saying "if Rome was not Rome, Cracow would be Rome."[74] Roughly four decades separate the observations of Stoppio and Mucante, yet the impression left by the two foreign observers testify to a shift Cracow underwent from an urban hub experiencing religious diversity and negotiating the character of its city space to an ecclesiastical centre "rich [...] in churches, in bodies of saints, innumerable places of worship, and non-stop religious services as if the city was another Rome."[75]

Although the city dwellers and daily incoming visitors remained religiously and confessionally heterogeneous, the public expression of their religious diversity was limited to the minimum. Both Jews and Protestants of different denominations were allowed to be present in the economic, juridical, and administrative sphere of the city, but only as long as their devotional practices were confined to the private sphere (in the case of Protestants) or to the separated residential quarter in adjacent town (in the case of Jews). The difference in the policies applied to Jews and Protestants was, among other issues, related to the challenge the two minorities posed to the sacred topography of the city. Since Polish Protestants were not visibly different from their Catholic neighbours, they could live in the city as long as they conformed to the norm of the distinction between public and private dictated by the Catholic politico-religious majority and practised their faith in private spaces marked by the threshold of domestic space inside or church space outside of the city. In the case of the Jews, it was not only their institutions or worship but their way of life in general that appropriated urban space and thus violated the sacral topography of Cracow, eventually leading to their exclusion from the urban residential space.

The coexistence in the public sphere was thus realised through the exclusion of religious minorities from the sacred topography of the city. With the victory of the Counter-Reformation, the once contested space of the urban centre became the heart of practical toleration, especially in the economic realm and the sphere of antagonistic tolerance granted by the Catholic authorities to religious minorities. The dominance of the Catholic creed was reflected in the physical transformation of urban space, in which there was no place for a Jewish Street, or for Protestant churches, or for "heretics [who] wreak havoc on the royal city."[76]

Notes

1 Fynes Moryson, *The Itinerary* (Glasgow: J. MacLehose and Sons, 1907), 3: 462.
2 Stanisław Kot, "Polska rajem dla Żydów, piekłem dla chłopów, niebem dla szlachty," *Kultura i Nauka* (Warsaw, 1937), 255–82.
3 Paweł Jasienica coined these terms for the sixteenth (the Golden Age) and the beginning of the seventeenth century (the Silver Age). *Rzeczpospolita Obojga Narodów* (Warsaw: P.I.W., 1986).
4 Leading up to the Reformation, only 40% of the population were ethnic Poles, some of whom were Orthodox. Moshe Rosman, "Innovative Tradition: Jewish Culture in the Polish-Lithuanian Commonwealth," in *Culture of the Jews. A New History*, ed. David Biale (New York: Schocken Books, 2002), 521.
5 The issue of religious tolerance was discussed in Poland as far back as the Middle Ages and found expression in a theological doctrine that opposed coercive religious missions. The most well-known pioneer of this approach was Paweł Włodkowic. See also: S. Sider, *Handbook to Life in Renaissance Europe* (New York: Facts on File, 2005), 16.
6 Roman Żelewski, *Materiały do dziejów Reformacji w Krakowie. Zaburzenia wyznaniowe w latach 1551–1598* (Cracow: Zakład Narodowy im. Ossolińskich, 1962), 15.
7 By the end of the sixteenth century, there were approximately 14,700–15,900 inhabitants in the city of Cracow proper. In the seventeenth century, 40% of the city council members were immigrants from abroad or other areas in Poland. Italians, Hungarians, and later Scots could be easily found in the Cracovian streets and markets. Among the 393 councillors in the sixteenth to eighteenth centuries, 55 (14%) were Italian. See Kamila Follprecht and Zdzisław Noga, "Kraków w 1598 r.," in *Atlas Historyczny Polski. Województwo krakowskie w drugiej połowie XVI wieku*, vol. 2, ed. Henryk Rutkowski (Warsaw: Wydawnictwo Neriton, 2008), 151; Janina Bieniarzówna, *Mieszczaństwo krakowskie VII w: z badań nad strukturą społeczną miasta* (Cracow: Wydawnictwo Literackie, 1969), 99.
8 The Evangelical community in Cracow included devotees of the Augsburg Evangelical Church (also known as the Lutheran Church) and the Evangelical Reformed Church (also known as the Calvinist Church). They referred to themselves as "Evangelicals" to emphasise their adherence to ancient Christian principles and as a form of protest to the names assigned to them by the Catholic establishment. See Urszula Augustyniak, *Historia Polski 1572–1795* (Warsaw: PWN, 2008), 177–8.
9 Małłek divided the history of Polish religious tolerance into four periods: 1517–1548, the subversive growth of the Reformation in defiance of the monarchy;

1548–1573, full tolerance under the reign of Sigismund II Augustus; 1573–1648, the age of tolerance with Counter-Reformation elements; and 1657–1768, the triumph of Catholic confessionalisation and Sarmatism. See Janusz Małłek, "Tolerancja religijna a konfesjonalizacja w Polsce i Szwecji w XVI i XVII wieku," *Przegląd Humanistyczny* 43, no. 2/3 (1999), 25–9.

10 Even as late as in the 1670s, 19% of personal signatures in Cracow city books were in German, 10% in Italian, and 24% those of foreign residents whose names had been translated to Polish. See Wacław Urban, "Skład narodowościowy mieszczaństwa krakowskiego w latach 1574–1660," in *Społeczeństwo Staropolskie*, vol. 3, ed. A. Wyczański (Warsaw: PWN, 1983), 124.

11 During the Middle Ages, intersecting blocks had no names.

12 Hanna Zaremska, *Żydzi w średniowiecznej Polsce. Gmina krakowska* (Warsaw: Instytut Historii PAN, 2010), 344–8.

13 Before 1469, the Jewish corner had one additional synagogue, in front of the house of Jan Tęczyn, the Palatine of Cracow, with a small adjacent cemetery and a hospital.

14 Zaremska, *Żydzi w średniowiecznej*, 359–60; B. Wyrozumska, *Żydzi w średniowiecznym Krakowie. Wypisy źródłowe z ksiąg miejskich krakowskich* (Cracow: Polska Akademia Umiejętności, 1995), no. 512.

15 Jan Długosz (1415–1480), a renowned chronicler, and his younger brother were both canons of Cracow. For more information about this process, see Zaremska, *Żydzi w średniowiecznej*, 346, 360, 375. On the location of the university in the Jewish neighbourhood, see *Codex diplomaticus Studii Generalis Universitatis Cracoviensis*, vol. 1 (Cracow: Sumptibus et typis Universitatis, 1870), nr 7–14.

16 In the seventeenth century, rabbis discussed whether the symbolic Eruv should include the entire city and not just the Jewish neighbourhood. For more information, see Micha J. Perry, "Imaginary Space Meets Actual Space in Thirteenth-Century Cologne: Eliezer Ben Joel and The Eruv," *Images* 5, no. 1 (2011), 26–36.

17 Babylonian Talmud: Shabbat, 119b.

18 Similar agreements, called pacta (ugody), between municipal authorities and Jewish communities became popular in Poland and Lithuania in the early modern period. They reflect Christian-Jewish relations and their contractual character in towns with a strong burgher class. See François Guesnet, "Agreements between Neighbours. The 'Ugody' as a Source on Jewish-Christian Relations in Early Modern Poland," *Jewish History* 24 (2010), 257–70.

19 Author's translation from pic. 8 in Majer Balaban, *Toldot ha-yehudim be-Krakov u-be-Kazhimiezh: 1304–1868*, vol. 1, trans. David Weinfeld et al. (Jerusalem: Magnes Press, 2003).

20 The trend to limit trade by foreign merchants had begun in the 1480s in centres on major regional and international trade routes. See Zaremska, *Żydzi w średniowiecznej*, 189, 211–2.

21 These required merchants to unload their goods in the city and to display them for sale for a certain period.

22 For example, in 1494 the number of Jewish butchers was restricted to four (instead of six).

23 Stefan Świszczowski, *Miasto Kazimierz pod Krakowem* (Cracow: Wydawnictwo Literackie, 1981), 183.

24 Stanisław Kutrzeba, "Ludność i majątek Kazimierza w końcu XVI stulecia," *Rocznik Krakowski* 3 (1900), 110.

25 For a discussion on different interpretations of Jewish relocation to Kazimierz, see, for example: Bożena Wyrozumska, "Czy Jan Olbracht wygnał Żydów z Krakowa?," *Rocznik Krakowski* 59 (1993), 5–11; Hanna Zaremska, "Crossing the River. How and Why the Jews of Kraków Settled in Kazimierz at the End of the Fifteenth Century," *Polin* 22 (2010), 174–92; Zaremska, *Żydzi w średniowiecznej*

Polsce, 493–6; Bałaban, *Historja Żydów w Krakowie i na Kazimierzu, 1304–1868* (Cracow: Nadzieja, 1931), 64; Janina Bieniarzówna et al., eds., *Dzieje Krakowa*, vol. 1 (Cracow, 1992), 150; Ilia M. Rodov, *The Torah Ark in Renaissance Poland: A Jewish Revival of Classical Antiquity* (Leiden and Boston: Brill, 2013), 6.

26 Rodov, *The Torah Ark*, 7.

27 In some places like Poznan, Jews continued living in the city, but as their numbers were restricted, they established a community in the nearby private town of Swarzędz (1621).

28 Danuta Dombrowska, Stefan Krakowski, and Arthur Cygielman, "Cracow," *Encyclopedia Judaica*, vol. 5, 2nd ed. (Jerusalem: Thomson Gale and Keter, 1973), 1028. Janina Bieniarzówna and Jan M. Małecki, eds., *Dzieje Krakowa. Kraków w wiekach XVI-XVIII*, vol. 2 (Cracow: Wydawnictwo Literackie), 152. Despite the gradual enlargement of the Jewish area, the demographic ratio remained constant until the Partitions.

29 For their detailed description, see Rodov, *The Torah Ark*.

30 The term "big community" was coined by Elchanan Reiner in his article "'Aliyyat ha-Kehillah ha-Gedolah': al Shorshe ha-Kehillah ha-Yehudit ha-Ironit be-Polin ba-Et ha-Hadashah ha-Mukdemet," *Gal-Ed* 20 (2006), 13–37.

31 Alicja Falniowska-Gradowska and Franciszek Lesniak, eds., *Lustracja województwa krakowskiego 1659–1664*, vol. 2 (Warsaw: Instytut Historii PAN, 2005), 354–5.

32 No original document of the privilege has been preserved. The other such privileges were probably granted to Jewish communities in Poznań and Lublin. In 1645, a privilege banning Christian residents was granted to all Jewish communities in the Grand Duchy of Lithuania.

33 It was referred to by voivodes and kings as well. See, for example, the edict of Sigismund I of 1527: "Sigismund I rex Poloniae ordinationem Ioannis Amor de Tarnow palatini Cracoviensis, de mercatura Iudaeorum a. 1485 factam, ratam esse iubet," quoted in Franciszek Piekosiński, *Prawa, przywileje i statuta miasta Krakowa (1507–1795)*, vol. 1 (1507–1586), part 1 (Cracow: Akademia Umiejętności, 1885), 43–5. In an attempt to better enforce local regulations, the Sejm in Piotrkow (1538) ruled that "Jews do not have unlimited freedom of trade, but they ought to follow the rules of our kingdom and observe the pacts which were signed in given cities." *Volumina Legum: Przedruk zbioru praw staraniem XX. Pijarów w Warszawie*, vol. 1 (St. Petersburg: Jozafat Ohryzko, 1860), 525.

34 Economically, Kazimierz was a satellite town that enjoyed a symbiosis both with the central city of Cracow and with the fellow satellite town of Kleparz.

35 J. Wyrozumski, *Dzieje Krakowa*, vol. 1. *Kraków do schyłku wieków średnich* (Cracow: Wydawnictwo Literackie, 1992), 243. Around 1600, the population of Kazimierz amounted to 26–8% of the population of Cracovian urban agglomeration. Leszek Belzyt, "Ludność i domy w Kazimierzu około roku 1600. Próba bilansu statystycznego," *Czasy Nowożytne* 3 (1997), 28.

36 According to the staple right, Jews, like other foreign merchants, were obligated to report their merchandise to the city clerk on the day of their arrival to the city or the morning after. Only upon reporting could the commodities be stored or displayed in shops rented by the Jews in the city. In the absence of a fair, the merchandise could be sold to clients directly or moved from the city a week after the reported arrival and under the condition that it was displayed in the market. If the staple right was violated, Jewish merchants could lose all their commodities: half of it to the voivode and half to the city. The staple right was to be exercised under the supervision of the city magistrate and the kahal of Kazimierz.

37 Cracow had two city weighing scales located on the main market square. One of the entrances to the small weighing scale was from the Jewish Market. See

Bieniarzówna & Małecki, *Dzieje Krakowa*, 181–3; Szymon Kazusek, *Żydzi w handlu Krakowa w połowie XVII wieku* (Cracow: Vistulana, 2000), 61.

38 Piekosiński, *Prawa, przywileje*, 257.

39 For example, in 1608, two out of four shops in the building belonging to the Cracovian castellan Janusz Ostrogski were rented by Jews. Kazusek, *Żydzi w handlu*, 81.

40 Walerian Nekanda Trepka, *Liber generationis plebanorum*, part 1, ed. W. Dworzaczek (Wrocław: Zakład Narodowy imienia Ossolińskich, 1963), 18.

41 Bałaban, *Historja Żydów*, 217–20.

42 Bałaban, *Historja Żydów*, 210–1.

43 The Akademia Krakowska was founded in 1364 and was the second university to be established in eastern Europe. Its current name – the Jagellonian University – was given to it only in the nineteenth century.

44 For example, the decree to establish a special committee overseeing bookstores and publishing houses in 1521, a decree permitting the Cracow bishop and town committee members to search private residences for forbidden books in 1523, and a ban on attending Protestant universities abroad. For a discussion on Luther's influence on the Reformation in Poland, see O. Bartel, "Marcin Luter w Polsce," *Odrodzenie i Reformacja w Polsce* [hereafter: *OiRP*] 7 (1962), 27–50.

45 G. Schramm, "Reformation und Gegenreformation in Krakau," *Zeitschrift für Ostforschungen Länder und Völker im östlichen Mitteleuropa* 19 (1970), 11.

46 It was a free-standing building in which Polish sermons were delivered until 1530.

47 Wacław Urban, *Dwa szkice z dziejów reformacji* (Kielce: Kieleckie Towarzystwo Naukowe, 1991), 47–53.

48 Janusz Tazbir, "Poland," in *The Reformation in National Context*, ed. Bob Scribner et al. (Cambridge: Cambridge University Press, 1994), 169. King Sigismund II Augustus' attitude to the Reformation is still under debate, but scholars agree that his religious policy was born of political pragmatism and in pursuit of political and dynastic interests. See Alicja Dybkowska, *Zygmunt August* (Lublin: Test, 2003), 64–8; Anna Sucheni-Grabowska, *Zygmunt August. Król polski i Wielki Książę Litewski* (Cracow: Universitas, 2010), 389–415.

49 Wojciech Węgierski, *Kronika Zboru Ewangelickiego Krakowskiego* (Cracow, 1817), 8.

50 Jan Boner (1516–1562), the eldest son of Seweryn Boner and an urban merchant and royal banker turned noble. Already at age 14, Boner travelled to Protestant centres and met with leading figures in the movement, such as Philip of Hesse and Philip Melanchthon, also befriending Erasmus, who dedicated one of his works to him in 1531. Boner initially supported Luther but later switched to the Calvinist faith. He was an advocate for the Protestant-Evangelical denomination and even tried to integrate Protestants and Jewish converts into the city council of Kazimierz. For further reading see Marian Hanik, *Trzy pokolenia z rodu Bonerów* (Cracow: Centralny Ośrodek Informacji Turystycznej, 1985), 49–58.

51 Walerjan Krasiński, *Zarys dziejów powstania i upadku reformacji w Polsce Reformacji w Polsce*, vol. 1 (Warsaw: Jul Bursche, 1903), 207. Another minister, Daniel Biliński, was appointed in 1558 for German-speaking adherents.

52 In 1550, the town council unsuccessfully attempted to place two Protestant preachers at St. Mary's and in 1564 a preacher to the church of St. Martin.

53 See complaints against these services: Archiwum Państwowe w Krakowie [hereafter APKr], *Inscr. Castr. Crac.* T. 76: 710, 976.

54 This internal schism was officially approved by the 1565 Protestant general assembly in Piotrków. Since the theology of the Polish Brethren was largely formulated by Faustus Socinius, the adherents of the Brethren were known in western Europe as the Socinians.

55 The exact date of the establishment of the Polish Brethren Church is disputed. Some date it as early as the beginning of 1565. See H. Merczyng, *Zbory i senatorowie protestanccy* (Warsaw: Druk Aleksandra Ginsa, 1904), 108–9.

56 Wacław Urban, "Heretycy parafii Mariackiej w Krakowkie w 1568 r.," *OiRP* 32 (1987), 168.

57 Urban, "Heretycy parafii," 168. In contrast, Kościelny argues – without specifying sources – that while 15–20% of the Polish nobility was Protestant in the 1570s, Protestants amounted to only about four percent of Cracow's residents. Piotr Kościelny, *Dzieje Reformacji w Polsce* (Warsaw: PAX, 2017), 290, 352. For 1572, a much lower number of 600 Protestants is given by J. Bieniarzówna, "Kraków pod wpływami reformacji," in *Dzieje Krakowa*, 2: 138.

58 Waldemar Kowalski, "The Reformation and Krakow Society, c. 1517–1637: Social Structures and Ethnicities," in *Stadt und Reformation: Krakau, Nüremberg und Prag (1500–1618)*, ed. Michael Diefenbacher et al. (Prague and Červený Kostelec: Archiv hlavního města Prahy, Pavel Mervart, 2019), 140.

59 Janusz Tazbir, "Społeczeństwo wober reformacji," in *Polska w epoce odrodzenia. Państwo-Społeczeństwo – Kultura*, ed. A. Wyczański (Warsaw: Muzeum Okręgowe, 1986), 340.

60 Mariusz Markiewicz, *Historia Polski, 1492–1795* (Cracow: Wydawnictwo Literackie, 2002), 118.

61 Roman Żelewski, "Zaburzenia wyznaniowe w Krakowie. Okres przewagi różnowierców 1551–1573," *OiRP* 6 (1961), 93.

62 Janina Bieniarzówna and ks. Karol Kubisz, *400 lat reformacji pod Wawelem, 1557–1957* (Warsaw: Strażnica Ewangeliczna, 1958), 17.

63 Previously, Cracow had one elementary school where the Lutheran faith was taught in German. As of 1572, the gymnasium's management was handed over to Jan Thenaudus. It continued to operate until the final destruction of the church building and followed the curriculum of German educator Johann Sturm. The emphasis was on the humanities and theology. It remains unclear whether Polish was also taught.

64 Krasiński, *Zarys dziejów*, 1: 207.

65 APKr, *Inscr. Castr. Crac.* T. 99: 744; *Prawa y wolności dissydentom w nabożeństwie chrześcijańskim w Koronie Polskiej y w W. X. L. Słuzące: z Przywileiow, Konstitucyi Seymowych, y Statutow W. X. L. y rożnych inszych [...] Authentykow zebrane, y dla Wiadomości Wszystkich do Druku Podane przez Daniela Ernesta Jabłońskiego* (n.p., 1767), 23–4. In this privilege, Protestants are referred to as Christians, not "heretics." According to Węgierski, the king granted the Cracowian community the privilege to establish a school and a hospital already in 1569, together with the permit for a church. This permit is not extant. We do, however, have the permit for the cemetery from August 8, 1569.

66 While the seat of the king was now in Warsaw, Cracow remained the legal capital up until 1795. See Bieniarzówna and Małecki, *Dzieje Krakowa*, 2: 168.

67 Samuel M.B. Linda, *Słownik języka polskiego* (Warsaw: Drukarnia XX. Piiarów, 1807), 1: 170.

68 Signed in 1570 between the Lutherans, the Calvinists, and the Bohemian Brethren – a more radical faction within the Bohemian Reformation, some of whose members resettled in Poland after being exiled in 1548.

69 See Żelewski, "Akta i relacje dotyczące zburzenia zboru kalwińsko-luterańskiego w Krakowie w r. 1574," in *Z dziejów Odrodzenia w Polsce. Teki Archiwalne* 2 (Warsaw, 1954), 111, n. 11.

70 *Prawa y wolności*, 10.

71 In the second half of the sixteenth century, the percentage of Protestants in the city council reached 40%. In 1574, Evangelicals constituted 70% of the acting

council responsible for city administration. Despite those high numbers, the magistrate could not prevent the riots. Zdzisław Noga, *Krakowska rada miejska w XVI wieku: studium o elicie władzy* (Cracow: Wydawnictwo Naukowe Akademii Pedagogicznej, 2003), 180–92.

72 APKr. *Cast. Crac. Rel.* vol. 3, 689–90, 1156–7; Biblioteka Jagiellońskiej, Ms. cim. nr. 8420.

73 Cardinal Hozjusz as quoted in Wacław Sobieki, *Nienawiść wyznaniowa tłumów za rządów Zygmunta IIIgo* (Warszawa: Wyd. Grafika, 1902), 32.

74 Jan Władysław Woś, ed., *Itinerario in Polonia del 1596 di Giovanni Paolo Mucante Cerimoniere Pontificio* (Rome: Il Centro di Ricerca, 1981), 89.

75 Almut Bues, *Die Aufzeichnungen des Dominikaners Martin Gruneweg (1562–ca. 1618) über seine Familie in Danzig, seine Handelsreisen in Osteuropa und sein Klosterleben in Polen* (Wiesbaden: Harrassowitz Verlag, 2009), 831.

76 See Note 6.

13 Confessional Boundaries and Transconfessional Spaces in Late Seventeenth- and Eighteenth-Century British North America

Susanne Lachenicht

Introduction

The United States of America and its predecessors, the English/British colonies in North America, have long been celebrated as safe havens for religious refugees, places where religious freedom, pluralism, and tolerance reigned.[1] This narrative, however, projects modern forms of coexistence between religious and ethnic groups onto past centuries.[2] Recent studies by Evan Haefeli and other scholars have made it clear that, in fact, the "religious politics of English expansion" were not dominated by ideas of tolerance or the protection of religious refugees.[3] Rather, a central aim of many imperial endeavours undertaken by the English/British, from the 1660s and especially from 1701, was to establish the Church of England. Viewed as the only "true" church, the latter was intended to form a bulwark against Protestant dissenters and Catholicism alike. In many of England's (from 1707 Britain's) North American and Caribbean colonies, the Church of England served as an instrument of empire-building.[4] It was hardly, though, the only religious body intent on establishing, maintaining, and spreading its own orthodoxy. It may have enjoyed unique support from the imperial state, but Puritans, Congregationalists, Huguenots, Moravians, Quakers, Catholics, and other religious dissenters were eager too, especially after having suffered persecution in Europe, to establish in the colonies their own communities, institutions, and belief systems.[5] They wished not only to maintain their orthodoxies but to ensure the conformity of their members to those orthodoxies. Their aim was to create well-defined confessional spaces with clear boundaries that believers were not supposed to transgress. By "confessional spaces" I mean both material and imagined spaces that were specific and exclusive to a particular Christian denomination (known also as a confession), such as churches, graveyards, and imaginings of this world and the hereafter.

In the colonial context of British North America, however, both established and dissenting churches confronted a lack of pastors, funds, and infrastructure. This difficulty forced them to accept, to some extent, transconfessional practices. The term "transconfessional" is preferable to "syncretism" or "hybridity" because it adopts the perspective of early modern religious

DOI: 10.4324/9781003030522-19

communities themselves. It refers to the violation or indeed elimination of boundaries between the spaces of different denominations. Transconfessional practices united believers of different denominations through the sharing of sacred spaces, including churches and meeting houses, clergy, and rituals. Entering transconfessional space meant that believers crossed the material and imagined boundaries created by the belief systems of their churches.

The practical challenges they confronted forced churches and religious communities to practise religious toleration if they wanted to satisfy their imperial and/or spiritual and social needs. As we shall see, pastors moved between denominations and congregations to conduct weddings, baptise children, preach, and bury the dead. Likewise, laypeople sought out the services of different pastors, attended religious services in various churches, joined several congregations, or concluded (religiously) exogamous marriages. Through their confessional and geographical mobility, both clergy and laity created relationships between diverse peoples and places – relationships often deemed undesirable by church, state, or dissenting believers – in the process creating transconfessional spaces.[6]

The frequent crossing of various confessional, "national," and other boundaries as well as the generation of links between diverse communities had implications beyond the creation of transconfessional spaces. For example, by forming and sustaining social relationships between people belonging to diverse confessional, ethnic, and national groups; by founding new parishes; by cultivating lands attached to their sinecures; and by missionising among African enslaved people and Native Americans, pastors contributed, alongside governors, assemblies, settlers, and merchants, to the development and integration of colonial spaces.[7]

This chapter will first consider how theories associated with the so-called "spatial turn" can be useful for understanding religious spaces and boundaries in English/British North America. It will then examine the imperial politics of settlement and the religious landscape of English/British North America. Thereafter, it will turn to transconfessional border-crossing in general before focusing on two examples, those of colonial South Carolina and colonial New York.

The *spatial turn* and confessional space

Space, especially geographical space, is often understood as a given, as something natural in which humans (and non-humans) move and place themselves. Since the 1980s, however, social sciences and cultural studies alike have critically assessed, enlarged, and fundamentally altered our definition of *space*. They have emphasised the constructed character of not only social, cultural, political, and economic space but also geographic space.[8] With the *spatial turn*, *space* has turned from a descriptive category into an analytical one – a multidimensional category that bridges the material and the imagined. Some academics still hold that *space* is something natural, material, and objective and thus have a substantialist definition of *space*. At the other end of the spectrum, social scientists and specialists in cultural studies see *space* as something that is always socially and culturally constructed – through imagination, narratives, and performative acts. This chapter holds that *space* is a dynamic, multidimensional set of relationships created by human (and non-human) beings. *Space* is never an objective *container* in which humans (or non-humans) move. *Space* arises from actors relating themselves to sites or places, objects, or other humans, through imaginations, narratives, and performative acts.

The following sections will focus on the construction of confessional space and of shared, transconfessional space. The actors creating and sharing confessional space come with identifications that are not only confessional but also ethnic, national,[9] social, economic, or cultural (cultural in terms of other cultural identifications than confessional ones). These identifications often overlap or come into conflict in one and the same context, place, or situation. While in many early modern contexts, the ritual actions performed by believers related to existing confessional places and spaces (such as churches), confessional space in English/British North America was in the beginning imagined space, imagined by the gatekeepers[10] of European denominations as sites of orthodox worship, as spaces where homogeneous confessional groups should have been formed or sustained (see also below).[11] These "life worlds" or "special worlds" were meant to establish not only homogeneously orthodox groups of believers but also boundaries dividing the latter from other denominations.[12] The following sections will show whether or not this was possible in English/British North America.

British North America and the imperial politics of settlement

The restoration of the Stuarts in 1660 was followed by the establishment, or re-establishment, of the Church of England as the official, established church of the English colonies in North America. Some colonies, such as Virginia, even anticipated Anglican conformity back in England by calling immediately for the suppression of dissenters, Quakers in particular.[13] Other colonies, such as the New England ones, preserved their congregationalist or dissenting character, while Pennsylvania was established in 1681 as a haven for persecuted Quakers and other dissenters.[14]

To gain more control over the colonies and the colonists' beliefs and practices – to create confessional space and boundaries – some elements within English imperial politics wished to establish an Anglican episcopate in North America.[15] More successful were the attempts to create a missionary arm of the Church of England, based on a royal charter. In 1701, the Reverend Thomas Bray founded the *Society for the Propagation of the Gospel in Foreign Parts* (SPG), to bring Anglican worship to the English, later British, colonies in North America and the Caribbean and to reduce the influence there of dissenters such as Quakers and, from the 1720s, Moravian brethren.[16] The SPG collected funds in the British Isles and other parts of Protestant Europe to hire missionaries and send them to the colonies. The aim was not only to eradicate Protestant dissent but also to convert African enslaved people and American Indians to the faith promoted by the Church of England.[17]

Due, however, to a shortage of Anglican pastors willing to serve in the colonies, the SPG also hired non-conformist ministers, who had to be re-ordained by the bishop of London or another member of the Anglican episcopate. Among the SPG's pastors, we therefore find French and Dutch Reformed pastors, Lutheran, and former Quaker and Moravian ones.[18] Re-ordained by and officially conforming to the Anglican Church, these pastors should have established and upheld the orthodoxy of English Anglicanism in the colonies. Some, nevertheless, held services and preached in non-conformist ways, wherever and whenever necessary, in the churches of their original denominations. They thus became transconfessional agents. Moreover, when SPG missionaries were sent to British North America, they moved from one place to another, preaching in New England churches, on Long Island, in Virginia, Pennsylvania, the Carolinas, and the Hudson Valley, sometimes for just a few days, other times for months or a couple of years.[19] Through this mobility, they linked disparate geographic and colonial places, created relationships between people of different denominations and national/ethnic backgrounds, and fashioned transconfessional spaces.

To restore the Church of England in North America and the Caribbean was important to English/British colonial governments. It was also important, though, to strengthen the colonies economically and militarily by attracting sufficient numbers of settlers. As before the Restoration, so after it, the Lords Proprietors, governors, and chartered companies that ran the various colonies remained responsible for immigration and settlement policies. They invited Irish Catholics, Scottish Presbyterians, German Lutherans, French Huguenots, Dutch and German Mennonites, Moravians, Ashkenazi and Sephardi Jews, and others to settle in British North America and the British Caribbean. Some of these groups also helped other empires expand control over territories and economies, as did the Sephardi Jews in the French and Dutch empires and Moravians, Mennonites, and Huguenots in the Dutch and Russian empires.[20] At times, empires competed for migrants who were deemed valuable, regardless of whether they were religious dissenters: for example, Huguenots in the 1680s.[21] In pursuing such policies, rulers were influenced by mercantilism and by population theories such as Samuel von Pufendorf's, which favoured the accommodation and settlement of diverse ethnic, national, and religious minorities in pursuit of imperial interests. The accommodation of heterodox migrants depended on their usefulness, real or assumed, which was a subject of the ongoing discussion.[22] Such accommodation, however, increased the confessional, national, and ethnic diversity of the colonies. It thus ran counter to the efforts of the Church of England to Anglicanise all English/British colonies in North America and the Caribbean.

The religious landscape of British North America

With the onset of the Reformation in the early sixteenth century, "Protestant heresies" had spread not only across Europe but also to European colonies overseas. Anabaptists, Hutterites, Mennonites, Walloons, Huguenots, Dutch Catholics, and Puritans in the sixteenth century; Puritans, Quakers, Protestant Bohemians, and Huguenots in the seventeenth; Moravians, Salzburg Protestants, Protestants from the Austrian Habsburg lands of Styria and Carinthia, French Catholics from Acadia, and Huguenots in the eighteenth century – to give only a partial list – were persecuted, fled their homes, and were invited to resettle in the territories of other imperial states.[23]

Starting in the 1620s, Puritans who had left England settled in the colonies of New England, where Baptists, Quakers, and Huguenots were later admitted.[24] Beginning in the 1630s, English Catholics established themselves in Maryland and elsewhere. Presbyterians and Quakers came to the English colonies from the 1650s onwards.[25] Pennsylvania accommodated Quakers, Moravians, and German Lutherans, while the Carolinas became a new home for Anglicans, Huguenots, Quakers, Baptists, and Scottish Presbyterians. In the 1730s, the Austrian Habsburgs and the Prince-Archbishop of Salzburg deported or expelled from their territories crypto-Protestants, who were resettled in Georgia to protect the frontier against Spanish, French, and American Indian attacks.[26] Moravian brethren, known also as Herrnhuters, who in the 1720s had moved from Saxony to Denmark, Sweden, and the Netherlands, travelled onwards to North America, where they settled in greater numbers in Pennsylvania and also in New York and the Carolinas.[27] Between 1755 and 1763, Britain deported some 11,000 French Catholics from Acadia (today Nova Scotia) and resettled them in other parts of the British Empire, not the least the Thirteen Colonies further south.[28] Sephardi Jews were admitted to many English/British colonies in North America and the Caribbean: Barbados and Jamaica (especially under Cromwell's so-called "Western Design" plan),[29] New York, Virginia, Maryland, and the Carolinas.[30]

Transconfessional spaces, confessional boundaries, and border-crossing in English/British North America

All denominations in English/British North America, at least their gatekeepers, sought to maintain the purity and orthodoxy of their faith. Even if religious institutions were eager, though, to keep their flocks away from other denominations, the demographic and geographic situation in British North America required some flexibility. In theory, transconfessional practices – for example, moving in and out of diverse religious institutions for baptism, marriage, funerals, social welfare, or Sunday services – were usually prohibited by church, state, and dissenting religious communities alike. Nevertheless, confessional border-crossing and the creation of transconfessional spaces was a common practice in the Atlantic World, part of the everyday experience of many individuals.[31] In the following sections, we will look at colonial New York and South Carolina as examples. Whereas New York, under Dutch and then English rule, has often been perceived as a safe haven for religious minorities and a model of tolerant policies, the Carolinas have often been described as homogeneously Anglican and intolerant. Both characterisations require qualification and nuancing.

Transgressing and integrating confessional and geographical space

Colonial South Carolina

When the colony of the "Carolinas" was founded in 1663, its Lords Proprietors initially expected to attract sufficient settlers from Barbados, New England, and Virginia. Some retained this hope even after the division of the colony into North and South in 1669. However, in the 1670s, it became clear to others that settlers would need to be recruited from the British Isles and continental Europe. One of the proprietors, the Whig politician Anthony Ashley Cooper, Earl of Shaftesbury, was particularly keen on inviting non-Anglican settlers to advance the colony's prosperity. He pushed his cause vigorously after becoming *Lord President of the Council of Trade and Plantations* in 1679.[32] In consequence, the colony's proprietors allowed and, in some instances, even invited Huguenots, Quakers, Baptists, English and Scottish Presbyterians, Swiss Reformed Protestants, and other religious groups to settle in colonial South Carolina. Some of these settlers were officially granted religious freedom. In addition, enslaved people from Africa and Native Americans lived amongst the white settlers or in the vicinity of their communities. Legally, however, Anglicanism was from the beginning the established religion of South Carolina, and pressure to conform to it increased when, in the wake of the Glorious Revolution (1688), English governments began to push for more control over their North American and Caribbean colonies. The *Fundamental Constitutions* of the colony required dissenting Protestants to conform to the Anglican Church, and this requirement was translated into law with the arrival of Sir Nathaniel Johnson as governor in 1702.[33] In May 1704, the South Carolina Assembly of colonial representatives passed a law prescribing that all its members take communion according to the rites of the Church of England. It thus excluded non-Anglicans from public office. After a wave of petitions by Protestant dissenters, it was reversed in 1706 and replaced with an *Act for the Establishment of Religious Worship in this Province, according to the Church of England; and for the Erecting of Churches for the public Worship of God; and also for the Maintenance of Ministers, and the building convenient Houses for them.* With this Act, the Church of England became the official state church of South Carolina. This policy softened from 1712 when Governor Charles Craven came to power.[34]

As an outcome of these developments, the South Carolina parishes of St. Philip's, Christ Church, St. Thomas, St. John's, St. James Goose Creek, St. Andrew's, St. Denis, St. Paul's, St. Bartholomew's, and St. James Santee all became officially Anglican, yet with a majority of parishioners from dissenting denominations. Even the Church of England commissioners who were sent to South Carolina, the reverends Gideon Johnston, William Treadwell Bull, and Alexander Garden, could not turn the officially Anglican colony into a colony with an Anglican majority of settlers.[35] Dissenting Protestants prevailed.

In its efforts to make South Carolina an Anglican colony, the Church of England attempted to increase the number of its missionaries and pastors there. It did not succeed, though, in overcoming an enduring shortage of clerical personnel and failed to establish a bishopric for British North America. South Carolina had only eight Anglican clergymen in 1710 and seven in 1720. This meant that the proprietors and governors of the colony depended on dissenting ministers to provide services for Protestant parishes.[36] Among the Church of England pastors, we thus find, for instance, the Huguenots Francis Le Jau and Jean LaPierre and the Swiss Reformed Pierre Stouppe. Born around 1690 in Switzerland, Stouppe had first been ordained in Geneva. In North America, he served the non-conforming French Reformed churches in Charleston and Orange Quarter in today's South Carolina. In 1724, he was re-ordained by the bishop of London, Edmund Gibson. He then served the officially Anglican French parish in New Rochelle, in the Province of New York, where he also preached in English to non-Huguenot parishioners.[37] As did many pastors in British North America, Stouppe linked congregations, parishes, and places. Preaching to very heterogeneous groups of believers, he remained in touch with former parishioners and established relationships between individuals in different colonies. Like other SPG pastors in the British colonies, Stouppe also ran a boarding school at his home, where he educated English Anglicans, Dutch Reformed Protestants, and Europeans of mixed descent, thus acculturating and amalgamating young people of different confessional, linguistic, and national origins.[38]

The SPG records for South Carolina document complex transconfessional practices that worried some SPG members and missionaries. Baptists, for example, attended Anglican church services, causing great scandal.[39] In 1709, Francis Le Jau complained in a letter to Lambeth Palace, the London seat of the archbishop of Canterbury, that many men and women who attended his Church of England services were dissenters or had never been baptised. In addition, enslaved Africans and Native Americans whom Le Jau was to catechise had been baptised by the Spanish and were therefore more Catholic than anything else.[40] French Reformed churches that were officially conforming, and thus nominally Anglican, not only accepted Dutch or French Reformed pastors who had been re-ordained by the Anglican Church,[41] such as Laurentius van Bosch, François Guichard, and Jean LaPierre;[42] even more problematic, in 1719 the French Reformed church in St. Denis/Orange Quarter hired as pastor a Moravian minister named Christian George.[43] In 1720, SPG missionary Peter Justian complained to the society that most of the settlers in the South Carolina parish of Saint Georges were dissenters, who nonetheless came to hear him preach in his church.[44]

Colonial New York

New Netherland had not only admitted Dutch Calvinists to the colony but also Huguenots, Congregationalists, Presbyterians, Jews, Quakers, and East European Calvinists, as well as Norwegian, Finnish, Swedish, and German Lutherans. Free and unfree Africans were also admitted, subject to varying degrees of discrimination.[45] After New Amsterdam was conquered by the English in 1664, the practice of religious toleration expanded to some extent, especially for Lutherans and Quakers, a development that was reversed in 1673/74 with the return of Dutch rule.[46] Following the English reconquest in 1674, Governor Edmund Andros once again expanded toleration, a situation that lasted until 1688/89. In the wake of Leisler's rebellion,[47] however, Governors Sloughter and Fletcher made attempts to impose Anglican conformity on the colony.[48] England's Toleration Act of 1689 exempted non-Anglican dissenters from the penal laws but did not grant them civil equality. It accommodated Catholics, Antitrinitarians, and non-Christians on even more discriminating terms. Anglican conformity became much more important in New York City than it did in small settlements on the upper Hudson River.[49] Around 1700, 200 French Reformed, 450 Dutch Reformed, and 90 Anglican families lived in what is today New York City, along with African and American Indian enslaved people.[50] In the Hudson Valley, we find Anglicans, Dutch Reformed Protestants, Presbyterians, Huguenots, Quakers, and German Lutherans as the major groups of free settlers.[51] Many of these religious groups enjoyed religious freedom and tried to form their own congregations and church administrations.[52]

For a number of reasons, however, transconfessional practices took root. Some of these reasons were similar to those in South Carolina and other English colonies in North America: from the beginning, congregations affiliated with different denominations shared the use of some church buildings. This arrangement sometimes produced major conflicts, as the congregations fought over schedules, pews, and the equipment of church buildings.[53] From 1624, Dutch, Walloon, and French Reformed immigrants in New Amsterdam utilised the same meeting houses. In 1658, New Haarlem saw the erection of an independent French Reformed church that later incorporated the Dutch congregation of this part of New York City.[54] In the later eighteenth century, the French Reformed church of New York shared its church building with the German Reformed congregation in town.[55]

In many communities, settlers of diverse confessional and national backgrounds lacked parishes and pastors. Colonial New York had no Anglican pastor prior to 1674 and no Church of England parish until the 1690s.[56] In many settlements, all Protestant denominations, Anglican and dissenter alike, shared one church building and were served by one Protestant pastor. The latter did not necessarily belong to the dominant denomination.[57] In some areas, Dutch Reformed churches became hotbeds of acculturation, as non-English and non-Anglican settlers who lacked pastors of their own denominations gravitated towards Dutch churches and communities.[58] With the establishment of Anglican churches in colonial New York – that is, from the early 1700s – Anglicans, Presbyterians, and Huguenots frequented the Anglican *Trinity Church* in New York City or moved between the French, Dutch Reformed, and Anglican churches in town. With ongoing colonisation, the arrival of new colonists, and the foundation of new settlements and parishes, this pattern slowly changed, as the case of Westchester shows: after initially forming a single parish with Anglicans and other Protestants, in 1700 Presbyterians there left the local Anglican church and founded their own parish of East Chester.[59] In other settlements in the Province of New York, however, the Anglican parish church accommodated dissenters of many denominations up to the 1720s, as missionary John Thomas in Hempstead reported to the SPG.[60]

Transconfessional practices were commonplace not only due to the lack of pastors. The consistory records of New York City's Huguenot *Église du Saint Esprit* indicate various reasons why its members frequented churches other than the French Reformed: some were dissatisfied with their pastor,[61] while others were interested in the spiritual offerings of other Protestant churches. In the 1760s, elder François Basset and other members of the *Église du Saint Esprit* consistory attended services in New York's Anglican, Presbyterian, and Dutch churches to listen to other pastors' sermons.[62]

In New Paltz, a Huguenot settlement, the French Reformed church had no pastor of its own from 1702 to 1730. During this long vacancy, a French Reformed pastor from another Huguenot community visited from time to time and conducted services. In the absence of a visiting cleric, the New Paltz Huguenots attended Dutch Reformed services in Kingston, where they also had their children baptised, or relied on lay preachers.[63] In 1731, Johannes van Driessen became pastor of the French Reformed church of New Paltz. Born in Wallonia, he had been ordained by a New Haven presbyter. The *classis* of the Amsterdam Walloon church, considering itself as holding authority over all French Reformed churches in the Province of New York, did not recognise Van Driessen as a properly ordained pastor. New Paltz's Huguenots ignored the judgement of the *classis*, accepted Van Driessen, and ceased to attend services in Kingston. Other non-orthodox pastors followed, including Theodore Frelinghuysen (1691–1747), a German Reformed pastor with Pietist tendencies.[64]

Intermarriage was another important reason for, and, to some extent, also a consequence of, transconfessional practices. The records of the Dutch Reformed church of New Amsterdam show that church members not only married Dutch Reformed men and women, but also Anglican English people, Reformed and Lutheran Germans, Lutheran Danes and Norwegians, Presbyterian Scots, Catholic Italians, and Huguenots. In the church registers, we also find wedding records for Africans from Angola.[65] The transconfessional space that was constructed through these practices, thus, furthered the integration of people of different ethnic, national, and denominational origins. Intermarriage often led families to attend more than one church and to share and discuss different liturgies, belief systems, and church organisations.[66]

Conclusions

The description of transconfessional practices offered above hopefully makes it clear that in colonial North America, attempts to establish religious orthodoxy and conformity, by the Church of England and dissenting churches alike, were from the beginning problematic. Efforts to construct confessional spaces and boundaries were in tension with everyday transconfessional practices. While some of these practices can also be found in parts of early modern Europe, as scholars have shown,[67] the question remains for English/British North America whether confessional spaces and boundaries were often not more imagined than real. In a colonial setting that lacked infrastructure such as parishes, church buildings, and pastors, transconfessional practices were common. They contributed to processes of confessional, ethnic, and national integration and acculturation, and in so doing tended to encourage toleration. A variety of sources, such as the records of the SPG and the New York French Reformed church, reveal Protestant denominations sharing transconfessional space in both colonial South Carolina and New York; in some cases, Catholics and non-Christian believers are known to have shared the same spaces. As the process of colonisation, and with it attempts to establish orthodoxy, continued, these transconfessional practices should have ceased to exist. Many settlers and pastors, though, continued to transgress confessional boundaries, often choosing their congregation on the basis of distance, social needs, spiritual preferences, or curiosity.

Whether boundaries and identifications other than the confessional became more important in the nineteenth century – boundaries such as ethnic, national, linguistic, and social ones such as class *avant la lettre* – is difficult to determine; the answer seems to have varied according to local and situational context. In the French Reformed church of New York, we do find nineteenth-century Reformed Protestants of French descent integrating more and more with Swiss Reformed immigrants. We also find church members with hybrid ethnic, national, confessional, and linguistic backgrounds – people whose ancestors had married English Anglicans, Scottish Presbyterians, Dutch Reformed Protestants, or German or Swedish Lutherans, and who thus had Dutch, English, Scottish, German, French, or Swedish backgrounds and family members. Such members often attended more than one church, a practice that also strengthened social and class ties. From these examples, it seems that not only confessional, but also ethnic, national, and linguistic boundaries were in many contexts dynamic and flexible, if flexibility served individual or family-related needs.[68]

In English/British North America, then, confessional space was from the beginning transconfessional space. Religious toleration aided the process of colonisation and empire-building. In the process, it became a common if conflict-laden feature of many colonies, both very Anglican and less Anglican ones.

Notes

1 I differentiate here between, on the one hand, "ideas of tolerance" and, on the other, the accommodation of religious dissenters for pragmatic reasons by states, cities, and ordinary people, defined as "toleration" (for the varieties in definitions of "toleration" and "tolerance," see Ned C. Landsman, "Roots, Routes, and Routedness. Diversity, Migration, and Toleration in Mid-Atlantic Pluralism," *Early American Studies* 2, no. 2 (2004), 267; Benjamin J. Kaplan, *Divided by Faith: Religious Conflict and the Practice of Toleration in Early Modern Europe* (Cambridge: Belknap Press of Harvard University Press, 2007), 8–10; Evan Haefeli, *New Netherland and the Dutch Origins of American Religious Liberty* (Philadelphia: University of Pennsylvania Press, 2012), 5–9; Evan Haefeli, *Accidental Pluralism. America and the Religious Politics of English Expansion, 1497–1662* (Chicago: The University of Chicago Press, 2021), 6–7. See also Alexandra Walsham, *Charitable Hatred: Tolerance and Intolerance in England, 1500–1700* (Manchester: Manchester University Press, 2006).
2 Cf. Carla Gardina Pestana, *Liberty of Conscience and the Growth of Religious Diversity in Early America, 1636–1786* (Providence: John Carter Brown Library, 1986); Landsman, "Roots."
3 Haefeli, *Accidental Pluralism.*
4 Cf. Nicholas Canny, "The Origins of Empire: An Introduction," in *The Oxford History of the British Empire, vol. 1: The Origins of Empire*, ed. Nicholas Canny (Oxford: Oxford University Press 1998), 4–5; David Armitage, *The Ideological Origins of the British Empire* (Cambridge: Cambridge University Press, 2000), 61–99; James B. Bell, *The Imperial Origins of the King's Church in Early America, 1607–1783* (Houndmills, Basingstoke, Hampshire: Palgrave MacMillan, 2004); Rowan Strong, *Anglicanism and the British Empire, c. 1700–1850* (Oxford, New York: Oxford University Press, 2007); Carla Gardina Pestana, *Protestant Empire: Religion and the Making of the British Atlantic World* (Philadelphia: University of Philadelphia Press, 2009); Travis Glasson, *Mastering Christianity: Missionary Anglicanism and Slavery in the Atlantic World* (Oxford: Oxford University Press, 2012).
5 On Puritans, cf. Francis J. Bremer, *The Puritan Experiment: New England Society from Bradford to Edwards* (Lebanon/NH: University Press of New England, 1995); on Moravians, cf. Michelle Gillespie and Robert Beachy, eds., *Pious Pursuits: German Moravians in the Atlantic World* (New York, Oxford: Berghahn Books, 2007); Craig D. Atwood, *Community of the Cross: Moravian Piety in Colonial Bethlehem* (University Park: Penn State University Press, 2004); on Huguenots, cf. Susanne Lachenicht, *Hugenotten in Europa und Nordamerika. Migration und Integration in der Frühen Neuzeit* (Frankfurt/Main, New York: Campus, 2010), 85–93, 297–324.
6 On the spatial turn, see below.
7 See cf. Society for the Propagation of the Gospel in Foreign Parts (SPG) series A letter books, vol. 1, letter from John Bartow to SPG, Westchester, New York

Province, November 4, 1702; letter from Edward Marston to Thomas Bray, Charleston, February 2, 1702; vol. 7, letter from Daniel Bondet to Secretary, November 21, 1711.

8 On the introduction of the concept of a "spatial turn" in human geography, see Edward Soja, *Postmodern Geographies. The Reassertion of Space in Critical Social Theory* (New York: Verso, 2010); Santa Arias and Barney Warf, eds., *The Spatial Turn. Interdisciplinary Perspectives* (London: Routledge, 2009). For an overview of the cultural turns more generally, and the spatial turn more specifically, see Doris Bachmann-Medick, *Cultural Turns: New Orientations in the Study of Culture* (Berlin, Boston: de Gruyter, 2016). For a synthesis of discussions about space, see Stephan Günzel, ed., *Raum. Ein interdisziplinäres Handbuch* (Stuttgart, Weimar: Böhlau, 2010), 121–32; or Jörg Döring and Tristan Thielmann, eds., *Spatial Turn. Das Raumparadigma in den Kultur- und Sozialwissenschaften* (Bielefeld: Transcript, 2008).

9 On early modern nationhood see, e.g. Susanne Lachenicht, "Early Modern Diasporas as Transnational Nations: The Examples of Sephardi Jews and Huguenots," *Yearbook of Transnational History* 5 (2022), 41–72, and the literature cited there.

10 *Gatekeepers* are political, spiritual, military, intellectual, or economic elites of nations and/or religions that foster narratives and practices serving group identifications through institutions such as laws, administration, families, churches, temples, synagogues, mosques, schools, media, and others.

11 On confessional space see, e.g. Renate Dürr, *Politische Kultur in der Frühen Neuzeit: Kirchenräume in Hildesheimer Stadt- und Landgemeinden 1550–1750* (Gütersloh: Gütersloher Verlagsgesellschaft, 2006); Susanne Rau, "Raum und Religion: Eine Forschungsskizze," in *Topo-graphien des Sakralen: Religion und Raumordnung in der Vormoderne*, ed. Susanne Rau and Gerd Schwerhoff (Munich: Dölling and Garlitz, 2008), 10–37; Martina Löw, *Raumsoziologie* (Frankfurt am Main: Suhrkamp, 2009); Gerd Schwerhoff, "Sakralitätsmanagement: Zur Analyse religiöser Räume im späten Mittelalter und in der Frühen Neuzeit," in *Topographien des Sakralen: Religion und Raumordnung in der Vormoderne*, 38–69.

12 On the concept of lifeworlds or special worlds, see Rupert Klieber, *Jüdische – christliche – muslimische Lebenswelten der Donaumonarchie 1848–1918* (Vienna-Böhlau 2010), 22, 163.

13 Haefeli, *Accidental Pluralism*, 305–7.

14 William Frost, *A Perfect Freedom: Religious Liberty in Pennsylvania* (University Park: Penn State University Press, 1993).

15 Landsman, "The Episcopate."

16 Cf. SPG A series letter books, letter from Thomas Keith to the SPG, November 29, 1702.

17 Strong, *Anglicanism*, 42–3.

18 SPG A series letter books, vol. 1, New York, letter from Thomas Keith to SPG, November 29, 1702; vol. 20, letter from Pierre Stouppe to SPG, December 11, 1727; vol. 21, letter from Pierre Stouppe to SPG, July 15, 1728.

19 Cf. SPG A series letter books, vol. 1, letter from Thomas Keith to SPG, November 29, 1702.

20 Roger Bartlett, *Human Capital. The Settlement of Foreigners in Russia 1762–1804* (Cambridge, New York: Cambridge University Press, 1979), 15–21; Michael Schippan, "Der Beginn der deutschen Russlandauswanderung im 18. Jahrhundert," in *Migration nach Ost- und Südosteuropa vom 18. bis zum Beginn des 19. Jahrhunderts*, ed. Matthias Beer and Dittmar Dahlmann (Stuttgart: Steiner, 1999), 47–70.

21 Jack P. Greene, *Selling a New World: Two Colonial South Carolina Pamphlets by Thomas Naire and John Norris* (Columbia: The University of South Carolina

Press, 1989); Bertrand van Ruymbeke, *From New Babylon to Eden? The Hugue-nots and Their Migration to Colonial South Carolina* (Columbia, SC: University of South Carolina Press, 2005), 38–43; Lachenicht, *Hugenotten*, 85–93.

22 Susanne Lachenicht, "Refugees and Refugee Protection in the Early Modern Period," *Journal of Refugee Studies*. Special issue. The History of Refugee Protection (2017), ed. Olaf Kleist, 261–81.

23 Cf. Kaplan, *Divided by Faith*, 2–4; Nicholas Terpstra, *Religious Refugees in the Early Modern World: An Alternative History of the Reformation* (Cambridge: Cambridge University Press, 2015), 1–7.

24 Andrew R. Murphy, *Conscience and Community: Revisiting Toleration and Religious Dissent in Early Modern England and America* (University Park: Penn State University Press, 2001), 27–73.

25 Bremer, *The Puritan Experiment*; Christina Hallowell Garrett, *The Marian Exiles: A Study in the Origins of Elizabethan Puritanism* (New York: Cambridge University Press, 2010); Thomas D. Hamm, *The Quakers in America* (New York: Columbia University Press, 2003).

26 Renate Wilson, "Land, Population, and Labor. Lutheran Immigrants in Colonial Georgia," in *In Search of Peace and Prosperity. New German Settlements in Eighteenth-Century Europe and America*, eds. Hartmut Lehmann, Hermann Wellenreuther, and Renate Wilson (University Park: Penn State University Press, 2000), 217–45; James van Horn Melton, "From Alpine Minder to Lowcountry Yeoman: Transatlantic Worlds of a Georgia Salzburger, 1693–1761," *Past & Present* 201, no. 1 (2008), 97–140; Mack Walker, "The Salzburger Migration to Prussia," in *In Search of Peace and Prosperity. New German Settlements in Eighteenth-Century Europe and America*, ed. Hartmut Lehmann, Hermann Wellenreuther, and Renate Wilson (University Park: Pennsylvania University Press, 2000), 68–76; Alexander Pyrges, *Das Kolonialprojekt Ebenezer: Formen und Mechanismen protestantischer Expansion in der atlantischen Welt des 18. Jahrhunderts* (Stuttgart: Steiner, 2015).

27 Hermann Wellenreuther, "The Herrnhuters in Europe and the British Colonies (1735–1776)," in *Religious Refugees in Europe, Asia and North America, 6th–21st century*, ed. Susanne Lachenicht (Hamburg: LIT, 2007), 171–95.

28 Christopher Hodson, "Idlers and Idolaters. Acadian Exiles and the Labor Regimes of British North America, 1755–1763," in *Religious Refugees in Europe, Asia and North America (6th-21st century)*, ed. Susanne Lachenicht (Hamburg: LIT, 2007), 197–212; Christopher Hodson, *The Acadian Diaspora: An Eighteenth-Century History* (New York: Oxford University Press, 2012).

29 Stephen A. Fortune, *Merchants and Jews: The Struggle for British West Indian Commerce, 1650–1750* (Gainesville: University Press of Florida, 1984), 33–4, 44.

30 Yitzchak Kerem, "Sephardic Settlement in the British Colonies of the Americas in the 17th and 18th centuries," in *From Strangers to Citizens: The Integration of Immigrant Communities in Britain, Ireland and Colonial America, 1550–1750*, eds. Randolph Vigne and Charles Littleton (Brighton, Portland: Sussex Academic Press, 2001), 286–7, 291–2.

31 For Pennsylvania, see cf. Charles H. Glatfelder, *Pastors and People: German Lutheran and Reformed Churches in the Pennsylvania Field, 1717–1793* (Breinigsville: Pennsylvania German Society, 1981); Mark Häberlein, *The Practice of Pluralism: Congregational Life and Religious Diversity in Lancaster, Pennsylvania, 1730–1820* (University Park: Pennsylvania State University Press, 2009).

32 Van Ruymbeke, *From New Babylon to Eden*, 36.

33 Van Ruymbeke, *From New Babylon to Eden*, 174.

34 Thomas J. Curry, *The First Freedoms: Church and State in America to the Passage of the First Amendment* (New York, Oxford: Oxford University Press, 1986), 58–9.

35 Charles S. Bolton, *Southern Anglicanism: The Church of England in Colonial South Carolina* (Westport: Greenwood, 1982).

36 Curry, *The First Freedoms*, 55, 59.

37 Paula Wheeler Carlo, *Huguenot Refugees in Colonial New York: Becoming American in the Hudson Valley* (Brighton, Portland: Sussex Academic Press, 2005), 62–3.

38 Wheeler Carlo, *Huguenot Refugees*, 65, 107–10. See also cf. SPG A series letter books, vol. 9, letter from Thomas Barclay to SPG, Albany, June 29, 1714.

39 SPG A series letter books, vol. 1, letter from Samuel Thomas to SPG, Carolina, January 29, 1702, see also vol. 14, letter from Thomas Hassel to the Society, March 20, 1719.

40 SPG A series, letter books, St. James, Goosecreek, S.C., letter from Francis Le Jau to the SPG, August 5, 1705, vol. 5, letter from Francis Le Jau to SPG, February 1, 1710.

41 SPG A series, letter books, vol. 5, letter from Jean LaPierre to Rival, January 20, 1723.

42 Van Ruymbeke, *From New Babylon to Eden*, 116–21.

43 SPG A series, letter books, vol. 17, letter from Jean LaPierre to SPG, June 24, 1710.

44 SPG A series, letter books, vol. 14, letter from Peter Justian to the Secretary, July 10, 1720.

45 Wheeler Carlo, *Huguenot Refugees*, 13; John Webb Pratt, *Religion, Politics, and Diversity: The Church-State Theme in New York History* (Ithaca, N.Y.: Cornell University Press, 1999), 11–3; Haefeli, *New Netherland*, 82–210.

46 Landsman, "Roots," 274; Haefeli, *New Netherland*, 253–78.

47 Leisler's rebellion is a famous New York uprising related to the Glorious Revolution. Jacob Leisler (c. 1640–1691), a German-Reformed subject of colonial New York, became leader of a rebellion against lieutenant governor Francis Nicholson, a supporter of James II and his policies in the Dominion of New England to which New York belonged. Leisler ruled the colony from 1689 to 1691. Under the reign of King William III, Leisler was imprisoned and sentenced to death.

48 Curry, *The First Freedoms*, 64–7.

49 Landsman, "Roots," 283.

50 Jon Butler, *The Huguenots in America: A Refugee People in New World Society* (Cambridge, MA: Harvard University Press, 1983), 47, 147; Graham Hodges, *Root and Branch: African Americans in New York and East Jersey 1613–1863* (Chapel Hill: University of North Carolina Press, 1999), 34–8.

51 David William Vorhees, "Jacob Leisler and the Huguenot Network in the English Atlantic World," in *From Strangers to Citizens. The Integration of Immigrant Communities in Britain, Ireland and Colonial America, 1550–1750*, ed. Randolph Vigne and Charles Littleton (Brighton, Portland: Sussex Academic Press, 2001), 322–31.

52 Curry, *First Freedoms*, 68–9; Haefeli, *New Netherland*, 95–6.

53 SPG A series, letter books, vol. 7, letter from Morris to the Secretary, January 1, 1711.

54 Joyce D. Goodfriend, *Before the Melting Pot: Society and Culture in Colonial New York City, 1664–1730* (Princeton: Princeton University Press, 1992), 84.

55 New York Historical Society, *Procédés des Trustees de l'Eglise Reformée Protestante Française dans la Ville de New York*, 1796–1818.

56 Haefeli, *New Netherland*, 257.

57 Curry, *First Freedoms*, 63; Landsman, "Roots," 281; Haefeli, *New Netherland*, 256–7.

58 Patricia U. Bonomi, *A Factious People: Politics and Society in Colonial New York* (New York: Columbia University Press, 1971); A.G. Roeber, "'The Origin

of Whatever Is Not English among Us': The Dutch-speaking and the German-speaking Peoples of Colonial British America," in *Strangers within the Realm: Cultural Margins of the First British Empire*, ed. Bernard Bailyn and Philip D. Morgan (Chapel Hill: University of North Carolina Press, 1991), 221, 226.

59 SPG A series, letter books, vol. 9, letter from John Bartow to Secretary of SPG, April 14, 1714.

60 SPG A series, letter books, vol. 14, letter from John Thomas to Secretary of SPG, December 5, 1720.

61 Lachenicht, *Hugenotten*, 309–24.

62 New York Historical Society, *Livre de Mémoire pour Jaques Buvelot*, entries of the summer of 1767 and of November and December 1767.

63 Wheeler Carlo, *Huguenot Refugees*, 44–7.

64 Wheeler Carlo, *Huguenot Refugees*, 48–53, 74–7.

65 *Marriages from 1639 to 1801 in the Reformed Dutch Church, New Amsterdam, New York City* (New York: New York Genealogical and Biographical Society, 1940).

66 New York Historical Society, *Records of the French Church du Saint Esprit New York, 1766–68, Livre de Mémoire pour Jaques Buvelot*, November 24, 1767, summer 1767.

67 Cf. Nicole Grochowina, *Indifferenz und Dissens in der Grafschaft Ostfriesland im 16. und 17. Jahrhundert* (Frankfurt: Peter Lang, 2003); Lachenicht, *Hugenotten*, 363–84.

68 Lachenicht, *Hugenotten*, 297–324.

Selected Readings

Concepts and theory

Bejczy, István. "Tolerantia: A Medieval Concept." *Journal of the History of Ideas* 58, no. 3 (1997), 365–84.

Brown, Wendy. *Regulating Aversion: Tolerance in the Age of Identity and Empire.* Princeton: Princeton University Press, 2006.

Brown, Wendy, et al. *The Power of Tolerance: A Debate.* New York: Columbia University Press, 2014.

Butterfield, Herbert. *The Whig Interpretation of History.* London: Bell, 1931.

Cannadine, David. *The Undivided Past: History Beyond Our Differences.* London: Allen Lane, 2013.

Coffey, John. "Milton, Locke and the New History of Toleration." *Modern Intellectual History* 5 (2008), 619–32.

Forst, Rainer. *Toleration in Conflict: Past and Present.* Translated by Ciaran Cronin. Cambridge: Cambridge University Press, 2013.

Guesnet, François, Lois Lee, and Cécile Laborde, eds. *Negotiating Religion: Cross-Disciplinary Perspectives.* Abingdon: Routledge, 2016.

Hayden, Robert M., et al. *Antagonistic Tolerance: Competitive Sharing of Religious Sites and Spaces.* London: Routledge, 2016.

Heyd, David, ed. *Toleration: An Elusive Virtue.* Princeton: Princeton University Press, 1996.

Johnson, Noel D., and Mark Koyama. *Persecution & Toleration: The Long Road to Religious Freedom.* Cambridge: Cambridge University Press, 2019.

Jütte, Daniel. "Interfaith Encounters between Jews and Christians in the Early Modern Period and Beyond: Towards a Framework." *American Historical Review* 118 (2013), 378–400.

Kymlicka, Will. "Two Models of Pluralism and Tolerance." In *Toleration: An Elusive Virtue,* edited by David Heyd, 81–105. Princeton: Princeton University Press, 1996.

Lotz-Heumann, U. "Confessionalization." In *Reformation and Early Modern Europe: A Guide to Research,* edited by D.M. Whitford, 136–57. Kirksville: Truman State University Press, 2008.

McKinnon, Catriona. *Toleration: A Critical Introduction.* London: Routledge, 2006.

Nirenberg, David. *Communities of Violence: Persecution of Minorities in the Middle Ages.* Princeton: Princeton University Press, 1995.

Stearns, Peter. *Tolerance in World History.* New York: Routledge, 2017.

Walzer, Michael. *On Toleration.* New Haven, CT: Yale University Press, 1997.

Overviews and essay collections

Bonney, Richard, and D.J.B. Trim, eds. *Persecution and Pluralism: Calvinists and Religious Minorities in Early Modern Europe, 1550–1700*. Bern: Peter Lang, 2006.

Christman, Victoria, and Marjorie Plummer, eds. *Topographies of Tolerance and Intolerance: Responses to Religious Pluralism in Reformation Europe*. Leiden: Brill, 2018.

Dixon, C. Scott, Dagmar Freist, and Mark Greengrass, eds. *Living with Religious Diversity in Early Modern Europe*. Farnham: Ashgate, 2009.

Fukasawa, Katsumi, Benjamin J. Kaplan, and Pierre-Yves Beaurepaire, eds. *Religious Interactions in Europe and the Mediterranean World: Coexistence and Dialogue from the Twelfth to the Twentieth Centuries*. Abingdon: Routledge, 2017.

Grell, Ole Peter, and Bob Scribner, eds. *Tolerance and Intolerance in the European Reformation*. Cambridge: Cambridge University Press, 1996.

Grell, Ole Peter, and Roy Porter, eds. *Toleration in Enlightenment Europe*. Cambridge: Cambridge University Press, 2000.

Israel, Jonathan I., *Radical Enlightenment: Philosophy and the Making of Modernity 1650–1750*. Oxford: Oxford University Press, 2001.

Israel, Jonathan I. *Enlightenment Contested: Philosophy, Modernity, and the Emancipation of Man, 1670–1752*. Oxford: Oxford University Press, 2006.

Kaplan, Benjamin J. "Coexistence, Conflict, and the Practice of Toleration." In *A Companion to the Reformation World*, edited by R. Po-chia Hsia, 486–505. Oxford: Blackwell, 2003.

Kaplan, Benjamin J. *Divided by Faith: Religious Conflict and the Practice of Toleration in Early Modern Europe*. Cambridge, MA: Harvard University Press, 2007.

Karremann, Isabel, Cornel Zwierlein, and Inga Mai Groote, eds. *Forgetting Faith? Negotiating Confessional Conflict in Early Modern Europe*. Berlin: De Gruyter, 2012.

Laursen, John Christian, and Cary J. Nederman, eds. *Beyond the Persecuting Society: Religious Toleration before the Enlightenment*. Philadelphia: University of Pennsylvania Press, 1998.

Lecler, Joseph. *Toleration and the Reformation*. Translated by T.L. Westow. 2 vols. London: Longmans, 1960.

Louthan, Howard, Gary B. Cohen, and Franz A.J. Szabo, eds. *Diversity and Dissent: Negotiating Religious Difference in Central Europe*. New York: Berghahn Books, 2011.

Safley, Thomas Max, ed. *A Companion to Multiconfessionalism in the Early Modern World*. Leiden: Brill, 2011.

Te Brake, Wayne P. *Religious War and Religious Peace in Early Modern Europe*. Cambridge: Cambridge University Press, 2017.

Terpstra, Nicholas, ed. *Global Reformations: Transforming Early Modern Religions, Societies, and Cultures*. New York: Routledge, 2019.

Senses

Baum, Jacob M. *Reformation of the Senses: The Paradox of Religious Belief and Practice in Germany*. Urbana: University of Illinois Press, 2018.

Boer, Wietse de. "The Counter-Reformation of the Senses." In *The Ashgate Research Companion to the Counter-Reformation*, edited by Alexandra Bamji, Geert H. Janssen, and Mary Laven, 243–60. Farnham: Ashgate, 2013.

Boer, Wietse de, and Christine Göttler, eds. *Religion and the Senses in Early Modern Europe*. Leiden: Brill, 2013.

Christ, Martin. "Sensing Multiconfessionality in Early Modern Germany." *German History* 40, no. 3 (2022), 317–39.

Cuffel, A., L. di Giacinto, and V. Krech. "Senses, Religion, and Religious Encounter: Literature Review and Research Perspectives." *Entangled Religions* 10 (2019), n.p.

Fisher, Alexander J. *Music, Piety, and Propaganda: The Soundscapes of Counter-Reformation Bavaria.* Oxford: Oxford University Press, 2014.

Fisher, Alexander J. "'Mit singen und klingen': Urban Processional Culture and the Soundscapes of Post-Reformation Germany." In *Listening to Early Modern Catholicism: Perspectives from Musicology,* edited by Daniele V. Filippi and Michael J. Noone, 187–203. Leiden: Brill, 2017.

Hahn, Philip. "Sensing Sacred Space: Ulm Minster, the Reformation, and Parishioners' Sensory Perception, c. 1470 to 1640." *Archiv für Reformationsgeschichte* 105, no. 1 (2014), 55–91.

Hall, Marcia B., and Tracy Elizabeth Cooper, eds. *The Sensuous in the Counter-Reformation Church.* Cambridge: Cambridge University Press, 2013.

Macdonald, Robin, Emilie K.M. Murphy, and Elizabeth L. Swann, eds. *Sensing the Sacred in Medieval and Early Modern Culture.* Abingdon: Routledge, 2018.

Smith, Mark M. *Sensing the Past: Seeing, Hearing, Smelling, Tasting, and Touching in History.* Berkely: University of California Press, 2007.

Smith, Mark M. *A Sensory History Manifesto.* University Park: Pennsylvania State University Press, 2021.

Identities

Bodian, Miriam. *Hebrews of the Portuguese Nation: Conversos and Community in Early Modern Amsterdam.* Bloomington: Indiana University Press, 1999.

Burke, Peter J., and Jan E. Stets. *Identity Theory.* Oxford: Oxford University Press, 2009.

Coulmas, Florian. *Identity: A Very Short Introduction.* Oxford: Oxford University Press, 2019.

Fisher, Alexander J. *Music and Religious Identity in Counter-Reformation Augsburg, 1580–1630.* Aldershot: Ashgate, 2004.

Forster, Marc R. *Catholic Revival in the Age of the Baroque: Religious Identity in Southwest Germany, 1550–1750.* Cambridge: Cambridge University Press, 2001.

Graizbord, David L. *Souls in Dispute: Converso Identities in Iberia and the Jewish Diaspora, 1580–1700.* Philadelphia: University of Pennsylvania Press, 2004.

Head, Randolph C. "Catholics and Protestants in Graubünden: Confessional Discipline and Confessional Identities without an Early Modern State?" *German History* 17, no. 3 (1999), 321–45.

Heal, Bridget. *A Magnificent Faith: Art and Identity in Lutheran Germany.* Oxford: Oxford University Press, 2017.

Janssen, Geert H. *The Dutch Revolt and Catholic Exile in Reformation Europe.* Oxford: Oxford University Press, 2014.

Kaplan, Yosef. *From Christianity to Judaism: The Story of Isaac Orobio de Castro.* Translated by Raphael Loewe. Oxford: Oxford University Press, 1989.

Kaplan, Yosef. "Political Concepts in the World of the Portuguese Jews of Amsterdam During the Seventeenth Century. The Problem of Exclusion and the Boundaries of Self-Identity." In *Menasseh Ben Israel and His World,* edited by Yosef Kaplan, Henry Méchoulan, and Richard H. Popkin, 45–62. Leiden: Brill, 1989.

Mentzer, Raymond A. *Blood & Belief: Family Survival and Confessional Identity among the Provincial Huguenot Nobility.* West Lafayette: Purdue University Press, 1994.

Lewycky, Nadine, and Adam Morton, eds. *Getting Along? Religious Identities and Confessional Relations in Early Modern England – Essays in Honour of Professor W.J. Sheils.* Farnham: Ashgate, 2012.

Parker, Charles H. "In partibus infidelium: Calvinism and Catholic Identity in the Dutch Republic." In *John Calvin and Roman Catholicism: Critique and Engagement, Then and Now,* edited by Randall C. Zachman, 119–44. Grand Rapids, MI: Baker Academic, 2008.

Pollmann, Judith. *Another Road to God: The Religious Development of Arnoldus Buchelius (1565–1641).* Manchester: Manchester University Press, 1999.

Spohnholz, Jesse, and Gary Waite, eds. *Exile and the Formation of Religious Identities in the Early Modern World.* London: Pickering & Chatto, 2014.

Boundaries

Barth, Fredrik. *Ethnic Groups and Boundaries: The Social Organization of Culture Difference.* London: Allen & Unwin, 1969.

Cohen, Mark R., ed. *The Autobiography of a Seventeenth-Century Venetian Rabbi: Leon Modena's Life of Judah.* Princeton: Princeton University Press, 1988.

Corpis, Duane. *Crossing the Boundaries of Belief: Geographies of Religious Conversion in Southern Germany, 1648–1800.* Charlottesville, VA.: University of Virginia Press, 2014.

François, Etienne. *Die unsichtbare Grenze: Protestanten und Katholiken in Augsburg 1648–1806.* Sigmaringen: Thorbecke, 1991. Also available in French as *Protestants et catholiques en Allemagne. Identités et pluralisme. Augsbourg, 1648–1806.* Paris: Albin Michel, 1993.

Harline, Craig. *Conversions: Two Family Stories from the Reformation and Modern America.* New Haven, CT: Yale University Press, 2011.

Lamont, Michèle, and Marcel Fournier. "Introduction." In *Cultivating Differences: Symbolic Boundaries and the Making of Inequality,* edited by Michèle Lamont and Marcel Fournier, 1–20. Chicago: University of Chicago Press, 1992.

Luebke, David M., ed. *Conversion and the Politics of Religion in Early Modern Europe.* New York: Berghahn Books, 2012.

Luria, Keith P. *Sacred Boundaries: Religious Coexistence and Conflict in Early-Modern France.* Washington, DC: Catholic University of American Press, 2005.

Mercedes García-Arenal, and Gerard Wiegers. *A Man of Three Worlds. Samuel Pallache, a Moroccan Jew in Catholic and Protestant Europe.* Translated by Martin Beagles. Baltimore: Johns Hopkins University Press, 2010.

Scholz, Maximilian Miguel. *Strange Brethren: Refugees, Religious Bonds, and Reformation in Frankfurt, 1554–1608.* Charlottesville, VA: University of Virginia Press, 2022.

Schwartz, Stuart B. *Blood and Boundaries: The Limits of Religious and Racial Exclusion in Early Modern Latin America.* Waltham: Brandeis University Press, 2020.

Siebenhüner, Kim. "Conversion, Mobility and the Roman Inquisition in Italy Around 1600." *Past & Present* 200, no. 1 (2008), 5–35.

Terpstra, Nicholas. *Religious Refugees in the Early Modern World: An Alternative History of the Reformation.* Cambridge: Cambridge University Press, 2015.

Interaction

Americas and the Atlantic World

Beneke, Chris. *Beyond Toleration: The Religious Origins of American Pluralism.* Oxford: Oxford University Press, 2006.

Beneke, Chris, and Christopher S. Grenda, eds. *The Lively Experiment: Religious Toleration in America from Roger Williams to the Present.* Lanham: Rowman & Littlefield, 2001.

Glaser, Elaine, ed. *Religious Tolerance in the Atlantic World: Early Modern and Contemporary Perspectives.* Basingstoke: Palgrave Macmillan, 2013.

Goodfriend, Joyce D. "Practicing Toleration in Dutch New Netherland." In *The First Prejudice: Religious Tolerance and Intolerance in Early America*, edited by Chris Beneke and Christopher S. Grenda, 98–122. Philadelphia: University of Pennsylvania Press, 2011.

Hanson, Charles P. *Necessary Virtue: The Pragmatic Origins of Religious Liberty in New England.* Charlottesville, VA: University Press of Virginia, 1998.

Häberlein, Mark. *The Practice of Pluralism. Congregational Life and Religious Diversity in Lancaster, Pennsylvania, 1730–1820.* University Park, PA: Pennsylvania State University Press, 2009.

Haefeli, Evan. *New Netherland and the Dutch Origins of American Religious Liberty.* Philadelphia: University of Pennsylvania Press, 2016.

Haefeli, Evan. *Accidental Pluralism: America and the Religious Politics of English Expansion, 1497–1662.* Chicago: University of Chicago Press, 2021.

Israel, Jonathan I., and Stuart B. Schwartz, eds. *The Expansion of Tolerance: Religion in Dutch Brazil (1624–1654).* Amsterdam: Amsterdam University Press, 2007.

Murphy, Andrew R. *Conscience and Community: Revisiting Toleration and Religious Dissent in Early Modern England and America.* University Park, PA: Pennsylvania State University Press, 2001.

Noorlander, D.L. *Heaven's Wrath: The Protestant Reformation and the Dutch West India Company in the Atlantic World.* Ithaca: Cornell University Press, 2019.

Schwartz, Stuart B. *All Can Be Saved: Religious Tolerance and Salvation in the Iberian Atlantic World.* New Haven, CT: Yale University Press, 2008.

British Isles

Brown, Carys. *Friends, Neighbours, Sinners. Religious Difference and English Society, 1689–1750.* Cambridge: Cambridge University Press, 2022.

Brown, Carys. "Women and Religious Coexistence in Eighteenth-Century England." In *Negotiating Exclusion in Early Modern England, 1550–1800*, edited by Naomi Pullin and Kathryn Woods, 68–87. New York: Routledge, 2021.

Cogan, Susan M. *Catholic Social Networks in Early Modern England: Kinship, Gender, and Coexistence.* Amsterdam: Amsterdam University Press, 2021.

Grell, Ole Peter, Jonathan I. Israel, and Nicholas Tyacke, eds. *From Persecution to Toleration: The Glorious Revolution and Religion in England.* Oxford: Oxford University Press, 1991.

Lake, Peter, and Michael Questier. *All Hail to the Archpriest: Confessional Conflict, Toleration, and the Politics of Publicity in Post-Reformation England.* Oxford: Oxford University Press, 2019.

Lotz-Heumann, Ute. "Between Conflict and Coexistence: The Catholic Community in Ireland as a 'Visible Underground Church' in the Late Sixteenth and Early Seventeenth Centuries." In *Catholic Communities in Protestant States: Britain and the Netherlands c. 1570–1720*, edited by Benjamin J. Kaplan, Bob Moore, H. van Nierop, and Judith Pollmann, 168–82. Manchester: Manchester University Press, 2009.

Marshall, John. *John Locke, Toleration and Early Enlightenment Culture: Religious Intolerance and Arguments for Religious Toleration in Early Modern and "Early Enlightenment" Europe*. Cambridge: Cambridge University Press, 2006.

Shagan, Ethan H., ed. *Catholics and the "Protestant Nation": Religious Politics and Identity in Early Modern England*. Manchester: Manchester University Press, 2005.

Sheils, William. "'Getting On' and 'Getting Along' in Parish and Town. Catholics and Their Neighbours in England." In *Catholic Communities in Protestant States: Britain and The Netherlands c. 1570–1720*, edited by Benjamin J. Kaplan, Bob Moore, H. van Nierop, and Judith Pollmann, 67–83. Manchester: Manchester University Press, 2009.

Sowerby, Scott. *Making Toleration: The Repealers and the Glorious Revolution*. Cambridge, MA: Harvard University Press, 2013.

Walsham, Alexandra. *Charitable Hatred: Tolerance and Intolerance in England, 1500–1700*. Manchester: Manchester University Press, 2006.

Walsham, Alexandra. "Supping with Satan's Disciples: Spiritual and Secular Sociability in Post-Reformation England." In *Getting Along? Religious Identities and Confessional Relations in Early Modern England – Essays in Honour of Professor W.J. Sheils*, edited by Adam Morton and Nadine Lewycky, 29–56. Farnham: Ashgate, 2012.

Walsham, Alexandra. "Cultures of Coexistence in Early Modern England: History, Literature and Religious Toleration." *The Seventeenth Century* 28, no. 2 (2013), 115–37.

Central and Eastern Europe

Bérenger, Jean. *Tolérance ou paix de religion en Europe centrale (1415–1792)*. Paris: Honoré Champion, 2000.

Fata, Márta. *Ungarn, das Reich der Stephanskrone, im Zeitalter der Reformation und Konfessionalisierung: Multiethnizität, Land und Konfession 1500 bis 1700*. Katholisches Leben und Kirchenreform im Zeitalter der Glaubensspaltung 60. Münster: Aschendorff, 2000.

Frick, David. *Kith, Kin, & Neighbors: Communities & Confessions in Seventeenth-Century Wilno*. Ithaca: Cornell University Press, 2013.

Head, Randolph C. "Religious Coexistence and Confessional Conflict in the Vier Dörfer: Practices of Toleration in Eastern Switzerland, 1525–1615." In *Beyond the Persecuting Society: Religious Toleration Before the Enlightenment*, edited by John C. Laursen and Cary J. Nederman, 145–65. Philadelphia: University of Pennsylvania Press, 1998.

Khordarkovsky, Michael. "'Not by Word Alone': Missionary Policies and Religious Conversion in Early Modern Russia." *Comparative Studies in Society and History* 38, no. 2 (1996), 267–293.

Louthan, Howard, Gary B. Cohen, and Franz A.J. Szabo, eds. *Diversity and Dissent: Negotiating Religious Difference in Central Europe*. New York: Berghahn Books, 2011.

Monter, E. William. "Toleration and Its Discontents in East-Central Europe." In *Ritual, Myth, and Magic in Early Modern Europe*, E. William Monter. Brighton: Harvester, 1983.

Müller, Michael G. "Protestant Confessionalisation in the Towns of Royal Prussia and the Practice of Religious Toleration in Poland-Lithuania." In *Tolerance and Intolerance in the European Reformation*, edited by Ole Peter Grell and Bob Scribner, 262–81. Cambridge: Cambridge University Press, 1996.

Murdock, Graeme. *Calvinism on the Frontier, 1600–1660: International Calvinism and the Reformed Church in Hungary and Transylvania.* New York: Clarendon Press, 2000.

Péter, Katalin. "Tolerance and Intolerance in Sixteenth-Century Hungary." In *Tolerance and Intolerance in the European Reformation*, edited by Ole Peter Grell and Bob Scribner, 249–61. Cambridge: Cambridge University Press, 1996.

Tazbir, Janusz. *A State without Stakes: Polish Religious Toleration in the Sixteenth and Seventeenth Centuries.* New York: Kościuszko Foundation, 1973.

Teter, Magda. *Jews and Heretics in Catholic Poland: A Beleaguered Church in the Post-Reformation Era.* Cambridge: Cambridge University Press, 2006.

Tollet, Daniel. "Religious Coexistence and Competition in the Polish-Lithuanian Commonwealth c. 1600." In *Religious and Cultural Exchange in Europe, 1400–1700*, edited by Heinz Schilling and István Tóth, 64–87. Cambridge: Cambridge University Press, 2006.

Volkland, Frauke. *Konfession und Selbstverständnis: reformierte Rituale in der gemischtkonfessionellen Kleinstadt Bischofszell im 17. Jahrhundert.* Veröffentlichungen des Max-Planck-Instituts für Geschichte. Göttingen: Vandenhoeck & Ruprecht, 2005.

Zdenek, V. David. "Confessional Accommodation in Early Modern Bohemia: Shifting Relations between Catholics and Utraquists." In *Conciliation and Confession: The Struggle for Unity in the Age of Reform, 1415–1648*, edited by H.P. Louthan and R.C. Zachman, 173–98. Notre Dame, IN: Notre Dame University Press, 2004.

Dutch Republic

Berkvens-Stevelinck, Christiane, Jonathan Irvine Israel, and G.H.M. Posthumus Meyes, eds. *The Emergence of Tolerance in the Dutch Republic.* Leiden: Brill, 1997.

Eijnatten, Joris van. *Liberty and Concord in the United Provinces: Religious Toleration and the Public in the Eighteenth-Century Netherlands.* Leiden: Brill, 2003.

Forclaz, Bertrand. *Catholiques au défi de la Réforme. La coexistence confessionelle à Utrecht au xviie siècle.* Paris: Honoré Champion, 2014.

Frijhoff, Willem. *Embodied Belief: Ten Essays on Religious Culture in Dutch History.* Hilversum: Verloren, 2002.

Hsia, R. Po-Chia, and H.F.K. van Nierop, eds. *Calvinism and Religious Toleration in the Dutch Golden Age.* Cambridge: Cambridge University Press, 2002.

Kaplan, Benjamin J. *Calvinists and Libertines: Confession and Community in Utrecht, 1578–1620.* Oxford: Clarendon Press, 1995.

Kaplan, Benjamin J. *Cunegonde's Kidnapping: A Story of Religious Conflict in the Age of Enlightenment.* New Haven, CT: Yale University Press, 2014.

Kaplan, Benjamin J. *Reformation and the Practice of Toleration.* Leiden: Brill, 2019.

Kooi, Christine. *Calvinists and Catholics during Holland's Golden Age: Heretics and Idolaters.* Cambridge: Cambridge University Press, 2012.

Lenarduzzi, Carolina. *Katholiek in de Republiek. De belevingswereld van een religieuze minderheid 1570–1750.* Nijmegen: Vantilt, 2019.

Pettegree, Andrew. "The Politics of Toleration in the Free Netherlands, 1572–1620." In *Tolerance and Intolerance in the European Reformation*, edited by Ole Peter Grell and Bob Scribner, 182–98. Cambridge: Cambridge University Press, 1996.

Pollmann, Judith. "Countering the Reformation in France and the Netherlands: Clerical Leadership and Catholic Violence 1560–1585." *Past & Present* 190, no. 1 (2006), 83–120.

Pollmann, Judith. "From Freedom of Conscience to Confessional Segregation? Religious Choice and Toleration in the Dutch Republic." In *Persecution and Pluralism: Calvinists and Religious Minorities in Early Modern Europe, 1550–1700*, edited by Richard Bonney and D.J.B. Trim, 123–48. Bern: Peter Lang, 2006.

Spaans, Joke. *Haarlem na de Reformatie: stedelijke cultuur en kerkelijk leven, 1577–1620.* The Hague: Stichting Hollandse Historische Reeks, 1989.

Spohnholz, Jesse. "Confessional Coexistence in the Early Modern Low Countries." In *A Companion to Multiconfessionalism in the Early Modern World*, edited by Thomas Max Safley, 47–74. Leiden: Brill, 2011.

Waite, Gary K. *Jews and Muslims in Seventeenth-Century Discourse: From Religious Enemies to Allies and Friends.* New York: Routledge, 2018.

Yasuhira, Genji. "Confessional Coexistence and Perceptions of the 'Public': Catholics' Agency in Negotiations on Poverty and Charity in Utrecht, 1620s–1670s." *BMGN – Low Countries Historical Review* 132 (2017), 3–24.

France

Benedict, Philip. *The Huguenot Population of France, 1600–1685: The Demographic Fate and Customs of a Religious Minority.* Philadelphia: American Philosophical Society, 1991.

Benedict, Philip. "*Un roi, une loi, deux fois*: Parameters for the History of Catholic-Reformed Coexistence in France, 1555–1685." In *The Faith and Fortunes of France's Huguenots, 1600–1685*, edited by Philip Benedict, 279–308. Aldershot: Ashgate, 2001.

Boisson, Didier, and Yves Krumenacker, eds. *La coexistence confessionnelle a l'épreuve: Études sur les relations entre protestants et catholiques dans la France moderne.* Lyon: Université Jean Moulin III, 2009.

Crouzet, Denis. *Les guerriers de Dieu: La violence au temps des troubles de religion (vers 1525-vers 1610).* 2 vols. Seyssel: Champ Valons, 1990.

Diefendorf, Barbara B. *Beneath the Cross: Catholics and Huguenots in Sixteenth-Century Paris.* Oxford: Oxford University Press, 1991.

Cameron, Keith, Mark Greengrass, and Penny Roberts, eds. *The Adventure of Religious Pluralism in Early Modern France: Papers from the Exeter Conference, April 1999.* Bern: Peter Lang, 2000.

Hanlon, Gregory. *Confession and Community in Seventeenth-Century France: Catholic and Protestant Coexistence in Aquitaine.* Philadelphia: University of Pennsylvania Press, 1993.

Konnert, Mark W. *Civic Agendas and Religious Passion: Châlons-sur-Marne during the French Wars of Religion.* Kirksville: Truman State University Press, 1997.

Linden, David van der. "The Sound of Memory: Acoustic Conflict and the Legacy of the French Wars of Religion in Seventeenth-Century Montpellier." *Early Modern French Studies* 41, no. 1 (2019), 7–20.

Luria, Keith P. *Sacred Boundaries: Religious Coexistence and Conflict in Early-Modern France.* Washington, DC: Catholic University of American Press, 2005.

Luria, Keith P. "France: An Overview." In *A Companion to Multiconfessionalism in the Early Modern World,* edited Thomas Max Safley, 207–38. Leiden: Brill, 2011.

Marzagalli, Silvia. "Trade across Religious and Confessional Boundaries in Early Modern France." In *Religion and Trade: Cross-Cultural Exchanges in World History, 1000–1900,* edited by Francesca Trivellato, Leor Halevi, and Catia Antunes, 169–91. Cambridge: Cambridge University Press, 2014.

Murdock, Graeme. "Do Good Fences Make Good Neighbors? Living with Heretics in Early Modern Savoy." In *Religious Interactions in Europe and the Mediterranean World: Coexistence and Dialogue from the Twelfth to the Twentieth Centuries,* edited by Katsumi Fukasawa, Benjamin J. Kaplan, and Pierre-Yves Beaurepaire, 67–78. London: Routledge, 2017.

Murdock, Graeme, et al., eds., *Ritual and Violence: Natalie Zemon Davis and Early Modern France.* Past and Present Supplement 7. Oxford: Oxford University Press, 2012.

Zemon Davis, Natalie. "The Rites of Violence: Religious Riot in Sixteenth-Century France." *Past & Present* 59 (1973), 51–91.

Holy Roman Empire

Asch, R.G. "Religious Toleration, the Peace of Westphalia and the German Territorial Estates." *Parliaments, Estates & representation/Parlements, états & représentation* 20, no. 1 (2000), 75–90.

Christ, Martin. *Biographies of a Reformation: Religious Change and Confessional Coexistence in Upper Lusatia, 1520–1635.* Oxford: Oxford University Press, 2021.

Dixon, C. Scott. "Urban Order and Religious Coexistence in the German Imperial City: Augsburg and Donauwörth, 1548–1608." *Central European History* 40, no. 1 (2007), 1–33.

Fehler, Timothy. "Coexistence and Confessionalization. Emden's Topography of Religious Pluralism." In *Topographies of Tolerance and Intolerance. Responses to Religious Pluralism in Reformation Europe,* edited by Marjorie Elizabeth Plummer and Victoria Christmann, 78–105. Leiden: Brill, 2018.

François, Etienne. *Die unsichtbare Grenze: Protestanten und Katholiken in Augsburg 1648–1806.* Sigmaringen: Thorbecke, 1991. Also available in French as *Protestants et catholiques en Allemagne. Identités et pluralisme. Augsbourg, 1648–1806.* Paris: Albin Michel, 1993.

Freist, Dagmar. "One Body, Two Confessions: Mixed Marriages in Germany." In *Gender in Early Modern Germany,* edited by Ulinka Rublack, 275–304. Cambridge: Cambridge University Press, 2002.

Freist, Dagmar. *Glaube – Liebe – Zwietracht. Religiös-konfessionell gemischte Ehen in der Frühen Neuzeit.* Berlin: De Gruyter, 2017.

Hsia, R. Po-chia, and Hartmut Lehmann, eds. *In and Out of the Ghetto: Jewish-Gentile Relations in Late Medieval and Early Modern Germany.* Washington, DC: German Historical Institute/Cambridge University Press, 1995.

Kaufmann, Thomas. "Religious, Confessional and Cultural Conflicts among Neighbors: Observations on the Sixteenth and Seventeenth Centuries." In *Orthodoxies and Heterodoxies in Early Modern German Culture,* edited by Randolph C. Head and Daniel Christensen, 91–115. Leiden: Brill, 2007.

Luebke, David M. *Hometown Religion: Regimes of Coexistence in Early Modern Westphalia.* Charlottesville: University of Virginia Press, 2016.

Luebke, David M. "A Multiconfessional Empire." In *A Companion to Multiconfessionalism in the Early Modern World*, edited by Thomas M. Safley, 129–154. Leiden: Brill, 2011.

Mayes, David. "Divided by Toleration: Paradoxical Effects of the 1648 Peace of Westphalia and Multiconfessionalism." *Archiv für Reformationsgeschichte* 106, no. 1 (2015), 290–313.

Schindling, Anton. "Neighbours of a Different Faith: Confessional Coexistence and Parity in the Territorial States and Towns of the Empire." In *1648: War and Peace in Europe*, edited by Klaus Bussmann and Heinz Schilling, 465–73. Munich: Bruckmann, 1998.

Spohnholz, Jesse. *The Tactics of Toleration: A Refugee Community in the Age of Religious Wars.* Newark: University of Delaware Press, 2010.

Warmbrunn, Paul. *Zwei Konfessionen in einer Stadt. Das Zusammenleben von Katholiken und Protestanten in den paritätischen Reichsstädten Augsburg, Biberach, Ravensburg und Dinkelsbühl von 1548 bis 1648.* Wiesbaden: F. Steiner, 1983.

Whaley, Joachim. *Religious Toleration and Social Change in Hamburg 1529–1819.* Cambridge: Cambridge University Press, 1985.

Zschunke, Peter. *Konfession und Alltag in Oppenheim: Beiträge zur Geschichte von Bevölkerung und Gesellschaft einer gemischtkonfessionellen Kleinstadt in der frühen Neuzeit.* Wiesbaden: F. Steiner, 1984.

Italy

Bonfil, Robert. *Jewish Life in Renaissance Italy.* Berkeley: University of California Press, 1994.

Cooperman, Bernard Dov. "Portuguese Conversos in Ancona: Jewish Political Activity in Early Modern Italy." In *Iberia and Beyond: Hispanic Jews Between Cultures. Proceedings of a Symposium to Mark the 500th Anniversary of the Expulsion of Spanish Jewry*, edited by Bernard Dov Cooperman, 297–352. Newark: University of Delaware Press, 1998.

Davis, Robert C., and Benjamin C.I. Ravid, eds. *The Jews of Early Modern Venice.* Baltimore: Johns Hopkins University Press, 2001

Francesconi, Francesca. "The Venetian Jewish Household as a Multireligious Community in Early Modern Italy." In *Global Reformations: Transforming Early Modern Religions, Societies, and Cultures*, edited by Nicholas Terpstra, 231–48. New York: Routledge, 2019.

Katz, Dana E. *The Jewish Ghetto and the Visual Imagination of Early Modern Venice.* Cambridge: Cambridge University Press, 2017.

Michelson, Emily. *Catholic Spectacle and Rome's Jews: Early Modern Conversion and Resistance.* Princeton: Princeton University Press, 2022.

Ortega, Stephen. "Across Religious and Ethnic Boundaries: Ottoman Networks and Spaces in Early Modern Venice." *Mediterranean Studies* 18 (2009), 66–89.

Pullan, Brian. *The Jews of Europe and the Inquisition of Venice, 1550–1670.* London: I.B. Tauris, 1997.

Ravid, Benjamin. *Studies on the Jews of Venice.* Aldershot: Ashgate, 2003.

Ruderman, David B., ed. *Essential Papers on Jewish Culture in Renaissance and Baroque Italy.* New York: New York University Press, 1992.

Stow, Kenneth. *Theatre of Acculturation: The Roman Ghetto in the Sixteenth Century.* Seattle: University of Washington Press, 2003.

Trivellato, Francesca, *The Familiarity of Strangers: The Sephardic Diaspora, Livorno, and Cross-Cultural Trade in the Early Modern Period.* New Haven, CT: Yale University Press, 2009.

Wainwright, Matthew Coneys, and Emily Michelson. *A Companion to Religious Minorities in Early Modern Rome.* Leiden: Brill, 2021.

Walden, Justine. "Before the Ghetto: Spatial Logistics, Ritual Humiliation, and Jewish-Christian Relations in Early Modern Florence." In *Global Reformations: Transforming Early Modern Religions, Societies, and Cultures,* edited by Nicholas Terpstra, 97–115. New York: Routledge, 2019.

Ottoman Empire

Baer, Marc. *Honored by the Glory of Islam: Conversion and Conquest in Ottoman Europe.* Oxford: Oxford University Press, 2008.

Barkey, Karen. *Empire of Difference: The Ottomans in Comparative Perspective.* Oxford: Oxford University Press, 2008.

Bracewell, Catherine Wendy. *The Uskoks of Senj: Piracy, Banditry, and Holy War in the Sixteenth-Century Adriatic.* Ithaca: Cornell University Press, 1992.

Doumanis, Nicholas. *Before the Nation: Muslim-Christian Coexistence and Its Destruction in Late-Ottoman Anatolia.* Oxford: Oxford University Press, 2012.

Dursteler, E.R. *Venetians in Constantinople: Nation, Identity, and Coexistence in the Early Modern Mediterranean.* Baltimore: Johns Hopkins University Press, 2006.

Gara, Eleni. "Conceptualizing Interreligious Relations in the Ottoman Empire: The Early Modern Centuries." *Acta Poloniae Historica* 116 (2017), 57–91.

Gelder, Maartje van. "The Republic's Renegades: Dutch Converts to Islam in Seventeenth-Century Diplomatic Relations with North Africa." *Journal of Early Modern History* 19 (2015), 175–98.

Greene, Molly. *A Shared World: Christians and Muslims in the Early Modern Mediterranean.* Princeton: Princeton University Press, 2000.

Ivetic, Egidio, and Drago Roksandic, eds. *Tolerance and Intolerance on the Triplex Confinium: Approaching the "Other" on the Borderlands: Eastern Adriatic and Beyond 1500–1800.* Padua: CLEUP, 2007.

Krstić, Tijana. *Contested Conversions to Islam: Narratives of Religious Change and Communal Politics in the Early Modern Ottoman Empire.* Stanford: Stanford University Press, 2011.

Masters, Bruce. *Christians and Jews in the Ottoman Arab World: The Roots of Sectarianism.* Cambridge: Cambridge University Press, 2001.

Mazower, Mark. *Salonica, City of Ghosts: Christians, Muslims, and Jews 1430–1950.* New York: Alfred A. Knopf, 2005.

Parker, Charles H. "Paying for the Privilege: The Management of Public Order and Religious Pluralism in Two Early Modern Societies." *Journal of World History* 17, no. 3 (2006), 267–96.

Rodrigue, Aron. "Difference and Tolerance in the Ottoman Empire." *Stanford Humanities Review* 5, no. 1 (1995), 81–90.

Rothman, E. Natalie. "Conversion and Convergence in the Venetian-Ottoman Borderlands." *Journal of Medieval and Early Modern Studies* 41, no. 3 (2011), 601–33.

Windler, Christian. "Ambiguous Belongings: How Catholic Missionaries in Persia and the Roman Curia Dealt with Communicatio in Sacris." In *A Companion to Early Modern Catholic Global Missions*, edited by R. Po-chia Hsia, 205–34. Leiden: Brill, 2018.

South(-East) Asia

Alberts, Tara. *Conflict and Conversion: Catholicism in Southeast Asia, 1500–1700.* Oxford: Oxford University Press, 2013.

Amaladass, Anand, and Ines G. Županov, eds. *Intercultural Encounter and the Jesuit Mission in South Asia (16th – 18th Centuries).* Bangalore: Asian Trading Corporation, 2014.

Andaya, L. *The World of Maluku. Eastern Indonesia in the Early Modern Period.* Honolulu: University of Hawaii Press, 1993.

Dalrymple, William. *White Mughals: Love and Betrayal in Eighteenth-Century India.* London: Harper Perennial, 2003.

Flüchter, Antje, and Rouven Wirbser, eds. *Translating Catechisms, Translating Cultures: The Expansion of Catholicism in the Early Modern World.* Leiden: Brill, 2017.

Niemeijer, Hendrik E. "Dividing the Islands: The Dutch Spice Monopoly and Religious Change in 17th-Century Maluku." In *The Propagation of Islam in the Indonesian-Malay Archipelago*, edited by Alijah Gordon, 251–83. Kuala Lumpur: Malaysian Sociological Research Institute, 2001.

Parker, Charles H. *Global Interactions in the Early Modern Age, 1400–1800.* Cambridge: Cambridge University Press, 2010.

Parker, Charles H. *Global Calvinism. Conversion and Commerce in the Dutch Empire, 1600–1800.* New Haven, CT: Yale University Press, 2022.

Vink, Markus P.M. "Church and State in Seventeenth-Century Colonial Asia: Dutch-Parava Relations in Southeast India in a Comparative Perspective." *Journal of Early Modern History* 4, no. 1 (2000), 1–43.

Županov, Ines G., and Pierre Antoine Fabre, eds. *The Rites Controversies in the Early Modern World.* Leiden: Brill, 2018.

Spain

Bernabé-Pons, Luis F. "Identity, Mixed Unions and Endogamy of the Moriscos: The Assimilation of the New Converts Revisited." *Mediterranean Historical Review* 35, no. 1 (2020), 79–99.

Dadson, Trevor J. *Tolerance and Coexistence in Early Modern Spain: Old Christians and Moriscos in the Campo de Calatrava.* Woodbridge: Tamesis, 2014.

Deardorff, Max. "The Ties That Bind: Intermarriage between Moriscos and Old Christians in Early Modern Spain, 1526–1614." *Journal of Family History* 42, no. 3 (2017), 250–70.

García-Arenal, Mercedes, and Yonatan Glazer-Eytan, eds. *Forced Conversion in Christianity, Judaism and Islam. Coercion and Faith in Premodern Iberia and Beyond.* Leiden: Brill, 2020.

García-Arenal, Mercedes, and Gerard Wiegers, eds. *The Expulsion of the Moriscos from Spain: A Mediterranean Diaspora.* Leiden: Brill, 2014.

García-Arenal, Mercedes. "Mi padre moro, yo moro: The Inheritance of Belief in Early Modern Iberia." In *After Conversion: Iberia and the Emergence of Modernity*, edited by Mercedes García-Arenal, 304–35. Leiden: Brill, 2019.

Melammed, Renee Levine. *Heretics or Daughters of Israel? The Crypto-Jewish Women of Castile*. New York: Oxford University Press, 1999.

Meyerson, Mark D. *The Muslims of Valencia in the Age of Fernando and Isabel: Between Coexistence and Crusade*. Berkeley: University of California Press, 1991.

Nirenberg, David. *Communities of Violence: Persecution of Minorities in the Middle Ages*. Princeton: Princeton University Press, 1995.

Nirenberg, David. "Violencia, memoria y convivencia: los judíos en el medioevo ibérico." *Memoria y civilización* 2 (1999), 31–53.

Nirenberg, David. "Mass Conversion and Genealogical Mentalities: Jews and Christians in Fifteenth-Century Spain." *Past & Present* 174, no. 1 (2002), 3–41.

Ray, Jonathan. "Beyond Tolerance and Persecution: Reassessing Our Approach to Medieval 'Convivencia'." *Jewish Social Studies* 11, no. 2 (2005), 1–18.

Soifer, Maya. "Beyond *convivencia*: Critical Reflections on the Historiography of Interfaith Relations in Christian Spain." *Journal of Medieval Iberian Studies* 1, no. 1 (2009), 19–35.

Weller, Thomas. "'He Knows Them by Their Dress': Dress and Otherness in Early Modern Spain." In *Dress and Cultural Difference in Early Modern Europe*, edited by Cornelia Aust, Denise Klein, and Thomas Weller, 52–72. Jahrbuch für Europäische Geschichte/European History Yearbook 20. Berlin: De Gruyter, 2019.

Southern Netherlands

Corens, Liesbeth. "Seasonable Coexistence: Temporality, Health Care and Confessional Relations in Spa, c. 1648–1740." *Past & Present* 256, no. 1 (2022), 129–64.

Christman, Victoria. *Pragmatic Toleration: The Politics of Religious Heterodoxy in Early Reformation Antwerp, 1515–1555*. Rochester: University of Rochester Press, 2015.

Duerloo, Luc. *Dynasty and Piety: Archduke Albert (1598–1621) and Habsburg Political Culture in an Age of Religious Wars*. Farnham: Ashgate, 2012.

Duke, Alastair C. *Dissident Identities in the Early Modern Low Countries*. Edited by Judith Pollman and Andrew Spicer. Aldershot: Ashgate, 2009.

Harline, Craig, and Eddy Put. *A Bishop's Tale: Matthias Hovius Among His Flock in Seventeenth-Century Flanders*. New Haven, CT: Yale University Press, 2000.

Marnef, Guido. *Antwerp in the Age of Reformation: Underground Protestantism in a Commercial Metropolis, 1550–1577*. Baltimore: Johns Hopkins University Press, 1995.

Marnef, Guido. "Multiconfessionalism in a Commercial Metropolis: The Case of 16th-Century Antwerp." In *A Companion to Multiconfessionalism in the Early Modern World*, edited by Thomas Max Safley, 75–97. Leiden: Brill, 2011.

Roobroeck, Roman, "Confessional Coexistence in the Habsburg Netherlands: The Case of the Geuzenhoek (1680–1730)." *BMGN – Low Countries Historical Review* 136, no. 4 (2021), 3–26.

Space

Coster, Will, and Andrew Spicer, eds. *Sacred Space in Early Modern Europe*. Cambridge: Cambridge University Press, 2005.

Nelson, Eric, and Johanthan Wright, eds. *Layered Landscapes: Early Modern Religious Space Across Faiths and Cultures*. New York: Routledge, 2017.

Fisher Gray, Emily. "'Good-Neighborhood' and Confessional Coexistence in Augsburg's Holy Cross Quarter, 1548–1629." *Archiv für Reformationsgeschichte* 107, no. 1 (2016), 61–82.

Fehler, Timothy. "Coexistence and Confessionalization. Emden's Topography of Religious Pluralism." In *Topographies of Tolerance and Intolerance. Responses to Religious Pluralism in Reformation Europe*, edited by Marjorie Elizabeth Plummer and Victoria Christmann, 78–105. Leiden: Brill, 2018.

Foa, Jérémie. "An Unequal Apportionment: The Conflict over Space between Protestants and Catholics at the Beginning of the Wars of Religion." *French History* 20 (2006), 369–386.

Frick, David. *Kith, Kin, and Neighbors: Communities & Confessions in Seventeenth-Century Wilno*. Ithaca-London: Cornell University Press, 2013.

Geraerts, Jaap. "Competing Sacred Spaces in the Dutch Republic: Confessional Integration and Segregation." *European History Quarterly* 51, no. 1 (2021), 7–44.

Hamilton, Sarah, and Andrew Spicer, eds. *Defining the Holy: Sacred Space in Medieval and Early Modern Europe*. Aldershot: Ashgate, 2005.

Hayden, Robert M., et al. *Antagonistic Tolerance: Competitive Sharing of Religious Sites and Spaces*. London: Routledge, 2016.

Jütte, Daniel. "'They Shall Not Keep Their Doors or Windows Open': Urban Space and the Dynamics of Conflict and Contact in Premodern Jewish–Christian Relations." *European History Quarterly* 46, no. 2 (2016), 209–37.

Kaplan, Benjamin J. "Fictions of Privacy: House Chapels and the Spatial Accommodation of Religious Dissent in Early Modern Europe." *The American Historical Review* 107, no. 4 (2002), 1031–64.

Luebke, David M. "Sharing Sacred Spaces. Reflections on the Westphalian Experience." In *The Cultural History of the Reformations: Theory and Applications*, edited by Susan Karant-Nunn and Ute Lotz-Heumann, 55–80. Wolfenbüttel: Harrassowitz Verlag, 2021.

Luria, Keith P. "Sharing Sacred Space. Protestant Temples and Religious Coexistence in the Seventeenth Century." In *Religious Differences in France: Past and Present*, edited by Kathleen P. Long, 51–72. Kirksville, MO: Truman State University Press, 2006.

Roberts, Penny. "Contesting Sacred Space: Burial Disputes in Sixteenth-Century France." In *The Place of the Dead: Death and Remembrance in Late Medieval and Early Modern Europe*, edited by Bruce Gordon and Peter Marshall, 131–48. Cambridge: Cambridge University Press, 2000.

Warf, Barney, and Santa Arias. *The Spatial Turn: Interdisciplinary Perspectives*. London: Routledge, 2009.

Yasuhira, Genji. "Transforming the Urban Space: Catholic Survival Through Spatial Practices in Post-Reformation Utrecht." *Past & Present* 255, no. 1 (2021), 39–86.

Index